Cleft Structures

Linguistik Aktuell/Linguistics Today (LA)

Linguistik Aktuell/Linguistics Today (LA) provides a platform for original monograph studies into synchronic and diachronic linguistics. Studies in LA confront empirical and theoretical problems as these are currently discussed in syntax, semantics, morphology, phonology, and systematic pragmatics with the aim to establish robust empirical generalizations within a universalistic perspective.

For an overview of all books published in this series, please see
http://benjamins.com/catalog/la

Volume 208

Cleft Structures
Edited by Katharina Hartmann and Tonjes Veenstra

Cleft Structures

Edited by

Katharina Hartmann
Universität Wien

Tonjes Veenstra
ZAS Berlin

John Benjamins Publishing Company
Amsterdam / Philadelphia

The paper used in this publication meets the minimum requirements of the American National Standard for Information Sciences – Permanence of Paper for Printed Library Materials, ANSI Z39.48-1984.

CIP data is available from the Library of Congress.

Linguistik Aktuell/Linguistics Today, ISSN 0166-0829 ; v. 208
ISBN 978 90 272 5591 4 (Hb ; alk. paper)
ISBN 978 90 272 7112 9 (Eb)

John Benjamins Publishing Co. · P.O. Box 36224 · 1020 ME Amsterdam · The Netherlands
John Benjamins North America · P.O. Box 27519 · Philadelphia PA 19118-0519 · USA

Table of contents

List of contributors

Edith Aldridge
Department of Linguistics
University of Washington
Box 354340
Seattle, WA 98195–4340
USA
aldr@uw.edu

Lisa Cheng
Leiden University
Department of Linguistics
P.O. Box 9515
2300 RA Leiden
The Netherlands
L.L.Cheng@hum.leidenuniv.nl

Marcel den Dikken
CUNY Graduate Center
Linguistics Program
365 Fifth Avenue
New York, NY 10016–4309
USA
MDen-Dikken@gc.cuny.edu

Laura Downing
Göteborgs Universitet
SPL
Box 200
SE 405 30 Göteborg
Sweden
laura.downing@sprak.gu.se

Mara Frascarelli
Università degli Studi Roma Tre
Dipartimento di Lingue, letterature e culture straniere
Via Ostiense 236
00146 Roma
Italy
mara.frascarelli@uniroma3.it

Katharina Hartmann
Universität Wien
Institut für Germanistik
Universitätsring 1
1010 Wien
Austria
katharina.hartmann@univie.ac.at

Daniel Hole
Universität Stuttgart
Institut für Linguistik/Germanistik
Keplerstr. 17
D-70174 Stuttgart
Germany
holedan@gmail.com

Nancy Hedberg
Simon Fraser University
Department of Linguistics
Burnaby, BC V5A 1S6
Canada
hedberg@sfu.ca

Rosmin Mathew
CASTL
Teorifagbygget,
Hus 4, Plan 3
Universitetet of Tromsø
NO-9037 Tromsø
Norway
rosmin@gmail.com

Punnappurath Madhavan
School of Language Sciences
The English and Foreign Languages
University
Hyderabad
India
500007
professorp.madhavan@gmail.com

Francesca Ramaglia
Università degli Studi Roma Tre
Dipartimento di Lingue, letterature e
culture straniere
Via Ostiense 236
00146 Roma
Italy
francesca.ramaglia@uniroma3.it

Matthew Reeve
University College London
UCL Linguistics
Chandler House
2 Wakefield Street
London, WC1N 1PF
UK
m.reeve@ucl.ac.uk

Petra Sleeman
University of Amsterdam
Department of Linguistics
Spuistraat 210
1012 VT Amsterdam
The Netherlands
p.sleeman@uva.nl

Harold Torrence
University of Kansas
Department of Linguistics
Blake Hall, Room 427
1541 Lilac Lane
Lawrence, KS 66044–3177
USA
torrence@ku.edu

Tonjes Veenstra
Zentrum für Allgemeine
Sprachwissenschaft
Schützenstraße 18
10117 Berlin
Germany
veenstra@zas.gwz-berlin.de

Malte Zimmermann
Universität Potsdam
Kognitionswissenschaft/Linguistik
Karl-Liebknecht-Str. 24–25
D-14476 Potsdam
Germany
mazimmer@uni-potsdam.de

Introduction*

Katharina Hartmann & Tonjes Veenstra
University of Vienna / ZAS Berlin

Part I: The theoretical context

1. Cleft desiderata

The term *cleft* describes a specific syntactic pattern which serves to separate a discourse prominent constituent structurally from the rest of the clause. Languages use a variety of different syntactic strategies to structure a sentence according to the information state of its parts. Clefts are peculiar in this respect in that they exhibit a rather uncommon syntactic form to achieve the separation of the prominent, i.e. focal or topical, sentence part from the background of the clause. In its classical form, a cleft is a bi-clausal copulative construction consisting of an impersonal pronoun (the *cleft pronoun*), a copular verb, the informationally prominent phrase (the *cleft phrase*) and an embedded relative clause (the *cleft clause*). An example is given in (1). In this introduction, we represent the cleft phrase in small capitals.

(1) It was CHICKEN WINGS that Peter ordered for lunch.

In the overwhelming majority of cases the cleft phrase expresses the focus of the clause in which it appears. In intonation languages, it carries the main, falling accent of the clause (Collins 1991: 54ff). The focus status of the cleft phrase can be tested by embedding clefts in contexts which typically trigger focus interpretations. Thus, (1) could be an answer to an object question, or it could be a correction to a preceding statement where Peter ordered something else for lunch. It is also possible to insert focus sensitive particles in the cleft phrase which associate with

* Financial support for the Workshop on Clefts was provided by the Collaborative Research Center (Sonderforschungsbereich/SFB 632) Information Structure, funded by the German Research Foundation (DFG), the Federal Ministry of Education and Research (BMBF) of Germany (grant number 01UG0711), and research funds allocated to Tonjes Veenstra by the DFG (VE 468/1-1). The editors hereby gratefully acknowledge the financial support of these institutions. . We also want to thank Katharina Nimz, Marianna Patak, and JakobSteixner for their support in preparing the manuscript.

the focused constituent, see (2). Specific aspects of the focus interpretation of clefts will be addressed in Section 4.

(2) It was ONLY CHICKEN WINGS that Peter ordered for lunch.

The cleft phrase can also be a topic, see the example in (3).

(3) [My professor was always very supportive.]
It was HIM who wrote the decisive letter of recommendation.

Apart from the prototypical *it*-cleft given in (1), there are other types of clefts. Variation concerns the form and the position of the embedded clause. In (4), a *pseudocleft* (often also referred to as *wh-cleft*, see Lambrecht 2001; Declerck 1988), the cleft clause is a free relative clause, which appears in sentence initial position.

(4) What she really needs is AN ORTHOPEDIC SPECIALIST.

A pseudocleft is called inverted if the free relative clause occurs in sentence final position. Inverted pseudoclefts can be construed with a cleft pronoun (5a) or without one (5b).

(5) a. It is AN ORTHOPEDIC SPECIALIST what she really needs.
b. AN ORTHOPEDIC SPECIALIST is what she really needs.

In many languages, cleft pronouns are excluded altogether, hence, in these languages the cleft phrase always appears as the subject of the predication, whether inverted or not, compare the American Spanish example in (6) (Di Tullio 2006: 488).

(6) a. *Es DE LA MUJER DEL PRESIDENTE que todos hablan.*
it about the wife of president that everybody talks
'It is about the president's wife that everybody talks.'
b. *DE LA MUJER DEL PRESIDENTE es que todos hablan.*

The special format of clefts has been challenging linguists for decades. It has, however, never lead to any agreement on most of the basic issues concerning the structure and interpretation of clefts. The most pertinent questions are listed below:

- What is the nature of the cleft pronoun? Is it an expletive or a referential pronoun?
- What is the syntactic position of the cleft phrase? Is it located within the relative clause or external to it? Does it appear in its base position or in a derived position?
- What is the syntactic position of the relative clause? Is it extraposed or situated in its base position?

- How is the cleft phrase interpreted? Is it necessarily the focus of the clause, or could it possibly also express given or topical information?
- Is the cleft phrase always interpreted exhaustively?
- Does a cleft have typical presuppositions? Where do they come from?
- Clefts appear to be quite common across languages. Yet, they are not used with the same frequency in the languages of the world. What is the reason for such usage restrictions?

In answering some of these questions, the present volume aims at contributing to a better understanding of cleft structures across languages. The articles compiled in the volume are based on presentations given at a workshop on cleft structures, which took place in November 2009 at the *Zentrum für Allgemeine Sprachwissenschaft* in Berlin.

In the remainder of this introduction, we will discuss some fundamental issues in the structure and interpretation of clefts. The intention is to lay the ground for the specific discussions in the chapters to follow. We will discuss typological variation in the landscape of clefts, basic structural aspects, as well as interpretational properties of clefts.

2. Typological variation

2.1 Clefting and focus marking

Clefting as a focus marking strategy is very common cross-linguistically. In some languages, it is the main strategy for expressing the information structural category of focus. This is the case, e.g. in Bura, an Afro-Asiatic language. Bura generally expresses focus on non-subject constituents by a cleft strategy (see Hartmann & Zimmermann 2012). (7a) is a context-free Bura declarative clause which reflects the basic SVO word order. (7b) expresses focus on the direct object. The example shows the typical properties of a cleft sentence: The cleft phrase is fronted; it is followed by a copula/focus marking element and a relative clause. Clefting is the only possibility to mark object focus in Bura.

(7) a. *Píndár tá dívà-r mphyì.*
P. cook mush-LINK sorghum
'Pindar cooked sorghum mush.'

b. *DÍVÀ-R MPHYÍ àn [tí Kùbílí tà].*
mush-LINK sorghum FOC REL K. prepare
'It's sorghum mush that Kubili cooked.'

In many other languages, clefting is a subsidiary strategy, which exists besides more prominent means of focus marking. This is briefly illustrated for languages that mark focus prosodically, morphologically, or syntactically. Prosodic focus marking can be observed in German, which marks focus with pitch accent on the most prominent syllable of the focused constituent. The focus usually stays *in situ* (8a), but it sometimes also appears sentence-initially, preceding the finite verb in second position (8b).

(8) a. *Ich habe* DEN WEIN *nicht vertragen.*
I have the wine not tolerated
'I didn't tolerate the wine.'

b. DEN WEIN *habe ich nicht vertragen.*

Apart from *in situ* and *ex situ* focus, German also has clefts, although they are rather infrequent. The main accent within a cleft is realized on the cleft phrase:

(9) *Es war* DER WEIN, *den*$_i$ *ich nicht* t$_i$ *vertragen habe.*
it was the wine that I NEG tolerate have
'It was the wine that I didn't tolerate.'

The three focus realizations exemplified in (8ab) and (9) all express object focus but they differ with respect to the interpretation of the focus: focus marking using cleft sentences signals an exhaustive interpretation that *in situ* focus lacks (see Section 4). Fronted non-subject focus as in (8b) is often said to express a contrast, which, again, is not necessarily associated with in situ focus.

Languages using morphological focus marking may also have access to a cleft strategy. An example in case is the West Chadic language Guruntum. Guruntum marks focus by the focus marker *a*, which obligatorily precedes *in situ* (10a) and *ex situ* focused constituents (10b). In the latter case, the predicate is a relative clause introduced by the relative clause marker *mài*. This gives rise to a cleft analysis of (non-subject) *ex situ* focus in Guruntum, see Hartmann and Zimmermann (2009).

(10) a. *Tí bà ná á* FÚL *à wálì.*
3SG PROG catch FOC cow at farm
'He is catching a cow at the farm.'

b. *Á* FÚL *mài tí ná à wálì.*
FOC cow REL 3SG catch at farm
'It is a cow that he caught at the farm.'

Finally, cleft formation also exists in languages that mark focus syntactically. In Turkish, for example, the focus constituent appears in the wimmediate preverbal position. Analyses of focus in Turkish differ in assuming either movement of the focus constituent to a preverbal focus position (Erguvanlı 1984 and Kornfilt 1997) or movement of non-focal constituents out of the focus domain (Kılıçaslan 2004; Göksel & Özsoy 2000). According to the latter assumption, Turkish does not exhibit a unitary focus position. Apart from this, (pseudo) cleft formation is possible, see the subject and object clefts in (11ab) from Kornfilt (1997: 193) (SBJP = subject particle, OBJP = object particle). In a Turkish cleft, the cleft phrase is "extraposed", i.e. it appears in postverbal position. Pseudoclefts differ from regular Turkish focus constructions semantically, see Section 4 for discussion.

(11) a. [*sinema-ya gid-en*] *HASAN-DI*
cinema-DAT go-SBJP H.-PAST
'Hasan was the one who went to the movies.'

b. [*sinema-da gör-dük-ler-im*] *ÖĞRENCI-LER-IM-DI*
cinema-LOC see-OBJP-PL-1SG student-PL-1SG-PAST
'My students were the ones whom I saw at the movies.'

2.2 Agreement

There is a lot of cross-linguistic variation with respect to the inventory of cleft constructions and their formal properties. While English has a rich inventory of different forms, other languages are more restricted in that they do not exhibit the same range of clefting options (e.g. Turkish, which only has pseudoclefts, see Kornfilt 1997: 193). Across languages, the form of the cleft constructions is also subject to much variation, which concerns all parts of the cleft: the relative clause, the copula, and the clefted XP, see e.g. Lambrecht (2001), Drubig and Schaffar (2001), Drubig (2006). The discussion will be restricted to an exemplary case of variation, namely agreement between the copula and the cleft phrase.

First, consider English. In English clefts, the copula agrees with the cleft pronoun; agreement with the cleft phrase is excluded.

(12) a. It is ME/JOHN/US/THE CHILDREN who will visit you soon.
b. *It am ME/ARE THE CHILDREN who will visit us soon.

In many languages, though, the copula and the cleft phrase agree. A language in case is German where the copula and the cleft phrase necessarily agree, see, e.g. Smits (1989: 212), and Grewendorf and Poletto (1991: 179) who note the same facts for Italian.

(13) a. *Es ist* HANS, *der es getan hat.*
it is H. who it done has
'It is Hans who did it.'

b. ICH *bin es, der es getan hat.*
I am it who it done has

c. *Es ist ich, der es getan hat.

Next, consider canonical clefts in European and Brazilian Portuguese. Both, the copula and the lexical verb in the cleft clause agree with the cleft phrase (data from Kato & Ribiero 2009), just as in German.

(14) a. *Sou* EU *que sou vadia.*
be.1SG.PRES 1SG that be.1SG.PRES lazy
'It is me that is lazy.'

b. *São* AS CRIANÇAS *que fazem barulho.*
be.3PS.PRES the children that make.3PL.PRES noise
'It is the children that are noisy.'

Interestingly, this person/number agreement disappears on the copula in inverted clefts:

(15) a. EU *é que sou vadia.*
1SG be.3SG.PRES that be.1SG.PRES lazy
'I am the one who is lazy.'

b. *EU *sou que sou vadia.*
1SG be.1SG.PRES that be.1SG.PRES lazy

Tense concord, which is obligatory in non-inverted clefts, becomes optional in inverted clefts, see (16). This can be interpreted as a further clear indication of (more advanced) syntactic partitioning and the greater independence between the two parts of the construction:

(16) a. EU *é que comi o bolo.*
1SG be.3SG.PRES that eat.1SG.PAST the cake
'I was the one who ate the cake.'

b. EU *fui que comi o bolo.*
1SG be.3SG.PAST that eat.1SG.PAST the cake
'I was the one who ate the cake.'

Kato and Ribeiro (2009) note that European and Brazilian Portuguese diverge in one important respect. Only in the popular variety of the latter (also known as Brazilian Vernacular Portuguese, cf. de Mello 1997), the restrictions on tense concord (see (17) below) and person/number agreement (as in (14)) have also been relaxed in the canonic cleft construction, which the authors identify as a clear case of the grammaticalization of the copula (see below).

(17) a. *É* EU *que comi o bolo.* tense concord
be.3SG.PRES 1SG that eat.1SG.PAST the cake
'It was me that ate the cake.'

b. *É* AS CRIANÇAS *que comeram o bolo.*
be.3SG.PRES the children that eat.3PL.PAST the cake
'It is the children that ate the cake.'

(18) a. *É* *EU* *que* *sou* *vadia.*
be.3SG.PRES 1SG that be.1SG.PRES lazy
'It is me that is lazy.'

b. *É* *AS* *CRIANÇAS* *que* *fazem* *barulho.*
be.3SG.PRES the children that make.3PL.PRES noise
'It is the children that are noisy.'

They note a further process of grammaticalization, in which the copula disappears completely, leading to *reduced clefts* in the terminology of Kato et al. (1996). If the copula is covert, the cleft construction can only be recognized by the relative form of the predicate clause. Example (19) is from Brazilian Vernacular Portuguese (Holm & Viera Machado 2010):

(19) a. *ELA* *que* *sabe.*
3SG that knows
'It is her who knows.'
Compare: "É ELA que sabe" (Brazilian Standard Portuguese)

b. *QUEM* *que* *foi* *lá?*
who that went there
'Who went there?'
Compare: "QUEM é que foi lá?" (European Portuguese)

The total disappearance of the agreement-carrying copula has been explicitly linked to the creole origin of Brazilian Vernacular Portuguese by Holm and Viera Machado (2010). In the majority of cases, however, it is the agreement on the copula that is lost, and not the copula itself. This leads to the situation that the copula is susceptible to reanalysis and/or (further) grammaticalization. In the next section we turn to one such possible path of grammaticalization, namely the reanalysis as markers of focus.

2.3 From copulas to focus markers

The tendency that copulas develop into syntactic focus markers is quite common across languages (see Heine & Reh 1984; Hopper & Traugott 1993; Givón 1990). It is typically accompanied by a syntactic reconstruction of the biclausal cleft structure into a monoclausal structure. Such a development can be observed, e.g. in Hausa, another Afro-Asiatic language. Hausa marks focus by syntactic fronting. The fronted focus constituent is optionally followed by the particle *nee/cee* (after masc./fem. nouns), see Newman (2000), Jaggar (2001), Hartmann and Zimmermann (2007b). Examples (20) and (21) illustrate subject and object focus fronting, respectively (Hartmann & Zimmermann 2007b: 367).

(20) [KÀNDE]$_{FOC}$ *cèe ta-kèe dafà kiifii.*
K. PRT 3SG-REL.CONT cooking fish
'Kande is cooking fish.'

(21) [KIIFII]$_{FOC}$ *nèe Kande ta-kèe dafàa-waa.*
fish PRT K. 3SG-REL.CONT cook-NOM
'Kande is cooking fish.'

Nee/cee is also the copula in Hausa. This nurtured an analysis of Hausa focus constructions as clefts (see McConvell 1973; Jaggar 1978). The analysis has been questioned, though, since the putative cleft clause may not be introduced by a relative pronoun. Tuller (1986), followed by Green (1997), reanalyses the particle as a focus marker. Green (1997, 2004) presents a unified account of focus and copula constructions assuming that the particle is a focus marker in both. Hartmann and Zimmermann (2007a) argue that *nee/cee* occurs if the preceding focus is exhaustively interpreted.

As pointed out with respect to Example (6), the Afro-Asiatic language Bura marks non-subject focus by the copula/focus marker *àn*, which appears between the fronted non-subject and a relative clause to the fronted constituent, see (22). Focus subjects appear in a mono-clause which lacks any sign of relative clause marking, see (23). Here, the marker *àn* rather resembles a focus marker. Hartmann and Zimmermann (2012) propose a unified semantic analysis of *àn* as a focus copula (FCOP). Thus, the data suggest an on-going grammaticalization process from a copula in a bi-sentential focus cleft to a focus marker in mono-sentential structure with focus fronting.

(22) [DÍVÀ-R MPHYÍ]$_{FOC}$ *àn* [$_{RelC}$ *tí Kùbílí tà*].
mush-LINK sorghum FCOP REL K. prepare
'Its sorghum mush that Kubili cooked.'

(23) [MWÀLÀ LÀGÁ] *àn kwàsà tsír nì.*
woman some FCOP eat beans DEF
'A woman ate the beans.'

To sum up, this section presented an array of data which showed that clefts share common features across languages. These are the presence of a focused phrase, a copula verb, and an embedded relative clause. Apart from this, clefts exhibit quite some variation concerning the position, composition, and the interaction of their individual parts. A selection of this variation has been discussed in this section, other typological aspects are analysed in the contributions to this volume.

3. Structural issues of *it*-clefts

Section 3 discusses the main tendencies in the analysis of clefts. It introduces the most important concepts and ideas with respect to the syntactic relation between the cleft clause and the cleft phrase, the nature of the copula as a predicate or a semantically empty element, as well as the properties of the cleft pronoun as an expletive or a semantically contentful element. Proposals will be evaluated with respect to agreement and several connectivity facts.

3.1 From pseudoclefts to it-clefts

One prominent line of approaches to the representation of clefts, which we shall refer to as the *extraposition approach*, consists in the assumption that *it*-clefts are derived from pseudoclefts. The idea, which goes back to Jespersen first analysis of clefts (1927: 88f), assumes that the relative clause forms a discontinuous constituent with the cleft pronoun at the syntactic surface. The first elaborated theory in this spirit is Akmajian (1970). Subsequent analyses, which smoothed some of the initial problems of the extraposition approach, are Pinkham and Hankamer (1975), Emonds (1976), Gundel (1977), Percus (1997), and Huber (2002). The central features of the extraposition approach are the following: (i) the cleft pronoun and the extraposed cleft clause form a discontinuous definite DP together, which is part of a (specificational) copula clause; (ii) the cleft clause is the subject of the cleft. It is extraposed and adjoined to IP; (iii) the cleft phrase is the predicate of the copula; (iv) the cleft pronoun is the phonological spell-out of $[_{DP}\ D_{def}\ [_{NP}\ \emptyset]\ t_{CP}]$, and is taken to be referential. The structure in (24) represents this approach and is from Percus (1997: 338).

(24)

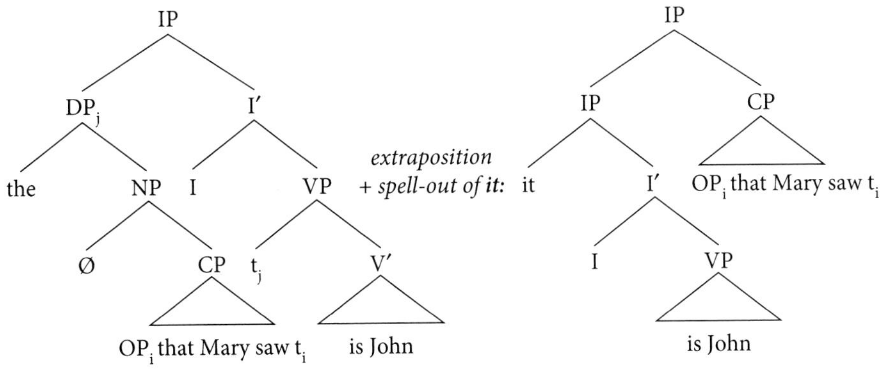

The extraposition approach predicts that clefts should have the same properties as (specificational) copular sentences, which appears to be borne out, see (25).

(25) a. It is GEORGE that came late.
b. [The one that came late] is GEORGE.

A good argument in favor of the extraposition approach comes from German where it can be shown that extraposition has to be available in clefts independent of the assumed approach. German is a verb-final language with verb second properties in main clauses. Even with verb second, participles (26a), verbal particles (26b) and other infinite elements remain in final position.

(26) a. *Hans ist nach Hause gekommen.*
H. is to home came
'Hans has come home.'

b. *Hans staubt das Regal ab.*
H. dusts the shelf PRT
'Hans dusts the shelf.'

Extraposed constituents generally appear to the right of the final verb or verbal part (27). With respect to clefts, it can be shown that the German cleft clause always appears extraposed since it has to *follow* the verb in final position (28a). A preverbal position of the cleft clause is ruled out, see (28b). This shows that extraposition of the cleft clause has to be assumed irrespective of the adopted approach, at least in German.

(27) *Hans staubt das Regal ab, das er auf dem Flohmarkt gekauft hat.*
H. dusts the shelf PRT that he at the flee.market bought has
'Hans dusts the shelf that he bought at the flee market.'

(28) a. *Es ist* UNSER NACHBAR *gewesen, der geklingelt hatte.*
it is our neighbor been who rang.the.bell has
'It was our neighbor who rang the bell.'

b. *Es ist unser Nachbar, der geklingelt hatte, gewesen.

The extraposition approach provides a good explanation for the English agreement facts within clefts. The complex DP in (24), which contains the unspecified nominal head, functions as the subject of the cleft. It follows that agreement takes place between the copula and the unspecified noun phrase spelled-out as *it* motivating default 3rd person agreement, see (29a). The extraposition approach naturally accounts for the fact that the copula may not agree with the cleft phrase, at least not in English, see (29b).

(29) a. It is ME/JOHN/US/THE CHILDREN who will visit you soon.
b. *It am ME/ARE THE CHILDREN who will visit us soon.

Akmajian (1970: 150) provides further evidence for the extraposition approach. He notes that a reflexive in the cleft clause does not have to be bound by the cleft phrase, see (30a) where the 3rd person reflexive *himself* is not bound by the 2nd person cleft phrase. According to Akmajian, (30a) is derived from the pseudocleft in (30b) in which the reflexive is bound by the indefinite quantifier. But Akmajian's argument is weakened by the fact that a 2nd person anaphor is also acceptable in the relative clause (30c) where binding of the anaphor by the cleft phrase appears to be possible.

(30) a. Was it YOU that saw himself in the crystal ball?
b. Was the one who saw himself in the crystal ball YOU?
c. Was it YOU that saw yourself in the crystal ball?

In short, the extraposition approach offers a natural account for the agreement facts in English clefts. However, it does not withstand closer scrutiny when it comes to cross-linguistic comparison (see e.g. Grewendorf & Poletto 1991). The examples in (31) are from German. As pointed out above, the copula does not agree with the cleft pronoun, but with the cleft phrase, irrespective of fronting of the cleft phrase. Agreement with the cleft phrase is also observable in Spanish, which does not use a cleft pronoun, see (32).

(31) a. *Es bin* ICH/ *bist* DU/ *ist* ER, *der gewählt wurde.*
it am I are you is he who elected was
'It is me/it is you/it is him who was elected.'
b. ICH *bin es*/DU *bist es* / ER *ist es, der gewählt wurde.*

(32) *Soy* YO / *eres* TU / *es* EL *quien fue elegido.*
am I are you is he who elected was
'It is me/it is you/it is him who was elected.'

The data in (31) and (32) are problematic for the extraposition approach since the copula apparently agrees with the cleft phrase. Such data show that the extraposition approach makes good predictions with respect to agreement in English, but is unable to cover cross-linguistic variation.

A further problem for the extraposition approach concerns PP-clefts, see (33a) from Huber (2002: 50). The assumed base-structure of the PP-cleft, given in (33b), is ungrammatical in English, which does not have PP-pseudoclefts.

(33) a. It was TO JOHN that I spoke.
b. *The one that/Who I spoke was to John.

Several proposals within the extraposition approach attempt to circumvent this problem by assuming additional rules for PP-clefts, see, e.g. Pinkham and Hankamer (1975), Emonds (1976), Gundel (1977).

With respect to anaphor binding and semantic binding, the extraposition approach makes the following predictions. (34) shows that an anaphor in the cleft phrase may be bound by an R-expression in the cleft clause. Thus, binding cannot apply at surface structure.

(34) a. It was [A PICTURE OF HIMSELF$_i$] [that Peter$_i$ was looking for].
b. It was HERSELF$_i$ [that Mary$_i$ saw first]. [Percus 1997: 343]
c. It was [HIS$_i$ MOTHER] [that every boy$_i$ saw first]. [Percus 1997: 344]
d. In the end, [it is THEIR$_i$ CHILD'S SAFETY] that every mother$_i$ is worried about. [Andrew Murphy, p.c.]

Percus (1997) argues that anaphor/pronoun binding in (34) can be derived from the underlying structure with the cleft clause preceding the cleft phrase. Yet, the extraposition approach has to assume anaphor/pronoun binding in the absence of c-command since the binder is embedded in the cleft clause.

The extraposition approach is able to account for negative polarity licensing in clefts. Following Percus (1997: 344), a negative copula licenses a negative polarity item in the cleft phrase, but not in the relative clause, see (35ab).

(35) a. It isn't [ANYONE I KNOW] [that John saw]
b. *It wasn't JOHN [who did anything to help] [Percus 1997: 344]

The ungrammaticality of (35b) is easily accomodated in the extraposition approach according to which the base-position of the relative clause is higher than the negated copula.

3.2 Predicative analyses

A different group of proposals rejects the assumption that it-clefts are derived from pseudoclefts. Instead, they analyze clefts similar to predicative constructions. In these approaches, the copula is treated as a non-expletive verb with an argument structure. The approaches differ with respect to kinds of arguments the copula selects and the status they attribute to the cleft pronoun. We discuss two variations of this analysis.

3.2.1 It-*as-subject*

The first group of analyses assumes that the copular verb in an *it*-cleft is a bivalent predicator taking the cleft pronoun and the cleft phrase as arguments. The cleft pronoun functions as the subject, and the cleft phrase (together with the attributive cleft clause) as the predicate of the copular verb. We refer to this approach as the "*it*-as-subject" analysis. Representative proponents of this approach are Smits (1989), Grewendorf and Poletto (1991), Hedberg (2000), Lambrecht (2001) and

Reeve (2011). The approaches take different views concerning the base-position of the cleft pronoun. Grewendorf and Poletto (G&P) argue for an "ergative analysis". They assume that the cleft pronoun is base-generated as the inner argument of the verb and raised to the subject position in order to receive case. Hedberg and Reeve, on the other hand, claim that the cleft pronoun, which they take to be referential, is base-generated in a subject position outside of VP (see also Huber 2002). The following cleft structure illustrates Grewendorf and Poletto's analysis for English (1991: 190ff). G&P assume extraposition of the predicative DP in addition, for information structural reasons. Since this move is controversial, and not required for the illustration of the analysis, it is not represented in (36).

(36)

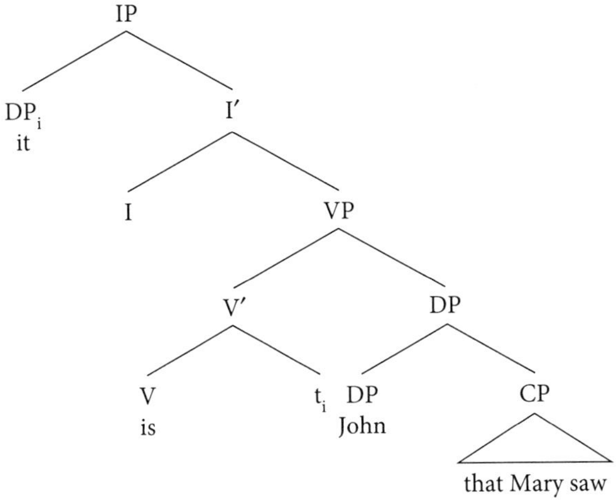

Hedberg (2000) differs from G&P in assuming that the cleft clause forms an interpretational chain with the cleft pronoun. This aspect of her theory is reminiscent of the extraposition analysis.

It-as-subject analyses are corroborated especially by agreement facts. A nominal cleft phrase agrees in case with the cleft-pronoun, irrespective of its grammatical role and case in the relative clause. This follows naturally from an analysis of a cleft as a predicative construction in which the nominal predicate agrees with the subject in case. Illustrating data are again from German, where case is morphologically expressed on determiners and pronouns, and, occasionally, also on nouns. The cleft pronoun receives nominative case from the finite copular verb. By case-agreement, the cleft phrase must appear in the nominative case, too, see (37) for subject clefts, and (8) and (9), repeated as (38a, b), for object clefts. It is always possible to reformulate the cleft sentence as a regular declarative clause which shows default case on the "cleft phrase".

(37) a. *Es war* PHILIP, *der*$_i$ *t*$_i$ *die Kette gefunden hat.*
it was Philip$_{NOM}$ who the necklace found has
'It was Philip who found the necklace.'

b. PHILIP$_{NOM}$ *hat die Kette gefunden.*

(38) a. *Es war* DER WEIN, *den*$_i$ *ich nicht t*$_i$ *vertragen habe.*
it was the$_{NOM}$ wine that I NEG tolerate have
'It was the wine that I didn't tolerate.'

b. *Ich habe* DEN$_{ACC}$ WEIN *nicht vertragen.*

If the cleft phrase does not agree in case with the nominative cleft pronoun, the construction is ruled out, see (39a) (Duden[7] 2005: 1044) and (40a) (see also Grewendorf & Poletto 1991):

(39) a. **Es war* EINEM JOURNALISTEN$_{DAT}$, *dem*$_i$ *er t*$_i$ *einen*
it was a journalist who he a
Hinweis verdankte.
hint owed
'It was to a journalist that he owed a hint.'

b. *Er verdankte den Hinweis einem Journalisten*$_{DAT}$.

(40) a. **Es war* EINEN JOURNALISTEN$_{ACC}$, *den*$_i$ *die Polizei t*$_i$ *verhaftete.*
it was a journalist that the police arrested
'It was a journalist who was arrested by the police.'

b. *Die Polizei verhaftete einen Journalisten*$_{ACC}$.

Given that the cleft phrase is the predicate of the copula, nominal cleft phrases succumb to the same case restrictions as nominal predicates in German copula constructions. As (41) shows, the predicative DP agrees with the subject in nominative case, which is assigned to the subject by the copula in I^0/$AgrS^0$. This fact directly accounts for the ban of accusative and dative case in clefts.

(41) a. *Dieser Jahrgang*$_{NOM}$ *ist ein Erfolg*$_{NOM}$.
this vintage is a success
'This vintage is a success.'

b. *Jürgen*$_{NOM}$ *ist mein bester Freund*$_{NOM}$.
J. is my best friend
'Jürgen is my best friend.'

Even prepositional case is excluded in the cleft position, as shown by the contrast between (42a) where the preposition is clefted along with the accusative pronoun, and (42b) where the preposition stays in the cleft clause and the cleft phrase appears in the nominative.

(42) a. **Es ist* AN IHN, *den$_i$ ich t$_i$ denke.*
it is to him$_{ACC}$ whom I think
'*It is of him that I think.'

b. *Es ist* ER$_{NOM}$, *an den$_i$ ich t$_i$ denke.*

c. *Ich denke an* IHN$_{ACC}$.

Notice that prepositional phrases can occur in the cleft position if they are modifiers, which do not receive case. In (43), the locative adverbial *in Las Vegas* is clefted:

(43) *Es war* IN LAS VEGAS, *wo sie geheiratet haben.*
it was in Las Vegas where they married have
'It was in Las Vegas where they got married.'

Apart from NPs and PPs, APs and VPs are also predicates. Since they cannot be relativized, they do not form proper clefts, but they do appear in cleft-like constructions as shown in (44).

(44) a. *Es war* SCHÖN, *wie sie gesungen hat.*
it was beautiful how she sung has
'It was beautiful how she sung.'

b. *Es war* BÜCHER ZU LESEN, *worauf er sich am meisten*
it was books to read what.for he REFL at most
gefreut hat.
look.forward has
'It was reading books what he was looking for most.'

Finally, the predicate analysis of cleft phrases is supported by the fact that the cleft phrase is generally interpreted as the focus of the sentences (see Sections 3.1 and 4). Since predicates are likely to be interpreted as focus (see, e.g. Lambrecht 1994, Chapter 3.1), the syntactic behaviour of the cleft phrase appears to be in line with its pragmatic interpretation.

As pointed out above, Grewendorf and Poletto (1991) claim that the cleft clause is adjoined to the cleft phrase. This assumption has been criticized by Huber (2002:65) who notes that the cleft phrase and the cleft clause do not form a constituent in the middlefield. (45b), where the DP+CP appear in the middle-field, only has a devious interpretation according to which it is the Peter who came (and not, e.g. the one who left).

(45) a. *dass es* PETER *ist, der kommt*
that it Peter is who comes
'that it is Peter who came'

b. *#dass es* PETER, *der kommt, ist*

Turning to anaphor/pronoun binding, the *it*-as-subject analysis has to assume a derivational relation between the cleft phrase and the cleft clause. This is suggested by the binding facts in (34a–c), repeated here:

(34) a. It was [A PICTURE OF HIMSELF$_i$] [that Peter$_i$ was looking for].
  b. It was HERSELF$_i$ [that Mary$_i$ saw first]. [Percus 1997: 343]
  c. It was [HIS$_i$ MOTHER] [that every boy$_i$ saw first]. [Percus 1997: 344]
  d. In the end, [it is THEIR$_i$ CHILD'S SAFETY] that every mother$_i$ is worried about. [Andrew Murphy, p.c.]

The fact that the cleft phrase can be bound from an element within the cleft clause suggests that the cleft phrase is reconstructed into the cleft clause. This is corroborated by the following ungrammatical Example (46) where reconstruction of the cleft phrase yields a principle C-violation.

(46) *It was [PETER$_i$] [that he$_i$ didn't want to help].

The proponents of the *it*-as-subject analysis do not dwell on this issue. Hedberg (2000) assumes "extraposition" of the cleft clause from the cleft pronoun to a position adjoined to the cleft phrase. According to her theory, relative clause extraposition is analyzed as an "interpretive relation […] established at LF between the extraposed [cleft] clause and the NP [DP] subject" (Hedberg 2000: 913). Thus, the cleft clause forms a semantic constituent with the cleft pronoun, but it is the non-restrictive embedded clause of the cleft phrase to which it is adjoined syntactically (see also Delahunty 1982). This theory is not compatible with the binding data in (34) and (46) since it does not account for the reconstruction effect of the cleft phrase with respect to the cleft clause.

Grewendorf and Poletto (1991), on the other hand, analyze the cleft phrase and the cleft clause as a syntactic and semantic constituent. They claim that the connectivity effects in English follow from the assumption of a chain of co-indexed elements. Thus, the operator chain of the cleft clause is co-indexed with the cleft phrase, a fact which, according to G&P, triggers reconstruction of the cleft phrase. The analysis of the cleft phrase as an attributive clause of the cleft phrase is reminiscent of Chomsky's (1977) analysis of relative clauses. However, English relative clauses and clefts exhibit a striking difference when it comes to connectivity effects. As illustrated in (47), the relativized DP does not reconstruct. In (47a) the anaphor cannot be bound by the R-expression within the relative clause; in (47b) the pronoun is not bound by the quantified DP.

(47) a. *I found [the picture of himself$_i$] [that Peter$_i$ was looking for].
  b. *In the end, I didn't question [their$_i$ child's safety] [that every mother$_i$ is worried about].

The failure of reconstructing the relativized DP into the relative clause could be due to the fact that reconstruction requires (A')-movement. Since the relativized DP is merely co-indexed with a movement chain, reconstruction is not possible in (47). By the same reasoning, though, reconstruction should be excluded in clefts as well, contrary to fact.

Concerning negative polarity licensing, the *it*-as-subject theory does account for the fact observed in (35) that a negative copula licenses an NPI in the cleft phrase (35a) or in the cleft phrase since both are embedded under the copular verb.

(35) a. It isn't [ANYONE I KNOW] [that John saw]
b. *It wasn't JOHN [who did anything to help]

3.2.2 *Expletive analyses*

In a related, prominent group of proposals the cleft phrase and the cleft clause do not form a constituent but represent the subject (cleft phrase) and the predicate (cleft clause) of the copular verb. The cleft pronoun is taken to be an expletive which blocks subject raising. The earliest proposal in this spirit is Jespersen (1937) who revised his analysis from 1927. Proponents of this approach are the cleft predication analyses of Williams (1980) and Delahunty (1982), the small clause analyses of Heggie (1988), and Svenonius (1998). Svenonius assumes, at least for cleft phrases introduced by the complementizer *that*, that raising of the cleft phrase is triggered by the focus status of the cleft phrase, see Section 3.3 for discussion. The representative structure in (48) is based on Delahunty (1982), who assumes, together with Heggie (1988) late insertion of *that/who*. The cleft phrase and the cleft clause are related by coindexing the cleft phrase and the A'-chain within the cleft clause.

(48)

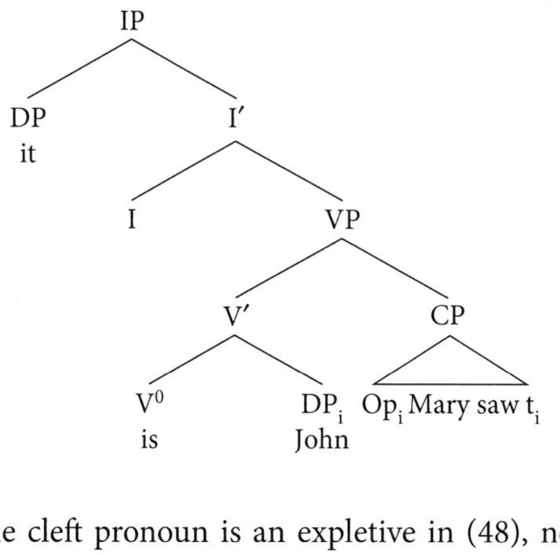

Since the cleft pronoun is an expletive in (48), nominative case marking of the cleft phrase cannot result from case agreement between *it* and the cleft phrase. Alternatively, the cleft phrase could receive nominative case as the subject of a small clause. However, small clause subjects do not carry nominative case, see (49ab) for English, (49c) for German. Thus, proper case assignment in clefts cannot be derived from the expletive analysis without further stipulations.

(49) a. They called me$_{\text{ACC}}$ a liar.

b. They named her$_{\text{ACC}}$ Gloria.

c. *Sie fegte den*$_{\text{ACC}}$ *Boden*$_{\text{ACC}}$ *sauber.*
she swept the floor clean
'She swept the floor clean.'

Expletive analyses assume an interpretational relation between the cleft phrase and the cleft clause without assuming a derivational relation between them. Thus, the expletive analyses are faced with the same problems as the *it*-as-subject analyses with respect to the observed connectivity effects: Since co-indexing of the cleft phrase and the operator chain within the cleft clause is merely interpretational, and does not derive from movement, neither syntactic nor semantic reconstruction is expected to take place.

The analysis of the cleft pronoun as an expletive element has been criticized first by Hedberg (2000) who argues that *it* is referential. One argument for the referential status of the pronoun is that it can be replaced by the referential propositional anaphors *this/that*. (50) is Hedberg's Example (3c):

(50) This/that was JOHN that I saw.

A second argument in favor of the referential analysis of the cleft pronoun is the fact that languages which have unequivocal expletive pronouns do not use them in cleft. This is the case in French, which uses the demonstrative pronoun *c'est* instead of the expletive pronoun *il* in clefts.

(51) *Au final, c'est* SARKOZY *qui fait le projet de 2012.*
at.the end it is S. who made the project of 2012
'At the end it is Sarkozy who made the project 2012.'
(Le Figaro, 12.1.2011)

According to Grewendorf and Poletto (1991) and Grewendorf (1989), the expletive in German is an empty element which occurs in impersonal passives, see (52). Since German does not have a lexicalized expletive pronoun, the cleft pronoun cannot be expletive either.

(52) *weil (*es) hier getanzt wurde*
because (it) here danced was
'because people danced here'

Another argument against the expletive status of the cleft pronoun is the positional variation of the cleft pronoun in German. As (53a) shows, the cleft pronoun may appear in the German prefield, i.e. SpecCP, the position preceding the finite verb in second position. A variation to the cleft in (53a) is (53b) where the cleft phrase is topicalized. In this case, the cleft pronoun must still be realized. Following G&P (1991), the cleft pronoun must be present since it represents an argument of the copular verb. In English, the cleft phrase cannot be fronted, see (53c).

(53) a. *Es war* PETER, *der die Vase zerbrochen hat.*
it was P. wh the vase broken has
'It was Peter who broke the vase.'

b. PETER *war* *(*es*), *der die Vase zerbrochen hat.*

c. *Peter was it who broke the vase.

On the basis of such arguments, proponents of the *it*-as-subject analyses of clefts take the cleft pronoun to be referential.

3.3 Focus-based analyses

Yet another family of related analyses exploits the informational focus status of the cleft phrase in assuming movement of the cleft phrase to the specifier of a focus projection. Such proposals strengthen the relation between focus movement and clefting. Both operations yield a syntactic partition of the clause into a focus (the cleft phrase), and a presupposition (the cleft clause). Focus-based analyses show commonalities with the predicative analyses. They share the assumption of the expletive analysis that the cleft pronoun is an expletive element inserted to block further movement of the cleft phrase. The analysis of the cleft phrase as an attributive clause of the cleft phrase, on the other hand, is reminiscent of the *it*-as subject approaches. It is assumed that the cleft phrase is selected by some kind of functional head, typically the head of a focus phrase. The following structure is taken from É. Kiss (1999: 224); the example is from Hedberg (2000: 10):

(54)

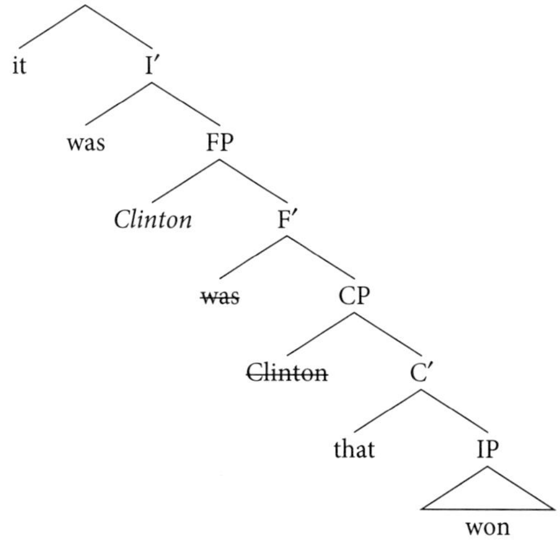

Focus-based analyses can also be traced back to Jespersen (1937) who assumes a transformational operation whereby the cleft phrase is raised to a high position in the clause. The first generative analysis in this spirit is Chomsky (1977) who assumes "topicalization" of the cleft phrase to a position corresponding to SpecCP in more recent phrase structure theories. In this early cleft theory the presence of the complementizer *that* is not motivated. The function of the cleft pronoun and the copula, which are both considered semantically empty, is not clarified. These problems carry over to Rochemont (1986) who assumes as a landing site of the focused cleft phrase an embedded position to the right of the copula. Rochemont himself points out that this assumption leads to problems with respect to proper binding of the movement trace. É. Kiss (1995, 1998) and Meinunger (1998) both assume proper focus projections which attract the focused cleft phrase. The cleft pronoun and the copula verb occupy higher functional positions, for example, the topic projection in Meinunger (1998).

The assumption of the focus-based theory that the cleft phrase is moved to a high functional projection predicts that the moved phrase may be bound by a lower constituent due to reconstruction of the A'-moved phrase. Thus, the challenges represented by anaphor and semantic binding in (34) are easily satisfied by this approach. With respect to NPI licensing, it is predicted that the negative copula licenses a negative polarity item in the cleft phrase, see (35a), repeated here. The ungrammaticality of (55b) (= (35b)) is unexpected, though, since the embedded clause is clearly in the scope of the copula in (55). Note that NPI-licensing is not subject to locality. (55) is therefore expected to be well-formed in the focus-based approaches.

(55) a. It isn't [ANYONE I KNOW] [that John saw].
b. *It wasn't JOHN [who did anything to help].

4. Semantic issues

Delin and Oberlander (2005) list the following essential interpretive features for cleft constructions in English:

(56) a. Clefts are presuppositional;
b. Clefts convey uniqueness/exhaustive listing;
c. Presupposition and information structure are separate, but information-structural generalisations are possible (in particular, there are no all-new cleft sentences).

With respect to the latter point, there is a widespread tendency in the literature to treat the cleft phrase as being the Focus (in terms of new information, e.g. Collins 1991), but as Delin and Oberlander (2005) stress time and again it is quite normal to find clefts in which the cleft phrase is given and the cleft clause presents the new information. An illustrative example from Prince (1978) suffices to drive this point home. The cleft clause is entirely new, while the cleft phrase consists solely of an anaphoric pronoun (which is taken as 'given' by definition):

(57) The leaders of the militant homophile movement in America generally have been young people. It was THEY who fought back during a violent police raid on a Greenwich Village bar in 1969 …

In fact, the corpus study reported on in Delin (1989) reports that the latter is even more common in natural-occurring data from English (see also Birner & Ward 2006).

The other two issues listed by Delin and Oberlander (2005), presupposionality and uniqueness/exhaustivity, have dominated the discussion on the semantic properties of cleft constructions in the literature so far. These have been argued to be absent from (or weaker in) their non-cleft counterparts (e.g. Akmajian 1970; Atlas & Levinson 1981; Bolinger 1972; Jackendoff 1972; Horn 1981; É. Kiss 1998; Percus 1997; Rooth 1999, and many others). Thus, in the following example, the *it*-cleft seems to introduce a presupposition to the effect that there exists an individual that satisfies the backgrounded predicate denoted by the cleft clause (i.e. John drank something):

(58) It was THE CHIANTI that John drank.

Initial evidence for treating the existence effect as being presuppositional in nature comes from standard tests for presuppositions (e.g. Karttunen & Peters 1979) and the comparison with their non-clefted alternatives (cf. Atlas & Levinson 1981). Consider the following minimal pair:

(59) a. Mary kissed John.
b. It was JOHN that Mary kissed.

Both sentences in (59) share the meaning core *Mary kissed someone*. However, the cleft in (59b) preserves this inference under denial (60) and questioning (61), while this is not the case for (59a):

(60) *Denial*
(60b) has the same truth conditions as (60a), but only (60b) presupposes (60c):
a. Mary did not kiss John.
b. It wasn't JOHN that Mary kissed.
c. Mary kissed someone.

(61) *Questioning*
The truth value of (61b) is the same as (61a), but only (61b) presupposes (61c):
a. Did Mary kiss John?
b. Was it JOHN that Mary kissed?
c. Mary kissed someone.

These standard tests for presuppositions strongly support the conclusion that the existence effect with *it*-clefts is a presupposition.

Further evidence for this presupposition of existence comes from the behavior of simple negative quantifiers. These are not possible in the cleft phrase of *it*-clefts (Percus 1997: 339):

(62) Q: Who saw John?
A_1: Nobody saw John.
A_2: *It was NOBODY that saw John.

Additional strong evidence comes from Rooth (1999). He constructs the following example to show that *it*-clefts are presuppositional (as opposed to constructions where Focus is signaled by a pitch accent). The context is the following. In my department, a football pool is held each week, where people bet on the outcomes of games. It is set up so that at most one person can win; if nobody wins, the prize money is carried over to the next week:

(63) a. A: Did anyone win the departmental football pool this week?
b. B: Probably not, because it's unlikely that $[\text{Mary}]_F$ won it, and she's the only person who ever wins.
c. B: #Probably not, because it's unlikely that it's MARY who won it, and she's the only person who ever wins.

Rooth points out that the *it*-cleft in (59c) conveys the presupposition that someone won the football pool and this is what makes this example incoherent and contradictory, because it contrasts with the explicit statement that 'probably no-one won'.

The conclusion we draw from the discussion so far is, therefore, that cleft constructions contain a presupposition of existence and, since this presuppositional effect is mandatory, it should be structurally encoded in these constructions. In other words, it is a hard, wired-in, property of the construction.

We turn now to the exhaustivity effect that has been ascribed to clefts. Percus (1997) notes that there is no association of cleft-foci with additive focus particles (*also*, *even*) which are incompatible with exhaustivity (König 1991; E. Kiss 1998):

(64) It was ??also/*even JOHN that drank the Barolo.

The account Percus (1997) gives derives the infelicity of (64) from the clash between the presupposition of the *it*-cleft (λx [x drank the Barolo]: x = John) and the (conflicting) presupposition that the additive particle triggers (λz [z ≠ John]: z drank the Barolo). Reeve (2008) even goes further suggesting that *it*-clefts seem to exhibit an even stronger version of exhaustivity, because of the impossibility of focusing a bare universal quantifier in them:

(65) *It was EVERY HAT that Mary picked for herself.

Wedgwood et al. (2008) counter this latter point by showing that given the proper context such quantifiers are well able to occur in *it*-clefts:

(66) It's EVERY CHILD that got frightened, not just the girls.

There seem to be two issues at stake. First, how is this exhaustivity effect derived? Is it due to the semantic nature of the construction or is it to be accounted for in pragmatic terms? Second, is this effect mandatory in clefts?

A first indication that the exhaustivity effect is not mandatory is the observation that children initially do not interpret *it*-clefts non-exhaustively (Heizmann 2007) suggesting that, at least at the early stages of acquisition, exhaustivity is not a wired-in property of the construction (whereas the presupposition of existence is). Furthermore, several authors have argued (and shown) that such additive particles can very well sometimes associate with the cleft phrase and these phrases need not receive an exhaustive interpretation (Prince 1978; Horn 1981; Dufter 2009). Some illustrative examples are presented below. In (63) we have two conjoined cleft phrases neither of which is exhaustive by itself, whereas (64) is an example with an additive focus particle inside the cleft phrase from EUROPARL which is a corpus of parallel text in 11 languages from the proceedings of the European Parliament (see Dufter 2009):

(67) Perhaps it was HITLER'S GRANITE WILL AND DETERMINATION and certainly it was THE FORTITUDE OF THE GERMAN SOLDIER that saved the armies of the Third Reich from a complete debacle. [Shirer, *Rise and Fall of the Third Reich*] (Horn 1981: 131, quoting Ellen Prince).

(68) Moreover, it is ALSO OUT OF RESPECT FOR YOUR ELECTORATE that, as President-in-Office of the Council, I do not wish to set myself up as judge. [EUROPARL] (Dufter 2009)

Horn (*to appear*) contrasts Focus constructions built on *only* with pure Focus constructions (clefts, pseudo-clefts, bare focus) and argues that the latter do not entail exhaustiveness. To be more precise, Focus constructions built on *only* **assert** exhaustivity, whereas pure Focus constructions merely **implicate** exhaustivity. Thus, as Horn (*to appear*) astutely points out, '[e]xhaustivity is part of what is "at issue" (cf. Potts 2005) in *only* statements, but not in (unadorned) clefts.' The following contrast in cancellability illustrates this point:

(69) A: It's PRESIDENT BUSH who's responsible for the abuse at Abu Ghraib.
B: Yes, you're right – Bush, and Cheney, and Rumsfeld.

(70) A: It's ONLY PRESIDENT BUSH who's responsible for the abuse at Abu Ghraib.
B: #Yes, you're right – Bush, and Cheney, and Rumsfeld.

Further evidence for his position, Horn (*to appear*) adduces from the behavior of NPIs which can only be licensed in clefts if a dedicated exhaustivity marker is present:

(71) *it*-cleft
  a. Of all our presidents, it's (ONLY) BUSH who has proposed tax cuts during a war.
  b. Of all our presidents, it's *(ONLY) BUSH who has ever proposed any tax cuts during a war.

(72) *th*-cleft
  a. The only one who could ever reach me was the son of a preacher man.
  b. *The one who could ever reach me was the son of a preacher man.

The upshot of the discussion is that the exhaustivity effect is not mandatory in cleft constructions. As such, this effect is different from the presuppositional effect discussed above, which is mandatory. Therefore, the exhaustive effect, in contrast, is not a hard, wired-in, property of the construction. It should not be structurally encoded in these constructions by means of an underlying exhaustivity marker.

The last question we want to address is how to account for the exhaustivity effect. Three proposals exist in the literature as to what this effect arises from: (i) truth-conditional import (Atlas & Levinson 1981; É. Kiss 1998); (ii) a presupposition/conventional implicature (Halvorsen 1978; Delin & Oberlander 2005; Percus 1997; Büring & Križ 2013); (iii) a generalized conversational implicature (Horn 1981; Drenhaus, Zimmermann & Vasishth 2011). Although we will not take a definite stand on this issue here, we like to note that Horn (1981) already showed that the exhaustiveness effect in *it*-clefts does not show the expected projection behavior of conventional implicatures in negative, question, and conditional contexts. This militates heavily against the second proposal. As for the first proposal, we showed above that *it*-clefts and *only*-foci are not synonymous, thereby ruling out this option. This leads to the preliminary conclusion that the third proposal seems to be a step forward in the direction of the right solution. Many questions, however, remain that have to be dealt with in future research.

Part II: The articles

Marcel den Dikken's contribution brings the dichotomy between specificational and predicational copular sentences into the realm of cleft constructions (see Declerck 1988 for an earlier proposal). Starting out with a discussion of pseudoclefts, where the relevance of these two types of copular sentences has been well-established, he shows on the basis of data from English and Dutch that this distinction also plays an important role in the analysis of clefts proper. He proposes a thoughtful analysis of specificational *it*-clefts, in which the cleft pronoun acts as a pro-predicate that inverts with its subject in the course of the syntactic derivation. He then proceeds with an analysis of contrastive-focus *it*-clefts, in which he argues that the relative clause is a right-dislocated headless relative licensed by the mechanism of 'parallel construal' (cf. Koster 2000). Finally, he discusses continuous-topic *it*-clefts, which are shown to be structurally assimilated to pseudo-relative constructions.

Edith Aldridge presents a comprehensive analysis of clefts in Austronesian languages. In many of them, *wh*-questions are formed on clefts. She proposes that the derivation of such *wh*-clefts is parallel to the derivation of basic word order. In the latter case the absolutive DP is treated as a Topic, and moves into a low Topic position in the C-domain, and the remnant clause is moved into a higher Focus position, thus deriving the VOS order. The trigger for the latter movement is a combination of the Focus head carrying a [T]-feature and the independently motivated Stranded DP Constraint, which ensures that it is the entire (remnant) TP that is attracted rather than just the T head. In the case of clefts, it is the cleft sentence realized as a headless relative that is analyzed as a Topic, which accounts for its presuppositional behaviour. The cleft phrase, on the other hand, is part of the remnant TP moved to the FocP position. Since the cleft phrase is a *wh*-word, it is inherently focused. Aldridge shows that this focused constituent can occur with elements, such as particles, negation and modals that typically occur with predicates but not with subjects. This is taken to be evidence for the claim that the cleft phrase is located within the surface predicate. This analysis also accounts for another characteristic of Austronesian clefts. Since the movements in the derivation target the left periphery directly, and place the cleft sentence and cleft phrase in the positions where they are interpreted, it follows that such clefts are irreversible. Finally, the bi-clausal status of the construction is determined on the basis of positional restrictions on pronominal clitics.

Mara Frascarelli and Francesca Ramaglia provide a syntactic, semantic, and intonational analysis of cleft (and pseudocleft) constructions. In their view, clefts qualify as specificational copular sentences in which the focused constituent is realized as the predicate and the presupposed part of the sentence is a relative clause merged in subject position. The free relative qualifies as a definite description headed by either a *pro* or a generic NP of a restricted class (e.g. person, thing) via a type-shifting operation. As such, this analysis accounts for a number of well-known phenomena like extraction, Case marking, and anti-agreement effects. In addition, they argue that clefts also instantiate a Topic-Comment structure. The cleft sentence constitutes a right-hand Topic in clefts, and a left-hand Topic in pseudo-clefts, thereby accounting for the presuppositional behaviour of these elements in the construction. It also accounts for some syntactic facts, such as the possibility to place right-dislocated adverbials between the cleft phrase and the cleft sentence, the deletion of the cleft sentence leading to reduced clefts, and the connectedness effects between the cleft phrase and the verb within the cleft sentence in subject clefting. They argue the analysis does not only capture the commonalities between clefts and pseudo-clefts, but also the asymmetries with respect to word order, the realisation of the cleft pronoun, the agreement pattern of the verb in the cleft sentence as well as of the copula. The intonational data they present seem also to support the analysis of cleft constructions as involving a Topic-Comment structure.

Lisa Cheng and Laura Downing investigate the structure of clefts in Durban Zulu. They provide prosodic and syntactic arguments to show that Zulu clefts have a bipartite structure. Durban clefts are formed by a copular sentence and, depending of the nature of the cleft phrase as nominal or non-nominal, an adjoined DP or CP. The copular sentence itself consists of a copula and the cleft phrase (the *pivot* in the author's terminology). These two parts of a cleft form two independent intonational phrases where the prosodic phrase boundaries are indicated by lengthening of the respective penultimate vowels. The copular phrase and the postcopular DP/CP are also syntactically independent from each other in that the two parts can appear in either order. Based on Adger and Ramchand's (2005) proposal for copular constructions in Scottish Gaelic, the authors assume that the copula of a Zulu cleft heads a predicate phrase which hosts the cleft phrase in its specifier. The predicate phrase is selected by T whose specifier provides a position for predicate inversion. The cleft phrase is adjoined to the copular phrase. With respect to information structure, it is shown that clefting is obligatory in Zulu subject focus constructions. Non-subjects clefts are commonly interpreted as contrastive.

Matthew Reeve presents detailed evidence for several revisions of the syntax of clefts. He first discusses the nature of the cleft pronoun. Giving numerous syntactic and semantic arguments, he shows that the cleft pronoun *it* does not behave like an expletive, as assumed e.g. by Percus (1997), but rather as a referential pronoun. The proposed non-expletive analysis of *it* assimilates clefts to specificational sentences, which, according to Reeve, represent the structural basis of clefts. The cleft pronoun is assumed to form a discontinuous definite description with the cleft phrase. This leads to an existential presupposition which typically appears in clefts. Reeve further proposes that the cleft clause is a restrictive relative clause which syntactically modifies the cleft phrase. Thus, it cannot be extraposed from the cleft pronoun. Here, the analysis clearly departs from most specificational analyses. The last issue Reeve brings up concerns the relation of the cleft phrase and relative clause. He shows that the cleft phrase exhibits connectivity effects with respect to the cleft clause, which he takes as evidence for raising of the cleft phrase out of the cleft clause.

Harold Torrence presents a morphosyntactic analysis of clefts in Wolof. He discusses a formal difference between subject and non-subject clefts. A clefted subject immediately precedes the copula *a*, the head of a copular phrase CopP. In non-subject clefts, an expletive pronoun *l-* is located in the specifier of the CopP. In predicative constructions, the copula has properties of a raising predicate. This property also causes raising of the focused cleft phrase. In subject clefts, the cleft phrase A-moves to SpecCopP for EPP feature checking. Subsequently, it A'-moves to the higher SpecFocP. A non-subject cleft phrase directly raises the SpecFocP. The promotion analysis of Wolof clefts is motivated by the following facts: Clefting exhibits island sensitivity and shows reconstruction effects. Thus, parts of idiomatic expressions can be clefted; an ideophone can be separated from a verb by clefting; the negative polarity item *dara* ('anything') can be clefted if it is associated with a negative element in the cleft phrase. Clefting in Wolof also shows principle A and C effects: Reflexive pronouns, which must be locally bound, can be clefted. Clefted quantifiers show narrow scope readings with respect to the cleft phrase. The A'-movement analysis of clefts is further corroborated by some Wolof specific constructions.

Nancy Hedberg lays out an approach to the integration of discourse-pragmatic theories and formal semantic theories to focus, topic and cleft sentences. She argues that clefts in English divide a proposition into two parts both syntactically and semantically. In her view, the cleft phrase expresses an exhaustive focus, whereas the cleft clause expresses a pragmatic presupposition. Furthermore, she shows that clefts can map variously onto topic/comment structure, so that the cleft as a whole can have topic-comment organization as well as comment-topic organization. The cleft phrase as well as the cleft clause can contain a prosodic focus. The innovative idea of this chapter is that the prosodic focus in both cases can be characterized as semantic focus in the sense of Krifka (2008) as representing alternatives. When the prosodic focus is realized on the cleft phrase, it is always associated with the (structural) exhaustive focus operator, but when it is realized in the cleft clause, it is associated with an assertive focus operator. From this, two things follow. First, the exclusive focus particle *only* can only appear if the prosodic focus is on the cleft phrase. Second, the additive focus particle *also* or a scalar focus particle like *even* can only be associated with a prosodic focus in the cleft clause.

Rosmin Mathew's chapter is concerned with clefts in Malayalam, especially their focus-related properties, and how they differ from other Focus constructions. She shows that constructions traditionally described as clefts in the literature on Malayalam are decided different from preverbal Focus constructions. In the latter we are dealing with Information Focus in the sense of É. Kiss (1998), whereas the cleft construction exhibits Identificational Focus. She adduces morphological (difference in Case retention), syntactic (restrictions on what can be moved), and semantic evidence (exhaustivity, scope interaction) for this division. Furthermore, she argues that the preverbal Focus construction is situated in the *v*P-Phase. The cleft, on the other hand, is situated in the CP-Phase. She adopts a mono-clausal analysis, along the lines of Hiraiwa and Ishihara (2002) for Japanese.

Punnapurath Madhavan also discusses cleft constructions in Malayalam, specifically relating them to question strategies. Although Malayalam is generally held to be a *wh*-in-situ language, Madhavan shows this only seems to be the case in (simple) matrix clauses, but not in embedded clauses. As such, it is different from run-of-the-mill in-situ language like Korean and Chinese where no such asymmetry is found. In addition to the (superficial) in-situ strategy, *wh*-questions can have the form of clefts, with either the *wh*-word in the cleft phrase or the whole clause containing the *wh*-word in that position. This strategy is available in both matrix and embedded contexts. Madhavan observes that when multiple *wh*-phrases occur in the embedded clause, only the latter strategy is possible, i.e. the whole clause must be moved. He develops a straightforward movement analysis of clefts in which Focus-features are responsible for movement of the cleft phrase (or the cleft clause) into the specifier position of the Focus phrase, which is headed by the copula.

Daniel Hole and Malte Zimmermann present a comparative overview of clefts and related focusing strategies in the (South) East Asian languages Japanese, Burmese, and Mandarin. They show that all three languages make use of copulas and nominalizers in their cleft constructions, although in different ways. In Japanese and Burmese, the cleft phrase and the copula form a constituent, and the nominalizer is part of the cleft clause, which is backgrounded (and optionally marked with a Topic marker).They argue that the copula links the cleft phrase to the cleft clause. In Chinese, on the other hand, it is the nominalizer that fulfils the function of linking the cleft phrase and the cleft clause. The copula precedes the complete cleft construction. Furthermore, they observe that, unlike Chinese, Japanese and Burmese allow for nominalized clauses with in-situ Focus. From a semantic point of view, they show that the cleft constructions in all three languages receive an exhaustive interpretation (as opposed to the in-situ Focus construction, which can also be interpreted non-exhaustively). Given that there is cross-linguistic variation with respect to exhaustivity in cleft constructions (see also above), they hypothesize that syntactic partitioning is a necessary, though not a sufficient condition for exhaustiveness effects with Focus. Still, they note differences between the languages. In Chinese the exhaustivity effect is linked to the nominalizer, but not in Japanese and Burmese, where it is linked to the presence of the Topic marker in the cleft clause.

Petra Sleeman discusses the licensing conditions of infinitival subject relatives in cleft constructions. In contrast to English and French, (subject) clefts in Italian can license such relatives. This is possible, she argues, because only in Italian the cleft phrase has to be a contrastive focus. Evidence mainly comes from Belletti's (2005, 2008) discussion of answering strategies in the three languages. In short, whereas in English and especially in French the use of clefts is a normal strategy to answer a question concerning the identification of the subject of the clause, in Italian the use of a cleft in this case is associated with a somewhat negative presupposition and thus expresses a [+contrastive] focus. She further shows that the cleft phrase is moved to a high position in the left periphery of the clause. Finally, she argues that the cleft clause is in a complement position, given that extraction is possible from infinitival subject relatives, and proposes an analysis in terms of the Kaynian framework.

References

Adger, David & Ramchand, Gillian. 2005. Merge and move. Wh-dependencies revisited. *Linguistic Inquiry* 36(2): 161–193.

Akmajian, Adrian. 1970. On deriving cleft-sentences from pseudo-cleft sentences. *Linguistic Inquiry* 1: 149–168.

Atlas, Jay David & Levinson, Stephen C. 1981. It-clefts, informativeness and logical form: Radical pragmatics (revised standard version). In *Radical Pragmatics*, Peter Cole (ed.), 1–62. New York NY: Academic Press.

Belletti, Adriana. 2005. Answering with a cleft: the role of the null subject parameter and the VP periphery. In *Proceedings of the Thirtieth Incontro di Grammatica Generativa*, Laura Brugè, Giuliana Giusti, Nicola Munaro, Walter Schweikert & Giuseppina Turano (eds) 63–82. Venice: Cafoscarina.

Belletti, Adriana. 2008. Answering strategies: new information subjects and the nature of clefts. Chapter 10 of *Structures and Strategies*. London: Routledge.

Birner, Betty J. & Ward, Gregory. 2006. Information structure. In *Handbook of English Linguistics*, Bas Aarts & April McMahon (eds), 291–317. Oxford: Basil Blackwell.

Bolinger, Dwight. 1972. A look at equations and cleft sentences. In *Studies for Einar Haugen Presented by Friends and Colleagues*, Evelyn Sherabon Firchow, Kaaren Grimstad, Nils Hasselmo & Wayne A. O'Neil. (eds) 69–114. The Hague: Mouton.

Büring, Daniel & Križ, Manuel. 2013. It's that, and that's it! Exhaustivity and homogeneity presuppositions in clefts (and definites). Semantics and Pragmatics 6, Article 6: 1–29. http://dx.doi.org/10.3765/SP.6.6.

Chomsky, Noam. 1977. On Wh-movement. In *Formal Syntax*, Peter Culicover, Tom Wasow & Adrian Akmajian (eds), 71–132. New York NY: Academic Press.

Collins, Peter. 1991. *Cleft and Pseudo-Cleft Constructions in English*. London: Routledge.

Declerck, Renaat. 1988. *Studies on Copular Sentences, Clefts, and Pseudo-Clefts*. Leuven & Dordrecht: Leuven University Press & Foris.

Delahunty, Gerald Patrick. 1982. *Topics on the Syntax and Semantics of Cleft Sentences*. Bloomington IN: Indiana University Linguistics Club.

Delin, Judy L. 1989. Cleft Constructions in English Discourse. Ph.D. dissertation, University of Edinburgh.

Delin, Judy L. & Oberlander, Jon. 2005. Cleft constructions in context: Some suggestions for research methodology. Ms, University of Stirling.

Drenhaus, Heiner, Zimmermann, Malte & Vasishth, Shravan. 2011. Exhaustiveness effects in clefts are not truth-functional. *Journal of Neurolinguistics* 24(3): 320–337.

Drubig, Bernhard. 2006. Phases and the typology of focus constructions. In *On Information Structure: Meaning and Form* [Linguistik Aktuell/Linguistics Today 100], Kerstin Schwabe & Susanne Winkler (eds) 33–66. Amsterdam: John Benjamins.

Drubig, Bernhard & Schaffar, Kazemin Wolfgang. 2001. Focus constructions. In *Language Typology and Language Universals: An International Handbook*, Martin Haspelmath, Ekkehard König, Wulf Oesterreicher & Wolfgang Raible (eds), 1079–1104. Berlin: Walter de Gruyter.

Dudenband 4 – Die Grammatik. 2005. Hg. von der Dudenredaktion, 7th edn. Mannheim: Dudenverlag.

Dufter, Andreas. 2009. Clefting and discourse organization: Comparing Germanic and Romance. In *Focus and Background in Romance Languages* [Studies in Language Companion Series 112], Andreas Dufter & Daniel Jacob (eds), 83–122. Amsterdam: John Benjamins.

É. Kiss, Katalin. 1995. *Discourse Configurational Languages*. Oxford: OUP.

É. Kiss, Katalin. 1998. Identificational focus versus information focus. *Language* 74: 245–273.

É. Kiss, Katalin. 1999. The English cleft construction as a focus phrase. In *Boundaries of Morphology and Syntax* [Current Issues in Linguistic Theory 180], Lunella Mereu (ed.), 217–229. Amsterdam: John Benjamins.

Emonds, Joseph. 1976. *A Transformational Approach to English Syntax*. New York NY: Academic Press.

Erguvanlı, Eser Emine. 1984. *The Function of Word Order in Turkish Grammar*. Berkeley CA: University of California Press.

Givón, T. 1990. *Syntax. A Functional-Typological Introduction*, Vol. II. Amsterdam: John Benjamins.

Göksel, Aslı & Öksoy, S. 2000. Is there a focus position in Turkish? In *Studies on Turkish and Turkic Languages*, Aslı Göksel & Celia Kerslake (eds), 219–228. Wiesbaden: Harrassowitz.

Green, Melanie. 1997. Focus and Copular Constructions in Hausa. Ph.D. dissertation, SOAS, London.

Green, Melanie. 2004. Predication, equation and information structure: Evidence from Hausa copular sentences. Ms, University of Sussex.

Grewendorf, Günther 1989. *Ergativity in German*. Dordrecht: Foris.

Grewendorf, Günther & Poletto, Cecilia. 1991. Die Cleft-Konstruktion im Deutschen, Englischen und Italienischen. In *Strukturen und Merkmale syntaktischer Kategorien*, Gisbert Fanselow & Sascha Felix (eds) 174–216. Tübingen: Narr.

Gundel, Jeanette. 1977. Where do cleft structures come from? *Language* 53: 543–559.

Halvorsen, Per-Kristian. 1978. The Syntax and Semantics of Clefts. Ph.D. dissertation, University of Texas (= TLF [Texas Linguistic Forum] #11).

Hartmann, Katharina & Zimmermann, Malte. 2007a. Exhaustivity particles in Hausa: A reevaluation of the particle nee/cee. In *Focus Strategies in African languages: The Interaction of Focus and Grammar in Niger-Congo and Afro-Asiatic*, Enoch Aboh, Katharina Hartmann & Malte Zimmermann (eds), 241–263. Berlin: Mouton de Gruyter.

Hartmann, Katharina & Zimmermann, Malte. 2007b. In place – out of place: Focus in Hausa. In *On Information Structure: Meaning and Form* [Linguistik Aktuell/Linguistics Today 100], Kerstin Schwabe & Susanne Winkler (eds), 365–403. Amsterdam: John Benjamins.

Hartmann, Katharina & Zimmermann, Malte. 2009. Morphological focus marking in Gùrùntùm (West Chadic). *Lingua* 119(9): 1340–1365.
Hartmann, Katharina & Zimmermann, Malte. 2012. Focus marking in Bura: Semantic uniformity matches syntactic heterogeneity. *Natural Language and Linguistic Theory* 30(4): 1061–1108.
Hedberg, Nancy. 2000. The referential status of clefts. *Language* 76: 891–920.
Heggie, Lorie. 1988. The Syntax of Copular Structures. Ph.D. dissertation, University of Southern California.
Heine, Bernd & Reh, Mechtild. 1984. *Grammaticalization and Reanalysis in African Languages.* Hamburg: Buske.
Heizmann, Tanja. 2007. Child acquisition of exhaustivity in clefts. In *Proceedings of the* 31st *Annual Boston University Conference on Language Development*, Heather Caunt-Nulton, Samantha Kulatilake & I-Hao Woo (eds), 298–309. Cascadilla MA: Somerville.
Hiraiwa, Ken & Ishihara, Shinichiro. 2002. Missing links: Cleft, sluicing, and no da construction in Japanese. *MIT Working Papers in Linguistics* 43: 35–54.
Holm, John & Vieira Machado, Patricia. 2010. "Copula deletion" in restructured Portuguese. *Revista de Crioulos de Base Lexical Portuguesa e Espanhola* 2: 52–62.
Hopper, Paul & Traugott, Elizabeth Closs. 1993. *Grammaticalization.* Cambridge: CUP.
Horn, Larry. 1981. Exhaustiveness and the semantics of clefts. *NELS* 11: 125–142.
Horn, Larry. To appear. Information structure and the landscape of (non-)at-issue meaning. In *Oxford Handbook of Information Structure,* Caroline Féry & Shin. Ishihara (eds). Oxford: OUP.
Huber, Stefan. 2002. Es-*Clefts und* det-*Clefts. Zur Syntax, Semantik und Informationsstruktur von Spaltsätzen im Deutschen und Schwedischen* [Lunder germanistische Forschungen 64]. Stockholm: Almqvist and Wiksell International.
Jackendoff, Ray. 1972. *Semantic Interpretation in Generative Grammar.* Cambridge MA: The MIT Press.
Jaggar, Philip J. 1978. 'And what about...'- Topicalization in Hausa". *Studies in African Linguistics* 9: 69–81.
Jaggar, Philip J. 2001. *Hausa* [Londen Oriental and African Language Library 7]. Amsterdam: John Benjamins.
Jespersen, Otto. 1927. *A Modern English Grammar,* Vol 3. London: George Allen and Unwin.
Jespersen, Otto. 1937. *Analytic Syntax.* New York NY: Holt, Rinehart and Winston.
Karttunen, Lauri & Peters, Stanley. 1979. Conventional implicature. In *Presupposition. Syntax and Semantics* 11, Choon-Kyu Oh & David A. Dinneen (eds), 1–56. New York NY: Academic Press.
Kato, Mary Aizawa & Ribeiro, Ilza. 2009. Cleft sentences from Old Portuguese to Modern Portuguese. In *Focus and Background in Romance Languages* [Studies in Language Companion Series 112], Andreas Dufter & David Jacob (eds) 123–154. Amsterdam: John Benjamins.
Kato, Mary Aizawa, Braga, Maria Luisa, Reche Corrêa, Vilma, Lopes Rossi, Maria Aparecida & Soares Sikansi, Nilmara. 1996. As construções-Q no português brasileiro falado: Perguntas, clivadas e relativas. In *Gramática do português Falado*, Ingedore Grunfeld Villaça Koch (ed.), 309–374. Campinas: Editora Unicamp.
Kılıçaslan, Yilmaz. 2004. The syntax of information structure in Turkish. *Linguistics* 42(4): 717–765.
König, Ekkehard. 1991. *The Meaning of Focus Particles: A Comparative Perspective.* London: Routledge.

Kornfilt, Jay. 1997. *Turkish*. London: Routledge.

Koster, Jan. 2000. Extraposition as parallel construal. Ms, University of Groningen.

Krifka, Manfred. 2008. Basic notions of information structure. *Acta Linguistica Hungarica* 55(3–4): 243–276.

Lambrecht, Knud. 1994. *Information Structure and Sentence Form. Topic, Focus, and the Mental Representations of Discourse Referents* [Cambridge Studies in Linguistics 71]. Cambridge: CUP.

Lambrecht, Knud. 2001. A framework for the analysis of cleft constructions. *Linguistics* 39(3): 463–516.

McConvell, Patrick. 1973. Cleft Sentences in Hausa? A Syntactic Study of Focus. Ph.D. dissertation, SOAS.

Meinunger, André. 1998. A monoclausal approach to cleft and pseudo-cleft sentences. *ZAS Papers in Linguistics* 10: 89–105.

de Mello, Heliana Ribeiro. 1997. Brazilian Vernacular Portuguese: Evidence of partial restructuring. CUNY dissertation. Ann Arbor MI: University Microfilms International.

Newman, Paul. 2000. *The Hausa Language*. New Haven CT: Yale University Press.

Percus, Orin. 1997. Prying open the cleft. In *Proceedings of NELS 27*, Kiyomi Kusumoto (ed.), 337–351. Amherst MA: GLSA.

Pinkham, Jessie & Hankamer, Jorge. 1975. Deep and shallow clefts. *Chicago Linguistic Society* 11: 429–450.

Potts, Christopher. 2005. *The Logic of Conventional Implicatures* [Oxford Studies in Theoretical Linguistics]. Oxford: OUP.

Prince, Ellen. 1978. A comparison of wh-clefts and it-clefts in discourse. *Language* 54: 883–906.

Reeve, Matthew. 2008. A 'pseudo-biclausal' analysis of Slavonic clefts. *UCL Working Papers in Linguistics* 20: 63–85.

Reeve, Matthew. 2011. The syntactic structure of English clefts. *Lingua* 121: 142–171.

Rochemont, Michael S. 1986. *Focus in Generative Grammar* [Studies in Generative Linguistic Analysis 4]. Amsterdam: John Benjamins.

Rooth, Mats. 1999. Association with focus or association with presupposition? In *Focus: Linguistic, Cognitive, and Computational Perspectives*, Peter Bosch & Rob van der Sandt (eds), 232–244. Cambridge: CUP.

Smits, Rile J.C. 1989. *Eurogrammar. The Relative and Cleft Construction of the Germanic and Romance Languages*. Dordrecht: Foris.

Svenonius, Peter. 1998. Clefts in Scandinavian. An investigation. *ZAS Papers in Linguistics* 10: 163–190.

Tuller, Laurie. 1986. Bijective Relations in Universal Grammar and the Syntax of Hausa. Ph.D. disseration, UCLA.

di Tullio, Ángela. 2006. Clefting in spoken discourse. In *Encyclopaedia of Language and Linguistics,* 2nd edn, Keith Brown (ed.), 483–491. Cambridge: Elsevier.

Wedgwood, Dan, Cann, Ronnie & Pethö, Gergly. 2008. A contrastive study of the focus position in Hungarian and it-clefts in English. Ms, University of Edinburgh & University of Debrecen.

Williams, Edwin. 1980. Predication. *Linguistic Inquiry* 11: 203–238.

PART I

Specificational/predicational clefts

Predication and specification in the syntax of cleft sentences

Marcel den Dikken
CUNY Graduate Center

This paper reviews the differences between predicational and specificational copular sentences in the realm of (pseudo-)cleft constructions, and proposes an analysis which treats the *it* of specificational *it*-clefts as a pro-predicate that inverts with its subject in the course of the syntactic derivation. In contrastive-focus *it*-clefts, the sentence-final relative clause is a right-dislocated headless relative dependent on a formal licensing relationship with the operator inside the relative clause and a content-licensing relationship with the focus. This dual licensing dependency explains the restrictions on the distribution of *which* as the relative clause operator in contrastive-focus *it*-clefts. Continuous-topic *it*-clefts are structurally assimilated to pseudorelative constructions, which accounts for the restrictions on the realisation of the left periphery of their relative clause.

Keywords: *it*-cleft; predication; specification; headless relative; asyndetic specification

1. A typology of cleft sentences

1.1 Pseudoclefts: Predicational vs specificational

Since Higgins' (1979) seminal work, a terminological difference between two types of copular sentences, between so-called *predicational* and *specificational* ones, is standardly made in the literature. The two pseudoclefts in (1) bring this difference out particularly clearly.

(1) a. what Brian_i is is important to him_i
→ predicational: *important to him* predicates a property of *what Brian is*

b. what Brian_i is is important to himself_i
→ specificational: *important to himself* specifies a VALUE for the variable in the *wh*-clause

For (1a), the term 'predicational pseudocleft' is really a misnomer: though 'predicational' is certainly appropriate, there is nothing 'cleft' about this kind of sentence – it represents a garden-variety predicational copular sentence, with the free relative as the subject and the postcopular AP as the predicate, entirely parallel to *Brian's job/status is important to him*. For (1b), on the other hand, the term 'specificational pseudocleft' is entirely apt – (1b) 'cleaves' the sentence *Brian is important to himself* into two portions on either side of the copula, with *important to himself* specifying a value for the variable in the *wh*-clause.

In specificational pseudoclefts, the postcopular constituent seems to be the underlying *subject* of the predicate denoted by the *wh*-clause in precopular position (i.e. the opposite of the situation in (1a)). The two major constituents of the specificational pseudocleft in (1b) can in fact change places, as in (4a, b) – on a par with specificational copular sentences of the type in (5). Such word-order alternation is impossible in predicational 'pseudoclefts', *unless* the AP predicate is degree-modified – and in this respect, (1a) behaves exactly like other garden-variety copular sentences with AP predicates (see (2b) and (2b′), and compare these to (3b, b′)).

(2) a. what $Brian_i$ is important to him_i
b. *important to him_i is what $Brian_i$ is
b′. most important to him_i is what $Brian_i$ is

(3) a. his job/status is important to him
b. *important to him is his job/status
b′. most important to him is his job/status

(4) a. what $Brian_i$ is is important to $himself_i$
b. important to $himself_i$ is what $Brian_i$ is

(5) a. the best candidate is Brian
b. Brian is the best candidate

Word-order flexibility is thus one formal criterion for the distinction between predicational and specificational copular sentences.

A second formal criterion is control. In specificational pseudoclefts with a *wh*-clause – *be* – VALUE word order, just as in simple specificational copular sentences with a predicate – *be* – subject order, the constituent in structural subject position fails to control PRO, as shown in (6) (modelled on examples presented in Huber 2002: 127, 134). In predicational pseudoclefts, on the other hand, control is unproblematic, just as in garden-variety predicational copular sentences in general. This we see in (7).

(6) a. *[who murdered $Brian]_i$ was Ryan, besides PRO_i being a bad guy
b. *the $murderer_i$ is Ryan, besides PRO_i being a bad guy

(7) a. [who murdered Brian]$_i$ was insane, besides PRO$_i$ being a bad guy
b. the murderer$_i$ was insane, besides PRO$_i$ being a bad guy

The third indication that a predicational/specificational distinction holds in the domain of pseudoclefts is the distribution of the copula in non-finite predications embedded under propositional attitude verbs such as *consider*. Here, predicational 'pseudoclefts' behave like predicational copular sentences in general in freely allowing the copula to be either present or absent (see (8) and (9)), while the specificational pseudoclefts in (10) pattern with the specificational copular sentences in (11) in forcing the copula to show up whenever the notional predicate precedes its subject (the VALUE), as in the b–sentences.

(8) I consider what Brian$_i$ is (to be) important to him$_i$

(9) I consider his job/status (to be) important to him

(10) a. I consider what Brian$_i$ is *(to be) important to himself$_i$
b. I consider important to himself$_i$?(to be) what Brian$_i$ is

(11) a. I consider the best candidate *(to be) Brian
b. I consider Brian (to be) the best candidate

The parallel between (10a) and (11a) (see Williams 1983; for some remarks on speaker variation, see Den Dikken 2005: §3.4) and between (10b) and (11b) is strongly suggestive of a parallel syntactic derivation for specificational pseudoclefts with *wh*-clause – *be* – VALUE order and inverse specificational copular sentences of the type in (5a).

The obligatoriness of the copula in (11b) can be made to follow from an analysis of inverse specificational copular sentences according to which the predicative noun phrase, *the best candidate*, is raised from its base position within the small-clause to a small-clause external A–position, across the base position of its subject (*Brian*), as depicted in (12b). To facilitate such apparently non-local movement, a linker (in the terminology of Den Dikken 2006) is required outside the small clause; this linker is obligatorily realised by a copular element.

(12) a. [$_{RP}$ [$_{Subject}$ *Brian*] [RELATOR [$_{Predicate}$ *the best candidate*]]]
b. [$_{FP}$ [$_{Predicate}$ *the best candidate*]$_k$ [RELATOR$_i$+LINKER=*be* [$_{RP}$ [$_{Subject}$ *Brian*] [t_i t_k]]]]

This analysis straightforwardly accommodates the obligatoriness of the copula in (10a) as well if specificational pseudoclefts are assumed to have an underlying representation in which the *wh*-clause is predicated of the VALUE. The structures in (13) embody this assumption.

(13) a. $[_{RP}$ $[_{Subject}$ *important to himself*] [RELATOR $[_{Predicate}$ *what Brian is*]]]

b. $[_{FP}$ $[_{Predicate}$ *what Brian is*$]_k$ [RELATOR$_i$+LINKER=*be* $[_{RP}$ $[_{Subject}$ *important to himself*] [t_i t_k]]]]

I will take (13) to be a grammatical derivation of specificational pseudoclefts. It is arguably not the only one made available by Universal Grammar (see Den Dikken, Meinunger & Wilder 2000 for discussion of an alternative Topic–Comment structure for a well-defined subset of specificational pseudoclefts), but it will be the only one of concern to us in this paper.

1.2 *It*-clefts: Predicational vs specificational

For pseudoclefts, the distinction between predicational and specificational specimens is entirely commonplace. Much less familiar is the fact that the same distinction can be made in the domain of *it*-clefts as well.

(14) it was an interesting meeting that I went to last night (Declerck 1988)

a. predicational – 'the meeting I went to last night was interesting'

b. specificational – 'I went to the following last night: an interesting meeting'

On the specificational reading of (14), paraphrased in (14b), the entire postcopular noun phrase is the focus of the *it*-cleft and supplies new information. On the predicational reading, by contrast, only the attributive adjective *interesting* seems to supply new information (and, concomitantly, only the adjective is focally stressed): *meeting* is discourse-old in (14a).

That predicational and specificational *it*-clefts are genuinely different syntactic creatures is perhaps particularly evident from the fact that the two resist being conjoined (Declerck 1988: 161). As Declerck notes correctly, the problem with (15c,d) is presumably of the same type as that with sentences such as **Brian is the tall one and also fat.*

(15) a. specificational & specificational
it was a BOOK that Brian gave me and a BIKE that Imogen gave me

b. predicational & predicational
it was an IMPORTANT meeting that I went to and an INTERESTING subject that they discussed

c. ??predicational & specificational
??it was an IMPORTANT meeting that I went to and BRIAN who was presenting a talk at it

d. ??specificational & predicational
??it was BRIAN who led the debate and an INTERESTING subject that they discussed

In his seminal study of cleft and pseudocleft constructions (centred mostly around facts from English), Declerck (1988: 158ff.) presents twenty characteristics that (14) on its predicational reading shares with predicational sentences (see also Reeve 2007 and Patten 2008 for discussion of predicational clefts). In my discussion here, I will focus on replicating in the domain of *it*-clefts the three formal criteria discussed for pseudoclefts in the previous section.

English *it*-clefts have rigid word order: *it* is invariably in structural subject position (*it was Bill who left*, **Bill was it who left*). But in languages such as Dutch (and also German, Swedish; see Huber 2002), the *it* of an *it*-cleft can surface to the right of the copula (even in non-root, non-Verb-Second constructions), under certain circumstances. Thus, the Dutch root clauses in (16a) and (16b) alternate freely; and even in the non-root contexts in (17), *het* 'it' may either precede or follow the VALUE.

(16) a. *het was zijn vrouw die...* (Dutch)
it was his wife who...

het waren ZIJN KINDEREN *die...*
it were his children who...

b. ZIJN VROUW *was het die...*
his wife was it who...

ZIJN KINDEREN *waren het die...*
his children were it who...

(17) a. *dat het* ZIJN VROUW *was die...*
that it his wife was who...

dat het ZIJN KINDEREN *waren die...*
that it his children were who...

b. *dat* ZIJN VROUW *het was die...*
that his wife it was who...

dat ZIJN KINDEREN *het waren die...*
that his children it were who...

But predicational *it*-clefts do not tolerate such word-order variation: they must have the *it* in structural subject position even in languages which otherwise allow flexibility in *it*-clefts. To see this, consider the examples in (18) and (19). The former have a lead-in question that explicitly identifies the *it*-clefts as specificational, and what we find is that the word orders in (18a) and (18b) both make felicitous answers to this question. The preamble in (19), by contrast, prepares for a predicational *it*-cleft in the answer – and this time, the word order in the b-sentence is distinctly infelicitous (whereas the a-sentence still works perfectly well). This demonstrates that predicational *it*-clefts, in a language whose specificational *it*-clefts show word-order flexibility, are linearly rigid.

(18) *was wat je gisteravond hebt bijgewoond een*
was what you yesterday evening have attended an
interessante bijeenkomst of een slaapverwekkende lezing?
interesting meeting or a soporific lecture
'was what you attended last night an interesting meeting or a soporific lecture?'

a. *het was een* INTERESSANTE BIJEENKOMST *die ik*
it was an interesting meeting that I
gisteravond heb bijgewoond
yesterday evening have attended

b. *een* INTERESSANTE BIJEENKOMST *was het die ik*
an interesting meeting was it that I
gisteravond heb bijgewoond
yesterday evening have attended

(19) *was de bijeenkomst die je gisteravond hebt*
was the meeting that you yesterday evening have
bijgewoond een interessante of een slaapverwekkende?
attended an interesting or a soporific
'was the meeting you attended last night an interesting one or a soporific one?'

a. *het was een* INTERESSANTE *bijeenkomst die ik*
it was an interesting meeting that I
gisteravond heb bijgewoond
yesterday evening have attended

b. #*een* INTERESSANTE *bijeenkomst was het die ik*
an interesting meeting was it that I
gisteravond heb bijgewoond
yesterday evening have attended

More microscopically, the word-order flexibility in Dutch specificational *it*-clefts disappears in non-root contexts when the VALUE is pronominal, as seen in (21), where the a–sentences are strongly degraded.[1] This strikingly enhances the parallel

1. Google statistics support this intuition robustly: while there are thousands of tokens of type (21b), there are exactly six hits for the string *dat het zij was die* and exactly three for the string *dat het zij waren die* (Nov 2008), and the hits returned for these strings all sound highly unnatural to me. Huber's (2002:79) observations regarding word order in German embedded *it*-clefts with the demonstrative *das* 'that' as the VALUE also show a restricted pattern in non-root contexts, though opposite to the one seen with Dutch personal pronouns in (21): *daß es das ist was mir Spaß macht* '(lit.) that it that is what me pleasure makes, i.e. that it's that which gives me pleasure' vs. ?*daß das es ist was mir Spaß macht* 'that that it is what me pleasure makes'. For personal pronoun VALUES, Huber's judgements show that there is actually

between specificational *it*-clefts and simple specificational copular sentences, which show the same pattern: (23a) contrasts markedly with (23b) (whereas in the root context in (22) no such contrast manifests itself, once again perfectly parallel to the absence of a contrast in (20)).

(20) a. *het was* ZIJ *die...* *het waren* ZIJ *die...*
it was she who... it were they who...
b. ZIJ *was het die...* ZIJ *waren het die...*
she was it who... they were it who...

(21) a. ?**dat het* ZIJ *was die...* ?**dat het* ZIJ *waren die...*
that it she was who... that it they were who...
b. *dat* ZIJ *het was die...* *dat* ZIJ *het waren die...*
that she it was who... that they it were who...

(22) a. *het grootste probleem was* ZIJ
the biggest problem was she
het grootste probleem waren ZIJ
the biggest problem were they
b. ZIJ *was het grootste probleem*
she was the biggest problem
ZIJ *waren het grootste probleem*
they were the biggest problem

(23) a. ?**dat het grootste probleem* ZIJ *was*
that the biggest problem she was
**dat het grootste probleem* ZIJ *waren*
that the biggest problem they were
b. *dat* ZIJ *het grootste probleem was*
that she the biggest problem was
dat ZIJ *het grootste probleem waren*
that they the biggest problem were

The fact that a contrastively stressed full pronoun does not want to stay *in situ* in the subject position of the small clause in these specificational contexts is quite surprising in light of the fact that elsewhere in the grammar, contrastively stressed pronouns typically differentiate themselves from weak pronouns precisely in being perfectly happy to stay *in situ*. Thus, in the English verb–particle construction,

slightly *more* word-order flexibility in the *non-root* context than there is in the root context (i.e. quite the opposite of the situation in (my) Dutch). I have nothing insightful to say about the German facts here.

weak pronouns resist placement to the right of the particle (*Brian sounded* ⟨*her*⟩ *out* ⟨**her*⟩) while a contrastively stressed pronoun is welcome to be pronounced in this position (*Brian sounded out* HER, *not* HIM). I do not profess to have a profound understanding of the roots of the problem with (21a) and (23a). But the empirical fact that specificational *it*-clefts pattern with other specificational copular sentences with respect to the word-order restrictions they impose in non-root clauses with a pronominal VALUE certainly enhances the conclusion that specificational *it*-clefts with *it*-initial order have the syntax of inverse specificational copular sentences like *the problem is the children*. What further underpins this conclusion are the agreement facts in the examples in the right-hand column of (17)–(18) and (20)–(23). No matter where the VALUE is placed, it always controls the agreement with the finite copula;[2] *het* never agrees with the copula in Dutch *it*-clefts.[3] In this respect as well, *it*-clefts behave like simple specificational copular sentences: in the right-hand examples in (22) and (23), the VALUE consistently controls agreement with the copula, too.

When it comes to control, the *it* of predicational *it*-clefts behaves exactly like the proleptic *it* of 'clausal extraposition' constructions, as shown by the facts in (24) and (25).[4]

(24) a. it_i was an INTERESTING meeting I went to last night, despite PRO_i being poorly organised

b. it_i was, despite PRO_i being poorly organised, an INTERESTING meeting I went to last night

2. For thoughtful disscussion of the problem of agreement in specificational copular sentences, see also Heycock (2009).

3. Though *het* never itself controls phi-feature agreement with the finite verb, it apparently prevents the postcopular subject from controlling phi-feature agreement if the postcopular subject is specified for first or second person: **het ben ik die...* 'it am I who...' and **het ben jij die...* 'it are you who...' are sharply ungrammatical (as are **het is ik/jij die...*); uninverted *ik ben het die...* and *jij bent het die...* are the only option with first and second person VALUES. The root of the agreement problem with **het ben ik/jij die...* remains unclear to me; but it seems to lie specifically in the fact that the inverted predicate in *it*-clefts is pronominal: in inverse copular sentences with a full-nominal predicate, such as *de beste kandidaat ben ik/jij* 'the best candidate is me/you', the form *ben* 'am/are(2sg-inv)' is perfectly fine.

4. Of the pair of sentences in (24), (24b) presumably makes the point more strongly than does (24a): in (24a), *an interesting meeting* could be understood as the controller of PRO, resulting in a reading that would not make the text point. But in (24b) it would be hard for *an interesting meeting* to control PRO (such would have to be backward control of a PRO in a sentence-internal adjunct).

(25) it_i finally became clear, after PRO_i having been explained ten times, that the earth is round

The fact that the *it* in (25) can control PRO is perhaps Bennis's (1986) strongest argument to the effect that the proleptic *it* of 'clausal extraposition' constructions is not an expletive but a referential pronoun. Now the fact that the predicational *it*-cleft in (24) allows *it* to serve as a controller as well leads us to the conclusion that the *it* of predicative *it*-clefts is likewise an argumental, referential pronoun.[5]

By contrast, the specificational *it*-cleft in (26) (cf. Huber 2002: 136) patterns with our earlier examples in (6) in resisting control: (26) is ungrammatical with the indexation provided there.[6,7]

5. Support for this conclusion comes from Ball's (1978) observation that predicational clefts with a *plural* VALUE take a *plural* pronoun/demonstrative rather than *it* (*those are real eye glasses that Micky is wearing*), whereas specificational clefts with a plural VALUE stick with *it*. Many of the examples of 'predicational *it*-clefts' in Declerck (1988) involve postcopular noun phrases that are predicable of non-humans, so *it* as the subject of these predicates is perfectly feasible for those cases. But there are also predicational *it*-clefts that have postcopular predicates that should be predicated of humans, like *it's no RELIABLE man that you have hired, but a crook!* (p. 160). The use of referential *it* as the subject here raises some questions; I cannot address them here.

6. The qualification 'with the indexation provided here' is quite important: it does not seem to be impossible for the postcopular VALUE of a specificational *it*-cleft to control the PRO subject of an adverbial clause. Thus, *it is Brian who is teaching without PRO actually being a teacher* is certainly grammatical; but it is demonstrably *Brian* (the VALUE) and not *it* that is controlling PRO here: when we make the adverbial clause finite, the only grammatical choice of subject is *he*, not *it* (*it is Brian who is teaching though he/*it isn't actually a teacher*). In the example in (26), the adverbial clause is supposed to contain a truncated cleft (cf. *it is a bad guy who...*).

7. Note that Reeve (2007) presents (ia, b) as grammatical, contradicting the text claim. I cannot weigh in on the English judgements here, but want to point out that my informants (speakers of American English, unlike Reeve) find (i) quite impossible. I add here that Dutch clearly resists control by *het* in specificational *it*-clefts. I will take such control to be generally impossible, leaving Reeve's examples aside. While one could in principle take (26) to indicate that the *it* of contrastive/stressed-focus *it*-clefts is an 'expletive', Huber (2002: 140) shows that in German it really does not behave as such. As is well known, 'truly expletive' *es* in German (as found e.g. in (ii)) occurs only in SpecCP of root clauses: (iib) is ungrammatical. By contrast, the *es* of German *it*-clefts does occur in non-SpecCP positions, as (iii) shows (see also Reeve 2007). So the *es* of *it*-clefts is certainly not an 'expletive'.

(i) a. it_i was John who Bill spent all his time with [despite PRO_i being Mary the day before] (Reeve 2007)

b. it_i was the furniture that annoyed John on Sunday [despite PRO_i being the décor the day before]

(26) *it$_i$ was Ryan who murdered Brian, besides PRO$_i$ being a bad guy

This suggests that the *it* of specificational *it*-clefts is not an argumental, referential pronoun, but instead behaves like the raised predicates of inverse specificational copular sentences and specificational pseudoclefts.

Finally, let us examine the distribution of the copula in the two types of *it*-clefts to fully round out our demonstration of the fact that *it*-clefts come in two types: predicational and specificational. Declerck (1988:171) observes the parallel between (27) and (28).

(27) a. I consider Brian (to be) his best friend
b. I consider his best friend *(to be) Brian

(28) a. I consider it (to be) an INTERESTING subject that they are discussing tonight
b. I consider it *(to be) BRIAN who is his best friend

The predicational *it*-cleft in (28a) does not force the presence of *to be*, which makes it behave on a par with canonical, non-inverted, predicational copular sentences of the type in (27a). This confirms what we had taken the control facts to indicate already: that *it* in (28a) is the subject of the predicate *an* INTERESTING *subject*, just as *Brian* in (27a) is the subject of the predicate *his best friend*. The *it* of (28b), by contrast, patterns with the inverted predicate of inverse specificational copular sentences of the type in (27b). So *it* in (28b) is the *predicate* of the VALUE *Brian*, its subject, just as *his best friend* in (28b) is the predicate of *Brian*.

The discussion of the word-order, control and copula distribution facts leads us to the partial derivation in (29) for specificational *it*-clefts. This derivation parallels the ones in (12), for inverse specificational copular sentences, and (13), for specificational pseudoclefts with a word order in which the *wh*-clause precedes *be*, which in turn precedes the VALUE.

(29) a. $[_{RP}$ $[_{Subject}$ VALUE] [RELATOR $[_{Predicate}$ *it*]]]
b. $[_{FP}$ $[_{Predicate}$ *it*$]_k$ [RELATOR$_i$+LINKER=*be* $[_{RP}$ $[_{Subject}$ VALUE] [t_i t_k]]]]

(ii) a. *es spielen Kinder auf der Straße*
it play children on the street
b. *Kinder spielen (*es) auf der Straße*
children play it on the street

(iii) a. *es ist Peter, der kommt*
it is Peter who comes
b. *Peter ist *(es), der kommt*
Peter is it who comes

The central claim of (29) about the syntax of *it*-clefts is that the *it* of specificational *it*-clefts is an underlying *predicate* that (in *it*-initial cases) inverts with its subject (cf. Moro's 1997 analysis of *it's that S* constructions, and Cheng & Downing's 2008 account of Zulu clefts), and *be* is a linker (in the sense of Den Dikken 2006).[8]

---

8. While the arguments reviewed in this section all robustly support the conclusion that the *it* of specificational *it*-clefts is the underlying predicate of a small clause that inverts with its subject (the VALUE) in the syntactic derivation, there is one important respect in which specificational *it*-clefts behave very differently from inverse specificational copular sentences – *wh*-extraction:

(i) a. I think the most important item on the reading list is this book
b. *which book do you think the most important item on the reading list is *t*?

(ii) a. I think what every linguistics student should read is this book
b. *which book do you think what every linguistics student should read is *t*?

(iii) a. I think it is this book that every linguistics student should read
b. which book do you think it is *t* that every linguistics student should read?

While the postcopular notional subject of an inverted predicate in specificational predicate nominal constructions like (i) and specificational pseudoclefts like (ii) is ineligible for *wh*-extraction, the postcopular VALUE of a specificational *it*-cleft is perfectly capable of undergoing A'–fronting, as seen in (iii). There is reason to believe, however, that this does not undermine the otherwise very robust syntactic parallelism between specificational *it*-clefts and other inverse specificational copular sentences.

Den Dikken (2006: 125) claims that the ban on (ib)/(iib) is reducible to the 'frozenness' of foci: 'A constituent that ends up in a syntactic configuration that leads it to be interpreted as a focus will inevitably be interpreted as the focus of the clause that it is in, and will literally be frozen in place'. Developing this account somewhat further, I believe there is a way of rendering (iiib) compatible with the general picture regarding extraction of the focus in specificational copular sentences. In all of the a–examples in (i)–(iii), focus is assigned in postcopular position. But only in (ia) and (iia) does the postcopular focus surface to the right of the topic. In the *it*-cleft in (iiia), the focus is to the *left* of the topic (i.e. the material in the *that*-clause): the *it* of *it*-clefts evidently is not itself the topic of the *it*-cleft (*it* is a mere pro-predicate, not serving as the meaningful topic of the sentence); the meaningful topic is the material in the relative clause, which *follows* the focus. So leftward *wh*-extraction of the focus of an *it*-cleft leaves the information-structural articulation of the sentence ('focus before topic') intact, precisely thanks to the fact that in *it*-clefts, the raised predicate does not represent the topic – unlike in other inverse specificational copular sentences such as (i) and (ii), whose raised predicates *are* the topics of the sentences. In (ib) and (iib), therefore, the focus is extracted *across the topic*, *reversing* the special information-structural pattern assigned as a result of predicate inversion. In (iiib), by contrast, extraction of the focus does not lead to a reversal of the information-structural pattern of the predicate inversion construction: the focus still precedes the topic after *wh*-extraction has taken place. On the assumption that extraction of the focus of a specificational copular sentence is grammatical so long as the information-structural pattern (foc<top or top<foc) of the input to extraction is kept intact,

It will be obvious, however, that the derivation in (29) is incomplete: we still need to find a way to incorporate the right-peripheral clause into the structure. This is the topic of Section 2, to which I now turn.

2. Integrating the relative clause

For specificational *pseudo*clefts, (13) gives us everything we need: the *wh*-clause is the small-clause predicate (a free relative); and it inverts (optionally) with its subject, the VALUE. But for specificational *it*-clefts, (29) gives us too little. Semantically, (29) seems rather uninformative: *it* by itself does not appear to be a very meaningful predicate for the VALUE. The relative clause at the end of the sentence would seem to be a natural predicate for the VALUE; but syntactically, this relative clause is hard to fit in: the structure in (29) provides no home for it as one of the major constituents of the structure.

One logical possibility would be to represent the relative clause of specificational *it*-clefts as a satellite specifying the content of *it*, as in (30a). The alternative would be to construe the relative clause with the VALUE of the *it*-cleft, as in (30b). In the latter case, we then have two further options in principle: the relationship between the relative clause and the VALUE could either be established *indirectly*, roughly as in (30b.*i*), or *directly*, roughly as in (30b.*ii*).

(30) a. $[_{\text{FP}}\ [_{\text{Predicate}}\ \underline{it}]_{\text{k}}$ [RELATOR$_{\text{i}}$+LINKER=*be* $[_{\text{RP}}\ [_{\text{Subject}}$ VALUE] [$t_{\text{i}}\ t_{\text{k}}$]]]] [RELATIVE CLAUSE]

b. *i.* $[_{\text{FP}}\ [_{\text{Predicate}}\ it]_{\text{k}}$ [RELATOR$_{\text{i}}$+LINKER=*be* $[_{\text{RP}}\ [_{\text{Subject}}$ VALUE] [$t_{\text{i}}\ t_{\text{k}}$]]]] [RELATIVE CLAUSE]

ii. $[_{\text{FP}}\ [_{\text{Predicate}}\ it]_{\text{k}}$ [RELATOR$_{\text{i}}$+LINKER=*be* $[_{\text{RP}}\ [_{\text{Subject}}$ VALUE [RELATIVE CLAUSE]] [$t_{\text{i}}\ t_{\text{k}}$]]]]

In what follows, I will show that (more detailed structures close to) (30b.*i*) and (30b.*ii*) are both available in principle, but that they result in different *subtypes* of specificational *it*-clefts: *indirect* association between the relative clause and the VALUE, *à la* (30b.*i*), delivers a *contrastive it*-cleft, while *direct* association, *à la* (30b.*ii*), yields a *continuous-topic it*-cleft. The difference between these two subtypes of specificational *it*-clefts is perhaps easiest to appreciate by looking at the pair of examples in (31a, b), where underlining marks new information.

---

it then follows that *wh*-extraction of the VALUE of an *it*-cleft is grammatical while extraction of the VALUE of other inverse specificational copular sentences (whose inverted predicate has information-structural content, unlike the proform *it* of *it*-clefts) systematically fails.

(31) a. contrastive or stressed-focus *it*-clefts
what got you interested in clefts? – it was Brian's book that got me interested in clefts

b. continuous-topic *it*-clefts
do you know Brian's book? – yes, in fact it was Brian's book that got me interested in clefts

None of the data that I will discuss in the remainder of this section would fall out from a structure of the type in (30a), in which the relative clause is associated with *it*. It seems to me, therefore, that (unless some other subtype of *it*-cleft is found for which (30a) could provide the right structure), (30a) should be rejected as a grammatical structure underlying clefts (*contra* esp. Percus 1997; also Hedberg 2000).

2.1 The relative clause of contrastive *it*-clefts: A headless relative

In my search for an analysis of the relative clause of contrastive *it*-clefts, I will take as my starting point the important (but easily overlooked) question of why this clause must obligatorily occur in right-peripheral, 'extraposed' position. The reason why I say this question is easily overlooked is that for English, it is not immediately evident that the relative clause must indeed be radically final.[9] But for an OV–language such as Dutch, this is plain from the facts in (32a, a′), which contrast markedly with (32b), involving a garden-variety headed relative (see Smits 1989 for an important antecedent of this observation).

(32) a. *dat het* ZIJN ZOON *⟨*die zojuist belde⟩* was ⟨√die *zojuist belde⟩* (Dutch)
that it his son who just called was who just called

a′. *dat* ZIJN ZOON *⟨*die zojuist belde⟩ het ⟨*die zojuist belde⟩ was ⟨√die zojuist belde⟩*
that his son who just called it who just called was who just called

b. *dat ik met zijn zoon ⟨die zojuist belde⟩ heb gestudeerd ⟨die zojuist belde⟩*
that I with his son who just called have studied who just called

9. Reeve (2007) presents empirical evidence for English *it*-clefts as well, however, to support the conclusion that the relative clause must be extraposed.

The key question that needs to be addressed in this connection is whether there any contexts, outside the realm of *it*-clefts, of obligatory relative clause extraposition. It is certainly not the case that a relative clause associated with the VALUE of an inverse specificational copular sentence is forced to extrapose. In the inverse predicate nominal constructions in (33a) and (34a), extraposition is perhaps preferred but by no means obligatory.[10]

(33) a. *dat het probleem zijn zoon ⟨(?)die zojuist belde⟩ is*
that the problem his son who just called is
⟨√die zojuist belde⟩
who just called

b. *dat zijn zoon ⟨die zojuist belde⟩ het probleem is*
that his son who just called the problem is
*⟨?*die zojuist belde⟩*
who just called

(34) a. *dat wat op tafel ligt het boek ⟨(?)dat Jan me gegeven*
that what on table lies the book that Jan me given
heeft⟩ is ⟨√dat Jan me gegeven heeft⟩
has is that Jan me given has

b. *dat het boek ⟨√dat Jan me gegeven heeft⟩ wat op*
that the book that Jan me given has what on
*tafel ligt is ⟨*dat Jan me gegeven heeft⟩*
table lies is that Jan me given has

So the relative clause of an *it*-cleft does not behave like a garden-variety restrictive relative clause associated to the subject of a predicate nominal construction – and more specifically, it does not even behave like a garden-variety restrictive relative clause associated to the VALUE of an inverse specificational copular sentence.

10. The preference for extraposition in (33a) and (34a) mostly has to do with the fact that the verbal cluster in these examples is very light: not extraposing the relative clause delivers a word order in which the only thing that follows the relatively bulky relative clause is the single-word, stressless copula that rounds out the matrix clause. But there are no restrictions on the composition of the verbal cluster in inverse specificational copular sentences – so this 'orphan effect' can be ameliorated by making the matrix verbal cluster bulkier: *dat het probleem zijn zoon die zojuist belde geweest zou kunnen zijn* 'that the problem his son who just called been would could have, i.e. that the problem could have been his son who just called' is perfectly fine. No matter how bulky the verbal complex of an *it*-cleft is made, however, the relative clause there can *never* precede it: it is systematically extraposed.

One context in which extraposition of something that looks like a relative clause is indeed obligatory is right dislocation, illustrated by English (35a–d) and their direct Dutch counterparts in (36a–d).[11]

(35) a. it was an explosion, what Bill heard
b. it's apples, what I have enough of
c. it was Alice, the one who just had the baby
d. it was a model train, what I bought
d′. it was a model train {that/which} I bought

(36) a. dat het een explosie ⟨*wat Bill gehoord heeft⟩ was, ⟨√wat Bill gehoord heeft⟩
b. dat het appels ⟨*waar ik genoeg van heb⟩ zijn, ⟨√waar ik genoeg van heb⟩
c. dat het Alice ⟨*degene die net een baby heeft gekregen⟩ was, <√degene die net een baby heeft gekregen>
d. dat het een modeltrein ⟨*wat ik gekocht heb⟩ was, ⟨√wat ik gekocht heb⟩
d′. dat het een modeltrein ⟨*die ik gekocht heb⟩ was ⟨√die ik gekocht heb⟩

The examples in (35) are from Gundel (1977), who takes them to be the source for *it*-clefts. I will not follow her in literally transformationally deriving *it*-clefts from right-dislocation constructions; but Gundel's (1977) insight that the relative clause in *it*-clefts is in the same structural position as right-dislocated constituents is certainly of significant interest. While a parallel treatment of, say, (35d) and (35d′) appears at first to be contradicted by the absence in clefts of the prosody typical of right-dislocation, it seems to be supported by the fact that the relative clause of clefts must indeed be radically final, like right-dislocated constituents.

To be able to gauge the syntactic significance of the parallel between right-dislocated constituents and the relative clause of *it*-clefts, we should now ask what the analysis of right dislocation is, and how it sheds light on the syntax of *it*-clefts. Here, I will adopt one specific approach to right dislocation – the 'asyndetic coordination' approach originally proposed by Jan Koster (for an easily accessible overview, I refer the reader to Koster 2000; see also Rijkhoek 1998; De Vries 1999). For Koster, the right-peripheral constituent is introduced as the complement of a null conjunction (annotated as ':') that heads a phrase whose specifier is the portion of the sentence that the right-peripheral constituent combines with. Concretely, for the Dutch right-dislocation construction in

11. On the link between *it*-clefts and right-dislocation constructions, see also Frascarelli and Ramaglia (2008: §4.2).

(36d), repeated in (37a), we end up with the structure in (37c), where the right-dislocated free relative *wat ik gekocht heb* is the complement of a ':' head whose specifier is the entire IP that precedes it.

(37) a. *dat het een modeltrein* ⟨**wat ik gekocht heb*⟩ *was,*
that it a model train what I bought have was
⟨$^{\surd}$*wat ik gekocht heb*⟩
what I bought have (= (36d))
b. *$[_{:P}$ $[_{DP}$ *een modeltrein*] [: [*wat ik gekocht heb*]]
c. $[_{:P}$ $[_{IP}$ *het een modeltrein was*] [: [*wat ik gekocht heb*]]

'Extraposition' can now be seen to transpire from a structure in which the ':P' takes as its specifier something larger than the noun phrase with which the right-dislocated phrase is associated. Such 'extraposition' is effectively forced in (37a) because a direct asyndetic specification relationship between the right-dislocated free relative and a DP cannot be established – (37b) is ill-formed. This follows from the fact that we are dealing in (37) with a *free* relative, introduced by *wat* 'what'. By their very nature, free relatives are 'free' or 'headless'. I take this to mean that they cannot be directly construed with an overt noun phrase.

This analysis of (37a) given in (37c) can now be extended to cover *it*-clefts. The structures in (38) illustrate this for our earlier examples in (35d′), from English, and (36d′), from Dutch.

(38) a. it was a model train {that/which} I bought (= (35d′))
*$[_{:P}$ $[_{DP}$ *a model train*] [: [{*that/which*} *I bought*]]
$[_{:P}$ $[_{IP}$ *it was a model train*] [: [{*that/which*} *I bought*]]
b. *dat het een modeltrein* ⟨**die ik gekocht heb*⟩ *was*
that it a model train that I bought have was
⟨$^{\surd}$*die ik gekocht heb*⟩
that I bought have (= (36d′))
*$[_{:P}$ $[_{DP}$ *een modeltrein*] [: [*die ik gekocht heb*]]
$[_{:P}$ $[_{IP}$ *het een modeltrein was*] [: [*die ik gekocht heb*]]

The ban on 'intraposition' of the relative clause in (38) will now follow analogously to the ban on 'intraposition' of the free relative in (37) *if* the relative in (38) is essentially a free relative.

The link between (35d′) and (35d), the latter unquestionably featuring a free relative, is certainly enhanced by the fact that *it*-clefts resist non-finite relatives (as pointed out by Declerck 1988: 152): non-finite relatives are grammatical in 'headed' contexts, but not in *free* relatives; so the fact that they are ungrammatical in *it*-clefts as well may give us an important clue to the effect that the relative clause in an *it*-cleft is very much like a free relative.[12]

(39) a. he was the third man to be arrested
b. *it was the President to be arrested
c. it was the President who was (to be) arrested

(40) a. what to do was unclear (infinitival *wh*-question)
b. *what to do was important (free relative)
c. what they should/would do was important

But a free relative approach to the relative clause of *it*-clefts would appear to be seriously compromised by the fact that typical free relatives are never introduced by *that, which* or Dutch *die*.

There is evidence, however, that *which* in the relative clause of *it*-clefts behaves differently from the way it does in garden-variety relatives. Something which, to my knowledge, has not been noted before in the literature on *it*-clefts is that *which* qua introducer of the relative clause seems to assert its inherent *specificity/D-linking* in ways that it systematically does not do when it is the relative operator in ordinary relatives. This specificity effect seems to underlie not just the relatively familiar observation that the relative clause of a contrastive *it*-cleft, when construed with a predicate nominal VALUE, can only be introduced by *that*, never

12. Declerck also notes that the relative clause of an *it*-cleft may not be a reduced relative (*it was* BRIAN **(who was) working in the garden*). This, too, carries over to free relatives (though rather trivially so: reduced relatives never have an overt operator in their left periphery, while free relatives demand an overt operator). At this time, I do not understand why the relative clause of English *it*-clefts and free relatives is always finite and non-reducible. Note that it does not seem to be a universal that the relative clause of *it*-clefts is always finite: Sleeman (2008) shows that, unlike English and French, Italian allows *it*-clefts with infinitival subject relatives:

(4) *è stato Gianni a darmi la chiave* (Italian)
is been Gianni to give-me the key
'it was Gianni who gave me the key'

Sleeman relates the contrast between Italian, on the one hand, and French and English, on the other, to the claim that Italian *it*-clefts always have a *contrastive* focus (whereas *it*-clefts in French and English have an *identificational* focus unmarked for contrastiveness), and that infinitival subject relatives are licensed specifically by contrastive focus. As a *general* claim about infinitival (subject) relatives this latter claim seems false (*I'm looking for a man to fix the sink* plainly does not require contrastive focus on *a man*). Note also that infinitival relatives remain ungrammatical in English/French *it*-clefts *even* when the VALUE *is* actually contrastive.

by *which* (cf. Declerck 1988: 152; Reeve 2007), as shown in (41) and (42), but also the novel observations built on (43)–(48), which I will go through step by step.[13]

(41) a. it is the president of the club that he has always wanted to be
c. Brian is the president of the club, {which/*that} Imogen has in fact always wanted to be

(42) a. *it is a doctor which I want to become, not a baker
b. it is a doctor that I want to become, not a baker

The aggregrate of the examples in (43)–(48) tells us that the relative clause of an *it*-cleft, when construed with a(n aggressively) non-specific/non-D-linked non-human VALUE, cannot be introduced by *which*, whereas a garden-variety relative clause with a non-specific/non-D-linked non-human head certainly can be so introduced. The examples in (43) and (44) show this with reference to *it*-clefts with *anything at all* or *nothing at all* as the VALUE: the a–sentences here are modelled on attested examples on the internet; and while the a–pattern is not common, it seems to me significant that the b–pattern is not found at all.[14]

(43) a. it is very unlikely that it is anything at all that you are doing wrong
b. *it is very unlikely that it is anything at all which you are doing wrong

(44) a. it is nothing at all that you are doing wrong
b. *it is nothing at all which you are doing wrong

The effect can perhaps be observed more clearly for *it*-clefts with *wh-the-hell* as the VALUE. *It*-clefts with a [+WH] VALUE generally disprefer a *wh*-operator in the relative clause (hence prefer *that*). But examples of the type in (45b), with *who*, and

---

13. Arguably in the same ballpark as the facts in (42) and (43)–(48) is Reeve's (2007) observation that, while idiom chunks are possible in *it*-clefts (unlike in pseudoclefts), they work only if *that* is chosen as the introducer of the relative clause. That *which* fails in (i) presumably has the same cause as the ungrammaticality of *which* in (42b), (43b), (44b) and (48b): a specificity mismatch between the VALUE and *which*.

(i) it was careful track {that/*which} she kept of her expenses

Reeve presents the possibility of idiom chunks in *it*-clefts as evidence for a raising analysis of the *it*-cleft. The analysis of the intimate relationship between the VALUE and the operator of the relative clause presented below should be able to preserve the desired result that idiom chunks are grammatical in *it*-clefts with an appeal to concord rather than raising.

14. There are very few examples of the type in (43a) and (44a) on Google, and my informants do not find it hugely natural to have *anything* or *nothing* as the VALUE of an *it*-cleft. But there are zero hits for "it is/was anything at all which" and "it is/was nothing which", and speakers sense a clear contrast between the a–examples and the b–sentences. It is this relative contrast that matters.

(47b), with *which*, can be found (though they tend to be rarer than corresponding examples with *that*).[15] By contrast, examples of the type in (48b), with *which*, are not found at all, and are judged to be sharply worse than (48a) and also distinctly worse than (47b), though *it*-clefts of the type in (46b) *are* found.[16]

(45) a. who is it that keeps sending me anonymous E-mails all the time?
b. ?who is it who keeps sending me anonymous E-mails all the time?

(46) a. who the hell is it that keeps sending me anonymous E-mails all the time?
b. ?who the hell is it who keeps sending me anonymous E-mails all the time?

(47) a. what is it that is bothering you?
what is it that you want?
b. ?what is it which is bothering you?
?what is it which you want?

---

15. The more contentious case here is the *which*-example in (47b). The number of hits for (47b) (search: "what is/was it which") is not huge (there are plenty of results that have "it" and "which" in separate clauses, such as *what is it? which type is best?* – but the number of clefts among the results is relatively small, and it may be significant that the bulk of the attested cases are *subject* clefts: (i.i), below, is one of the rare cases of an object cleft with *which*), but there definitely are numerous examples of this type, so it would not be right to exclude (47b) altogether. Below are some attested examples, culled from the internet with the aid of Google. For good measure, I have also included some attested examples of type (45b) (search: "who is/was it who"). Note that example in (iib) has a clearly non-specific/non-D-linked interpretation for *who* qua VALUE: so *who* does not have to be read as a D-linked element to make a relative clause introduced by *who* legitimate in an *it*-cleft.

(i) a. what is it which makes your product stand out from the rest?
b. what is it which draws her into anger?
c. what is it which makes say gold denser than aluminum?
d. what is it which, if changed, makes a document essentially different?
e. what is it which saves a soul?
f. what was it which led him to be such an effective double-agent?
g. what was it which we set out to accomplish?
h. what was it which got you interested in photography?

(ii) a. who is it who gets expensive jeans? is it Tutter or Malory?
b. who is it who still thinks George W. Bush has the judgement, maturity, and emotional stability required to lead the most powerful nation on earth?

16. Though (46b) may be much rarer than (46a) (just five hits on the web for "who the hell is it who", and a few more than five for "who the hell was it who"; but several thousands of the type in (46a)), it is significant that it is not radically impossible for *who* to be used as the relative operator in *it*-clefts with *who the hell* as the VALUE.

(48) a. what the hell is it that is bothering you?
what the hell is it that you want?

b. *what the hell is it which is bothering you?
*what the hell is it which you want?

So the specificity or D-linking effect seems to manifest itself only in *it ... which* clefts, not in *it ... who* clefts.

This can plausibly be related to the fact that *which* is itself [+specific]/D-linked in *wh*-phrases like *which book*, whereas *who* is not inherently marked for specificity or D-linking. But the specificity of *which* does not normally 'assert itself' on the head of a relative clause introduced by *which* – that is, in (49a) *as well as* (49b) we see an ambiguity between *de dicto* (non-specific) and *de re* (specific) interpretations. The same is true for (50): though, to my knowledge, no specific book exists that actually solves the mystery of *it*-clefts, (50b) is perfectly felicitous, which, if *which*-relatives were to force a specific interpretation on the relativised noun phrase, would be difficult to reconcile with our (or, at least, *my*) knowledge of the world.

(49) a. he wants to buy a car that is easy to park in small spaces
b. he wants to buy a car which is easy to park in small spaces

(50) a. he wants to find a book that solves the mystery of *it*-clefts
b. he wants to find a book which solves the mystery of *it*-clefts

These observations taken together suggest that *which* is, in some way, in a concord relationship with the VALUE of the cleft. Specifically, I propose that the structure of the extraposed relative of an *it*-cleft involves a null head that shows obligatory concord in specificity *(a)* with *which* (even though heads of relative clauses do not normally 'agree' with *which* in specificity) and *(b)* with the VALUE of the *it*-cleft. The structure in (51) sums it up.

(51) $[_{:P}$ [*it's* VALUE–XP$^{[\alpha SPEC]}$] [':' $[_{XP}$ ø $^{[\alpha SPEC]}$ $[_{CP}$ {*which*$_i$/Op$_i$}$^{[\alpha SPEC]}$
$[_{C'}$ {*that*/ ø } $[_{IP}$ (...) t_i (...)]]]]]]

Assuming that *which* is inherently specified as [+SPEC], and that the ø head of the relativised XP must show CONCORD for the feature [αSPEC] with both the operator in SpecCP and the VALUE–XP, we now derive the fact that whenever *which* is chosen as the operator of the relative clause in *it*-clefts, the VALUE–XP must be [+SPEC]: because *which* is inherently [+SPEC], and because it is in a concord relationship with ø, ø must also be [+SPEC], to ensure feature matching under concord; and because ø is in turn in another concord relationship with the VALUE, the VALUE must have a matching value for [±SPEC] as well, which prevents it from being non-specific whenever *which* is chosen as the operator in the relative clause.

This correctly rules out (42a), (43b), (44b), and (48b): in all of these cases, the nature of the VALUE–XP is such that it radically resists being in a concord relationship with a [+SPEC] element. When the VALUE is radically non-specific, ø is also [−SPEC], and in turn the operator in the left periphery of the relative clause must [−SPEC] as well, all as a result of concord. The inherently [+SPEC] operator *which* is incompatible with the [−SPEC] specification imposed via concord, so *which* cannot be used in (42a), (43b), (44b), and (48b). By contrast, the versions of these examples featuring *that* instead of *which* are grammatical because, unlike *which*, the null operator in the specifier of *that* is not inherently specified for specificity, hence may assume any specification for [αSPEC] that is appropriate in the structural environment.

The structure in (51) is a more detailed instantiation of the schema in (30b.*i*), repeated below. The obligatory concord relationship that we have found to hold between *which*, ø, and the VALUE supplies a powerful argument against approaches to *it*-clefts that take *it* and the relative clause to form a 'discontinuous constituent' (esp. à *la* Percus 1997, but see also Hedberg 2000), as represented by (30a).

(30) a. $[_{FP}\ [_{Predicate}\ \underline{\textit{it}}]_k$ [RELATOR$_i$+LINKER=*be* $[_{RP}\ [_{Subject}$ VALUE] $[t_i\ t_k]]]]$
[<u>RELATIVE CLAUSE</u>]

b. *i.* $[_{FP}\ [_{Predicate}\ \textit{it}]_k$ [RELATOR$_i$+LINKER=*be* $[_{RP}\ [_{Subject}$ <u>VALUE</u>] $[t_i\ t_k]]]]$
[<u>RELATIVE CLAUSE</u>]

Three serious questions arise at this point: *(a)* why must the null head ø necessarily be in a concord relationship with the relative operator and the VALUE–XP; *(b)* what is the difference between the relative clause of an *it*-cleft (which (51) treats as null-headed) and a free relative; and *(c)* what is the nature of ø, the null head of the relativised XP in *it*-clefts? I will address these questions in order.

The first question should be teased apart into two subquestions – one about the concord relation between ø and the relative operator, and the other about the concord relation between ø and the VALUE–XP. Regarding the former, I would like to present the following hypothesis: ø must show concord with the relative operator in order to be *formally licensed*. ø is a null category that, like other null categories, is in need of formal licensing. It cannot be licensed all by itself, nor can the head in its immediate structural environment, the ':' head in (51), help it out – ':' cannot formally license anything because it is itself featureless.[17] The radically null head of the relative clause in extraposition is structurally too distant from the VALUE–XP (embedded within the specifier of ':P') to be able to be formally

17. It is here that my adoption of Koster's ':P' analysis is significant, even though it is otherwise mostly a matter of representational convenience.

licensed by it. So only one possibility remains: the ø head depends for its formal licensing on the relative operator, with which it must entertain a concord relation in order for formal licensing to be in effect. And as regards the obligatory concord relationship between the null head and the VALUE, I hypothesise that it is this concord relationship that allows the ø head to be *content-licensed.* So ø depends for its licensing on *both* the relative operator *and* the VALUE–XP: the former takes care of *formal licensing*, and the latter of *content licensing.*

How then is the relativised XP in (51) different from a *free* relative (which cannot be used in an *it*-cleft)? Or put differently: what makes *which-* or *that*-relatives the only grammatical choice in the *it*-cleft in (52a) while a *what*-relative (a *free* relative) is the only grammatical choice in the pseudocleft in (52b)?

(52) a. it's KIMCHI {which/that/*what} I'd like to have
b. {what/*which/*that} I'd like to have is KIMCHI

In the *it*-cleft in (52a), the relationship between the null-headed relative and (the container of) the VALUE–XP is established via asyndetic specification (see (55a), further below). Asyndetic specification of this type is subject to a strict concord requirement, as is evident from (54): the intraclausal plural pronouns can only be associated with right-dislocated asyndetic specifiers that match their number feature. By contrast, nominal predication constructions are well known for allowing number mismatches between subjects and predicate nominals perfectly happily, as for instance in (53).

(53) *dat zij ons grootste probleem zijn*
that they our biggest problem are
'that they are our biggest problem'

(54) a. *dat zij me irriteren, {die kinderen/*ons grootste* probleem}
that they me irritate those children/our biggest problem
b. *dat ik hen haat, {die kinderen/*ons grootste probleem}*
that I them hate those children/our biggest problem

It is this strict concord relationship chacterising asyndetic specification that facilitates the licensing of the ø head in the *it*-cleft in (55a). In the pseudocleft in (55b), on the other hand, the relationship between the free relative and the VALUE–XP is established via predication, which, as we saw in (53), is not subject to strict concord between the subject and the predicate. Due to the lack of a strict concord relationship, the ø head cannot be licensed in pseudoclefts. Since the head of the relativised noun phrase is not allowed to be radically empty, something that has feature content must head the relativised noun phrase in a pseudocleft. That 'something' is a phonologically null but semantically contentful operator: ∀ or Def(inite) (cf. 'maximisation' effects in free relatives; this is naturally related to the 'exhaustivity' property of specificational pseudoclefts); cf. Percus (1997) (who extends this to clefts, wrongly so if I am right).

(55) a. $[_{:P}$ [*it's* VALUE–XP] [: $[_{XP}$ ø $[_{CP}$ {*which*$_i$/Op$_i$/**what*$_i$} $[_{C'}$ C $[_{IP}$ (…) t_i (…)]]]]]]

b. $[_{RP}$ VALUE–XP [RELATOR $[_{XP}$ ∀/Def $[_{CP}$ {*what*$_i$/*Op$_i$/**which*$_i$} $[_{C'}$ C $[_{IP}$ (…) t_i (…)]]]]]]

∀/Def is an 'unusual' external head of a restrictive relative, forcing *what* as the relative operator (see, for instance, Dutch *alles wat/*dat je ziet* 'everything what you see' and *dat wat/*dat je ziet* 'that what you see'). A classic approach to the *what* of English free relatives is to treat it as the surface realisation of the combination of *it* (the pronominal external head) and *which* ('*what* = *it*+*which*') – an approach that of course makes very little morphophonological sense (there is no plausible way to get from physical *it*+*which* to *what*) but hits the nail on the head when it comes to (at least one side of) the semantics of *what*. With *what* analysed as *what*=∀/Def+*which*, we have the outlines of an account of why free relatives are introduced by a 'special' operator.[18] The null head in (55a), on the other hand, is for all intents and purposes a 'regular' external head of a restrictive relative, being relativised with *which* or the null operator. So when the external head is radically empty (ø), the relative operator is the one expected for a garden-variety restrictive relative; it is only when the external head is phonologically null but semantically specified (as ∀ or Def) that the form of the relative operator is 'unusual'.

At this point let me add up what we have so far discovered regarding the null head of the relative clause of *it*-clefts: *(i)* it is obligatorily null (i.e. it does not alternate with anything overt); *(ii)* it is in need of formal licensing; and *(iii)* it is itself contentless, hence fully dependent on its environment for content licensing. Where does this leave us when it comes to determining the nature of the null head ø? Is there anything elsewhere in the grammar of English and/or other languages that resembles or is identical to this null element?

Null nouns lacking descriptive content certainly exist. Panagiotidis (2003), surveying the literature, discusses a variety of them, including such cases as *the poor* [*e*] in (56a), or *the tallest/shortest* [*e*] in (56b).

(56) a. the poor [*e*] are usually ignored by politicians because they tend not to vote

b. as for basketball players, the tallest [*e*] are usually paid more than the shortest [*e*]

18. The details of the analysis of free relatives are certainly beyond the scope of this paper.

But though there is a venerable tradition in the literature to treat the null head of such expressions as *pro* and to require of it that it be formally licensed and content-licensed (see esp. Kester 1996 and Sleeman 1996), Panagiotidis argues against the idea that empty nouns require licensing, at least in any of the ways suggested in the literature on null nouns (i.e. null nominal complements to D). Panagiotidis' strongest argument to this effect comes from the distribution of so-called Indefinite Argument Drop in Greek (Giannakidou & Merchant 1996), as in *i Maria puluse ftina isitiria*$_i$ *ki o Phoevos aghoraze* e_i 'Maria was selling cheap tickets and Phoevos was buying (them)'. Giannakidou and Merchant assign 'e_i' (which can be understood either as 'cheap tickets' or simply 'tickets') a DP structure in which an empty noun is embedded in a null-headed DP: $[_{DP}\ ø\ [_{NP}\ e]]$. Panagiotidis points out that with such argument drop, 'there do not seem to exist any special requirements for determiners' (p. 405): the form and distribution of the null determiner 'are those required for LF reasons in ordinary indefinite DPs', and the nullness of the determiner would make it difficult to pin down the licensing of the null noun e_N on specific properties of the determiner. This is well taken. It probably would not be right to imposed D-related formal licensing requirements on the empty noun e_N (whether analysed as *pro* or something else) within the null-headed DP of Greek Indefinite Argument Drop constructions. But the distribution of Indefinite Argument Drop in Greek is certainly not unrestricted – though not subject to licensing restrictions that differ from those of ordinary null-headed DPs, the null D-head in Indefinite Argument Drop contexts (just like null D in general) must be appear in a structural context in which it is formally licensed to be null; and the content of the null noun e_N in the complement of D must, in turn, be recoverable as well (in the Greek case, from the discourse antecedent, as marked by the coindexation). Viewed this way, formal licensing and content licensing do actually remain as hallmarks of empty nominal phrases (i.e. 'doubly null' noun phrases, whose NP and DP layers are both null-headed) – but the two requirements are distributed over two different ingredients: formal licensing becomes a requirement imposed on the D portion of the structure of the dropped argument, and content licensing is identified as a requirement imposed on the N portion. In (51)/(55a), the relative clause is headed by a nominal phrase that is 'doubly null' in this sense, and in this respect it resembles the DP in Greek Indefinite Argument Drop; and like the DP in Greek Indefinite Argument Drop constructions, its N- and D-heads are both subject to licensing requirements, but each to a different one: the empty noun N must be content-licensed (in the *it*-cleft case by being in a concord relationship with the VALUE), and the null D must be formally licensed (by being in a concord relationship with the operator in the relative clause).

In the free relative case in (55b), the D-head of the noun phrase heading the relative clause is not empty: it has semantic features, and depending on one's analysis of the way *what* comes about, it might even have some phonological features as well. So D here is not subject to a formal licensing requirement. And the fact that D has semantic content allows it to content-license the null noun in its complement. In free relatives, therefore, no concord requirements arise, and a predicational structure of the sort in (55b) converges.

In sum, what I have tried to argue in this section is that there are significant structural similarities but also important differences between the relative clauses in *it*-clefts and pseudoclefts. In particular:

(i) both *it*-clefts and pseudoclefts feature a null-headed relative clause
(ii) in *it*-clefts, the null head is *radically* empty (i.e. devoid of both phonological and semantic features), hence dependent for its *licensing* on a concord relation with the relative operator and the VALUE–XP
(iii) the concord relation between the ø head, the relative operator, and the VALUE–XP is responsible for the *specificity effects* seen in *it*-clefts featuring *which* as the relative operator (see (42)–(44) and (48))
(iv) the fact that a strict concord relation is established in an asyndetic specification structure but *not* in a predication structure (a 'small clause') is responsible for the unavailability of the ø-headed relative (the default option) in pseudoclefts

2.2 Explaining the properties of *it*-clefts with the aid of the headless relative analysis

Now that we have the analysis of the *it*-cleft in place, let me briefly demonstrate how it accounts for some of the key properties of the construction – besides the specificity effect that has driven the analysis.

Declerck (1988: 152) points out that the relative clause of an *it*-cleft 'can follow a uniquely referring "antecedent" such as a personal pronoun (*I, me*) or a proper name not preceded by an article, whereas a restrictive relative clause cannot' (Declerck 1988: 152), as illustrated in (57).

(57) a. it is me that they invited
b. they were thinking of {a linguist/*me} that they could invite
c. it is John that they invited
d. *(the) John that they invited (was John Smith, not John Jones)

This would be puzzling from the point of view of an analysis of *it*-clefts that treats the relative clause as *directly* related to the VALUE. But on the analysis proposed in Section 2.1, the relative clause is *not* construed directly with the VALUE: instead, it is associated with a ø-head that entertains a concord relationship with but is not identical to the VALUE. The facts in (57) thus fall into place.

Also relatable to the null-headedness of the relative clause construction in the *it*-cleft is the relatively microscopic observation (again made in Declerck 1988: 152) that the relative clause of an *it*-cleft, when construed with a VALUE containing *such*, cannot be introduced by *as* and must be introduced by *that* instead, whereas a garden-variety restrictive relative clause construed with a head containing *such* must be introduced by *as*, not by *that*. This is illustrated in (58).

(58) a. it is such a doll {that/*as} I'd like to have
b. this is such a doll {as/*that} I'd like to have

It is natural to hypothesise that *as* is only licensed as a relative operator in relative clauses whose external heads include the word *such*. Since the relative clause of *it*-cleft constructions is headed by ø, which does not include *such*, no *as* is licensed in (58a).

A better-known property of the relative clause of an *it*-cleft is that, when construed with a non-locative PP VALUE, hence containing a non-locative PP–gap, it is introduced by *that*, whereas a garden-variety restrictive relative clause with a PP–gap cannot be (see (59)).

(59) a. it was of Brian {that/*of whom} I was thinking
b. Brian was thinking of the woman {of whom/*that} Ryan was thinking

To explain the difference in the distribution of *that* across (59a) and (59b), we can capitalise on the concord requirement that we relied on in the account of the specificity effect in *it*-clefts with *which*. Concretely, the difference between (60a) and (60b) follows from concord, this time for 'prepositionality' – concord (for content-licensing) between ø and the prepositional VALUE identifies the former as a PP, and concord (for formal licensing) between ø and Op identifies the latter, and thereby its trace, as a PP; (60b) crashes because of lack of concord. Conversely, it is the lack of concord in regular headed relatives that explains the ungrammaticality of (59b) with *that*.

(60) a. it is [$_{PP}$ of Mary] [$_{XP=PP}$ ø [$_{CP}$ Op=PP [that I was thinking t_{PP}]]]
b. *it is [$_{PP}$ of Mary] [$_{XP=DP}$ ø [$_{CP}$ Op=DP [that I was thinking of t_{DP}]]]

And the fact that (60a) also becomes ungrammatical when the null operator is replaced with a PP pied-piped by *whom* (as in the version of (59a) with *of whom*) again recalls the structural similarity between the relative clause of *it*-clefts and a free relative: pied-piping in free relative constructions, including specificational pseudoclefts, is severely restricted:

(61) *of whom I was thinking was (of) Brian

So far in this section, I capitalised on ways in which the relative clause of an *it*-cleft *differs* from ordinary headed relatives. But there are also important properties that the two types of relative clause share, and which make it intuitively plausible from the outset to call the *that/wh*-clause of *it*-clefts a relative clause. Thus, for English, it is well known that in many (though, as we have seen, not all) cases, the *that/wh*-clause *it*-clefts can be introduced by either *that* or a *wh*-element, as is also the case in the typical (non-subject) restrictive relative clause.[19] And in Dutch and German, *it*-clefts with a demonstrative pronoun as the VALUE, just like as headed relatives associated with a demonstrative pronoun, force the operator in the relative clause to be *wat/was* 'what' rather than the d-pronoun that otherwise introduces relatives (see German *das was/*das mir Spaß macht* 'that which gives me pleasure' and *dass es* DAS *ist was/*das mir Spaß macht* 'that it that is what/d-pronoun me pleasure makes, i.e. that it is that which gives me pleasure'; Huber 2002: 79). And in Cypriot Greek clefts, according to Gryllia and Lekakou (2007), the *pu*-clause of an *it*-cleft shows the same pattern of resumption as do restrictive and free relatives: resumption is impossible with accusative arguments, and obligatory with non-arguments, in all these contexts. These parallels between the relative clause of *it*-clefts and ordinary relatives follow from the proposed analysis as well, thanks in particular to the obligatory CONCORD relationship between the ø head in (51)/(55a) and the VALUE.

2.3 The relative clause of continuous-topic *it*-clefts: A pseudorelative

The discussion in Section 2.1 has revealed that (30a) is not an adequate vehicle for the analysis of the relative clause in *it*-clefts, and that (30b.*i*), developed in more detail as (51)/(55a), seems just right for the purpose of explaining the unusual

19. Declerck (1988: 152) points out that the relative pronoun of an *it*-cleft 'may sometimes be deleted in subject position ..., whereas a subject relative pronoun can otherwise never be omitted (except in *there*-constructions)' (see also Pavey 2004). The fact that the relative clause of an *it*-cleft with a highest-subject gap seems to admit of a null left periphery somewhat more liberally than does a headed relative (as illustrated in (i)) is something that does not follow immediately from the structure proposed but may be related, perhaps, to the fact that the head of the relative clause in *it*-clefts is itself null. This needs further thought – if only because the empirical fact of the matter is not perfectly straightforward. A null left periphery in the highest-subject relative clause of an *it*-cleft, as in (ia), is not universally possible among native speakers of English. It seems to be distinctly uncommon among American English speakers. Note also that (ib) does not universally block a null left periphery in the English-speaking world: there are many dialects, both in the Old World and in the New World, that accept so-called subject contact relatives.

(i) a. it was John saw it first
b. the police would like to talk to the person *(who/that) saw it first

properties of the relative clause in contrastive *it*-clefts – in particular, its obligatory extraposition, and the specificity effect seen with *which* as the relative operator.

(30) a. $[_{\text{FP}}\ [_{\text{Predicate}}\ \textit{it}]_{\text{k}}\ [\text{RELATOR}_{\text{i}}\text{+LINKER=}\textit{be}\ [_{\text{RP}}\ [_{\text{Subject}}\ \text{VALUE}]\ [t_{\text{i}}\ t_{\text{k}}]]]]$
[RELATIVE CLAUSE]

b. *i.* $[_{\text{FP}}\ [_{\text{Predicate}}\ \textit{it}]_{\text{k}}\ [\text{RELATOR}_{\text{i}}\text{+LINKER=}\textit{be}\ [_{\text{RP}}\ [_{\text{Subject}}\ \text{VALUE}]\ [t_{\text{i}}\ t_{\text{k}}]]]]$
[RELATIVE CLAUSE]

ii. $[_{\text{FP}}\ [_{\text{Predicate}}\ \textit{it}]_{\text{k}}\ [\text{RELATOR}_{\text{i}}\text{+LINKER=}\textit{be}\ [_{\text{RP}}\ [_{\text{Subject}}\ \text{VALUE}$
$[\text{RELATIVE CLAUSE}]]\ [t_{\text{i}}\ t_{\text{k}}]]]]$

What I would now like to argue that (30b.*ii*) is close to right for the analysis of so-called *continuous-topic it*-clefts of the type in (31b), repeated here (along with a typical *contrastive it*-cleft):

(31) a. contrastive or stressed-focus *it*-clefts
what got you interested in clefts? – it was Brian's book that got me interested in clefts

b. continuous-topic *it*-clefts
do you know Brian's book? – yes, in fact it was Brian's book that got me interested in clefts

Before I turn to the two key structural properties that differentiate continuous-topic *it*-clefts from contrastive *it*-clefts, let me make it clear that both types of *it*-clefts belong to the family of *specificational it*-clefts. In Section 1, I reviewed three diagnostics that allow us to tell apart predicational and specificational copular sentences, and demonstrated that they apply to *it*-clefts, proving that *it*-clefts come in both predicational and specificational flavours. Perhaps the most powerful test is the distribution of the copula. Recall that a copula shows up obligatorily in inverse specificational copular constructions when these are embedded below a propositional attitude verb like *consider* – and recall, more specifically, that some *it*-clefts pattern exactly like inverse specificational copular constructions in this regard, while others do not. The contrast in (28), repeated below, will bring this back to memory.

(28) a. I consider it (to be) an INTERESTING subject that they are discussing tonight

b. I consider it *(to be) BRIAN who is his best friend

The *it*-cleft in (28a) is a predicational construction, with *it* serving as the subject of *an interesting subject*; (28b), on the other hand, is a specificational *it*-cleft, with *it* being the raised predicate of the VALUE, *Brian*. Now, (28b) is of course a *contrastive it*-cleft, of type (31a). Contrastive *it*-clefts clearly belong to the family of specificational *it*-clefts. To determine whether *continuous-topic it*-clefts also belong to this family, all we now need to do is to verify whether the copula is optional or obligatory when a continuous-topic *it*-cleft is embedded under *consider* – and as (62) shows clearly, the copula distribution facts put the continuous-topic *it*-cleft squarely in the family of inverse specificational constructions.

(62) A: do you know Brian's book?
B: yes, in fact I consider it *(to be) Brian's book that got me interested in clefts

So the *it* of sentences like (31b) is an underlying predicate that inverts with its subject in the course of the syntactic derivation, forcing the presence of *to be* in (62B). To probe more deeply into the rest of the syntax of continuous-topic *it*-clefts, it will be useful to look closely at two important structural restrictions on such *it*-clefts identified in the literature. These are reproduced in (*i*) and (*ii*):

(i) 'Informative-presupposition *it*-clefts are formally and unambiguously identifiable. First, unlike stressed-focus *it*-clefts, they have normally (vs. weakly) stressed *that*-clauses.[fn. omitted] Second, they generally have a short and anaphoric focus, which, in my data, is either a (subject) NP or an adverbial, generally of time, place, or reason ... Third, in such sentences, <u>*that/wh-* is not deletable</u>.' (Prince 1978: 898; my underscore)[20]

(63) a. I want you to agree with me, no matter who it is {that/ø} you think is right
b. The leaders of the militant homophile movement in America generally have been young people. It was they {who/*ø} everyone knows fought back during a violent police raid on a Greenwich Village bar in 1969

(ii) <u>*that* cannot be used</u> in <u>highest-subject</u> *it*-clefts of the continuous-topic (or informative-presupposition) type <u>if the VALUE is [+human]</u> (Kayne 1981: §3.3.3)

(64) A: do you know Mary's book?
B: yes, in fact it was Mary's book {which/that} got me interested in clefts

(65) A: do you know Mary?
B: yes, in fact it was Mary {who/?*that} got me interested in clefts

(66) A: do you know Mary?
B: yes, in fact it was Mary {who/that} everybody knows got me interested in clefts

20. Erades (1962) makes this observation as well, though he does not state it in categorical terms.

Kayne's observation is relatable to Belletti's (2008) recent suggestion that the specifier position of the relative clause in highest-subject *it*-clefts is an *A–position* – which suggests a link with pseudorelatives (cf. (67)), as Belletti notes (but she does not develop this in any detail).

(67) *j'ai vu Marie qui mangeait une pomme* (French)
I'have seen Marie who ate an apple
'I saw Marie eat an apple'

The claim that the specifier position of the relative clause of highest-subject *it*-clefts is an A–position is not obviously correct as a *general* claim about ALL highest-subject *it*-clefts. But it seems to me that it is highly plausible that it *is* correct on a more modest scale, confined in scope to continuous-topic *it*-clefts.

In particular, imagine that in the structure of a highest-subject continuous-topic *it*-cleft, the VALUE is actually base-generated in SpecCP, with the *wh*-constituent occupying the SpecIP position and being linked to the VALUE in SpecCP, as in (68) – a structure that closely resembles Guasti's (1993) analysis of pseudorelatives of the type in (67) (which base-generates the 'head' of the pseudorelative in the specifier of 'AgrCP', the projection in the C–domain that has an A–specifier position).

(68) $[_{SC}$ $[_{CP}$ VALUE$_{[+human]}$ $[_{C'}$ (**that*) $[_{IP}$ *who* $[_{I'}$ I …]]]] $[_{Predicate}$ *it*]]
(cf. (30b.*ii*))

If the VALUE is in SpecCP in highest-subject continuous-topic *it*-clefts, as in (68), and if SpecCP in these *it*-clefts is an A–position (as Guasti 1993 proposed for the SpecCP of pseudorelatives), the ban on *that*-relatives with [+human] VALUES can be made sense of as follows. Assume first, uncontroversially, that a [+human] occupant of SpecCP *qua* A–position must agree with C. Secondly, let us follow Kayne (2008) in taking seriously the fact that *that* is a grammaticalisation of the distal demonstrative pronoun, which cannot refer to humans: we can say *he/she talks too much*, but not **that talks to much* (except insultingly or with reference to a parrot). So in (68), the [+human] specification of the VALUE clashes with a lexicalisation of C as *that*, which is incompatible with [+human]. This then captures Kayne's observation in (65).

I should note that I have found that there are quite a number of speakers who do not object strongly at all to the use of *that* in (65B). What could we say about such speakers? The answer, from the point of view of the proposal for continuous-topic *it*-clefts, is simple: for such speakers, the complementiser *that* does NOT share with the distal demonstrative *that* its [–human] feature specification. Thus, the difference between speakers with respect to the allowability of *that* in (65B) is, at the end of the day, a question of whether *that*, in the speaker's lexicon, is listed once (as a demonstrative, with the feature [–human], thus always prevented from referring deictically to a human or being in a Spec–Head relationship with something specified as [+human])[21] or more than once (as a demonstrative *and* as a complementiser).[22] For speakers who list *that* just once, the Kayne judgement is in effect; for the homonyms group, it is not.

The account of Kayne's observation in (65) that I have just presented is predicated on the premise that the relative of a highest-subject continuous-topic *it*-cleft is a *pseudorelative*, and that, more specifically, the entire pseudorelative (including the 'head') occupies the subject position of the small clause whose predicate is *it* (as in (68)). Precisely by virtue of the fact that it structurally represents the entire pseudorelative CP as the subject of the small clause, (68) predicts that the *entire CP* is the focus of the cleft, not just the 'head' of the pseudorelative – after all, it is the subject of the raised predicate of an inverse specificational copular sentence that qualifies as the focus; and the subject of *it* in (62) is the entire pseudorelative CP. This is in fact exactly the right result for continuous-topic *it*-clefts, which have the peculiar property that it is not the VALUE *per se* that is the focus of the construction but rather the predication established between the VALUE and the predicate denoted by the pseudorelative clause. This point is made forcefully in important work on pseudorelatives and a particular subtype of clefts in French by Lambrecht (2002).

Going much further than Belletti in empirical detail, Lambrecht (2002) *explicitly* establishes a parallel between pseudorelatives and a particular subtype of clefts in French – esp. constructions like (69) (so-called *avoir*-clefts).

(69) a. *j'ai une dent qui manque* (French)
I'have a tooth that misses
'I have a tooth missing'

b. *y a la téléphone qui sonne*
there has the phone that rings
'the phone is ringing'

21. As Kayne (2008) points out, *that man* and *that mat* are both grammatical, indicating that the demonstrative when used as a determiner neither refers deictically (instead the whole noun phrase *that man/mat* refers deictically) nor entertains a Spec–Head relationship with something [+human] (i.e. the head noun's projection, in *that man/mat*, is not in a Spec–Head relationship with the demonstrative; in (68), by contrast, a Spec–Head relation *is* inevitably established).

22. I take it for granted that for all speakers of English, *that* qua demonstrative pronoun is restricted to non-humans (i.e. I do not anticipate finding an English speaker who will happily say *that talks too much*, pointing to a person, except in an attempt to insult the person in question); so arguably, *that* qua demonstrative is always specified as [–human].

Lambrecht uses the label 'presentational relative construction' (PRC) for all his examples, including his *avoir* clefts and perception constructions with pseudo-relatives. He observes that 'the discourse function of this construction type is to introduce a new entity into a given discourse world and at the same time to express some piece of new information involving this entity' (p. 171) – so, crucially, they have in common with continuous-topic *it*-clefts the fact that the relative clause is not presuppositional but new. For Lambrecht, in pseudorelatives and *avoir*-clefts '[t]he RC denotatum … has a FOCUS relation to the global proposition' (p. 178). For continuous-topic clefts at least (I have nothing to say here about pseudorelatives), I would argue that this is because it is the relative clause as a whole that serves as the subject of the specificational copular sentence, as depicted in (68).

Thus (68) allows us to explain both the ban on *that* in highest-subject continuous-topic *it*-clefts with a [+human] VALUE and the information-structural profile of these constructions (as distinct from contrastive *it*-clefts).[23]

The structure in (68) as it stands caters specifically for *highest-subject* continuous-topic *it*-clefts. This is basically a good result: according to Prince (1978: 899), continuous-topic *it*-clefts are overwhelmingly more common (in corpora) with highest subjects than with objects or other constituents.[24] Prince was successful, though, in constructing (63b) on the basis of an attested example with a highest-subject focus; and Kayne (2008) gives a made-up example of a continuous-topic *it*-cleft with an object gap in the relative clause: *do you know Mary? – yes, in fact it was Mary {who/$^?$that} I learned linguistics from in the first place*. So continuous-topic *it*-clefts are not strictly confined to highest subjects, though they tend to be particularly common in corpora with highest subjects.

Let me tentatively take this to mean that (68) (which fits the information-structural profile of these clefts perfectly) is actually correct as the schema for continuous-topic *it*-clefts *in general*, and that non-(highest-)subject continuous-topic *it*-clefts are 'squeezed into' this general schema. Specifically, let me assume that non-(highest-)subject continuous-topic *it*-clefts *are* in fact (surface appearances notwithstanding) instances of highest-subject continuous-topic *it*-clefts – but that

23. One thing that (68) does not account for as it stands is the fact that the (pseudo)relative clause of a continuous-topic *it*-cleft, just like the relative clause of other specificational pseudoclefts, must be radically clause-final. This remains to be addressed.

24. Prince (1978: 899) points out that of the 50+ examples of informative-presupposition *it*-clefts with a nominal focus that she had gathered, every one of them involved a *subject* – 'While I certainly am not claiming that focused objects never occur in this construction, I do consider this an important area for further investigation'.

the portion of the relative clause in which the VALUE identifies the highest subject is *elliptical*, in either of the two ways in (70).[25]

(70) a. [$_{SC}$ [$_{CP}$ VALUE$_{[+human]}$ [$_{C'}$ (**that*) [$_{IP}$ *who* ~~*is the person [who/that*~~ ...]]]]] [$_{Predicate}$ *it*]]

b. [$_{SC}$ [$_{CP}$ VALUE$_{[+human]}$ [$_{C'}$ (**that*) [$_{IP}$ ~~*who is the person*~~ [*who/that* ...]]]]] [$_{Predicate}$ *it*]]

(70a, b) present the two logically possible ellipsis choices. Of these, (70a) makes exactly the same predictions regarding the physical left periphery of the relative clause as does (68): only *who* should be allowed with a [+human] VALUE. (70b), by contrast, predicts that the physical left periphery of the relative clause should be subject to exactly the same restrictions that a restrictive relative clause associated with a [+human] predicate nominal is normally subject to – i.e. (70b) allows *that* for the same reason that *the person that...* is grammatical. So via (70b), we can accommodate the possible occurrence of *that* in non-(highest-) subject continuous-topic *it*-clefts. And interestingly, we also get a straightforward handle on the fact that a *null* left periphery is disallowed in such clefts – Prince's observation in *(i)*, illustrated by (63b). Here is how.

The ellipsis derivation in (70a) predicts that *who* must show up for the same reason that *who* must show up in (68) (the EPP). (70b), on the other hand, elides the *wh*-word of the pseudorelative, and preserves the 'regular' relative clause embedded within the pseudorelative. Under 'normal' (i.e. non-elliptical) circumstances, the left periphery of a regular non-highest-subject relative clause is allowed to be null. But in the special circumstances that the regular non-highest-subject relative in (70b) finds itself in, its left periphery must be overtly realised, by either *who* or *that*. This is so because the fact that the matrix is elliptical prevents licensing of a null left periphery in the embedded relative clause – basically for the same reason that complementiser deletion in the clausal complement of a gapped bridge verb is impossible: *John said (that) Mary had done it, and Bill* ~~*said*~~ **(that) Sue had.*

Prince's (1978) observation that continuous-topic *it*-clefts disallow a null left periphery is thus accounted for. What remains to be said is that, apparently, an

25. If ellipsis is the way to derive non-highest-subject pseudorelatives on the basis of a core structure that admits only highest-subject gaps, the fact that Romance pseudorelatives are strictly confined *on the surface* to highest-subject cases suggests that the kinds of ellipsis depicted in (70a, b) are not available in the Romance pseudorelative. While I have no rationale to offer for why this is the case, it is clear that (if this way of looking at the world is on the right track) the question of whether or not the pseudorelatives of a particular language are confined *on the surface* to highest subjects must be a function of the constraints on ellipsis in the language.

elliptical derivation for a highest-subject continuous-topic *it*-cleft is unavailable. For plainly, if we allowed (70b) as the underlier for highest-subject continuous-topic *it*-clefts, we would lose our account of Kayne's observation in (65B). An elliptical derivation for continuous-topic *it*-clefts apparently is only available as a last resort – so only for non-(highest-)subject cases, for which (68) as it stands is not applicable. Since (68) itself takes care directly of highest-subject continuous-topic *it*-clefts, the more complex source in (70b) is not available. Though this makes intuitive sense, formalising it as part of a general theory of the distribution of elliptical underliers is by no means trivial. Since I am currently unable to do more than this, however, I must leave the pursuit of a principled theory of this sort for some future occasion.

3. Some conclusions on predication and specification

Having come to the end of this exploration of predication and specification in the realm of cleft sentences, what I think we can say with confidence, now that the entire range of types of specificational copular sentences has been taken into account, is that all specificational copular sentences have a predicational source. More specifically, it seems to me true that all *inverse* copular sentences (i.e. the ones derived via Predicate Inversion) are specificational copular sentences (with 'equatives' arguably subsumed under this label; see Den Dikken 2006 for a suggestion regarding the analysis of equative copular sentences). But it is not the case that, conversely, all specificational copular sentences are inverse copular sentences: copular sentences with a canonical subject – predicate order can support a specificational interpretation as well. Finally, we have found that specificational *it*-clefts are a particular subtype of inverse specificational copular sentences – in particular, copular sentences featuring a pro-predicate, *it*. In contrastive specificational *it*-clefts, this pro-predicate takes as its subject the projection of the focus, which in its turn is structurally related to a radically headless relative via asyndetic specification (not predication). In continuous-topic *it*-clefts, on the other hand, pro-predicate *it* is predicated of the pseudorelative constituted by the VALUE and the relative clause, a constituent that, as a whole, is the focus of the cleft.

Acknowledgements

Versions of this paper were presented at the workshop on clefts organised by the editors of this volume (Zentrum für Allgemeine Sprachwissenschaft, Berlin, 28–29 November 2008), at Harvard University (23 February 2009), and the workshop on non-canonical predication held at the University of Western Ontario (16 May 2009). The paper also served as material for a portion of my Advanced Syntax seminar on the syntax of cleft sentences at the CUNY Graduate Center in the spring of 2009. I thank the participants in these events, and especially David Adger, Mark Baker and Caroline Heycock, for their feedback.

References

Ball, Catherine. 1978. It-clefts and th-clefts. Paper presented at the LSA summer meeting, Urbana-Champaign IL.

Belletti, Adriana. 2008. Answering strategies: New information subjects and the nature of clefts. Chapter 10 of *Structures and Strategies*, London: Routledge.

Bennis, Hans. 1986. *Gaps and Dummies*. Dordrecht: Foris.

Cheng, Lisa & Downing, Laura. 2008. Clefts in Durban Zulu. Paper presented at the workshop on clefts, ZAS Berlin.

Declerck, Renaat. 1988. *Studies on Copular Sentences, Clefts and Pseudo-clefts*. Leuven: Leuven University Press/Dordrecht: Foris.

den Dikken, Marcel. 2005. Specificational copular sentences and pseudoclefts. In *The Blackwell Companion to Syntax*, Vol. IV, Henk van Riemsdijk & Martin Everaert (eds). Oxford: Blackwell.

den Dikken, Marcel. 2006. *Relators and Linkers: The Syntax of Predication, Predicate Inversion, and Copulas*. Cambridge MA: The MIT Press.

Dikken, Marcel, Meinunger, André & Wilder, Chris. 2000. Pseudoclefts and ellipsis. *Studia Linguistica* 54: 41–89.

Erades, Pieter. 1962. Points of modern English syntax. *English Studies* 43: 136–41.

Frascarelli, Mara & Ramaglia, Francesca. 2008. (Pseudo)cleft constructions at the interfaces. Ms, University of Rome.

Giannakidou, Anastasia & Merchant, Jason. 1996. On the interpretation of null indefinite objects in Modern Greek. *Studies in Greek Linguistics, Proceedings of the* 10th *Annual Meeting of the Department of Linguistics*. Thessaloniki: Faculty of Philosophy, Aristototle University.

Gryllia, Stella & Lekakou, Marika. 2007. Clefts in Cypriot Greek. Ms, Leiden University & Meertens Institute, Amsterdam.

Guasti, Maria Teresa 1993. *Causative and Perception Verbs: A Comparative Study*. Turin: Rosenberg & Sellier.

Gundel, Jeanette. 1977. Where do cleft sentences come from? *Language* 53: 543–59.

Hedberg, Nancy. 2000. The referential status of clefts. *Language* 76: 891–920.

Heycock, Caroline. 2009. Specificational sentences, scrambling, and special nouns. Paper presented at the workshop on noncanonical predication, University of Western Ontario. Ms, University of Edinburgh.

Higgins, F. Roger. 1979. *The Pseudocleft Construction in English*. New York NY: Garland.

Huber, Stefan. 2002. Es-*Clefts und* det-*Clefts: Zur Syntax, Semantik und Informationsstruktur von Spaltsätzen im Deutschen und Schwedischen*. Stockholm: Almqvist & Wiksell International.

Kayne, Richard. 1981. ECP extensions. *Linguistic Inquiry* 12: 93–133.

Kayne, Richard. 2008. Why isn't *this* a complementizer? Ms, New York University.
Kester, Ellen-Petra. 1996. The Nature of Adjectival Inflection. Ph.D. dissertation, OTS, Utrecht University.
Koster, Jan. 2000. Extraposition as parallel construal. Ms, University of Groningen.
Lambrecht, Knud. 2002. Topic, focus and secondary predication: The French presentational relative construction. In *Romance Languages and Linguistic Theory 2000*. [Current Issues in Linguistic Theory 232], Claire Beyssade, Reineke Bok-Bennema, Frank Drijkoningen & Paula Monachesi (eds), 171–212. Amsterdam: John Benjamins.
Moro, Andrea. 1997. *The Raising of Predicates*. Cambridge: CUP.
Panagiotidis, Phoevos. 2003. Empty nouns. *Natural Language & Linguistic Theory* 21: 381–432.
Patten, Amanda. 2008. On the specificational/predicational distinction in *it*-clefts. Paper presented at the workshop on clefts, ZAS Berlin.
Pavey, Emma Louise. 2004. The English *It*-cleft Construction: A Role and Reference Grammar Analysis. Ph.D. dissertation, University of Sussex.
Percus, Orin. 1997. Prying open the cleft. In *Proceedings of NELS 27*, 337–351. Amherst MA: GLSA.
Prince, Ellen. 1978. A comparison of *wh*-clefts and *it*-clefts in discourse. *Language* 54: 883–906.
Reeve, Matthew. 2007. Relatives and pronouns in the English cleft construction. Ms, University College London.
Rijkhoek, Paulien. 1998. On Degree Phrases and Result Clauses. Ph.D. dissertation, University of Groningen.
Sleeman, Petra. 1996. Licensing Empty Nouns in French. Ph.D. dissertation, OTS, Utrecht University.
Sleeman, Petra. 2008. Clefts and the licensing of infinitival subject relatives. Paper presented at the workshop on clefts, ZAS Berlin.
Smits, Rik. 1989. *Eurogrammar. The Relative and Cleft Constructions of the Germanic and Romance Languages*. Dordrecht: Foris.
de Vries, Mark. 1999. Extraposition of relative clauses as specifying coordination. In *Proceedings of ConSOLE 7*.
Williams, Edwin. 1983. Semantic vs. syntactic categories. *Linguistics and Philosophy* 6: 423–46.

Wh-clefts and verb-initial word order in Austronesian languages

Edith Aldridge
University of Washington

Wh-questions are formed on clefts in many Austronesian languages, a fact which is generally assumed to be related to their verb-initial basic word order. What is less clear is the precise relationship between verb-initial word order and the cleft strategy for questions. This paper proposes that the derivation of clefts is parallel to the derivation of basic word order in VOS languages. The absolutive DP is analyzed as a topic and moves to the left periphery of the clause. Following this, the remnant clause is fronted to a higher focus position. I further show how this parallelism accounts for certain distinguishing characteristics of clefts in Austronesian languages.

Keywords: Cleft; *wh*-question; verb-initial word order; predicate-fronting; Austronesian

1. Introduction

It is well known that *wh*-questions frequently take the form of clefts in a great many Austronesian languages (Georgopoulos 1991; Paul 2000; Pearson 2001; Massam 2003; Aldridge 2004; Potsdam 2006, 2007, 2009; among others). It is also generally agreed that the structure is some type of pseudocleft, in which the focused constituent, i.e. the *wh*-word, functions as the matrix predicate, while the remainder of the utterance forms a headless relative clause in matrix subject position. (1a) shows a cleft in which a predicate nominal is focused. Since the languages in question are generally verb- or predicate-initial, the focused predicate appears clause-initially. It is followed by the headless relative, which is a bare CP with an absolutive case marker. (1b) shows a *wh*-cleft in which the *wh*-word is the matrix predicate.

(1) *Seediq*
   a. *Rulu* [$_{DP}$ *ka* [$_{CP}$ *b⟨n⟩ari=na*]].
      car ABS ⟨PERF⟩buy=3SG.ERG
      'What he/she bought is a car.'

b. *Maanu* [$_{DP}$ *ka* [$_{CP}$ *b⟨n⟩ari=na*]]?
what ABS ⟨PERF⟩buy=3SG.ERG
'What did he/she buy?'

Recent research has attempted to account for *wh*-clefting within a general analysis of basic word order in these languages. Massam (2000, 2001, 2003) and Oda (2002) have proposed that *wh*-movement is generally disallowed in verb-initial languages, because clause-initial position is reserved for predicative material. The proposal is essentially that the EPP feature on T or Infl attracts the predicate in verb-initial languages rather than the DP subject.

(2) *Massam (2003), Oda (2002)*
Infl has a [Pred] feature and not a [D] feature.

This effectively ensures that these languages have predicate-initial word order and that DPs do not move to clause-initial position. In the derivation of basic word order, the VP is attracted to [Spec, IP].

(3) *Niuean* (Massam 2001: 157)

a. [$_{VP}$ *Tagafaga* ika] *tumau* *ni* *a* *ia*.
hunt fish always Emph ABS he
'He is always fishing.'

b.

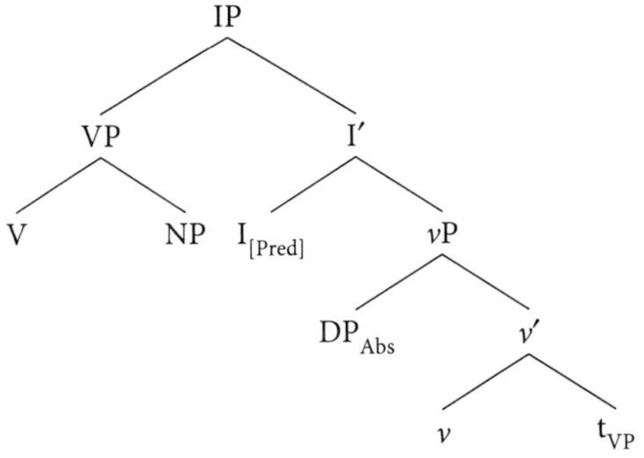

In *wh*-questions, there is no DP *wh*-movement to [Spec, CP]. As evidence, Massam (2003) notes that bare DP *wh*-words cannot appear in clause-initial position but must be preceded by a predicate particle. Rather, *ko* and the *wh*-word form the predicate in [Spec, IP].

(4) *Niuean* (Massam 2003: 97)
[$_{IP}$ [Ko *hai*] [$_{I'}$ [$_{DP}$ [$_{CP}$ *ne* *lalaga* *e* *kato* *e:*]]]]?
PRED who C weave ABS basket this
'Who wove this basket?'

The analysis I pursue in this paper shares the fundamental insight of Massam's approach that the derivation of clefts is parallel to the derivation of VOS basic word order. However, this derivation crucially employs A'-movements into the left periphery. Another point of departure is the motivation I assume for movement of the predicate. It is not the case that a predicate must appear in clause-initial position, but rather the true generalization is that a DP *cannot* occur in this position.

(5) *Stranded DP Constraint* (SDPC)[1]
The highest constituent in the CP phase edge cannot be a DP.

The reader is referred to Aldridge (2004) for detailed discussion and motivation of the SDPC. For reasons of space, I will not attempt a full justification of the constraint in this paper, though I will point out certain phenomena which are accounted for by the SDPC but not necessarily predicted by other approaches to predicate-fronting. One of these is the asymmetry between the two types of Tagalog *wh*-question shown in (6). DP *wh*-phrases must be clefted, as in (6a). But non-DP *wh*-phrases are allowed to move to clause-initial position, as in (6b). Note the absence of an absolutive case marker in (6b), indicating that what follows the *wh*-word is not a relative clause. The fact that the clitic pronoun attaches to the *wh*-word also shows that (6b) is a monoclausal construction. Note in (6a) that the clitic remains in the relative clause, not being able to cross a tensed clause boundary.

(6) *Tagalog*
a. **Ano** $[_{DP}$ *ang* $[_{CP}$ *ga-gaw-in*=mo]]?
what ABS FUT-do-TR=2SG.ERG
'What are you going to do?'
b. $[_{CP}$ **Saan**=siya $[_{TP}$ *bi-bili* *ng* *bahay* t_{saan}]].
where=3SG.ABS FUT-buy OBL house
'Where will he/she buy a house?'

The locative *wh*-phrase in (6b) cannot be analyzed as having moved to [Spec, IP] to check the [Pred] feature on Infl, as per Massam's (2003) proposal. This is because clause-initial focus position in Tagalog is not restricted to main predicates. (7b) shows a focused PP in preverbal position. Note in (7a) that unmarked word order in Tagalog is verb-initial.

1. I assume that this constraint applies at the point in the derivation at which chains are linearized, meaning that structural relations are still preserved but only the member of a chain to be spelled out overtly will be assessed.

(7) *Tagalog*

a. *Bi-bili si Maria ng bahay* **sa Maynila.**
FUT-buy ABS Maria OBL house in Manila
'Maria will buy a house in Manila.'

b. **Sa Maynila** *bi-bili si Maria ng bahay.*
in Manila FUT-buy ABS Maria OBL house
'Maria will buy a house *in Manila*.'

These adjuncts cannot be analyzed as occupying the position for the primary predicate, since PPs in this function must be preceded by a predicativizing prefix *na-*.

(8) *Tagalog*

a. ***Sa** *Maynila si Maria.*
in Manila ABS Maria
'Maria is in Manila.'

b. **Na-sa** *Maynila si Maria.*
be-in Manila ABS Maria
'Maria is in Manila.'

I assume that VSO word order in Tagalog is derived through head-movement of the verb to T or an aspectual position above *v*P (c.f. Richards 2000; Rackowski 2002; Aldridge 2004, 2005, 2008; and Rackowski & Richards 2005). This leaves [Spec, CP] available for movement of an adverb or PP, as in (6b) and (7b). The lack of *wh*-movement in (6a) is accounted for by the SDPC, since it prohibits spelling out of the DP *wh*-phrase in the edge of the CP phase. Therefore, DP *wh*-questions must be formed on clefts, with the *wh*-phrase embedded in the matrix predicate.

The derivation of Austronesian clefts I propose in this paper is parallel to the derivation of basic word order in a VOS language. Since the subject or absolutive argument in a VOS language has a fixed position at the end of the clause, movement of this DP is required for deriving basic word order. Recent work on VOS word order in Austronesian languages (Massam 2000, 2001, 2003 for Niuean; Rackowski & Travis 2000; Pearson 2001 for Malagasy; Cole & Hermon 2008 for Toba Batak) has converged on a derivation involving leftward movement of the absolutive DP to a position external to *v*P or TP, followed by fronting of the remnant predicate or clause. I propose in Section 2 that the absolutive moves to a topic position above TP. Subsequently, the remnant TP fronts to a higher position in the C domain. I assume that the SDPC provides the motivation for TP-fronting. Specifically, if TP-fronting did not take place, then the absolutive DP would be spelled out in the highest position in the CP phase edge, thereby violating the SDPC.

(9)

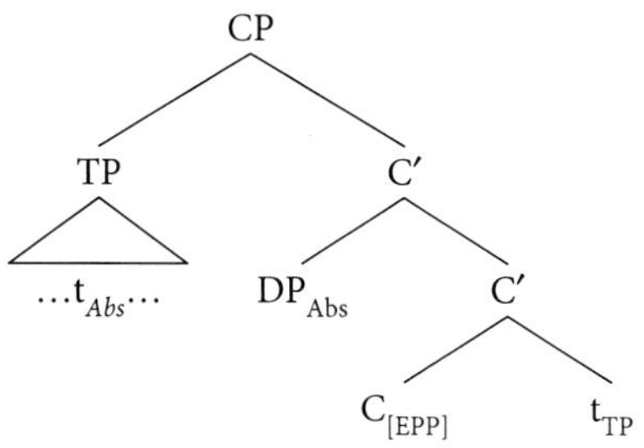

Section 2 presents arguments from Seediq for the topicalization of the absolutive DP and subsequent fronting of the remnant TP shown in (9). In Section 3, I discuss the structure of clefts and show them to be derived in the same way, by raising the headless relative clause to the topic position in the CP layer, followed by fronting the remnant TP which contains the focused constituent. Section 4 offers some cross-linguistic evidence for the SDPC, which I assume to be the motivation for TP fronting.

2. Basic word order in Seediq

This paper focuses on word order in the VOS language Seediq, an Ataylic language spoken in Taiwan. Seediq has an ergative-absolutive case-marking system. The absolutive DP is optionally marked with the case-marker *ka*, but regardless of the presence of the case-marker, the absolutive obligatorily follows the predicate, yielding VOS word order, with the absolutive in the 'S' position. The verb, together with auxiliary verbs indicating tense/aspect and negation, if there are any, occur in clause-initial position. In the transitive example in (10a), the ergative DP immediately follows the verb, with the absolutive DP following the ergative. In the applicative construction in (10b), the applied argument has absolutive status and occurs clause-finally. The ergative argument in this example is a clitic pronoun, attaching to the first prosodic word in the sentence, here the tense auxiliary. (10c) is an antipassive. Intransitive morphology appears on the verb; the direct object is treated as an oblique; and the external argument has absolutive status and appears in clause-final position.

(10) a. *Wada burig-un na Ape* ka patis.
PAST buy-TR ERG Ape ABS book
'Ape bought the book.'

b. *Wada=na s-tabu huling* ka buuts rodux.
PAST=3SG.ERG APP-feed dog ABS bone chicken
'She fed the chicken bones to a/the dog.'

c. *Wada m-ari hulama* ka Ape.
PAST INTR-buy treat ABS Ape
'Ape bought a treat.'

The analysis of absolutive-final word order is spelled out below. In essence, the absolutive DP moves to a topic position above TP. This movement is followed by fronting of the remnant TP to a higher specifier in the C domain. Absolutive movement is triggered by EPP features on transitive *v* and C. C also has a [T] feature, which could be satisfied by T-to-C head movement or by remnant TP fronting. The choice is determined by the SDPC. If head movement were to take place, the absolutive DP would be stranded in the edge of CP. Therefore, TP fronting is required in order to prevent the derivation from crashing.

(11) a. *Wada burig-un na Ape* ka patis.
PAST buy-TR ERG Ape ABS book
'Ape bought the book.'

b.

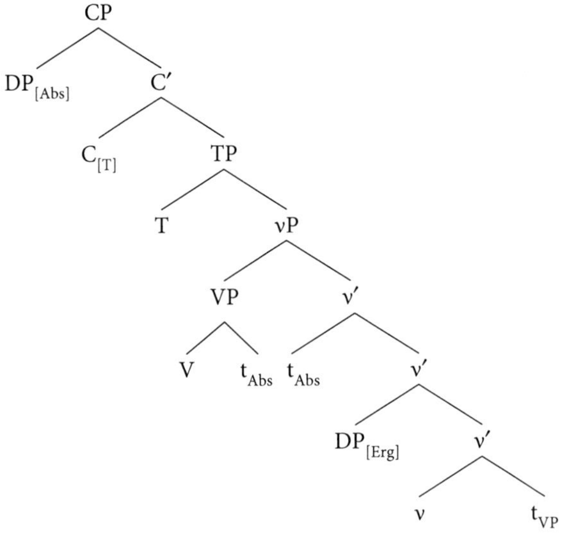

c.

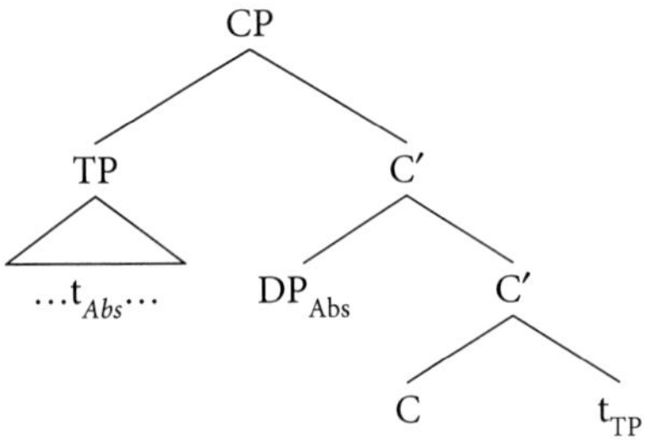

Let me also elaborate further on the movement of the absolutive. Topicalization of the absolutive involves first movement to the edge of *v*P. Aldridge (2004, 2005, 2008) has argued that transitive *v* has an EPP feature which draws the absolutive internal argument to the edge of the *v*P phase, from which position it can undergo further movement, e.g. topicalization in VOS ergative languages like Seediq.

(12) *Transitivity and EPP*
v_{Tr}: [D] feature
v_{Intr}: No [D] feature

Raising to the outer specifier of *v* also allows the object DP to check absolutive case with T. Ergative case is inherent, assigned by transitive *v* to its specifier.[2]

(13)

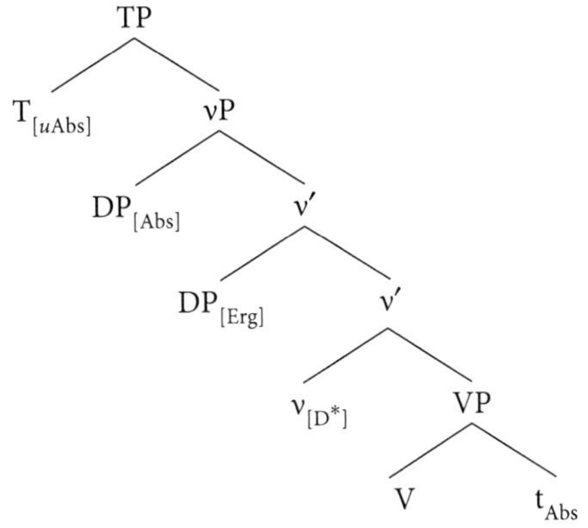

Furthermore, the ergative DP, which is located in a lower specifier of *v*P, will not be attracted to [Spec, CP] over the absolutive DP in the outer specifier of *v*P, assuming that this feature enters into an Agree relation with the closest matching element in its c-command domain.[3]

This analysis of movement of the absolutive DP also accounts for the restriction in Austronesian languages, according to which only absolutives are eligible to undergo A'-extraction.[4] Since transitive *v* has an EPP feature which attracts the absolutive DP in (14a) to its outer specifier, this DP can be further attracted to the specifier of CP. But the ergative DP will always be blocked from moving in transitive clauses.

2. See Mahajan (1989), Woolford (1997, 2006), and Legate (2002, 2008) for similar proposals.

3. The fact that the ergative DP does not move over the absolutive would be surprising if we were to assume that both specifiers of *v*P are equidistant from C. However, there is a recent trend away from the notion of equidistance (Fox & Pesetsky 2005; Rackowski & Richards 2005; among others). For example, if we consider the approach in Rackowski and Richards (2005), they ensure that only the highest (closest) specifier in *v*P can enter into an Agree relation with a probe on C.

4. This is the well-known subject or topic restriction on A'-movement in Austronesian languages. Accordingly, numerous disparate analyses have been proposed to account for this fact in a variety of Austronesian languages (Schachter & Otanes 1972; Richards 2000; Rackowski 2002 for Tagalog; Holmer 1996; Chang 1997 for Seediq; Keenan 1976; Pearson 2001 for Malagasy; Chung 1994, 1998 for Chamorro; Georgopoulos 1991 for Palauan; among many others). The approach proposed in this paper, however, suggests a uniform account of this phenomenon across languages, though development of this cross-linguistic mechanism is beyond the scope of this paper.

(14) a. sapah *b⟨n⟩ari* *na* *tama*
house TR⟨PERF⟩buy ERG father
'house which Father bought'

b. *seediq *b⟨n⟩ari* *sapah*
person TR⟨PERF⟩buy house.ABS
'person who bought the house'

2.1 Evidence for movement of the absolutive

The next two subsections provide evidence for the predicate-fronting derivation of Seediq basic word order. I first show that the absolutive DP moves out of TP. Initial evidence is provided by structural relations. In Seediq, only absolutives in antipassives can antecede reflexives. Recall that antipassives are a type of intransitive, meaning that the external argument has absolutive status. (15) shows that the agent absolutive in an antipassive can bind a benefactive reflexive. This is accounted for on the current analysis, since the external argument c-commands the reflexive in VP. Since antipassive *v* is intransitive, it does not have an EPP feature, so the internal argument never raises out of VP. Assuming cyclic, phase-based application of Binding Principle A (Lee-Schoenfeld 2008; Quicoli 2008, and others), binding is established in the *v*P phase. In subsequent phases, no other Binding Principles are violated, since the reflexive will never c-command the intended antecedent, so the derivation converges.

(15) a. *Wada=nak* *m-ari* *rulu* *ka* *Ape.*
PAST=REFL INTR-buy car ABS Ape
'Ape bought herself a car.'

b.
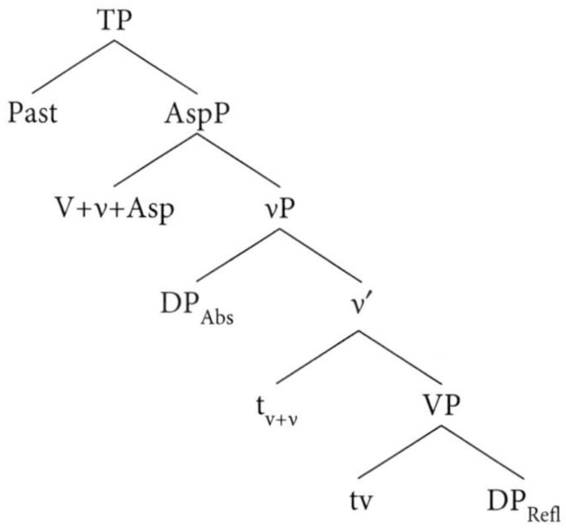

The transitive version of (15) is not grammatical. In this sentence, the intended antecedent has ergative status. The reflexive is the absolutive, licensed by the benefactive applicative morphology on the verb. In their base positions, the ergative DP c-commands the reflexive, satisfying Condition A. However, c-command relations will be reversed when the absolutive DP moves out of its base position to the outer specifier of *v*. In this position, the absolutive reflexive c-commands and binds the intended antecedent, invoking a Condition C violation.[5]

(16) a. **Wada=nak s-bari rulu na Ape.*
PAST=REFL.ABS APP-buy car ERG Ape
'Ape bought herself a car.'

b.

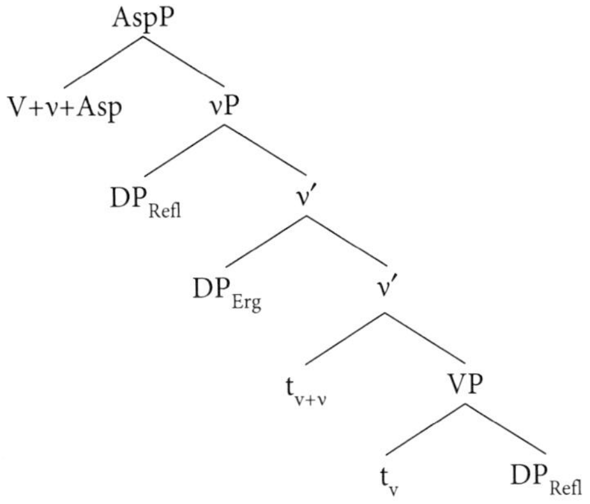

NPI licensing also provides evidence that absolutives reside in a high position at the relevant point in the derivation. Neg licenses a VP-internal oblique object NPI in an antipassive, as in (17a). This is because the object remains in VP, where it is c-commanded by negation, while the external argument values absolutive case and moves to [Spec, CP]. However, Neg does not license an absolutive NPI, as in (17b), indicating that absolutives move out of the c-command domain of negation.

(17) a. [$_{TP}$ *Wada ini bari* ani mumaanu] *ka Ape.*
PAST NEG buy any thing ABS Ape
'Ape didn't buy anything.'

b. *[$_{TP}$ *Ini burig-i na Ape*]
NEG buy-TR.IRR ERG Ape
ka ani mumaanu.
ABS any thing
'Ape didn't buy anything.'

5. Hoji (1985), Tada (1993), Oka (1996), Takano (1997), McGinnis (1999), and others have shown that short scrambling in Japanese also alters binding relations.

Next, I examine clitic doubling. In (18a, b), the absolutive *yaku* is resumed by clitic pronouns in second position in TP.

(18) a. [$_{TP}$ *Gaga*=ku=*daha* *ngal-un*] *ka* yaku *duri.*
PRES=1.SG.ABS=3.PL choose-TR ABS 1.SG even
'They have chosen even me.'

b. [$_{TP}$ *M-usa*=ku *mu-huma* *kyuuri=na*] ka *yaku.*
INTR-go=1.SG.ABS INTR-plant cucumber=3.SG.GEN ABS 1.SG
'I went to plant his cucumbers.'

Chang (1997) proposes that these clitics register agreement with a TP-internal absolutive. However there is evidence that arguments doubled by are not positioned internal to TP. This can be seen in the behavior of ergative clitics. In (19a), a clitic pronoun functions as the ergative argument. However, when a full DP ergative argument occurs in [Spec, *v*P], it cannot be resumed by a clitic pronoun, as shown in (19b).

(19) a. [$_{TP}$ *Wada*=na *biq-un* *hulama*] *laqi*
PAST=3.SG.ERG give-TR treat child.ABS
'He/she gave the child a treat.'

b. [$_{TP}$ *Wada*(*=na) *burig-un* na Ape] *ka* *patis-ni.*
PAST(=3.SG.ERG) buy-TR ERG Ape ABS book-DEM
'Ape bought this book.'

This suggests indirectly that the absolutive DPs in (18) are also located in TP-external positions.

Coordination also provides evidence that absolutives move out of TP. Clauses can be coordinated to the exclusion of the absolutive DP. In (20a) the ATB extracted DP is an internal argument in transitive clauses. (20b) conjoins an intransitive and an antipassive, in which the extracted absolutive is an external argument.

(20) a. [$_{TP}$ *S-bari=na* t_{Abs} *hulama*] *ma*
APP-buy=3.SG.ERG treat and
[$_{TP}$ *s-smalu=na* t_{Abs} *lukus* *dungan*]
APP-make=3.SG.ERG clothes also
ka *laqi=na.*
ABS child=3.SG.GEN
'She buys a treat for and also makes clothes for her child.'

b. [$_{TP}$ *M-usa* t_{Abs} *Purishia*] [$_{TP}$ *m-ari* t_{Ab} *sama*] ka *Ape.*
INTR-go Puli INTR.buy vegetable ABS Ape
'Ape went to Puli and bought vegetables.'

Additional evidence for movement of the absolutive comes from information structure. In a typical declarative clause in Seediq, new or focused information tends to appear first in the clause, inside the predicate, while definite material follows, generally in the form of the absolutive DP in clause-final position. Consequently, non-absolutive internal arguments, e.g. obliques in antipassives, surface in immediate post-verbal position and tend to be indefinite, while absolutive DPs must be definite or generic. For example, the antipassive in (21a) is used to introduce *qushia mutaso* 'clean water', where it has oblique status and appears immediately following the verb. In (21b), where this DP represents old information, it has absolutive status, while the DP representing new information *lukus* 'clothes' immediately follows the verb.

(21) a. *M⟨n⟩oda* *m-ari* qushia mutaso *Hori* *ka* *Ape.*
INTR⟨PERF⟩go INTR-buy water clean Puli ABS Ape
'Ape went to Puli to buy clean water.'

b. *Wada=na* *s-pahu* *lukus* *ka* qushia mutaso.
PAST=3.SG.ERG APP-wash clothes ABS water clean
'She washed clothes with the clean water.'

A final related asymmetry is that observed between strong and weakly quantified DPs. Strongly quantified DPs tend to be given absolutive status, as in (22a). On the other hand, weakly quantified DPs cannot appear in absolutive position (22c). If they appear in situ in the clause, they must have oblique status, e.g. as the object of an antipassive verb (22b).

(22) a. *Wada=na* *burig-un* kanna patis.
PAST=3.SG.ERG buy-TR all book.ABS
'He/she bought all the books.'

b. *Wada* *m-ari* egu nashi *ka* *Awe-ni.*
PAST INTR-buy many pear Abs Awe-DEF
'Awe bought a lot of pears.'

c. ?* *Wada=na* *burig-un* egu nashi.
PAST=3.SG.ERG buy-TR many pear.ABS
'He/she bought a lot of pears.'

Building on work by Milsark (1974), Diesing (1992) proposes that strong quantifiers, but not necessarily weak quantifiers, presuppose the existence of the entities they are applied to. This dichotomy is captured easily in the current analysis. Strongly quantified DPs move into topic position, where they will be mapped onto the presupposition, while weakly quantified DPs are contained inside the predicate and are mapped to the focused – or nonpresupposed – part of the clause. Therefore, it can be concluded that absolutives must reside in a position where they receive a presuppositional interpretation, such as a topic position outside TP.

2.2 Evidence for predicate-fronting

The previous subsection showed that the absolutive DP moves to a topic position in the C domain. Following this, the remnant TP also fronts, which I assume to be indirectly motivated by the SDPC. In this subsection, I offer evidence that phrasal TP-fronting takes place. First, let us consider a possible alternative analysis of VOS word order involving rightward movement of the absolutive along the lines of Holmer (1996) and Chang (1997), based on Guilfoyle et al. (1992). On this approach, transitive clauses are treated as a kind of passive, in which the absolutive moves to an A-position in order to be case-licensed.

(23) a. *Wada s-bari hulama na Ape ka laqi.*
PAST APP-buy treat ERG Ape ABS child
'Ape bought the child a treat.'

b. (based on Holmer 1996)

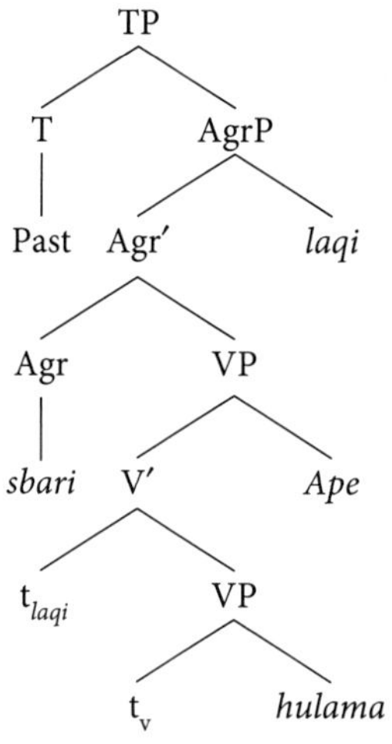

This analysis faces at least one serious empirical challenge, even if we ignore the obvious theoretical problem of allowing the internal argument to undergo A-movement over the external argument to [Spec, AgrP]. Recall from Section 1 that adjunct *wh*-phrases are able to front in Tagalog. Tagalog is a VSO language in which basic word order is generated by head-movement of the verb to a position above *v*P. The TP is therefore not expected to be an island to extraction, accounting for the extractability of adjuncts.

(24) *Tagalog*
a. *B⟨in⟩ili ni Maria ang bahay sa Maynila.*
⟨TR.PERF⟩buy ERG Maria ABS house in Manila
'Maria bought the house in Manila.'

b. *Saan b⟨in⟩ili ni Maria ang bahay?*
where ⟨TR.PERF⟩buy ERG Maria ABS house
'Where did Maria buy the house?'

c.

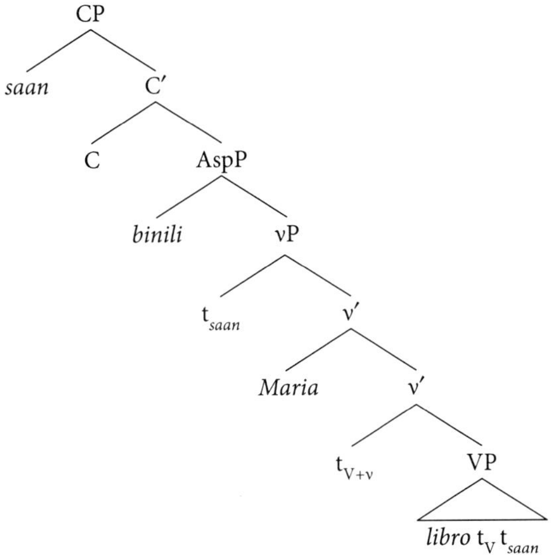

A key difference between the TP-fronting approach and the rightward movement approach is that the fronted TP in the former is predicted to be an island to extraction (based on the 'freezing effect' of Wexler & Culicover 1980 or the Condition on Extraction Domain of Huang 1982), while this is not the case in the latter approach.[6] We have already seen in (14) above that absolutive DPs can undergo A'-movement, while other DP arguments cannot. Adjuncts are also unable to front, as shown in (25). On the TP-fronting account, all clause-internal material except the absolutive is contained within TP and therefore frozen in place after TP-fronting.

(25) *Seediq*
a. *M⟨n⟩ari* inu *patis Ape?*
INTR⟨PERF⟩buy where book Ape
'Where did Ape buy books?'

b. *Inu$_i$ *m⟨n⟩ari* t$_i$ *patis Ape?*
where INTR⟨PERF⟩buy book Ape

---

6. See Nunes and Uriagereka (2000), Stepanov (2007), and others for more recent approaches to CED effects.

c.

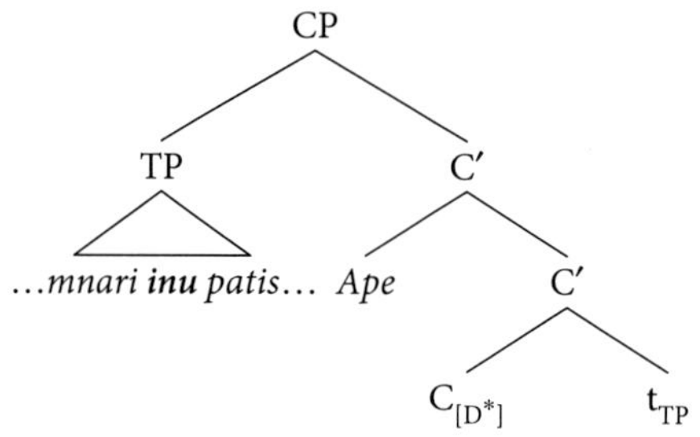

To summarize the discussion in Section 2, VOS word order in Seediq is derived by movement of the absolutive to a topic position in the C domain. The remnant TP then fronts to its left, forming an island to extraction, which prevents TP-internal material from moving to clause-initial position.[7]

3. Structure of *Wh*-clefts

In this section, I discuss the structure of *wh*-clefts in Austronesian languages. A *wh*-question in which the *wh*-phrase is a DP has to take the form of a cleft, which is a natural consequence of the derivation of basic word order developed in Section 2. To review that derivation, first recall that absolutive DPs are always topicalized or presupposed, while new information is contained inside the fronted TP.

(26) *Seediq*

a. [$_{TP}$ *M⟨n⟩oda* *m-ari* qushia mutaso
INTR⟨PERF⟩go INTR-buy water clean

Hori] *ka* *Ape.*
Puli ABS Ape

'Ape went to Puli to buy clean water.'

b. [$_{TP}$ *Wada=na* *s-pahu* *lukus*]
PAST=3.SG.ERG APP-wash clothes

ka qushia mutaso.
ABS water clean

'She washed clothes with the clean water.'

This can be accounted for straightforwardly by assuming that the position in the CP layer which the absolutive DP moves to is a low topic position (in the sense of

7. Time adverbs are allowed to appear in clause-initial position. I assume that these can be merged high, presumably adjoined to TP.

Rizzi 1997). The head which carries the [T] feature to attract the remnant TP is a focus position above the landing site for the absolutive. The SDPC will ensure that the phrasal TP will be attracted rather than just the T head.

(27)

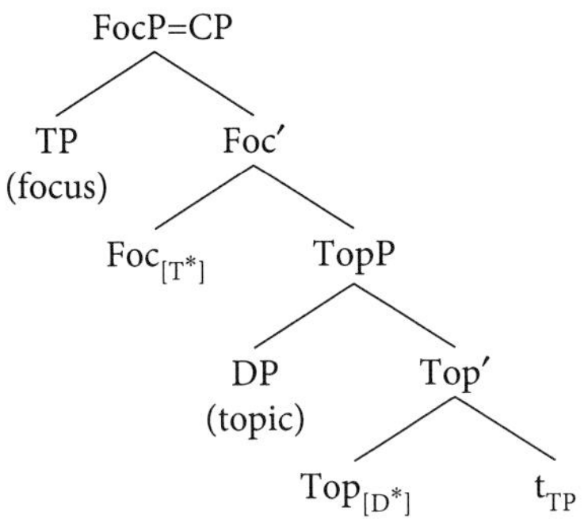

In regard to *wh*-questions, if a DP *wh*-phrase were to move to the left periphery, it would target the topic position in order to check the [D] feature there, since Foc carries a [T] feature. However, this would result in an anomalous interpretation, since *wh*-phrases are inherently focused. Interestingly, *wh*-phrases are indeed barred from absolutive position in VOS (as well as many SVO) Austronesian languages. Chang (1997) cites evidence from Seediq. See also Sabel (2003), Cole et al. (2005), Potsdam (2006), and others for discussion of a similar constraint in other Austronesian languages.

(28) *Seediq* (Chang 1997: 146)

a. Ima (*ka*) [$_{CP}$ Op [$_{TP}$ *s⟨m⟩ebut* t_{Op} *laqi*]]
who ABS ⟨INTR⟩hit child
'Who hits a child?'

b. **S⟨m⟩ebut laqi ka* ima?
⟨INTR⟩hit child ABS who
'Who hits a child?'

This problem is circumvented, however, if DP *wh*-questions are formed as clefts. The headless relative clause in this case checks absolutive case and moves to the topic position. The focused constituent is contained inside the fronted TP, which moves to [Spec, FocP].

(29) *Seediq*

a. *Maanu ka b⟨n⟩ari=na?*
what ABS ⟨PERF⟩buy=3.SG.ERG
'What did she buy?'

b.

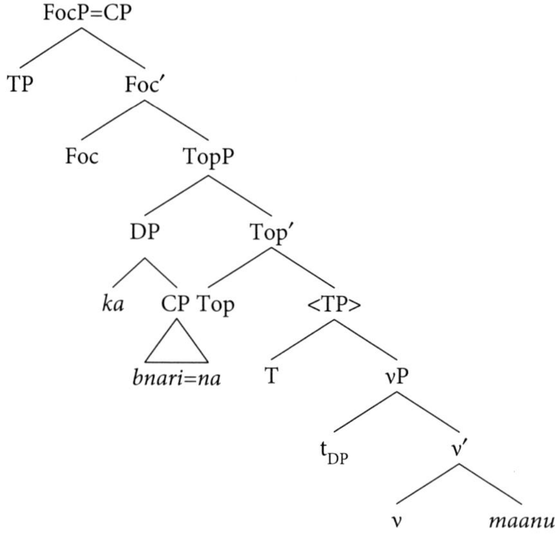

In the remainder of this section, I present evidence in favor of the derivation of *wh*-clefts sketched above. First I consider evidence that the constituent following the absolutive case marker is a headless relative clause. (30) is a predicational copula construction in which the headless relative *bnari na* ('what he/she bought') is the subject predicated of *malu uqun* 'taste good'. This indicates that a bare CP preceded by the absolutive case-marker can appear in nominal argument position.

(30) *Seediq*
Malu uqun [$_{DP}$ *ka* [$_{CP}$ *b⟨n⟩ari=na*]].
good eat ABS ⟨PERF⟩buy=3.SG.ERG
'What he/she bought tastes good.'

Aldridge (2002, 2004) argues for the biclausal status of DP *wh*-questions in Tagalog and Seediq on the basis of positional restrictions on pronominal clitics. As in Tagalog, pronominal clitics in Seediq attach to the first prosodic word within CP. In (31), a clitic raises to the question particle *yo*, which I assume to be located in the C domain. Clitics, then, should be able to raise into the CP layer of the clause.

(31) *Seediq*
[$_{CP}$ [$_{C'}$ *Yo*=su$_i$ [$_{TP}$ *kula-un* t$_i$
Q=2.SG.ERG know-TR
[$_{DP}$ *seedaq* [*m⟨n⟩huma* *bulebun-ni*]]]?
person INTR⟨PERF⟩plant banana-DEM
'Do you know the person who planted these bananas?'

In a cleft, however, the clitic has to stay below the predicate nominal and absolutive case-marker which follows it. In (32), the 3rd person Seediq ergative clitic attaches to the tense auxiliary. This clitic cannot move up to attach to the *wh*-word or the absolutive case marker.

(32) *Seediq*

a. *Ima ka wada*=na *s-bari hulama*?
who ABS PAST=3.SG.ERG APP-buy treat
'Who did she buy a treat (for)?'

b. **Ima*=na *ka wada s-bari hulama*?
who=3.SG ABS PAST APP-buy treat
"Who did she buy a treat (for)?"

c. **Ima ka*=na *wada s-bari hulama*?
who ABS=3.SG.ERG PAST APP-buy treat

Clitic placement can be accounted for if we assume that the clitic attaches to the highest head within the embedded CP, which is the auxiliary *wada*. The operator in [Spec, CP] is phonetically null and so cannot host a clitic.

(33) *Seediq*
Ima_i *ka* $[_{CP}$ Op_i $[_{TP}$ *wada*=na *s-bari hulama* t_i]]?
who ABS PAST=3.SG.ERG APP-buy treat
'Who did she buy a treat (for)?'

The preceding discussion has argued that DP *wh*-questions in Seediq are biclausal, containing a headless relative clause, as is expected of pseudo-clefts. Next I show that the *wh*-word forms part of the predicate, which is contained in the fronted remnant TP. This is by no means an uncontroversial claim when the structure of clefts is considered cross-linguistically. For English clefts, for example, some treat the relative clause as the subject (Boskovic 1997), while others take the focused constituent to be the subject (Williams 1983, 1994; Heggie 1988; Den Dikken 2006, this volume; and others). Here, I argue for the traditional view of Austronesian clefts, specifically, that the focus must be part of the predicate and crucially is not the subject.

Following Paul (2000) for Malagasy, Aldridge (2004) shows that the focused part of a cleft can be negated in Tagalog. (34a) shows that the negator generally precedes a verbal predicate. (34b) shows that the same negator can precede the clefted constituent.

(34) *Tagalog*

a. Hindi *p⟨um⟩unta si Maria sa Maynila*.
NEG ⟨INTR.PERF⟩go ABS Maria to Manila
'Maria didn't go to Manila.'

b. [Hindi *si* *Maria*] *ang* *p⟨um⟩unta* *sa* *Maynila.*
NEG Abs Maria ABS ⟨INTR.PERF⟩go to Manila
'It wasn't Maria who went to Manila.'

(35b) shows that a modal auxiliary appears before the clefted constituent. (35a) shows this modal selecting a verbal predicate.

(35) *Malagasy* (Potsdam 2006)
a. tokony *hamangy* *an-dRabe* *Rasoa*
should visit ACC-Rabe Rasoa
'Rasoa should visit Rabe.' (p. 2165)
b. [tokony *Rasoa*] *no* *hamangy* *an-dRabe*
should Rasoa PART visit ACC-dRabe
'It should be Rasoa who visits Rabe?' (p. 2170)

It has also frequently been pointed out that post-predicate particles can follow clefted constituents (Cole et al. to appear; Pearson 2001; Massam 2003; Potsdam 2009; Kroeger 2009; and others). (36) shows that the particle *tale* 'again' can follow the predicate it modifies but not the subject.

(36) *Fijian* (Potsdam 2009: 765)
a. [*e* *na* *lagasere*] tale *o* *Pita*
3SG.SUBJ FUT sing again D Peter
'Peter will sing again.'
b. *[*e* *na* *lagasere*] *o* *Pita* tale
3SG.SUBJ FUT sing D Peter again
'Peter will sing again.'

In the clefts in (37), this particle can follow either the embedded predicate or the clefted constituent. The fact that the particle can modify the clefted phrases shows that this constituent must be a predicate and not a subject.

(37) *Fijian* (Potsdam 2009: 765)
a. [*o* *cei*] [[*e* *na* *lagasere*] tale]
D who 3SG.SUBJ FUT sing again
'Who will sing again?'
b. [*o* *cei*] tale] *e* *na* *lagasere*
D who again 3SG.SUBJ FUT sing
'Who else will sing?'

Similarly, in Seediq, the absolutive case marker always appears between the fronted TP and the absolutive DP. It is not possible for the case marker to precede the focused constituent in a monoclausal construction, as in (38a), or in a cleft, as in (38b).

(38) *Seediq*

a. (**ka*) *malu uqun* [$_{DP}$ *ka* [$_{CP}$ *b⟨n⟩ari=na*]].
ABS good eat ABS ⟨PERF⟩buy=3.SG.ERG
'What he/she bought tastes good.'

b. (*ka) bulebun ka b⟨n⟩ari=na.
ABS banana ABS ⟨PERF⟩buy=3.SG.ERG
'What he/she bought was a/the banana.'

The facts in (34) to (38) show that the focused constituent in a cleft occurs with particles, negation, and modals, all elements which typically occur with predicates and, crucially, not with subjects. These facts also suggest that the clause-initial constituent contains more material than just the nuclear predicate. Specifically, there must be positions for negation and an auxiliary verb, which is accounted for on the TP-fronting analysis, since these elements will be pied-piped with the remnant clause when it moves to [Spec, FocP].

Another characteristic of Austronesian clefts accounted for on the TP-fronting analysis is the lack of reversibility. English specificational pseudoclefts are known to be reversible, i.e. the focus and clause can appear in either order.

(39) a. *Proud* is what John is. (Pseudocleft)
b. What John is is *proud*. (Inverse pseudocleft)

The general approach to this alternation is to analyze the clause as moving to a position above the focus. In the pseudocleft, the focus moves from an embedded small clause to [Spec, IP] subject position (Heggie 1988; Moro 1997, and Den Dikken 2006), as in (40a). In the inverse pseudocleft, the clause moves to either the subject [Spec, IP] position (Moro 1997; Den Dikken 2006), as in (40b), or to [Spec, CP] (Heggie 1988), as in (40c).

(40) a. [$_{IP}$ Proud [$_{VP}$ is [$_{SC}$ *t* [what John is]]]]
b. [$_{IP}$ what John is [$_{VP}$ is [$_{SC}$ proud *t*]]]
c. [$_{CP3}$ [$_{CP1}$ what John is]$_j$ is [$_{IP}$ [proud]$_i$ [$_{VP}$ [$_{CP2}$ t_i t_j]]]

I assume that the availability of landing sites in either [Spec, IP] or [Spec, CP] is what accounts for the reversibility. In contrast to this, specificational copula constructions are not reversible in the Austronesian languages which I am familiar with. If the order of the major constituents is reversed, the information sructure is also reversed. Since I have no relevant examples in my Seediq corpus, I use Tagalog examples for illustration.

(41) *Tagalog*

a. [*Ang lalaki*] *ang na-kita ng babae.*
ABS man ABS PERF-see ERG woman
'It is the man that the woman saw.'

b. [*Ang na-kita ng babae*] *ang lalaki.*
ABS PERF-see ERG woman ABS man
'It the one that the woman saw which is the man.'

What is important to note here is that the initial constituent must be focused. This falls out naturally in the analysis in (29b), since the clause will be attracted to [Spec, TopP], while the focus will be contained within the remnant TP moving above this position. Since both of these constituents already occupy the positions in the left periphery where they will be interpreted, there are no other potential landing sites for further movement which would change the word order, while maintaining the interpretation.

Let me note here also that Massam's (2003) analysis does not seem to make the correct prediction for reversibility in Austronesian clefts, since the focused constituent checks the [Pred] feature on Infl, while [Spec, CP] remains vacant. Given Heggie's (1988) analysis of English, I do not see how the clause could be prevented from moving to [Spec, CP].

(42) *Tagalog*
a. [Ang lalaki] *ang na-kita ng babae.*
ABS man ABS perf-see ERG woman
'It is the man that the woman saw.'

b.
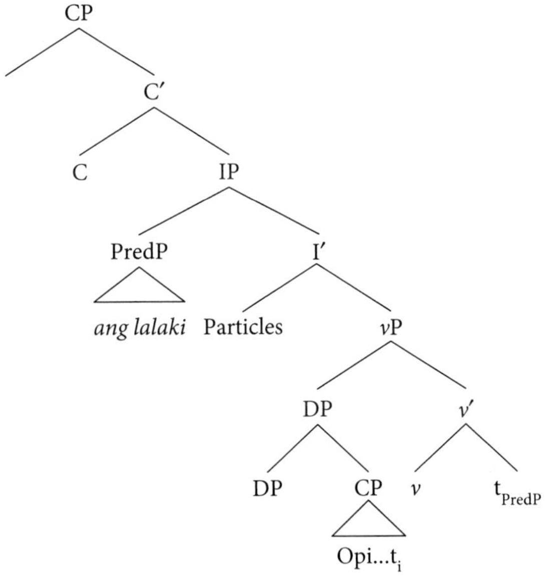

Thus, my postulation that movements in the derivation of clefts target the CP layer accounts for the lack of reversibility in Tagalog. I have no empirical evidence regarding the reversibility of clefts in Niuean, but there is evidence that that predicate-fronting in this language also accesses the left periphery. (43a) shows that the fronted predicate precedes the *yes/no* question particle. (43b) shows that an adjunct *wh*-phrase is pied-piped along with the fronted predicate, presumably to the position where a [wh] feature can be checked. Note that (43b) is not simply a case of *wh*-in-situ, since a non-interrogative locative phrase cannot be pied-piped with the fronted predicate, as shown in (43c).

(43) *Niuean*

a. [*Manako manu*] nakai *a* *koe*?
like animal Q Abs you
'Do you like animals?' (Massam 2001: 180)

b. [*Totou* he mena fe:] *e* *Mele* *e* *pepa*?
Read Loc thing which Erg Mele Abs paper
'Where did Mary read the book?' (Massam 2003)

c. *[*Totou* he peito] *e* *Mele* *e* *pepa*?
Read Loc kitchen Erg Mele Abs paper
'Mary read the book in the kitchen' (Massam 2003)

Recall further that the VSO language Tagalog, which does not employ movements to the left periphery in basic word order derivation, does allow adjunct *wh*-phrases to move to preverbal position. Since the verb raises only as far as T, the *wh*-phrase is able to move to [Spec, FocP] and precede the verb in surface order.

(44) *Tagalog*

a. *Bi-bili* *si* *Maria* *ng* *bahay* sa Maynila.
FUT-buy ABS Maria OBL house in Manila
'Maria will buy a house in Manila.'

b. Saan *bi-bili* *si* *Maria* *ng* *bahay*.
where FUT-buy ABS Maria OBL house
'Where will Maria buy a house?'

This asymmetry between Tagalog and Niuean suggests that the predicate moves to the left periphery in the latter, while the verb remains in TP in the former.

However, Tagalog, like Seediq and Niuean, does employ the cleft strategy when the *wh*-phrase is a DP, as discussed in Section 1. As also mentioned in Section 1, this suggests a role for the SDPC in the derivation of *wh*-questions. Specifically, Tagalog is not a VOS predicate (or TP) fronting language like Seediq and Niuean in declarative clauses. Therefore, we cannot say that *wh*-questions in Tagalog are clefts because TP is always attracted to the left periphery. Rather, the true generalization is that the SDPC forces TP-fronting if and when a DP moves to [Spec, TopP]. In Tagalog, this happens in a cleft because the interpretation forces the presupposed relative clause to move to the left periphery. Thus, Tagalog is a counterexample to Potsdam's (2009) proposal that *wh*-clefts are found in languages whose basic word order is generated through predicate-fronting. Hermon (2009) further points out that the SVO language Indonesian also employs the cleft strategy but is not otherwise a predicate-fronting language.

To summarize this section, I have argued that the derivation of clefts in Seediq and other Austronesian languages is parallel to the derivation of predicate-initial word order in VOS languages. The headless relative clause functions as the matrix subject (absolutive) and moves to a topic position in the left periphery. The focused constituent is pied-piped within the remnant TP to a focus position above the absolutive. This analysis accounts for two additional distinguishing characteristics of Austronesian clefts. TP-fronting ensures that the focused constituent is located within the surface predicate, rather than in subject position. Furthermore, since the movements involved in the derivation target the left periphery, hence serving to place the surface subject and predicate in the positions where they will be interpreted, Austronesian clefts are not reversible.

4. Evidence for the stranded DP constraint

Throughout this paper, I have suggested that the SDPC forces TP-fronting when a DP is moved to the left periphery of a clause. In this section, I provide supporting evidence for the SDPC.

In (28b) in Section 3, I showed that *wh*-phrases are generally disfavored in absolutive position in VOS Austronesian languages. This is expected under the analysis presented here, since absolutives move to a topic position. A problem, then, is introduced by the Malagasy construction in (45a). This is a multiple *wh*-question in which a DP *wh*-phrase appears in the left periphery of the clause. Multiple *wh*-fronting is a subtype of the construction first identified by Keenan (1976) as the 'bodyguard' construction. When a DP appears in the left periphery of the clause, it must be preceded by a second constituent, in this case an adjunct *wh*-phrase. The DP cannot precede the adjunct.

(45) *Malagasy* (Sabel 2003)

a. Aiza iza *no* *mividy* *ny* *vary*?
where who FOC PRES.AT.buy the rice
'Where does who buy the rice?'

b. *Iza aiza *no* *mividy* *ny* *vary*?
who where FOC PRES.AT.buy the rice
'Where does who buy the rice?'

Two DP *wh*-phrases likewise cannot be fronted.

(46) *Malagasy* (Sabel 2003)

a. *Iza inona *no* *mividy*?
who what FOC PRES.AT.buy
'What does who buy?'

b. *Inona iza *no* *mividy*?
what who FOC PRES.AT.buy
'What does who buy?'

The generalization, then, is that a DP can move to the left periphery only if it is preceded in surface order by a non-DP. This sensitivity to the category of the clause-initial constituent is readily accounted for by the SDPC. When a DP is moved to the left periphery, another XP of a different category is also required to be fronted. Note further that the DP *wh*-phrase must be D-linked, in the sense of Pesetsky (1987) (Paul 2000). In other words, a sentence like (45a) is only felicitous when there is "a context-specified set of people, known to both the speaker and hearer, that restricts the range of possible answers." (Paul 2000: 201). This interpretive restriction falls out on the analysis in which the DP *wh*-phrase moves to [Spec, TopP], while the adjunct is located in the higher [Spec, FocP].

(47)

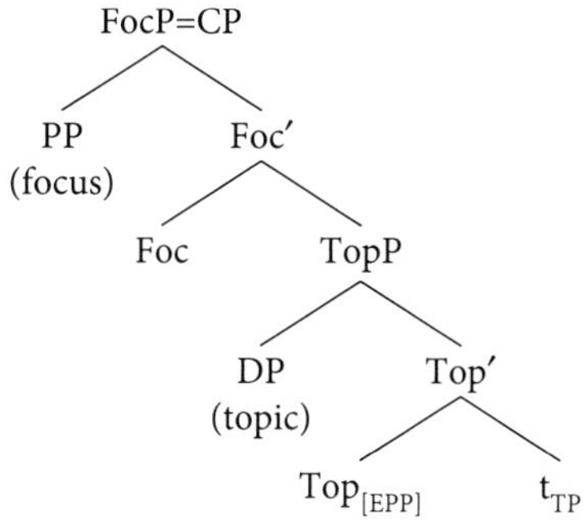

5. Conclusion

This paper has proposed an analysis of cleft constructions in Austronesian languages which is parallel to VOS basic word order derivation. The absolutive DP moves to a topic position in the left periphery, followed by fronting of the remnant TP to a focus position above the topic. This analysis accounts for key characteristics of Austronesian clefts, specifically the fact that the focus is contained within the fronted predicate and the fact that Austronesian clefts are not reversible. I have suggested that the requirement that DP *wh*-questions take the form of clefts is related to a prohibition on stranding a DP in the left edge of CP.

Although motivation for this Stranded DP Constraint has not been the specific focus of this paper, I have shown how it can provide a uniform account for a broad range *wh*-constructions found in Austronesian languages.

References

Aldridge, Edith. 2002. *Wh*-movement in Seediq and Tagalog. In *Proceedings of AFLA 8: The 8th Meeting of the Austronesian Formal Linguistics Association* [MIT Working Papers in Linguistics 44], Andrea Rackowski & Norvin Richards (eds), 1–28. Cambridge MA: MITWPL.

Aldridge, Edith. 2004. Ergativity and Word Order in Austronesian Languages. Ph.D. dissertation, Cornell University.

Aldridge, Edith. 2005. Phase theory account of absolutive extraction in Taglog. In *Perspectives on Phases* [MIT Working Papers in Linguistics 49], Martha McGinnis & Norvin Richards (eds), 1–27. Cambridge MA: MIT WPL.

Aldridge, Edith. 2008. Phase-based account of extraction in Indonesian. *Lingua* 118 (10): 1440–1469.

Boskovic, Zeljko. 1997. Pseudoclefts. *Studia Linguistica* 51(3): 235–277.

Chang, Yung-li. 1997. Voice, Case and Agreement in Seediq and Kavalan. Ph.D. dissertation, National Tsing Hua University.

Chung, Sandra. 1994. *Wh*-Agreement and referentiality in Chamorro. *Linguistic Inquiry* 25(1): 1–44.

Chung, Sandra. 1998. *The Design of Agreement*. Chicago IL: University of Chicago Press.

Cole, Peter & Hermon, Gabriella. 2008. VP Raising in a VOS language. *Syntax* 11(2): 144–197.

Cole, Peter, Hermon, Gabriella & Aman, Norhaida. To appear. Clefted questions in Malay. In *Malay/Indonesian Linguistics*, David Gil & James Collins (eds). London: Curzon Press.

Cole, Peter, Hermon, Gabriella & Tjung, Yassir N. 2005. How irregular is WH in situ in Indonesian? *Studies in Language* 29(3): 553–581.

Diesing, Molly. 1992. *Indefinites* [Linguistic Inquiry Monograph 20]. Cambridge MA: The MIT Press.

den Dikken, Marcel. 2006. *Relators and Linkers: The Syntax of Predication, Predicate Inversion, and Copulas*. Cambridge MA: The MIT Press.

Fox, Danny & Pesetsky, David. 2005. Cyclic linearization. *Theoretical Linguistics* 31: 1–45.

Georgopoulos, Carol. 1991. *Syntactic Variables*. Dordrecht: Kluwer.

Guilfoyle, Eithne, Hung, Henrietta & Travis, Lisa. 1992. Spec of IP and spec of VP: Two subjects in Austronesian languages. *Natural Language and Linguistic Theory* 10: 375–414.

Heggie, Lorie. 1988. The Syntax of Copular Structures. Ph.D. dissertation, University of Southern California.

Hermon, Gabriella. 2009. Language typology and universal grammar: A commentary on the paper by Eric Potsdam. *Natural Language and Linguistic Theory* 27: 773–787.

Hoji, Hajime. 1985. Logical Form Constraints and Configurational Structures in Japanese. Ph.D. dissertation, University of Washington.

Holmer, Arthur. 1996. *A Parametric Grammar of Seediq*. Lund: Lund University Press.

Huang, James C.-T. 1982. Logical Relations in Chinese and the Theory of Grammar. Ph.D. dissertation, MIT.

Keenan, Edward. 1976. Remarkable subjects in Malagasy. In *Subject and Topic*, Charles Li (ed.), 249–299. New York NY: Academic Press.

Kroeger, Paul. 2009. Malagasy clefts from a Western Malayo-Polynesian perspective: Commentary on the paper by Mans-Martin Gaertner. *Natural Language and Linguistic Theory* 27: 817–838.

Legate, Julie. 2002. Warlpiri: Theoretical Implications. Ph.D. dissertation, MIT.

Legate, Julie. 2008. Morphological and abstract case. *Linguistic Inquiry* 39: 55–101.

Lee-Schoenfeld, Vera. 2008. Binding, phases, and locality. *Syntax* 11(3): 281–298.

Mahajan, Anoop. 1989. Agreement and agreement projections. In *Functional Heads and Clause Structure* [MIT Working Papers in Linguistics 10], Itziar Laka & Anoop K. Mahajan (eds.), 217–252. Cambridge MA: MITWPL.

Massam, Diane. 2000. VSO and VOS: Aspects of Niuean word order. In *The Syntax of Verb Initial Languages*, Andrew Carnie & Eithne Guilfoyle (eds), 97–116. Oxford: OUP.

Massam, Diane. 2001. Pseudo noun incorporation in Niuean. *Natural Language and Linguistic Theory* 19: 153–197.

Massam, Diane. 2003. Questions and the left periphery in Niuean. In *Proceedings of the Ninth Annual Meeting of the Austronesia Formal Linguistics Association (AFLA 9)* [Cornell Working Papers in Linguistics 19], Anastasia Riehl & Thess Savella (eds), 94–106. Ithaca NY: Cornell Linguistics Circle Publications.

McGinnis, Martha. 1999. Evidence for feature-driven A-scrambling. In *Proceedings of the Eighteenth West Coast Conference on Formal Linguistics*, Sonya Bird, Andrew Carnie, Jason D. Haugen & Peter Norquest (eds), 364–378. Somerville MA: Cascadilla Press.

Milsark, Gary L. 1974. Existential Sentences in English. Ph.D. dissertation, MIT.

Moro, Andrea. 1997. *The Raising of Predicates*. Cambridge: CUP.

Nunes, Jairo & Uriagereka, Juan. 2000. Cyclicity and extraction domains. *Syntax* 3(1): 20–43.

Oda, Kenji. 2002. *Wh*-questions in V-initial Languages. MA thesis, University of Toronto.

Oka, Toshifusa. 1996. Scrambling in Japanese and English. *MIT Working Papers in Linguistics* 29: 361–388.

Paul, Ileana. 2000. Malagasy Clause Structure. Ph.D. dissertation, McGill University.

Pearson, Matthew. 2001. The Clause Structure of Malagasy: A Minimalist Approach. Ph.D. dissertation, UCLA.

Pesetsky, David. 1987. Wh-in-situ: Movement and unselective binding. In *The Representation of (In)definiteness*, Eric J. Reuland & Alice ter Meulen (eds), 98–129. Cambridge MA: The MIT Press.

Potsdam, Eric. 2006. More concealed pseudoclefts in Malagasy and the Clausal Typing Hypothesis. *Lingua* 116: 2154–2182.

Potsdam, Eric. 2007. Malagasy sluicing and its consequences for the identity requirement on ellipsis. *Natural Language and Linguistic Theory* 25: 577–613.

Potsdam, Eric. 2009. Austronesian verb-initial languages and *Wh*-question strategies. *Natural Language and Linguistic Theory* 27: 737–771.

Quicoli, A. Carlos. 2008. Anaphora by phase. *Syntax* 11(3): 299–329.

Rackowski, Andrea. 2002. The Structure of Tagalog: Specificity, Voice, and the Distribution of Arguments. Ph.D. dissertation, MIT.

Rackowski, Andrea & Richards, Norvin. 2005. Phase edge and extraction: A Tagalog case study. *Linguistic Inquiry* 36(4): 565–599.

Rackowski, Andrea & Travis, Lisa. 2000. V-initial languages: X or XP movement and adverbial placement. In *The Syntax of Verb Initial Languages*, Andrew Carnie & Eithne Guilfoyle (eds), 117–142. Oxford: OUP.

Richards, Norvin. 2000. Another look at Tagalog subjects. In *Formal Issues in Austronesian Linguistics*, Ileana Paul, Vivianne Phillips & Lisa Travis (eds), 105–116. Dordrecht: Kluwer.

Rizzi, Luigi. 1997. The fine structure of the left periphery. In *Elements of Grammar*, Liliane Haegeman (ed.), 281–337. Dordrecht: Kluwer.

Sabel, Joachim. 2003. Malagasy as an optional multiple *Wh*-fronting language. In *Multiple Wh-fronting* [Linguistik Aktuell/Linguistics Today 64], Cedric Boeckx & Kleanthes Grohmann (eds), 229–254. Amsterdam: John Benjamins.

Schachter, Paul & Otanes, Fe T. 1972. *Tagalog Reference Grammar*. Berkeley CA: University of California Press.

Stepanov, Arthur. 2007. The end of CED? Minimalism and extraction domains. *Syntax* 10(1): 80–126.

Tada, Hiroaki. 1993. The A/A-bar Partition in Derivation. Ph.D. dissertation, MIT.

Takano, Yuji. 1997. Linear Order and Parametric Variation in Syntax. Ph.D. dissertation, University of California, Irvine.

Wexler, Kenneth & Culicover, Peter. 1980. *Formal Principles of Language Acquisition*. Cambridge MA: The MIT Press.

Williams, Edwin. 1983. Semantic and syntactic categories. Linguistics and Philosophy 6: 423–446.

Williams, Edwin. 1994. *Thematic Structure in Syntax*. Cambridge MA: The MIT Press.

Woolford, Ellen. 1997. Four-way case systems: Ergative, nominative, objective, and accusative. *Natural Language and Linguistic Theory* 11: 679–728.

Woolford, Ellen. 2006. Lexical case, inherent case, and argument structure. *Linguistic Inquiry* 37(1): 111–130.

(Pseudo)clefts at the syntax-prosody-discourse interface

Mara Frascarelli & Francesca Ramaglia
Università degli Studi Roma Tre

This paper proposes an interface approach to (pseudo)cleft constructions, in which their semantic, syntactic, discourse and intonational properties are examined in a cross-linguistic perspective. Following most influential studies, the relevant constructions are analyzed as specificational copular sentences, in which the two major constituents – a (free) relative DP and the (to be) focused phrase – are merged in a SC structure. However, based on formal evidence and discourse considerations, we take the clefted constituent to be merged as the predicate of the relevant construction, thus departing from the general view. Finally, (pseudo)clefts are also shown to imply a Topic strategy. This proposal is substantiated by intonational investigation, showing a crucial correlation between tonal events and the information-structural articulation activated by clefting.

Keywords: Focus; interface; (pseudo)clefts; specificational copular sentences; (different types of) Topic(s)

1. (Pseudo)cleft constructions: An introduction

This paper offers a syntactic, semantic and intonational analysis of cleft and pseudocleft constructions. Specifically, it will be concerned with sentences of the following type:

(1) It is a book that I gave John (cleft)

(2) What I gave John is a book (pseudocleft)

Both structures are constituted by a copular construction in which a focused constituent (i.e. the clefted phrase *a book* in both examples) follows the copula while a relative DP is realized on the right of the Focus in clefts (cf. (1)) and in pre-copular position in pseudoclefts (cf. (2)).[1]

Though copular constructions may implement different types of semantic relations between the two major constituents (cf. among others, Safir 1985; Den Dikken 2001), (pseudo)clefts are generally analyzed as specificational copular sentences (cf. Declerck 1984, 1988; Den Dikken et al. 2000) insofar as one of the two constituents (i.e. the predicate) specifies the value of the variable represented by the other (i.e. the subject):

> A sentence is specificational if the NP that is subject of *be* in underlying structure represents a variable for which the predicate nominal specifies a value. Such sentences are identifying in that the specification of a value makes it possible to identify the variable, i.e. to pick out the person, thing, etc. represented by the variable from a set. […] [On the other hand, a] copular sentence is predicational if it does not specify a value for a variable but merely predicates something of the subject NP. (Declerck 1984: 252)

The specificational nature we assume for (pseudo)cleft constructions is supported by a number of formal and interpretive properties, as is briefly outlined below. First of all, predicational structures do not alternate with clefts (cf. Declerck 1988: 69, 260; Den Dikken 2001: 4), as the ungrammaticality of (3b) clearly illustrates:

(3) a. John is a teacher
b. *It is a teacher that John is

Another piece of evidence is provided by Den Dikken et al. (2000: 78), who show that APs can only receive an individual-level reading when pseudoclefted, whereas they also allow for a stage-level interpretation when they occur in predicational copular sentences. Consider for instance the interpretation of *available* in the copular sentence (4) and in the pseudocleft (5):

(4) a. A fireman is available (ambiguous)
b. 'There is a fireman available (right now)'
(stage-level reading)
c. 'A fireman has the intrinsic property of being available'
(individual-level reading)

1. As far as pseudoclefts are concerned, our analysis will be limited to structures like (2), in which the wh-clause precedes the copula, that is to say to Den Dikken et al.'s (2000) "Type A" pseudoclefts, whereas "Type B" constructions (showing the two nominal constituents in reversed order, as in (i)) will not be discussed:

(i) A book is what I gave John

(5) a. What a fireman is is available (unambiguous)
b. #'There is a fireman available (right now)'
(stage-level reading)
c. 'A fireman has the intrinsic property of being available'
(individual-level reading)

As illustrated, the ambiguity of *available* in (4) disappears if it occurs in a pseudocleft construction like (5). Following Ramaglia (2011), the ambiguity in (4) can be attributed to a different derivation of predicative adjectives: on the one hand, they can be directly merged as predicates of the DP to which they refer; on the other, they can function as modifiers of a null (generic) noun within a predicative NP. These two structures, associated with the stage-level and the individual-level interpretation of (4) respectively, are illustrated below:[2]

(6) is [$_{SC}$ [$_{DP}$ a fireman] [$_{AP}$ available]]
(stage-level reading)

(7) is [$_{SC}$ [$_{DP}$ a fireman] [$_{NP}$ ⟨an⟩ available ⟨person⟩]]
(individual-level reading)

As is shown, while (6) can only be analyzed as a predicational copular sentence (in which the property of being available is predicated about the subject), (7) receives a specificational interpretation (in which the individual having the property of being *an available person* specifies a value for its subject).[3] Since pseudoclefts only

2. In this work, the 'NP' label will be invariably used to indicate all types of predicative noun phrases, independently of the functional structure they project.

3. We surmise that the relevant (null) generic noun is licensed through a matching of semantic features ([+person], [+thing], [+place], etc.) with the subject DP, which is ensured by contextually given sortal restrictions on predicates (this also functions when ruling out otherwise grammatical predications like *#Rome is a person*, *#Leo is a city*, and so on).

Given this analysis, we expect individual-level AP predicates to be inflected like attributive adjectives in languages that mark this distinction. This prediction is borne out in Russian (cf. Bailyn 1994: 8):

(i) a. *Umnaja devuška*
smart$_{long}$ girl
b. **Umna devuška*
smart$_{short}$ girl
'A/the smart girl'

(2) a. *Devuška umnaja*
girl smart$_{long}$
'The girl is smart'
[intended: 'The girl is a smart one/a smart person']

allow for an individual-level interpretation, we conclude that this type of copular sentence must be specificational.

Finally, the specificational nature of pseudoclefts is also confirmed by the existence of specific restrictions on the realization of the copular element. The copula of a pseudocleft like (8) cannot be replaced by any other copular verb (such as *seem*, *become*, etc.; cf. (9a)) and shows restrictions in terms of tense marking (cf. (9b)) and adverbial modification (cf. (9c)) (cf. Higgins 1979; Den Dikken et al. 2000: §§ 3.5–3.6):[4]

(8) What I saw is a man (ambiguous: specificational/predicational)

(9) a. What I saw seems (to be) a man (unamb.: only predicational)
b. What I saw will be a man (unamb.: only predicational)
c. What I saw is still a man (unamb.: only predicational)

The paper is organized as follows. Section 2 discusses the semantic properties of (pseudo)cleft sentences while Section 3 deals with the syntactic implementation of the present approach. Section 4 is dedicated to an illustration of the Topic-Comment articulation in the structures at issue. Our syntactic analysis is addressed in Section 5 and further evidence from an intonational perspective is provided in Section 6. Section 7 summarizes the results.

2. Semantic properties of (Pseudo)clefts

As we have seen, (pseudo)clefts are copular sentences composed of a relative clause and a nominal expression representing the Focus of assertion.[5]

---

b. *Devuška umna*
girl smart$_{short}$
'The girl is smart'

For languages like German, which seem to disconfirm this prediction, we can tentatively suggest that a parameter is at work, requiring overt NP-heads to trigger inflection.

4. These restrictions suggest that the copula used in (pseudo)clefts should not be analyzed as a fully inflected verb: rather, it should be conceived as a functional head, which acts as a linker (a 'functor', in Partee's 2002 [1987] terms; see Section 2).

5. Since the notion of Focus plays a crucial role throughout the paper, it is important to clarify the characterization we assume for it (including its various implementations). In information-structural terms, Focus operates a partition of the sentence: it defines that part of information that the speaker assumes is not shared by the hearer, while unfocused material provides backgrounded information (the "presuppositional skeleton" in Jackendoff 1972;

According to the general (traditional) view (Gazdar 1979; Delahunty 1982; Klein & Sag 1985; Hedberg 1990), the relative clause corresponds to the (logical) predicate (type ⟨e,t⟩) of the relevant copular sentence, while the (to be focused) referential term is the subject (type ⟨e⟩). From this perspective, a cleft sentence like (10a) is semantically analyzed as in (10b):[6]

(10) a. It was John that Mary kissed
b. λx.kissed'(Mary, x) (John')
⟨e,t⟩ ⟨e⟩

Here the denotation 'John' is an individual, while the relative clause is a function applied to an individual. Specifically, the truth conditions expressed by the formula in (10b) can be restated by saying that the relevant sentence is true if the individual denoted as 'John' belongs to the set of individuals who have the property of having been kissed by Mary. Hence, on a purely semantic level, this analysis renders the cleft in (10a) totally equivalent to a simple (*in situ* Focus) sentence like (11):

(11) Mary kissed John

The semantic representation in (10b), however, fails to make the semantic and pragmatic data cohere. Several problems can be outlined.

First of all, Focus in cleft sentences entails an *exhaustive reading* (cf. Kiss 1999), which is not implied in simple sentences like (11). A second problem concerns *presuppositional behavior* (cf. Atlas & Levinson 1981). Sentences (10a) and (11) share the meaning stated in (12) below; however, the cleft in (10a) preserves the inference in (12) under denial (13a) and questioning (13b), while this is not the case for (11):

(12) Mary kissed someone

(13) a. It wasn't John that Mary kissed
b. Was it John that Mary kissed?

cf. also Krifka's 1992 Structured Meaning approach). From a semantic viewpoint, Focus is assumed to introduce a set of alternatives (cf. Rooth 1992). In particular, in the case of *Information* Focus, the alternative set of the answer must correspond to other conceivable answers to the relevant question; on the other hand, the alternative set of a *contrast* (or correction) must include the meaning of the utterance corrected. Finally, a Focus is *exhaustive* when its denotation can only lead to a true proposition (for an overview, cf. Krifka 2007).

6. Notice that, according to Gazdar (quoted in Atlas & Levinson 1981:17), pseudoclefts have the same semantic analysis.

More specifically, a negative sentence like (14b) has the same truth conditions as (14a), but only (14b) presupposes (14c) and (14d). Analogously, the denotation of (15b) is the same as (15a), but only (15b) presupposes (15c) and (15d):

(14) a. Mary did not kiss John
b. It wasn't John that Mary kissed
c. Mary kissed someone
d. There is one only person that Mary kissed

(15) a. Did Mary kiss John?
b. Was it John that Mary kissed?
c. Mary kissed someone
d. There is one only person that Mary kissed

A semantic theory of clefts must account for these entailments in a coherent way and must also account for the fact that (10a) is 'about' the person that Mary kissed (which is specified as John), while this is not the case for (11). This means that sentences (10a) and (11) must have different logical forms.

Hence, in line with Atlas & Levinson (1981: 50-ff.), we assume that sentence (10a) involves a λ-abstraction (Carnap 1958: 129–131) to formulate a complex one-place predicate-symbol and, following Partee (2002 [1987]), a ι-operator which, applied to the relative clause, defines the "maximal individual" having the property of being kissed by Mary. This yields the assertion that the relevant individual has the property of being identical to John:

(16) $\lambda x\ (x = \text{John})\ (\iota x\ \text{kissed'}\ (\text{Mary}, x))$

The semantics of cleft sentences thus implies a *type-shifting* operation. Assuming with Partee (2002 [1987]) that each category corresponds to a family of types (rather than just a single type) and that NPs all have basically a quantificational meaning (type ⟨<e,t>,t⟩), we propose that the denotation of the NP *John* has shifted (i.e. lowered) to type ⟨e⟩ and that the IDENT type-shifting rule is thus applied (⟨e⟩ → ⟨e,t⟩; Partee 2002 [1987]: 363). This produces the function that is characteristic of the individuals who have the property of being identical to the individual named John. On the other hand, the relative clause has shifted to type ⟨e⟩ through the ι-operator. In particular, following Percus (1997), we assume that the relevant relative clause corresponds to a definite description; as such, it has a presupposition of existence and uniqueness and contains a definite article at LF. This accounts for the exhaustive interpretation that the relevant focused constituents typically obtain. This means that there is an important difference between (17a) on the one hand and (17b–c) on the other:

(17) a. Mary is intelligent
b. MARY is intelligent
c. It is MARY that is intelligent

(17a) is a predicational sentence (i.e. a categorical judgment in Kuroda's 1972 terms) composed of two separate acts: the recognition of *Mary* as the subject and the act of affirming what is expressed by the predicate about the subject. In (17b–c), on the other hand, *Mary* is not the subject of a categorical judgment and the predicate has an NP-like denotation; in other words, (17b–c) imply the recognition of [someone who is intelligent] as the subject of the predication realized by *Mary*, which in turn specifies the entity having such a property.[7]

The type-shifting proposed is a legitimate operation, which accounts for nominal predicates in general (see Partee 2002 [1987]) and, in particular, for the restrictions imposed on the syntactic categories that can be clefted; phrases such as AdvPs,[8] NPIs and 'non-referential QPs' cannot be clefted because they cannot be shifted to the ⟨e,t⟩ type (cf. Heggie 1993: 54-ff; Hedberg 2000: Footnote 1).[9]

Following this line of analysis, the copula of a cleft construction has no meaning at all (cf. also Stowell 1981; Heggie 1988; Guéron 1992; Den Dikken 1995): it is

7. As a reviewer points out, the idea of Focus as a predicate is not totally new. We acknowledge that this analysis is part of a long tradition (Hermann 1880; Higgins 1973; von Stechow 1991; see Frascarelli 2010 for an overview) and different accounts have been proposed by several scholars (cf. Heggie 1988; Green 1997, among others). However, the originality of the present proposal rests in its *information-structural* characterization in which the focused DP is the *syntactic predicate* of a Small Clause (see details in Section 3).

8. As a matter of fact, some adverbs allow clefting, though this possibility seems to be strongly restricted to adverbs of space and (punctual) time (cf. Hasselgård 2004). Consider the following examples:

(i) a. *It's always/often that he is late
b. *It's probably/necessarily that he will come
c. *It's already that I've gone

(ii) a. It's here that I met him
b. It's now that I want to leave

Such a restriction can be connected with the potential for the relevant adverbial to denote an 'individual point' in time or space. Further research is needed on this matter.

9. In the same spirit, APs can only be clefted when they modify a null NP-head (cf. (5) and (7)), that is to say, when they are part of a nominal structure that can be shifted to type ⟨e,t⟩.

a functional element, namely a LINKER (Den Dikken 2006) between the two major constituents of the sentence (see also Adger & Ramchand 2001 for discussion).[10]

The next section will address the question of how this semantic analysis of (pseudo)clefts can be implemented in syntax.

3. Syntactic implementation

According to the semantic approach we assume, (pseudo)cleft constructions qualify as specificational copular sentences, in which the focused constituent is realized as the predicate and the presupposed part of the sentence is a relative clause merged in subject position.

In this line of analysis, the relative clause of clefts contains a semantic variable.[11] This qualifies as a pronominal form, as pronouns are the substitutional resource a language has for fully specified DP positions (cf. Adger & Ramchand 2005). Specifically, it is a *pro*, just like the NP heading the dependency (since we are dealing with headless relatives). Since all pronouns share the property of being referentially dependent (Frascarelli 2007), they must be assigned a value that relies on either the relevant pronoun being identified via antecedent-binding or by means of a referent associated with a predicate abstraction operator (cf. Adger & Ramchand 2005). In this picture, the variable *pro* is valued through connection with the null operator in Spec,CP, while the φ-features of the *pro* heading the relative clause must be specified (i.e. checked) by means of antecedent-binding.[12] Since the NP-head is external to the embedded CP (see diagram (18b) below),[13] its φ-features must be specified by a discourse antecedent in the left periphery of the matrix C-domain. The focused constituent, raised to Spec,FocP, can serve this function; it matches its φ-features (through AGREE) with those of the null NP-head, which is thus licensed

10. For further details and discussion on this semantic analysis and its implications, cf. Frascarelli (2010).

11. In the case of pseudoclefts, on the other hand, the wh-phrase in the relative clause functions as a variable ranging over given semantic roles.

12. This mechanism is reminiscent of *pro* interpretation in Topic constructions, as is argued in Frascarelli (2007).

13. Notice that we assume the structure proposed in den Dikken & Singhapreecha (2004) for (free) relatives, in which the relative DP takes a SC as its complement, having the NP-head merged in subject position and the CP as its predicate.

(on the relevant licensing conditions, cf. Footnote 3).[14] Notice that Focus movement is independently required for the interpretation of the [+foc] feature, merged in the Foc head.

To provide an illustration, consider sentence (18a) and the construction in (18b), which must be considered a preliminary version of the Merge structure we assume (a refinement will be proposed in Section 5):

(18) a. It is JOHN that kissed Mary

b.

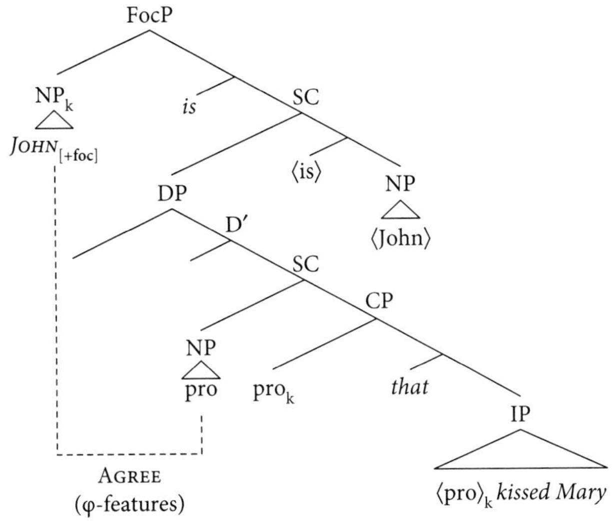

14. This theory predicts that, when the relative clause contains an overt (generic) NP-head, no checking is required for the φ-features of overt NPs. This can explain the difference in reversability between clefts and pseudoclefts:

(i) a. It's John that left
b. *That left is John

(ii) a. The one who left is John
b. John is the one who left

It is also important to notice that the ungrammaticality of a sentence like (iii) can be ascribed to its being a subjectless construction:

(iii) *John is that left

As is shown in (18b), the pre-copular constituent *John* cannot qualify as a structural subject. Therefore, sentence (iii) is ungrammatical in languages like English in which the copula has a verbal status and, as such, requires a subject; on the other hand, a sentence like (iii) is grammatical in languages in which the copula has been grammaticalized into a Focus Marker, losing its verbal properties (for more details on this point, cf. Section 5 and Footnote 35).

To summarize, (pseudo)cleft constructions take the form of a SC having the (to be) focused constituent as its main predicate. The presupposed part of the sentence is contained in a free relative that qualifies as a definite description headed by either a *pro* or a generic NP of a restricted class ('person', 'thing', etc.).[15] This kind of analysis can provide an explanation for a number of well-known phenomena, some of which will be briefly addressed below (for further discussion, cf. Frascarelli 2010a).[16]

3.1 Extraction effects

As is commonly agreed, extraction is not allowed from subject DPs (Moro 1997; Heycock & Kroch 1999; Den Dikken 2006), while no restriction is imposed on the

---

15. The analysis of the initial wh-clause of pseudoclefts as a free relative is also confirmed by the existence of a 'generic-headed' pseudocleft, in which the initial clause is a full relative headed by a generic noun:

(i) What I gave John is a book (subject = free (i.e. headless) relative)
(ii) The thing I gave John is a book (subject = relative headed by a generic noun)

As is clear, the wh-phrase heading the relative DP in pseudocleft constructions (as in (i)) has no interrogative features and simply counts as a generic NP. The use of wh-phrases as indefinites is largely attested cross-linguistically. Following Kratzer & Shimoyama (2002), we can assume that wh-phrases universally denote sets of individual alternatives and, in their indefinite use, they combine immediately with an existential quantifier which in many languages is null.

16. A reviewer has objected that contrasts such as the following challenge the proposal that the presupposition is realized as a free relative DP in subject position. As is shown below for German, it is not possible to use a free relative clause as a subject if the relative pronoun is dative, while the relative clause of a cleft can be introduced by a dative item:

(i)	*Wer/*Wem*	*Maria*	*vertraut*	*wird*	*einen*	*Vorteil*	*haben*
	who.NOM/*DAT	Maria	trust.3SG	will.3SG	a.ACC	benefit	have

'The one who Maria trusts will have a benefit'

(ii)	*Es*	*ist*	*der*	*Chef,*	*dem*	*Maria*	*vertraut*
	3SG.N	be.3SG	DET.NOM	boss	DET.DAT	Maria	trust.3SG

'It is THE BOSS that Maria trusts'

We surmise that this difference relies on the nature of the element introducing the relative clause: a relative *pronoun* in (i) vs. a relative *determiner* in (ii). Therefore, a gapped generic NOM NP-head can be assumed in (ii) (i.e. '*it is the boss* ⟨the person.NOM⟩ *to whom*.DAT...'), which is consistent with the subject function of the relative clause, while a 'silent' noun cannot be assumed in (i), given the presence of a pronoun heading the relevant DP. Ungrammaticality thus arises from its DAT Case, which is incompatible with a subject function. A similar case is discussed in Section 5.3.

movement of predicate-internal material. The present proposal therefore predicts that no constituent can be extracted from the relative clause of a (pseudo)cleft construction, while no movement restriction should be imposed on predicate-internal material. This prediction is borne out by data, as illustrated below for English and Italian (cf. Frascarelli 2000a):[17]

(19) a. It is [the photograph of the wall] [that I gave John]

b. *È* *[la* *foto* *del* *muro]* *[che* *ho*
be.3SG the photograph of.the wall that have.1SG

dato *a* *John]*
give.PST.PART to John

(20) a. What$_i$ do you think [what I gave John] is [the photograph of t_i]?

a′. *Di* *cosa$_i$* *pensi* *che* *[quello* *che* *ho* *dato*
of what think.2SG that DEM that have.1SG give.PST.PART

a *John]* *sia* *[la* *foto* t$_i$]?
to John be.SUBJ.3SG the photograph

b. *Who$_i$ do you think [what I gave to t_i] is [the photograph of the wall]?

b′. **A* *chi$_i$* *pensi* *che* *[quello* *che* *ho*
to who think.2SG that DEM that have.1SG

dato t$_i$] *sia* *[la* *foto* *del* *muro]*?
give.PST.PART be.SUBJ.3SG the photograph of.the wall

As we can see, while it is not possible to wh-move material from within the relative clause (cf. (20b–b′)), extraction from the predicative NP is fully grammatical (cf. (20a–a′)). This suggests that in cleft constructions too, it is the focused NP (rather than the relative clause) that constitutes the predicate.[18]

---

17. The list of the abbreviations used in the glosses is the following: ACC = accusative; DAT = dative; DECL = declarative; DEM = demonstrative; DET = determiner; F = feminine; FM = Focus Marker; FUT = future; M = masculine; N = neuter; NEG = negation; NOM = nominative; NOMIN = nominalizer; NONNOM = non-nominative; PART = participle; PL = plural; POSS = possessive; PRES = present; PROG = progressive; PST = past; RED = reduced paradigm; REFL = reflexive; REL = relative; SCL = subject clitic; SG = singular; SUBJ = subjunctive.

18. We acknowledge that the ungrammaticality of the examples (20b-b') could also be ascribed to the (generally assumed) impossibility of extraction from a relative clause. However, the grammaticality of (20a-a') unambiguously shows the predicative nature of *the photograph of the wall/la foto del muro*, so the relative DP cannot itself be taken as the predicate (for further details, see below).

3.2 Case marking and antiagreement effects

Additional evidence supporting the present analysis is provided by the Case marking of the two major constituents in (pseudo)cleft constructions.

First of all, it should be considered that, in a number of languages, when a 'subject' is clefted, it does not show NOM Case, but the default (i.e. unmarked) Case marking available in the relevant language. This is, for instance, the case of Somali, as illustrated in (21) (for comparative data and an extensive discussion, cf. Frascarelli & Puglielli 2005a; Frascarelli 2010a):

(21) *Hilib-ka* *NIMAN-KA* *baa* *cunayá*
meat-DET.NONNOM[19] men-DET.NONNOM FM eat.PRES.PROG.REL(RED)
'THE MEN are eating the meat'

It should be noted that NONNOM Case in Somali is also used to mark predicative NPs. Hence, in copular sentences in which Focus is not involved, a 'declarative marker' (*waa*) is present and the subject DP is marked for NOM Case, while the predicative NP shows NONNOM Case:

(22) *Wiilk*-u/**wiilk*-a *waa* *gabarta*
boy.DET-*NOM*/**NONNOM* DECL girl.DET
walaalkeed-a/**walaalkeed*-u
brother.POSS3SG.M-*NONNOM*/**NOM*
'The boy is the girl's brother'

(23) *Shukri* *waa* *naag*/**naag*-i
Shukri.NOM DECL woman.*NONNOM*/**NOM*
'Shukri is a woman'

It is therefore particularly interesting to notice that NOM Case can on the contrary appear on the relative DP of cleft constructions. This is clearly shown in 'dependent-marking' languages (cf. Nichols 1986), like Somali and Afar, in which Case marking appears on the rightmost constituent within a DP (from Frascarelli & Puglielli 2005b):

19. Somali marks non-subject functions with the same Case marking, which is distinct from NOM Case. This is the reason why we prefer to indicate it as 'non-nominative' (NONNOM), rather than using the (more specific) ACC(usative) label.

(24) *WIIL*-KAAS *baa* [*aan* *af* *Talyaani-ga*
boy-DEM.*NONNOM* FM NEG language Italian-DET.NONNOM
ku *hadlin*]-i (SOMALI)
in speak.NEG-*NOM*
'THAT BOY cannot speak Italian'

(25) *ÀWKA* [*huurí-h* *adda-l* *kullumta* *habte*]-m (AFAR)
boy.*ACC* boat-of inside-in fish leave.PST.3SG.F-NOMIN.*NOM*
'THE BOY left the fish inside the boat'

Case marking shows that what follows the Focus is a relative clause (cf. also Schachter 1973) connected to the subject position (the sense of this 'connection' will be fully clarified in Section 5). On the other hand, clefted 'subjects' are predicative elements whose subject interpretation is a by-product of their connection to the NP *pro* heading the relative DP (cf. (18b)).

This analysis is further supported by the fact that in a number of languages, subject agreement in cleft constructions is either dispensed with or 'reduced' by means of a special paradigm (specific of relative clauses).[20] This complex phenomenon (which cannot be explained by operator-movement *per se*) is generally defined as the 'Antiagreement effect' (cf. Ouhalla 1993; Frascarelli 1999, 2010a) and can be aptly illustrated through (21), repeated below as (26):

(26) *Hilib-ka* *NIMAN-KA* *baa* *cunayá*
meat-DET.NONNOM men-DET.NONNOM FM eat.PRES.PROG.REL(RED)
'THE MEN are eating the meat'

(27) a. **Hilibka* *NIMAN*-KU *baa* *cunayá*
men-DET.*NOM*

b. **Hilibka* NIMANKA *baa* *cunay*aan
eat.PRES.PROG.*3PL*

c. **Hilibka* NIMANKA bay *cunayá*
FM.*SCL3PL*

As we can see, when a 'subject' is clefted in Somali, the verb is realized in a reduced paradigm (RED) in which agreement is limited to gender and number features (cf. (27b))[21] and the relevant Focus cannot be resumed by a clitic (27c), while clitic resumption is obligatory in all other cases.

---

20. An explanation of full agreement in cleft constructions in some languages is addressed in Section 5.

21. In particular, the reduced paradigm has three forms: one for 3SG.F, one for 1PL and one for all other persons (the latter is the case for *cunayá* in (26)).

4. The information-structural articulation of (Pseudo)clefts

4.1 The information packaging in (pseudo)clefts

(Pseudo)cleft constructions are traditionally classified as Focus-related structures. We suggest, however, that they also implement a Topic-Comment structure. Specifically, evidence will be provided that the relative DP is dislocated in both constructions, thus constituting a right-hand Topic in clefts and a left-hand Topic in pseudoclefts. An illustration of the information-structural role of (pseudo)cleft constituents is therefore in order to concentrate on syntactic and intonational evidence in Sections 5 and 6, respectively.

Let us first consider the information packaging of pseudocleft constituents. A pseudocleft sentence like (28) is only appropriate in contexts in which it is presupposed that the speaker gave something to John. For this reason, the wh-clause is generally assumed to convey given information.

(28) What I gave John is a book

However, given our assumption that the relative clause is subject to a type-shifting operation that makes it denote an individual (see Section 2), we suggest that the information encoded by the wh-clause should be analyzed as an *existential presupposition* (on this point, cf. also Collins 1991: 71-ff.). In other words, what is presupposed in a sentence like (28) is the *existence* of an *individual* such that I gave it to John. Since its existence is presupposed, it seems plausible to argue that the relevant relative DP constitutes a Topic. Incidentally notice that a similar analysis is suggested in Prince (1978: 887), who argues that "[i]f we compare the logico-semantic notion of presupposition with the discourse notion of known/old/given information, we find that, in the case of the [pseudocleft], they seem to match quite closely".

This analysis is assumed for clefts as well. However, the different position of the relative DP suggests that this cannot have exactly the same (discourse) function in the two sentence types. In this respect, Prince (1978: 896) argues that

> [t]he difference [between clefts and pseudoclefts] lies in the communicative value of the presupposition. In the [pseudocleft] [...] the WH-clause represents what the speaker is assuming the hearer is or can be thinking about; as such, it may be seen as the THEME of that particular stretch of discourse. In the [cleft], the *that*-clause represents known or old information, which is not marked as assumed to be in the hearer's consciousness and which is not the theme.

It thus seems that the relative DP constitutes a topical element both in clefts and pseudoclefts, and that its realization in different positions (i.e. as a right-hand

Topic and a left-hand Topic respectively) is related to a different interpretation in the two cases. In particular, following Frascarelli & Hinterhölzl (henceforth, F&H, 2007), we can distinguish three types of Topics on the basis of their discourse functions and formal (phonological and syntactic) properties:[22]

> Topics [...] do 'different things' and, at least, three types of topics should be distinguished: (a) *aboutness[-shift] topic*: "what the sentence is about" (Reinhart 1981; Lambrecht 1994); in particular, a constituent that is "newly introduced, newly changed or newly returned to" (Givón 1983: 8), a constituent which is proposed as "a matter of standing and current interest or concern" (Strawson 1964); (b) *contrastive topic*: an element that induces alternatives which have no impact on the focus value and creates oppositional pairs with respect to other topics (Kuno 1976; Büring 1999); (c) *familiar topic*: a given or accessible (cf. Chafe 1987) constituent, which is typically destressed and realized in a pronominal form (Pesetsky 1987); when a familiar topic is textually given and d-linked with a pre-established aboutness[-shift] topic, it is defined as a *continuing topic* (cf. Givón 1983). (F&H 2007: 88)

Since right-hand Topics can only be of the familiar type, the right-hand dislocated wh/*that*-clause of clefts necessarily implements a Familiar Topic, whereas the relative DP in pseudoclefts qualifies as a left-hand Topic of any type (its specific nature depending on discourse grammar).[23]

22. For a discourse-semantic description of these three types of Topics and their impact on conversational dynamics in different languages, see also Bianchi & Frascarelli (2010a).

23. This means that a shifting or contrastive function is excluded for the (right-dislocated) relative DP of a cleft, as the following examples illustrate:

(i) [A great amount of delicious food has been prepared and is ready on the table]
A: *Chi è che ha preparato tutta questa roba?*
who be.3SG that have.3SG prepare.PST.PART all this stuff
'Who is it that prepared all this food?'

B1: *Chi ha cotto il riso è Sara, (mentre)*
who have.3SG cook.PST.PART the rice be.3SG Sara while
chi ha fatto il dolce è Leo
who have.3SG make.PST.PART the cake be.3SG Leo
'The one who cooked the rice is Sara, (while) the one who made the cake is Leo'

B2: *#È* SARA *che ha cotto il riso, (mentre)*
be.3SG Sara that have.3SG cook.PST.PART the rice while
è leo che ha fatto il dolce
be.3SG LEO that have.3SG make.PST.PART the cake
'It is SARA that cooked the rice, (while) it is LEO that made the cake'

Interestingly, an analysis of clefts as the right-dislocation counterpart of pseudo-clefts has already been proposed in Gundel (1977, 1985), according to which

> cleft sentences [like *It was an explosion that you heard*] are reduced forms of structures underlying right-dislocated pseudoclefts like [*It was an explosion, what you heard*], where the pronoun in the main sentence is a copy of the right-dislocated NP. (from Gundel 1977: 543)

In this view, "*it* [in clefts] is not empty at all, but is a pronominal reference to the topic of the sentence". We will resume this matter in Section 4.2, also discussing the syntactic evidence for this dislocation analysis.

As for the interpretation of the clefted phrase, the latter is the undisputed Focus of the sentence. In some languages (e.g. Somali, Tagalog, Tigrinya, Ingbo) it is interpreted as an (Exhaustive) *Information* Focus (though a contrastive interpretation can be obtained by means of intonation), whereas in others (e.g. Italian, English, Basque) a *contrastive* reading is normally induced (on the difference between Information and Contrastive Focus, cf. Footnote 5). However, it should

---

(ii) [Speaker B is watching the news on TV; speaker A has just entered the room]

A: *Ci sono novità? Chi è che ha rapito*
there be.3PL news who be.3SG that have.3SG kidnap.PST.PART
la ragazza?
the girl
'What's new? Who is it that kidnapped the girl?'

B1: *Non lo so. Ma chi ha ucciso la madre è*
NEG it know.1SG but who have.3SG kill.PST.PART the mother be.3SG
il vicino
the neighbor
'I do not know. But the one who killed her mother is their neighbor'

B2: *#Non lo so. Ma è* IL VICINO *che ha*
NEG it know.1SG but be.3SG the neighbor that have.3SG
ucciso la madre
kill.PST.PART the mother
'I do not know. But it is THEIR NEIGHBOR that killed her mother'

The context provided in (i) requires a Contrastive Topic value for the relative DPs in the conjoined clauses of B's answer and, as the examples show, only the pseudocleft (iB1) is appropriate. On the other hand, a shifting function is required for the relative DP in (ii) and, also in this case, the cleft in (iiB2) is clearly inappropriate. These examples support our proposal: the right-dislocated relative DP of clefts can only constitute a Familiar Topic, while the relative DP of pseudoclefts, which is left-dislocated, can qualify as an Aboutness-shift or a Contrastive Topic. This conclusion is also supported by intonational evidence, which will be provided and discussed in Section 6.

be noted that even in languages of the latter type, clefts can be used as answers to wh-questions (hence, to obtain Information Focus). The possibility of a non-contrastive interpretation for cleft sentences in languages like Italian is also argued in Belletti (2008), who observes that in this case clefts are normally realized in a reduced form and constitute "the preferred option when either a cleft is contained in the question [...] or else with agentive predicates expressing a somewhat negative presupposition".[24] This is illustrated in (29–30):

(29) Q. *Chi è che ha rotto il vaso?*
who be.3SG that have.3SG break.PST.PART the vase
'Who is it that broke the vase?'

A. *È (stato) GIANNI*
be.3SG be.PST.PART Gianni
'It is/was GIANNI'

(30) Q. *Chi ha urlato?*
who have.3SG scream.PST.PART
'Who screamed?'

A. *È stato GIANNI*
be.3SG be.PST.PART Gianni
'It was GIANNI'

Given the exhaustiveness effect associated with clefts (cf. Section 2), the sentence in (30A) (unlike the corresponding postverbal Focus construction, i.e. *L'ha fatto GIANNI* 'GIANNI did it') implies that there is only one person who screamed; hence, any individual other than Gianni is excluded from being the one (or among the ones) who screamed (cf. the notion of "exclusion by identification" in Kiss 1998). This is what makes this structure different from its non-cleft counterpart.

These examples show that the traditional observation that clefts can only convey Contrastive Focus in languages like Italian is not correct: clefted phrases have basically an exhaustive reading, which can but does not need to be associated with contrast.

4.2 The relative DP as a dislocated constituent: Syntactic evidence

The topical status of the initial wh-clause in pseudoclefts has been acknowledged in several studies, either on discourse and/or on syntactic grounds (cf. Gundel 1977, 1985; Prince 1978; Collins 1991; Frascarelli 2000a; Den Dikken et al. 2000; Den Dikken 2005). The hypothesis that the *that*-clause of clefts represents a

24. On the possibility for clefts to be used as answers to cleft-questions in Italian, see also Belletti (2005a: § 3.2).

right-hand Topic, however, might sound more controversial.[25] The present section is dedicated to an illustration of the syntactic arguments supporting this proposal.

One piece of evidence is the possibility to realize right-dislocated adverbial constituents between the Focus and the *that*-clause:

(31) *Sono io, alla fine, che parto*
be.1SG 1SG.NOM at.the end that leave.1SG
'It's ME, in the end, that leaves'

Given the right-dislocated nature of the adverbial PP *alla fine* in (31), the following *that*-clause can only constitute a right-hand Topic.[26]

Additional evidence is provided by deletion possibilities; consider the following data from Brazilian Portuguese, taken from Belletti (2008: § 3) (for Italian, see (29–30) above):

(32) (Q: Who spoke?)
A. *Foi UM RAPAZ (que falou)*
be.PST.3SG a boy that speak.PST.3SG
'It was A BOY (that spoke)'

As can be observed, the relative DP in (32) can be omitted, producing a reduced cleft; this confirms our hypothesis that it encodes given information.

As already mentioned, the assumption that the relative DP is right-dislocated in clefts implies that the initial *it* is not an expletive (as is generally assumed) but a non-expletive pronoun, which is coreferent with the right-hand Topic (on this point, see also Reeve 2007). Strong evidence for the nature of *it* as "a pronominal reference to the Topic at the end of the sentence" is provided in Gundel (1977: § 4). As the following examples show, the initial pronoun of clefts in many languages is (or, at least, can be) formally identical to a referential pronoun, thus differing from the dummy subject used in purely expletive constructions (e.g. in the presence of weather verbs) (cf. Hedberg 2000; Rialland et al. 2002; Belletti 2008):

(33) English: (Hedberg 2000: 892)
a. It/*this/*that is snowing
b. It/this/that was JOHN that I saw

25. Though several studies of this topic can be found (see, for instance, Jespersen 1927; Akmajian 1970; Emonds 1976; Gundel 1977, 1985; Hedberg 2000).

26. Since Focus is the rightmost constituent within the sentential Intonational Phrase, right-dislocation of *alla fine* in (31) is proved by its post-focal position (cf. Frascarelli 2000b, Samek-Lodovici 2006 and Bocci 2009 for Interface evidence; cf. also Cinque 1993). In this line of analysis, the same conclusion can be reached for the post-focal constituent in Portuguese (32).

(34) German:

a. *Es/*das* *regnet*
3SG.N/DET.N rain.3SG
'It's raining'

b. *Es/das* *war* *JOHN,* *den* *ich*
3SG.N/DET.N be.PST.3SG John DET.ACC 1SG.NOM
gesehen *habe*
see.PST.PART have.1SG
'It was JOHN that I saw'

(35) French: (Hedberg 2000: 893)[27]

a. *Il/*ce/?ça* *neige*
3SG.M/DEM snow.3SG
'It's snowing'

b. **Il/c'* *est* *JOHN* *que* *j'* *ai* *vu*
3SG.M/DEM be.3SG John that 1SG have.1SG see.PST.PART
'It's JOHN that I saw'

(36) Russian (Gundel 1977: 550, 553)

a. (**Èto*) *morozit*[28]
3SG.N freeze.3SG
'It's freezing'

b. *(*Èto*) *IVANA* *ja* *videl*
3SG.N Ivan.ACC 1SG.NOM see.PST.1SG
'It was IVAN I saw'

This section has discussed the discourse properties of (pseudo)cleft constituents, showing that a clefted phrase has an exhaustive reading (which may or may not be contrastive) while the relative DP qualifies as a Topic. In the next section, the structural analysis sketched in Section 3 will be refined in order to account for these properties.

27. An anonymous reviewer points out that not only *il* but also *ce* and *ça* can qualify as expletives in French (as in *c'est une honte de dire cela* 'it is a shame to say that' and *ça me ferait plaisir de sortir* 'it would give me the pleasure to go out'). However, what this paper proposes is that in the case of (pseudo)cleft constructions, the pronoun *ce* constitutes a referential (rather than an expletive) pronoun. Note that the analysis of *ce* as a referential pronoun in French clefts is also suggested in Rialland et al. (2002: 3): on the basis of a prosodic analysis, it is claimed that the relevant pronoun refers to the relative clause which realizes the coda.

28. Of course, the realization of *éto* in (36a) yields an acceptable sentence if the relevant pronoun is interpreted as referential.

5. Derivation

So far, it has been argued that the clefted phrase of (pseudo)cleft sentences has the properties of a main predicate in a copular construction. Furthermore, we have observed that, contrary to the traditional view, the relative DP should be analyzed as a dislocated constituent (specifically, as a right-hand Topic in clefts and a left-hand Topic in pseudoclefts), which is merged as (or connected with) the subject within a SC structure.[29] Given these results, we will first (Section 5.1) reconsider the preliminary structure in (18b) and see how clefts are derived. Pseudoclefts will then be addressed (Section 5.2), also showing that the present analysis can account for a number of similarities and asymmetries between the two sentence types (cf. Section 5.3).

5.1 Clefts

Before discussing the derivation of clefts, it is necessary to consider the structure we assume for the left periphery of the sentence. Based on F&H's (2007) and Frascarelli's (2010a) analyses of Focus and Topic constructions, we assume the hierarchy of functional projections in the CP-system as illustrated in (37) below (the asterisk indicates recursivity). Notice that this hierarchy also includes the Ground Phrase projection (GP; cf. Poletto & Pollock 2004), which is the landing site for backgrounded (i.e. unfocused) material. Its position with respect to other projections is based on distributional evidence from naturalistic data (cf. F&H 2007 and Frascarelli 2007):[30]

(37) $[_{ForceP}\ [_{ShiftP}\ [_{GP}\ [_{ContrP}\ [_{FocP}\ [_{FamP*}[_{FinP}\ [_{IP}$

As for the derivation of right-hand Topics, we assume that they are "merged [or moved] in the left periphery of the sentence and that their right-peripheral position is derived through IP-inversion" (from F&H 2007: 99). In other words, right-hand Topics are located in Spec,FamP (much like left-hand Familiar Topics) and are crossed by IP raising to Spec,GP:[31]

29. As will be shown below, the relative DP can either be merged as the subject or else be generated in an extrasentential position (i.e. in the left periphery of the clause); in the latter case, it is interpreted as coreferent with the structural subject, with which it establishes an AGREE relation (cf. Frascarelli 2007).

30. The mutual position of GP and FocP can also be ascribed to a prosodic well-formedness condition that requires Focus to be the rightmost constituent within the sentential Intonational Phrase (cf. Footnote 26).

31. Evidence for IP-inversion to derive right-dislocation (*contra* Cecchetto 1999 and Belletti 2001, 2005b) is provided in Cardinaletti (2002), Frascarelli (2004, 2008) and Samek-Lodovici

(38) [$_{\text{ShiftP}}$ [$_{\text{GP}}$ [$_{\text{IP}}$ … pron/t_k …] [$_{\text{ContrP}}$ [$_{\text{FocP}}$ [$_{\text{FamP}}$ Topic$_k$ t_{IP}

We can now turn to the derivation of clefts, which will initially be concerned with the analysis of English structures such as (39):

(39) It is ME that you saw

Given our syntactic analysis, the derivation of (39) requires movement of the clefted phrase *ME* to a left-peripheral Focus-related projection[32] (cf. (40a)) and IP-movement to Spec,GP to derive right-dislocation of the relative DP (cf. (40b)):[33]

(40) a. [$_{\text{FocP}}$ [$_{\text{NP}}$ ME] [$_{\text{FamP}}$ [$_{\text{DP}}$ [$_{\text{SC}}$ [$_{\text{NP}}$ *pro*] [$_{\text{CP}}$ that you saw]]] [$_{\text{IP}}$ it is [$_{\text{SC}}$ t_{it} t_{NP}]]]

b. [$_{\text{GP}}$ [$_{\text{IP}}$ it is [$_{\text{SC}}$ t_{it} t_{NP}]] [$_{\text{FocP}}$ [$_{\text{NP}}$ ME] [$_{\text{FamP}}$ [$_{\text{DP}}$ [$_{\text{SC}}$ [$_{\text{NP}}$ *pro*] [$_{\text{CP}}$ that you saw]]] t_{IP}]]]

It is now important to observe that in contrast to English, in a pro-drop language like Italian two agreement patterns are available when the clefted constituent is interpreted as the direct object of the relative verb. Specifically, a non-3rd person clefted phrase can be marked either with NOM (cf. (41a)) or ACC Case (cf. (41b)); in the former case, the copula agrees with the clefted constituent, whereas in the latter it shows a default 3SG agreement:

(41) a. *Sono* *IO* *che* pro *hai* *visto*
be.*1SG* 1SG.*NOM* that have.2SG see.PST.PART
'It is ME that you saw'

b. *È* *ME* *che* pro *hai* *visto*
be.*3SG* 1SG.*ACC* that have.2SG see.PST.PART
'id.'

(2006). Note that the notion of 'ground' that is assumed here to characterize the GP projection is different from what is intended in Vallduví (1992), where 'ground' is a topical notion. In the Structured Meaning approach that we assume (cf. Footnote 5), backgrounded (i.e. unfocused) material conveys *presupposed* information including a variable to be specified (by the Focus). This is why neither a Focus nor a Topic can move to GP.

32. Specifically, the clefted phrase moves either to Spec,FocP or Spec,ContrP, depending on whether it serves as an *Information* or a *Contrastive* Focus. For the sake of simplicity, in the following structures the relevant projection is uniformly indicated as FocP.

33. For the sake of simplicity, in (40) and in the following structures, the indication of the operator *pro* and its variable within the relative CP (cf. (18b)) will be omitted.

We would like to demonstrate that agreement and Case marking possibilities are related to the Null Subject parameter, as well as to the existence of two types of derivation for right-hand Topics in Italian. As for the latter point, it has often been claimed that right-hand Topics can either be merged in a left-peripheral (Familiar) Topic projection or derived from an IP-internal position (i.e. "marginalized"; cf. Cardinaletti 2002; F&H 2007; Frascarelli 2008). The existence of a twofold derivation for right-hand Topics is the very reason for the existence of the two constructions in (41).

First of all, consider sentence (41a), in which the clefted constituent shows NOM Case marking and determines agreement with the copula. This kind of construction can be explained along the lines of rightward copular agreement in Italian in cases like *La causa della rivolta sono/*è Gianni e Maria* (lit. 'The cause of the riot are/*is Gianni and Maria'). Following Moro's (1997) suggestion, we propose that the SC subject position is filled by a null pronoun, namely a *pro*, while the relative DP is merged in an extrasentential position as a Familiar Topic that is coreferent with the relevant null subject pronoun. Let us consider the relevant derivation step-by-step.

Within the SC the subject *pro* and the (to be) focused NP share both Case and φ-features since they are in a predicative relation (cf. (42a)). Case and φ-features are then checked by *pro* after it is raised to Spec,IP (cf. (42b)):

(42) a. [$_{SC}$ [$_{DP}$ *pro*] [$_{NP}$ io]]
NOM
1SG

b. [$_{IP}$ [$_{DP}$ *pro*] sono [$_{SC}$ t_{DP} [$_{NP}$ io]]]
1SG

At this stage of the derivation, the relative DP, merged in Spec,FamP, establishes a coreference relation (through AGREE) with the null subject (cf. (43a)). The derivation then proceeds with the discourse-related movements illustrated in (40), namely predicate raising to Spec,FocP (cf. (43b)) and remnant-IP movement (cf. (43c)). This determines the spell-out of the relative DP as a right-hand Topic:

(43) a. [$_{FamP}$ [$_{DP}$ [$_{SC}$ [$_{NP}$ *pro*] [$_{CP}$ che *pro* hai visto]]]$_i$ [$_{IP}$ [$_{DP}$ *pro*]$_i$ sono [$_{SC}$ t_{DP} [$_{NP}$ io]]]]
AGREE

b. $[_{FocP}\ [_{NP}$ IO$]\ [_{FamP}\ [_{DP}\ [_{SC}\ [_{NP}$ *pro*$]\ [_{CP}$ che *pro* hai visto$]]]_i\ [_{IP}\ [_{DP}$ *pro*$]_i$ sono $[_{SC}\ t_{DP}\ t_{NP}]]]]$

c. $[_{GP}\ [_{IP}\ [_{DP}$ *pro*$]_i$ sono $[_{SC}\ t_{DP}\ t_{NP}]]\ [_{FocP}\ [_{NP}$ IO$]\ [_{FamP}\ [_{DP}\ [_{SC}\ [_{NP}$ *pro*$]\ [_{CP}$ che …$]]]_i\ t_{IP}]]]$

The agreement pattern in (41b), on the other hand, is determined by the presence of a marginalized Topic. The derivation proceeds as follows: the relative DP is merged as the subject of the SC and raises to Spec,IP (cf. (44a)); in this position, it determines 3SG agreement with the copula through a Spec-Head configuration.[34] It is subsequently marginalized to Spec,FamP, where it can receive its interpretation as a Familiar Topic (cf. (44b)), while the predicate *me* is attracted to Spec,FocP (cf. (44c)). Finally, the relative DP is crossed by the movement of the remnant-IP (containing the copula) to Spec,GP (cf. (44d)):[35]

(44) a. $[_{IP}\ [_{DP}\ [_{SC}\ [_{NP}$ *pro*$]\ [_{CP}$ che *pro* hai visto$]]]$ è $[_{SC}\ t_{DP}\ [_{NP}$ me$]]]$

3SG

34. Unlike the case in (42), we can assume that in this structure, Case and φ-feature agreement within the SC is blocked because the subject is not a referential *pro* (a null pronoun taking its features via discourse antecedent), but a relative DP headed by an *indefinite pro* (a sort of 'null wh-pronoun', cf. Footnote 15), which is inherently specified as 3rd person.

35. For the sake of simplicity, we indicate the functional projection containing the copula as IP. However, given the analysis of copulas as linkers in (pseudo)cleft constructions (cf. Section 2), the functional structure of this IP projection should be seen as reduced. The extent of this reduction is dependent on the degree of grammaticalization of the copula, which is complete in languages that make use of FMs. As a matter of fact, unlike copulas, these 'particles' are no longer considered as auxiliaries by speakers and do not behave like auxiliaries syntactically (cf. Frascarelli & Ramaglia 2009: § 5.3 for details). We will not deal with Focus marking languages here, but limit ourselves to suggesting that an analysis along these lines might explain the different location shown by copular elements in cleft constructions cross-linguistically, namely either before the Focus (Italian, French, English, Kikuyu, etc.) or immediately after it (Somali, Hausa, Wolof, Chaha, etc.). Specifically, our hypothesis is that FMs move to Foc^0, where they establish a Spec-Head relation with the fronted Focus (in Spec,FocP); on the contrary, in languages in which the copula still maintains some inflectional features, this element reaches I^0 and is then raised to a pre-focal position by means of the IP-movement to Spec,GP (cf. for instance, (40b), (43c) and (44d)).

b. $[_{FamP}\ [_{DP}\ [_{SC}\ [_{NP}\ pro]\ [_{CP}$ che *pro* hai visto$]]]\ [_{IP}\ t'_{DP}$ è $[_{SC}\ t_{DP}\ [_{NP}$ me$]]]]$

c. $[_{FocP}\ [_{NP}$ ME$]\ [_{FamP}\ [_{DP}\ [_{SC}\ [_{NP}\ pro]\ [_{CP}$ che *pro* hai visto$]]]\ [_{IP}\ t'_{DP}$ è $[_{SC}\ t_{DP}\ t_{NP}]]]]$

d. $[_{GP}\ [_{IP}\ t'_{DP}$ è $[_{SC}\ t_{DP}\ t_{NP}]]\ [_{FocP}\ [_{NP}$ ME$]\ [_{FamP}\ [_{DP}\ [_{SC}\ [_{NP}\ pro]\ [_{CP}$ che *pro* hai visto$]]]\ t_{IP}]]]$

Under the present proposal the existence of two types of cleft structures in Italian (cf. (41)) is motivated by two independent syntactic properties, namely the syntax of Familiar Topics and the setting of the Null Subject parameter. As a matter of fact, the two derivations illustrated in (43) and (44) are distinguished by the merged vs. derived nature of the right-hand Familiar Topic (i.e. the *that*-clause) and the type of empty category hosted in Spec,IP (i.e. either a *pro* or a trace, respectively).

This line of analysis can also explain one of the most famous (and still unresolved) problems related to these constructions, namely *(anti)connectedness effects* between the Focus constituent and the relative verb in the case of subject clefting. In particular, when the clefted NP is (interpreted as) the subject of the subordinate clause, grammatical connectedness (person agreement and Case marking) is blocked in languages like English, while it is fully realized in languages like Italian. Consider the following:

(45) a. It is *ME* that/who/Ø *goes* to America

b. *Sono* IO *che* *vado* *in* *America*
be.1SG 1SG.*NOM* that go.*1SG* to America

b′. **È* ME *che* va *in* *America*
be.3SG 1SG.*ACC* that go.*3SG* to America

(46) a. It is not *ME* that always *looks* at *himself* in the mirror

b. *Non* *sono* IO *che* mi *guardo* *sempre*
NEG be.1SG 1SG.*NOM* that *1SG.REFL* look.*1SG* always
allo *specchio*
to.the mirror

b′. **Non* *è* ME *che* si *guarda* *sempre*
NEG be.3SG 1SG.*ACC* that *3SG.REFL* look.*3SG* always
allo *specchio*
to.the mirror

(47) a. Was it YOU that held *his* breath for five minutes?

b. *Sei* *stato* TU *che* hai
be.2SG be.PST.PART 2SG.NOM that have.2SG
trattenuto *il* *respiro* *per* *cinque* *minuti*?
hold.PST.PART the breath for five minutes

b′. **È* *stato* TE *che* ha *trattenuto*
be.3SG be.PST.PART 2SG.ACC that have.3SG hold.PST.PART
il *respiro* *per* *cinque* *minuti*?
the breath for five minutes

The (a) sentences illustrate the lack of syntactic connectedness in English as far as verb personal inflection (45–46), reflexive binding (46) and pronoun binding in idiom chunks (47) are concerned. Italian translations (cf. examples (b–b′)), on the other hand, illustrate the opposite behavior. In particular, English copula always agrees with the subject *it*, Focus is marked with ACC Case and the relative verb invariably shows 3rd person agreement (thus determining 3rd person reflexive binding).[36] In Italian, on the contrary, the focused NP shows NOM Case and triggers agreement both on the relative verb and the matrix copula.

The asymmetry between Italian and English regarding Case marking and copular agreement has already been discussed (cf. (39–40) vs. (41–44)). We would now like to show how the present analysis can explain the opposition concerning relative verb agreement. Let us consider the English sentence in (45a) above; the

36. An anonymous reviewer points out that connectedness effects are apparently attested in sentences like (ia-b) below and wonders if and how the present proposal can account for it.

(i) a. It was a picture of herself$_k$ that Mary$_k$ bought
b. It is his$_k$ dissertation that everybody$_k$ admires

Indeed, the anaphoric interpretation in (ia) and the distributive interpretation in (ib) seem to show that *Mary* and *everybody* must assume scope over the relevant pronouns at some point of the derivation, while this is excluded by the present proposal (and supported by a significant amount of evidence). This is a very complex and tricky question that cannot be fully treated in a footnote. In brief, we suggest that cases like (ia) can be explained following Frascarelli's (2007) idea that a null (Aboutness) Topic can be assumed in the relevant structure. In other words, since the relative DP is a right-hand Familiar Topic, the discourse referents it contains must have been previously mentioned in the discourse. Hence, in (ia) the DP *Mary* in the relative clause can be considered the *low copy* of a left-hand Topic c-commanding the relevant anaphor:

(ii) [⟨Mary$_k$⟩ [it was a picture of herself$_k$ that Mary$_k$ bought]]

As for (ib) notice that all the situations that verify the scope relation $\exists>\forall$ also verify the inverse scope relation $\forall>\exists$ (cf. Schwarzschild 2002). Hence, the distributive interpretation at issue is not really germane in endorsing the syntactic wide scope of the universal quantifier.

structure in (48) represents the stage of the derivation in which the clefted phrase is raised to Spec,FocP:

(48) $[_{FocP}\ [_{NP}$ ME$]\ [_{FamP}\ [_{DP}\ [_{SC}\ [_{NP}\ \textit{pro}]\ [_{CP}\ \textit{pro}_k$ that $\langle \textit{pro} \rangle_k$ goes to America$]]]\ [_{IP}$ it is $[_{SC}\ t_{it}\ t_{NP}]]]]$

Given the present analysis, 3SG agreement (as well as reflexive and pronoun binding) is due to the presence of a variable *pro* in subject position (cf. Section 3); since English is not a pro-drop language, this empty category is not licensed and a default (i.e. 3rd person) agreement shows up on the verb.[37] On the contrary, a pro-drop language like Italian allows for the presence of a null subject, which is valued through AGREE against the clefted phrase. This explains the grammaticality of the (b) examples in (45–47), where the relative verb presents grammatical agreement with the clefted constituent (which is mediated by the subject *pro*). Finally, this analysis can also account for the ungrammaticality of the (b′) sentences. As already mentioned, null subjects require an antecedent for their interpretation (cf. Frascarelli 2007). However, the ACC clefted phrases in (45–47b′) do not constitute appropriate antecedents for *pro* because of a Case mismatch.

5.2 Pseudoclefts

We can now focus on the derivation of pseudoclefts. In Section 4 we proposed that the relative DP is a left-dislocated constituent in these constructions. In particular, under F&H's (2007) approach sketched in Section 4.1, we take this constituent to be located in a specific Topic projection (depending on discourse requirements), from which it is connected with a null category in subject position. This is illustrated in (49) for Italian, assuming that the relative DP is an Aboutness-shift Topic:

---

37. As an anonymous reviewer points out, the default 3rd person agreement on the relative verb cannot be exclusively ascribed to the pro-drop parameter, as a non-pro-drop language like French shows full agreement on the relative verb when the clefted constituent is interpreted as the subject of the relative clause:

(i) *C'* *est* MOI *qui* vais *en Amérique*
DEM be.3SG 1SG.ACC who go.*1SG* to America
'It is me who goes to America'

We surmise that the pattern shown in (i) is related to the *que*/*qui* alternation in French relative clauses, as is widely discussed in Rizzi (1990); accordingly, the presence of *qui* suggests that agreement in Comp is involved in cases like (i) triggering full verb agreement.

(49) a. *Chi parte sono io*
who leave.3SG be.1SG 1SG.NOM
'The one who leaves is me'

b. [$_{\text{ShiftP}}$ [$_{\text{DP}}$ chi parte]$_i$ [$_{\text{IP}}$ [$_{\text{DP}}$ *pro*]$_i$ sono [$_{\text{SC}}$ t_{DP} [$_{\text{NP}}$ io]]]]]
AGREE 1SG NOM 1SG

As can be observed, the IP-internal structure of the pseudocleft in (49b) is equivalent to the type of cleft illustrated in (43) (i.e. the type with NOM clefted phrase and copular agreement). As a matter of fact, these two constructions differ in the position in which the relative DP is realized: a right-hand Topic in clefts and a left-hand Topic in pseudoclefts.[38]

The dislocation analysis proposed in (49b) is supported by French pseudoclefts. Since this is a non-pro-drop language, the presence of a null subject in Spec,IP is excluded; the prediction is therefore that the subject position will be filled by a resumptive pronoun. This is borne out by data (from Clech-Darbon et al. 1999: 92):[39]

(50) a. *Ce que tu vois, *(c') est ce qui sortira*
DEM that 2SG see.2SG *DEM* be.3SG DEM who come.out.FUT.3SG
'What you see is what will come out'

38. As for the predicative NP, it moves to the left periphery in clefts where it assumes a specific Focus interpretation (cf. (43b)), while it remains *in situ* in pseudoclefts. Indeed, as is argued in Section 4.1, pseudoclefts implement a Topic-Comment structure in which the post-copular phrase is interpreted as a Narrow Focus simply because it is the only constituent within the Comment (this is supported by intonational evidence; see Section 6). Notice that a similar conclusion can also be drawn from Den Dikken et al.'s (2000) and Den Dikken's (2005) approach to "Type A" (i.e. standard) pseudoclefts. The authors argue that the copula (the "linker") is located in Top^0 and that the IP-internal material is partially elided (e.g. *What John bought was [~~he bought~~ some wine]*) in such a way that the clefted phrase constitutes the only phonologically realized element within the Comment. Although their proposal is convincing in most respects (e.g. for connectivity effects), the present analysis is advantageous insofar as it can account for the semantic and syntactic similarities between clefts and pseudoclefts.

39. A reviewer objects that the use of *ce* in French is not really compulsory since sentences like *ce que je crains est d'être surpris* 'what I fear is being surprised' are fully grammatical. This is true, but sentences of this type only imply a *predicational* interpretation of the relevant construction. Our claim is in fact that *ce* must be present in a pseudocleft (specificational) structure, given the dislocated status of the initial relative clause. Notice that Clech-Darbon et al. (1999: 92–93) also show "the sharp contrast with real predicational sentences, which do not require dislocation: *Ce que je vois est laid* 'What I see is ugly'; *Ce que Marie aime est bon* 'What Marie likes is good'".

b. *Ce que Marie aime,* *(c') *est le riz*
DEM that Marie love.3SG *DEM* be.3SG the rice
'What Marie likes is rice'

If the asymmetry between Italian (cf. (49)) and French (cf. (50)) can be ascribed to the different value of the Null Subject parameter in the two languages, the question becomes why the resumptive subject pronoun is not required in another non-pro-drop language like English:

(51) a. The one who leaves (**it*) is me
b. What I saw (**it*) is a man

In order to account for the absence of a subject pronoun in English (vs. its presence in French), we suggest that the crucial point lies in the syntax of left-hand Topics in the two languages: they are merged in the left-periphery in French (De Cat 2002) but in a clause-internal position (and then moved to the left periphery) in English (cf. Culicover 1991; Lasnik & Saito 1992). As a consequence, the realization of a resumptive pronoun is excluded in the latter, as the subject position is filled by the trace (or copy) of the relative DP, as is illustrated in (52):

(52) $[_{ShiftP}\ [_{DP}$ what I saw] $[_{IP}\ t'_{DP}$ is $[_{SC}\ t_{DP}\ [_{NP}$ a man]]]]

5.3 Asymmetries between clefts and pseudoclefts

While explaining the well-known semantic and syntactic similarities between clefts and pseudoclefts, the present analysis can also account for a number of properties distinguishing the two constructions. Consider the following examples from Italian:

(53) a. *Sono* IO *che parto*
be.1SG 1SG.NOM that leave.1SG
'It is ME that leaves'

b. *Chi parte sono io*
who leave.3SG be.1SG 1SG.NOM
'The one who leaves is me'

b'. *La persona che parte sono io*
the person that leave.3SG be.1SG 1SG.NOM
'The one who leaves (lit. 'The person that leaves') is me'

Apart from word order, the examples in (53) differ in the realization of the element introducing the relative DP: a complementizer (*che* 'that') in clefts (cf. (53a)) and a relative pronoun (*chi* 'who' in (53b)) or a full generic noun (*persona* 'person' in (53b')) in pseudoclefts. Compare (53a–b) with the following ungrammatical sentences:

(54) a. **Sono* IO chi *parto*
be.1SG 1SG.NOM *who* leave.1SG

b. *Che *parte sono io*
that leave.3SG be.1SG 1SG.NOM

Moreover, when the clefted constituent is interpreted as the subject of the relative clause (as in (53)), the relative verb agrees with it in the case of cleft sentences, while it shows a default 3SG agreement in pseudoclefts. The obligatoriness of this agreement pattern is shown by the ungrammaticality of sentences like (55):

(55) a. **Sono* IO *che parte*
be.1SG 1SG.NOM that leave.*3SG*

b. **Chi parto sono io*
who leave.*1SG* be.1SG 1SG.NOM

We propose that both asymmetries between clefts and pseudoclefts can be explained by taking into account the scopal relations between the Focus and the relative DP.

Let us consider clefts first. In Section 5.1 we have seen that the clefted phrase takes scope over the relative DP after its movement to Spec,FocP (cf. (43b), (44c)). In this configuration, the *pro* heading the relative DP checks its φ-features with the Focus and is licensed. The relevant *pro*-head enters a predicative relation with the relative CP and transmits its φ-features to the null subject of the relative verb. In other words, agreement of the relative verb with the clefted phrase is mediated by the null relative head:

(56) [$_{FocP}$ [$_{NP}$ IO] [$_{FamP}$ [$_{DP}$ [$_{SC}$ [$_{NP}$ *pro*] [$_{CP}$ che *pro* parto]]] [$_{IP}$ *copula*…

AGREE (φ-features) (φ-features) (1SG) *Spec-Head Agreement* (1SG)

In the case of pseudoclefts, on the other hand, the agreement pattern illustrated in (56) is not available. As a matter of fact, the relative head in these constructions is not under the scope of the clefted phrase at any point of the derivation. As a consequence, it cannot be licensed as a *pro* and needs to be overtly realized as a relative pronoun (as in (53b)) or a generic noun (as in (53b′)) in order to be interpreted at the semantic component. Hence, the subject position within the relative DP is filled by (a copy of) the relative pronoun and obligatory 3SG agreement is triggered on the relative verb (independent of the φ-features of the pseudoclefted constituent).

Finally, it is important to consider a third asymmetry between the two constructions, which regards copular agreement. As observed in Section 5.1, when the Focus is interpreted as the direct object of the relative verb, clefts allow for two possible realizations of the copula and the clefted phrase. This is shown again in (57a). However, only one inflectional pattern is allowed in pseudoclefts, as the copula can only agree with a NOM predicate, as is illustrated in (57b):

(57) a. Sono IO/ è ME *che hai visto* (= 41)
be.*1*SG 1SG.*NOM* be.*3*SG 1SG.*ACC* that have.2SG see.PST.PART
'It is ME that you saw'

b. *Chi hai visto* sono io/ *è me
who have.2SG see.PST.PART be.*1*SG 1SG.*NOM* be.*3*SG 1SG.*ACC*
'The one that you saw (lit. 'Who you saw') is me'

As is argued in Section 5.1, the existence of two inflectional patterns in clefts is due to the syntax of right-hand Topics in Italian, which can either be merged extrasententially (cf. (43)) or derived from an IP-internal position (cf. (44)). Pseudoclefts, however, involve a left-hand Topic, which can only be merged in the left periphery in languages like Italian.[40] Therefore, the ungrammaticality of a 3SG copular inflection and ACC Case marking on the clefted phrase is fully expected under the present analysis. As a matter of fact, this would require the topical relative DP to be extracted from its subject position, which is excluded in Italian left-hand Topic constructions for independent reasons (cf. Cinque 1990; Frascarelli 2000b, 2008; Bianchi & Frascarelli 2010a).[41] The different properties distinguishing clefts and pseudoclefts thus confirm our analysis of these constructions as involving different types of Topics.

6. (Pseudo)clefts: Intonational analysis

In this paper we have proposed that both cleft and pseudocleft constructions implement a Topic-Comment structure, but involve different types of Topics. In particular, syntactic evidence has shown that cleft constructions imply – besides exhaustive focalization – the realization of a right-hand Familiar Topic, while the relative DP in pseudoclefts is a left-hand Topic; the latter is usually of the aboutness-shift type, but can also be contrastive (if more Topics are opposed)[42]

40. This is argued for Aboutness-shift and Contrastive Topics in F&H (2007). As for Familiar Topics, which generally allow either a merge or a derivation analysis (cf. Frascarelli 2008), the French data in (50), as well as intonational patterns, show that only a merge analysis can be assumed for pseudoclefts.

41. On the contrary, this agreement pattern is the only one admitted in English, as is to be expected from the derived nature of left-hand Topics in this language (see (52) above).

42. Aboutness-shift and Contrastive Topics can be distinguished for their syntactic and interpretive properties and for their impact on conversational dynamics (cf. Bianchi & Frascarelli

or familiar (when the relevant DP does not induce a shift, but is continuous with respect to the current Topic). In this section we will substantiate this proposal by means of intonational evidence.[43]

As already illustrated in Section 4.1, F&H (2007) singled out three different types of Topics based on the existence of a systematic correlation between their formal properties and discourse function. In particular, the complex L*+H tone is realized with Topics that are inherently associated with a shift in the conversation (Aboutness-shift Topics), while a H* tone is associated with Contrastive Topics and a L* tone is realized with Topics that refer to discourse-given information (Familiar Topics).[44] As already shown in (37), these types of Topics are located in the C-domain according to a specific order. We can now 'complete' the relevant hierarchy associating each functional projection to its PF interpretation (for further details and data, cf. Frascarelli 2007, 2008; for a semantic analysis of the different types of Topics, cf. Bianchi & Frascarelli 2010a):

(58) $[_{ForceP}$ $[_{ShiftP}$ $[_{GP}$ $[_{ContrP}$ $[_{FocP}$ $[_{FamP*}$ $[_{FinP}$ $[_{IP}$ …
L*+H H* L*

Let us first concentrate on the prosodic analysis of (pseudo)cleft sentences. Consider first the following passage:

(59) A: *quando adesso vai al Colosseo quando entri quello che vedi al centro non è dove-*
B: *sì l'arena stava più in alto*

2010a,b). We should bear in mind that 'contrast' assumes different characterizations when combined with either a Focus or a Topic. A Contrastive Focus implies a set of alternatives including the meaning of the utterance corrected (cf. Footnote 5), while the denotation of a Contrastive Topic refers to a *salient* set of alternatives and no correction is implied (on the notion of 'salient set', cf. Rooth 1992; Wagner 2008). Other members of the salient set need not be explicitly mentioned: a Contrastive Topic gives rise to the implicature that the predicate denoted by the Comment does not hold for the other members. The implicature arises (by the maxim of Quantity) because the set of entities is introduced by the presupposition associated with the [+contrast] feature (cf. Büring 2003; Bianchi & Frascarelli 2010b).

43. This research is based on a corpus of naturalistic data recorded in the Rome area with speakers of the Roman variety (for detailed information on the corpus, cf. Bonvino 2005). The relevant speakers (3 women and 1 man) have at least a high school education and their ages range from 29 to 33.

44. This prosodic characterization, originally based on Italian and German data, was later supported cross-linguistically by evidence from Somali (Frascarelli & Puglielli 2009) and Tagalog (Frascarelli 2010b). Also note that prosodic differences between left-dislocated constituents related to their pragmatic function have been observed for French (Doetjes et al. 2002; Marandin et al. 2002), although the tones are characterized differently.

A: *-si lottava no non era più in alto era lì solo che era coperta cioè* <u>*quello che si vede è è il sotterraneo*</u> [Figure 1] *sono i diciamo gli ambienti di servizio per dire no – questi ambienti di servizio erano coperti da un tavolato di legno sul quale poi loro combattevano…* [colosseo-02]

'A: now, when you go to the Colosseum, when you enter, what you see in the middle is not where- B: yes, the arena would be higher A: -they would fight, no, it was not in a higher position, it was there, simply it was covered, that is to say, what you see is the part underground, it's – let's say, the service area, that is to say – this service area was covered by a wooden platform, on which they used to fight…'

In this passage speaker A – a woman, who is a tourist guide – is describing the architecture inside the Colosseum and, specifically, the part dedicated to gladiator fights. In her first sentence, after a temporal clause, she introduces the discourse Topic by means of a relative DP, namely *quello che vedi al centro* 'what you see in the middle'. This relative DP thus qualifies as an Aboutness-shift Topic and, accordingly, it is realized with a rising tone (L*+H). Speaker A is then interrupted by speaker B who says something wrong about the Colosseum. Hence speaker A feels obliged to 'suspend' the Topic she proposed (*quello che vedi al centro*) in order to correct speaker B's assertion. She thus produces a null subject sentence (*no,* pro *non era più in alto* 'no, it was not in a higher position'), in which the interpretation of *pro* depends on the Aboutness-shift Topic proposed by speaker B (namely, 'the arena'). Consequently, when she resumes her explanation, she has to shift back to her former Topic (namely, *quello che si vede* 'what you see') and a rising contour is realized again on the relevant relative clause. The Comment follows with a downgrading contour, as is typical of Broad Focus sentences:

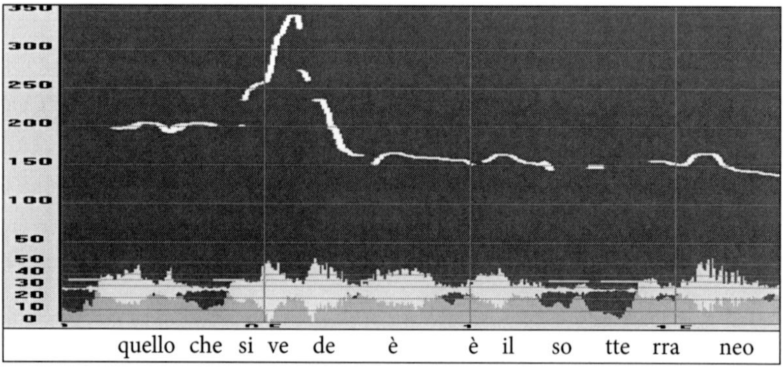

Figure 1. Pseudocleft structure with an Aboutness-shift Topic

The rising tonal event characterizing the relative DP in Figure 1 must not be ascribed to its initial position. Indeed, intonational analysis reveals that when the relative DP of a pseudocleft does not propose a Topic shift but maintains the current Topic, it is realized with a flat contour, as expected for a Familiar Topic. Consider, for instance, the following passage and the intonational contour in Figure 2 below:

(60) *il mio capo è un ex reporter è stato corrispondente per Panorama dall'Afganistan dal Libano è stato in giro per il mondo ma veramente uno di quelli pioniere sai di quelli che andavano in giro con la macchina fotografica e la macchina da scrivere a tracolla [...] quello che c'ha però è che è durissimo* [Figure 2] *sai una persona che al primo errore fa saltare la gente...* [chiacchiere-01]
'My boss is a former reporter he was correspondent for Panorama in Afghanistan and Lebanon, he has been all over the world but really he's one of those pioneers, you know, one who would go around with a camera and a typewriter slung over his shoulder [...] what he has, however, is that he is really tough, you know, a person that fires people at their first mistake...'

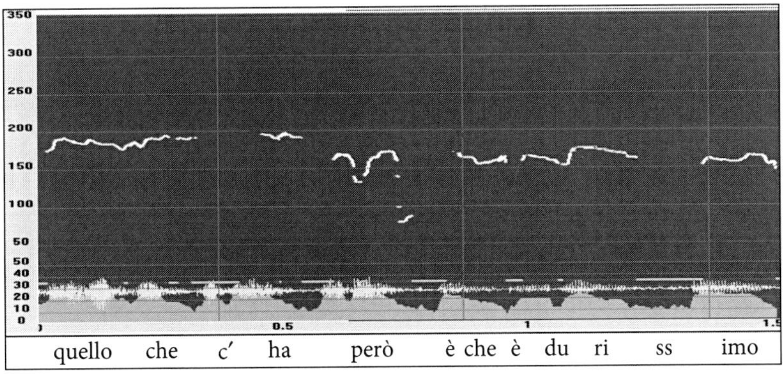

Figure 2. Pseudocleft structure with a Familiar Topic

As we can see, no rise characterizes the relative DP *quello che c'ha* ('what he has'), as the entire passage is dedicated to the description of the personality of the speaker's boss. The relevant Topic is therefore prosodically destressed and realized using a low tone.

Let us now consider the intonational properties of cleft sentences. According to our proposal, the relative DP following the copula is a right-hand Familiar Topic and, as such, a flat contour is expected. This prediction is borne out by data. Consider the following passage:

(61) A: *e poi lei mi guardava*

B: *ma ti guardava nel senso che rispondeva ai tuoi sguardi o proprio era LEI che ti guardava?* [Figure 3]

C: *sii onesto!*

A: *potevo anche essere io che rispondevo ai suoi sguardi* [Figure 4]

C: *che bugiardo!* [incontro-01]

'A: and then she was looking at me B: but she was looking at you in the sense that she responded to your looks, or was it really HER who was looking at you? C: be honest! A: it might have also been ME who was responding to her looks C: what a liar!'

In this passage speaker B (a man) is 'interviewing' speaker A about how he started to go out with his present girlfriend (speaker C). Specifically, he wants to know whether they got interested in each other at the same time or, rather, if he noticed her because it was (exclusively) her who was continually looking at him initially. The sentence in question (*o proprio era* LEI *che ti guardava*) is produced as illustrated in Figure 3:

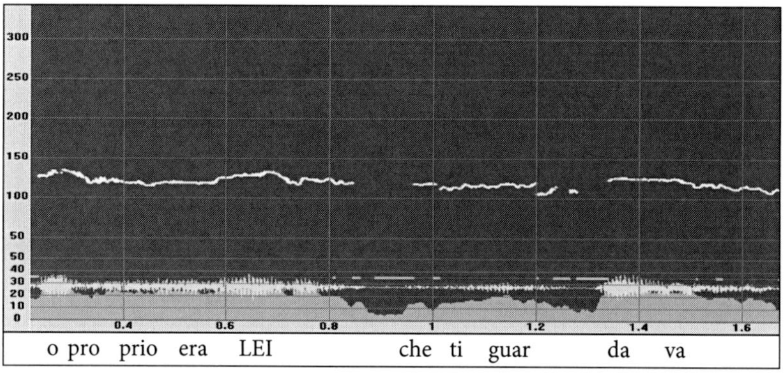

Figure 3. Non-contrastive cleft construction

As expected, the relevant *that*-clause (*che ti guardava*) is realized as an independent prosodic group (notice the clear break after the Focus) with a low, flat contour. Therefore, the relative DP fully qualifies as a Familiar Topic. This pattern can be found consistently throughout the corpus, providing additional support to our analysis.

As far as Focus is concerned, prosodic analysis shows that Focus prominence in clefts is not as marked as might be expected from its initial position and the emphatic character that is normally ascribed to this type of construction. In the sentence examined in Figure 3, for instance, the clefted constituent (*LEI*) is marked by only a slight prominence, despite the presence of the focusing adverb *proprio* ('exactly') which requires a H* tone on the element included in its scope.

In other cases, however, a significant pitch can be found on the clefted Focus. As an illustration, let us return to the passage in (61). After the first intervention of speaker C, speaker A produces another cleft sentence, namely *potevo anche essere* *IO che rispondevo ai suoi sguardi* ('it might have also been ME who was responding to her looks'), which is realized as illustrated in Figure 4:

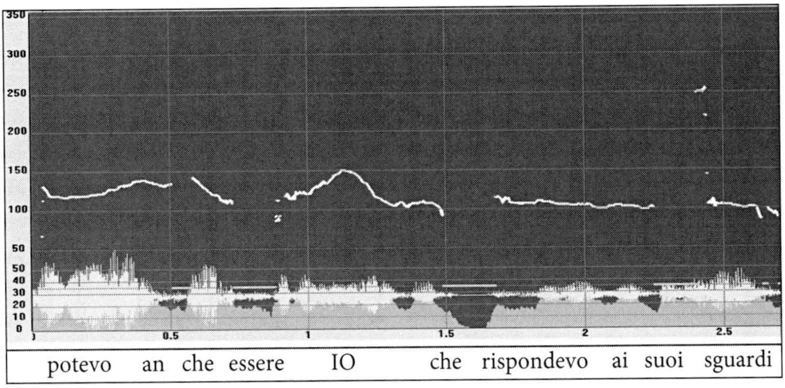

Figure 4. Contrastive cleft construction

As we can see, unlike the case examined above, a hat contour marks the tonic vowel of the clefted Focus *IO* (while the topical status of the relative clause remains unchanged).

In order to account for this difference, we propose that prominence on the clefted phrase depends on its interpretation as a Contrastive Focus. It should be borne in mind that clefted Foci are inherently characterized by exhaustiveness (cf. Section 2), while contrast is an additional meaning which depends on the context and requires Interface visibility for interpretation. Division of labour can be invoked to explain this case: exhaustiveness is obtained through syntactic markedness, hence no extra work is necessary at the level of phonetic form. On the other hand, when an Exhaustive Focus is also contrasted, we assume that the relevant phrase moves to Spec,ContrP and this operation is associated with a special prominence in order to signal this extra discourse value to Interface interpretation.[45]

Discourse analysis supports this proposal. The clefted Focus in Figure 3 does not have a contrastive reading and only expresses exhaustiveness. On the contrary, speaker A in Figure 4 wants to provide a contrast between what he is going to say and what his girlfriend would like him to admit (when she says *sii onesto* 'be honest').

45. This analysis clearly implies that a composition between discourse features is possible. To deal with this interesting and complex issue is, however, beyond the scope of this paper.

To conclude, we can say that intonational data strongly support our analysis of (pseudo)cleft sentences as Topic-Comment structures, in which different types of Topics are realized either in the left or in the right periphery of the sentence. Prosody also provides evidence for a correlation between intonation and different types of Foci.

7. Conclusions

In this paper an Interface approach to cleft and pseudocleft constructions has been put forward in order to account for their interpretation at different levels of analysis. According to the present proposal the (to be) focused constituent is merged as the predicate of a SC having the relative DP merged in (or connected to) the subject position. This analysis has been discussed regarding its semantic properties and syntactic implementation, while considering the advantages it offers for a comprehensive explanation of a number of phenomena (Sections 2 and 3). As for discourse analysis, the relevant constructions have been shown to realize not only a Focus strategy (as is generally acknowledged), but also a Topic-Comment structure; as a matter of fact, the relative DP is a definite description and, as such, it is a perfect candidate to be a Topic of a different type in clefts and pseudoclefts. Intonational properties of the two copular constructions in Italian supports the validity of the present analysis (cf. Section 6), also showing a different PF-interpretation for clefted Foci when exhaustiveness (an inherent property) is associated with contrast (a discourse-dependent option).

References

Adger, David & Ramchand, Gillian. 2001. Phases and Interpretability. In *WCCFL 20 Proceedings*, Karine Megerdoomian & Leora A. Barel (eds), 1–14. Somerville MA: Cascadilla Press.

Adger, David & Ramchand, Gillian. 2005. Merge and Move: Wh-dependencies revisited. *Linguistic Inquiry* 36(2): 161–193.

Akmajian, Adrian. 1970. Aspects of the Grammar of Focus in English. Ph.D. dissertation, MIT.

Atlas, Jay David & Levinson, Stephen C. 1981. *It*-Clefts, Informativeness, and Logical Form: Radical Pragmatics (Revised Standard Version). In *Radical Pragmatics*, Peter Cole (ed), 1–61. New York NY: Academic Press.

Bailyn, John F. 1994. The syntax and semantics of Russian long and short adjectives: An X′-theoretic account. In *Formal Approaches to Slavic Linguistics. The Ann Arbor Meeting*, Jindrich Toman (ed.), 1–30. Ann Arbor MI: Michigan Slavic Publications.

Belletti, Adriana. 2001. Inversion as focalization. In *Subject Inversion in Romance and the Theory of Universal Grammar*, Aafke Hulk & Jean-Yves Pollock (eds), 60–90. Oxford: OUP.

Belletti, Adriana. 2005a. Answering with a "cleft": The role of the null subject parameter and the VP periphery. In *Contributions to the Thirtieth Incontro di Grammatica Generativa*, Laura Brugè, Giuliana Giusti, Nicola Munaro, Walter Schweikert & Giuseppina Turano (eds), 63–82. Venezia: Cafoscarina.
Belletti, Adriana. 2005b. Extended doubling and the VP periphery. *Probus* 17(1): 1–35.
Belletti, Adriana. 2008. Answering strategies: New information subjects and the nature of clefts. In *Structure and Strategies*, Adriana Belletti (ed), 242–265. London: Routledge.
Bianchi, Valentina & Frascarelli, Mara. 2010a. Is topic a root phenomenon? *Iberia: An International Journal of Theoretical Linguistics* 2(1): 43–88.
Bianchi, Valentina & Frascarelli, Mara. 2010b. Topics, phases, and contexts of interpretation. Paper presented at *GLOW XXXIII* (Workshop on Recursivity of Information Structure – University of Wrocław).
Bocci, Giuliano. 2009. On the Syntax and Prosody in Italian. Ph.D. dissertation, University of Siena.
Bonvino, Elisabetta. 2005. *Le sujet postverbal en italien parlé: Syntaxe, zones et intonation*. Paris: Ophrys.
Büring, Daniel. 1999. Topic. In *Focus – Linguistic Cognitive and Computational Perspectives*, Peter Bosch & Rob van der Sandt (eds), 142–165. Cambridge: CUP.
Büring, Daniel. 2003. On D-trees, Beans and B-Accents. *Linguistics and Philosophy* 26(5): 511–545.
Cardinaletti, Anna. 2002. Against optional and null clitics. Right dislocation vs. marginalization. *Studia Linguistica* 56(1): 29–57.
Carnap, Rudolf. 1958. *Introduction to Symbolic Logic and its Applications*. New York NY: Dover.
Cecchetto, Carlo. 1999. A comparative analysis of left and right disclocation in Romance. *Studia Linguistica* 53(1): 40–67.
Chafe, Wallace. 1987. Cognitive constraints on information flow. In *Coherence and Grounding in Discourse* [Typological Studies in Language 11], Russel S. Tomlin (ed.), 21–51. Amsterdam: John Benjamins.
Cinque, Guglielmo. 1990. *Types of A'-Dependencies*. Cambridge MA: The MIT Press.
Cinque, Guglielmo. 1993. A null theory of phrase and compound stress. *Linguistic Inquiry* 24(2): 239–297.
Clech-Darbon, Anne, Rebuschi, Georges & Rialland, Annie. 1999. Are there cleft sentences in French? In *The Grammar of Focus* [Linguistik Aktuell/Linguistics Today 24], Georges Rebuschi & Laurice Tuller (eds), 83–118. Amsterdam: John Benjamins.
Collins, Peter C. 1991. *Cleft and Pseudo-Cleft Constructions in English*. London: Routledge.
Culicover, Peter W. 1991. Topicalization, inversion, and complementizers in English. In *OTS Working Papers. Going Romance, and Beyond, Fifth Symposium*, Denis Delfitto, Martin Everaert, Arnold Evers & Frits Stuurman (eds), 1–45. Utrecht: Utrecht Institute of Linguistics OTS.
De Cat, Cécile. 2002. French Dislocation. Ph.D. dissertation, University of York.
Declerck, Renaat. 1984. The pragmatics of *it*-clefts and WH-clefts. *Lingua* 64(4): 251–289.
Declerck, Renaat. 1988. *Studies on Copular Sentences, Clefts and Pseudo-clefts*. Dordrecht: Foris.
Delahunty, Gerald P. 1982. *Topics in the Syntax and Semantics of English Cleft Sentences*. Bloomington IN: Indiana University Linguistics Club.
den Dikken, Marcel. 1995. *Particles: On the Syntax of Verb-Particle, Triadic, and Causative Constructions*. Oxford: OUP.

den Dikken, Marcel. 2001. Specificational copular sentences and pseudoclefts. Ms, CUNY. (Published in *The Blackwell Companion to Syntax*, Vol. 4, Martin Everaert & Henk van Riemsdijk (eds), 2006, 292–409. Oxford: Blackwell).

den Dikken, Marcel. 2005. A comment on the topic of topic-comment. *Lingua* 115(5): 691–710.

den Dikken, Marcel. 2006. *Relators and Linkers. The Syntax of Predication, Predicate Inversion, and Copulas*. Cambridge MA: The MIT Press.

den Dikken, Marcel, Meinunger, André & Wilder, Chris. 2000. Pseudoclefts and ellipsis. *Studia Linguistica* 54(1): 41–89.

den Dikken, Marcel & Singhapreecha, Pornsiri. 2004. Complex noun phrases and linkers. *Syntax* 7(1): 1–54.

Doetjes, Jenny, Delais-Roussarie, Elisabeth & Sleeman, Petra. 2002. The Prosody of left detached constituents in French. In *Proceedings Speech Prosody 2002*, Bernard Bel & Isabelle Marlien (eds), 247–250. Aix-en-Provence: Laboratoire Parole et Langage, University of Provence. ⟨http://www.isca-speech.org/archive/sp2002/sp02_247.pdf⟩ (24 April 2010).

Emonds, Joseph. 1976. *A Transformational Approach to English Syntax*. New York NY: Academic Press.

Frascarelli, Mara. 1999. Subject, nominative case, agreement and focus. In *Boundaries of Morphology and Syntax* [Current Issues in Linguistic Theory 180], Lunella Mereu (ed.), 195–215. Amsterdam: John Benjamins.

Frascarelli, Mara. 2000a. Frasi scisse e 'small clauses': Un'analisi dell'inglese. *Lingua e Stile* 35(3): 417–446.

Frascarelli, Mara. 2000b. *The Syntax-Phonology Interface in Focus and Topic Constructions in Italian*. Dordrecht: Kluwer.

Frascarelli, Mara. 2004. Dislocation, clitic resumption and minimality: A comparative analysis of left and right topic construction in Italian. In *Romance Languages and Linguistic Theory 2002. Selected Papers from 'Going Romance' (Groningen, 28–30 November 2002)* [Current Issues in Linguistic Theory 256], Reineke Bok-Bennema, Bart Hollebrandse, Brigitte Kampers-Manhe & Petra Sleeman (eds), 98–118. Amsterdam: John Benjamins.

Frascarelli, Mara. 2007. Subjects, topics and the interpretation of referential *pro*. An interface approach to the linking of (null) pronouns. *Natural Language and Linguistic Theory* 25(4): 691–734.

Frascarelli, Mara. 2008. The Fine Structure of the Topic Field. In *The Bantu-Romance Connection. A Comparative Investigation of Verbal Agreement, DPs, and Information Structure* [Linguistik Aktuell/Linguistics Today 131], Cécile De Cat & Katherine Demuth (eds), 261–292. Amsterdam: John Benjamins.

Frascarelli, Mara. 2010a. Narrow focus, clefting and predicate inversion. *Lingua* 120(9): 2121–2147.

Frascarelli, Mara. 2010b. Intonation, information structure and the derivation of inverse VO languages: An interface analysis of Tagalog and Malagasy. In *Austronesian and Theoretical Linguistics* [Linguistik Aktuell/Linguistics Today 167], Raphael Mercado, Eric Potsdam & Lisa Travis (eds), 81–102. Amsterdam: John Benjamins.

Frascarelli, Mara & Hinterhölzl, Roland. 2007. Types of topics in German and Italian. In *On Information Structure, Meaning and Form* [Linguistik Aktuell/Linguistics Today 100], Kerstin Schwabe & Susanne Winkler (eds), 87–116. Amsterdam: John Benjamins.

Frascarelli, Mara & Puglielli, Annarita. 2005a. The focus system in Cushitic languages. In *Proceedings of the 10th Meeting of Hamito-Semitic (Afroasiatic) Linguistics*, Pelio Fronzaroli & Paolo Marrassini (eds), 333–358. Florence: Department of Linguistics, University of Florence.

Frascarelli, Mara & Puglielli, Annarita. 2005b. A comparative analysis of restrictive and appositive relative clauses in Cushitic languages. In *Contributions to the Thirtieth Incontro di Grammatica Generativa*, Laura Brugè, Giuliana Giusti, Nicola Munaro, Walter Schweikert & Giuseppina Turano (eds), 307–332. Venezia: Cafoscarina.
Frascarelli, Mara & Puglielli, Annarita. 2009. Position, function and interpretation of topics in Somali. In *Information Structure and Its Interfaces*, Lunella Mereu (ed.), 325–348. Berlin: Mouton de Gruyter.
Frascarelli, Mara & Ramaglia, Francesca. 2009. (Pseudo)cleft constructions at the Interfaces. Ms, University of Roma Tre, ⟨http://ling.auf.net/lingBuzz/000841⟩ (23 April 2010).
Gazdar, Gerald. 1979. *Pragmatics: Implicature, Presupposition, and Logical Form*. New York NY: Academic Press.
Givón, Talmy. 1983. Topic continuity in discourse: An introduction. In *Topic Continuity in Discourse: A Quantitative Crosslanguage Study*, Talmy Givón (ed), 5–41. Amsterdam: John Benjamins.
Green, Melanie. 1997. Focus and Copular Constructions in Hausa. Ph.D. dissertation, SOAS.
Guéron, Jaquelin. 1992. Types syntaxiques et types sémantiques: La phrase copulative comme palimpseste. *Revue Québécoise de Linguistique* 22(1): 77–115.
Gundel, Jeanette K. 1977. Where do Cleft Sentences Come From? *Language* 53(3): 543–559.
Gundel, Jeanette K. 1985. Shared knowledge and topicality. *Journal of pragmatics* 9(1): 83–107.
Hasselgård, Hilde. 2004. Adverbials in *it*-cleft constructions. In *Advances in Corpus Linguistics: Papers from the 23rd International Conference on English Language Research on Computerized Corpora (ICAME 23) Göteborg 22–26 May 2002*, Karin Aijmer & Bengt Altenberg (eds), 195–211. Amsterdam: Rodopi.
Hedberg, Nancy. 1990. Discourse Pragmatics and Cleft Sentences in English. Ph.D. dissertation, University of Minnesota.
Hedberg, Nancy. 2000. The Referential Status of Clefts. *Language* 76(4): 891–920.
Heggie, Lorie. 1988. The Syntax of Copular Structures. Ph.D. dissertation, University of Southern California.
Heggie, Lorie. 1993. The Range of Null Operators: Evidence from Clefting. *Natural Language and Linguistic Theory* 11(1): 45–84.
Hermann, Paul. 1880. *Prinzipien der Sprachgeschichte*. Tübingen: Niemeyer.
Heycock, Caroline & Kroch, Anthony. 1999. Pseudocleft Connectedness: Implications for the LF Interface Level. *Linguistic Inquiry* 30(3): 365–397.
Higgins, Francis Roger. 1973. The Pseudo-cleft Construction in English. Ph.D. dissertation, MIT.
Higgins, Francis Roger. 1979. *The Pseudo-Cleft Construction in English*. New York NY: Garland.
Jackendoff, Ray. 1972. *Semantic Interpretation in Generative Grammar*. Cambridge MA: The MIT Press.
Jespersen, Otto. 1927. *A Modern English Grammar*, Vol. 3. London: Allen and Unwin.
Kiss, Katalin É. 1998. Identificational focus versus information focus. *Language* 74(2): 245–273.
Kiss, Katalin É. 1999. The English cleft construction as a focus phrase. In *Boundaries of Morphology and Syntax*, Lunella Mereu (ed.), 217–229. Amsterdam: John Benjamins.
Klein, Ewan & Sag, Ivan. 1985. Type driven translation. *Linguistics and Philosophy* 8(2): 163–201.
Kratzer, Angelica & Shimoyama, Junko. 2002. Indeterminate pronouns: The view from Japanese. In *The Proceedings of the Third Tokyo Conference on Psycholinguistics*, Yukio Otsu (ed.), 1–25. Tokyo: Hituzi Syobo.
Krifka, Manfred. 1992. A compositional semantics for multiple focus constructions. In *Informationsstruktur und Grammatik* [Linguistische Berichte, Sonderheft 4], Joachim Jacobs (ed.), 17–53. Opladen: Westdeutscher Verlag.

Krifka, Manfred. 2007. Basic notions of information structure. In *Interdisciplinary Studies on Information Structure*, Vol. 6. [ISIS, Working Papers of the SFB 632], Caroline Féry, Gisbert Fanselow & Manfred Krifka (eds), 13–55. Potsdam: University of Potsdam.

Kuno, Susumu. 1976. Subject, theme, and the speaker's empathy. A reexamination of relativization phenomena. In *Subject and Topic*, Charles N. Li (ed.), 417–444. New York NY: Academic Press.

Kuroda, Sige-Yuki. 1972. The categorical and thetic judgment. *Foundations of Language* 9: 153–185.

Lambrecht, Knud. 1994. *Information Structure and Sentence Form: Topic, Focus and the Mental Representations of Discourse Referents*. Cambridge: CUP.

Lasnik, Howard & Saito, Mamoru. 1992. *Move α*. Cambridge MA: The MIT Press.

Marandin, Jean-Marie, Beyssade, Claire, Delais-Roussarie, Elisabeth & Rialland, Annie. 2002. Discourse marking in French: C accent and discourse moves. In *Proceedings Speech Prosody 2002*, Bernard Bel & Isabelle Marlien (eds), 471–474. Aix-en-Provence: Laboratoire Parole et Langage, University of Provence. ⟨http://www.isca-speech.org/archive/sp2002/sp02_471.pdf⟩ (24 April 2010).

Moro, Andrea. 1997. *The Raising of Predicates*. Cambridge: CUP.

Nichols, Johanna. 1986. Head-marking and dependent-marking grammar. *Language* 62(1): 56–119.

Ouhalla, Jamal. 1993. Subject-extraction, negation and the antiagreement effect. *Natural Language and Linguistic Theory* 11(3): 477–518.

Partee, Barbara H. 2002. Noun phrase interpretation and type-shifting principles. In *Formal Semantics: The Essential Readings*, Paul Portner & Barbara H. Partee (eds), 357–381. Oxford: Blackwell. (Originally published in *Studies in Discourse Representation Theory and the Theory of Generalized Quantifiers*, Jeroen Groenendijk, Dick de Jongh & Martin Stokhof (eds), 1987, 115–143. Dordrecht: Foris).

Percus, Orin. 1997. Prying open the cleft. In *Proceedings of the 27th Annual Meeting of the North East Linguistics Society*, Kiyomi Kusumoto (ed.), 337–351. Amherst MA: GLSA.

Pesetsky, David. 1987. *Wh*-in-situ: Movement and unselective binding. In *The Representation of (In)definiteness*, Eric J. Reuland & Alice G. B. ter Meulen (eds), 98–129. Cambridge MA: The MIT Press.

Poletto, Cecilia & Pollock, Jean-Yves. 2004. On the left periphery of some Romance wh-questions. In *The Structure of CP and IP* (The Cartography of Syntactic Structures 2), Luigi Rizzi (ed.), 251–296. Oxford: OUP.

Prince, Ellen F. 1978. A comparison of wh-clefts and it-clefts in discourse. *Language* 54(4): 883–906.

Ramaglia, Francesca. 2011. *Adjectives at the Syntax-Semantics Interface*. München: Lincom.

Reeve, Matthew. 2007. Relatives and pronouns in the English cleft construction. *UCL Working Papers in Linguistics* 19: 157–182.

Reinhart, Tanya. 1981. Pragmatics and linguistics: An analysis of sentence topics. *Philosophica* 27(1): 53–94.

Rialland, Annie, Doetjes, Jenny & Rebuschi, Georges. 2002. What is focused in *C'est XP qui/que* cleft sentences in French? In *Proceedings Speech Prosody 2002*, Bernard Bel & Isabelle Marlien (eds), 471–474. Aix-en-Provence: Laboratoire Parole et Langage. University of Provence. ⟨http://www.isca-speech.org/archive/sp2002/sp02_595.pdf⟩ (25 April 2010).

Rizzi, Luigi. 1990. *Relativized Minimality*. Cambridge MA: The MIT Press.

Rooth, Math. 1992. A theory of focus interpretation. *Natural Language Semantics* 1(1): 75–116.

Safir, Kenneth, J. 1985. *Syntactic Chains*. Cambridge: CUP.
Samek-Lodovici, Vieri. 2006. When right dislocation meets the left-periphery. A unified analysis of Italian non-final focus. *Lingua* 116(6): 836–873.
Schachter, Paul. 1973. Focus and relativization. *Language* 49(1): 19–46.
Schwarzschild, Roger. 2002. Singleton indefinites. *Journal of Semantics* 19(3): 289–314.
Stowell, Timothy A. 1981. Origins of Phrase Structure. Ph.D. dissertation, MIT.
Strawson, Peter Frederick. 1964. Identifying reference and truth values. *Theoria* 30(2): 96–118.
Vallduví, Enric. 1992. *The Informational Component*. New York NY: Garland.
von Stechow, Arnim. 1991. Focusing and backgrounding operators. In *Discourse Particles* [Pragmatics & Beyond New Series 12], Abraham Werner (ed.), 37–84. Amsterdam: John Benjamins.
Wagner, Michael. 2008. A compositional theory of contrastive topics. In *Proceedings of NELS 38*, Muhammad Abdurrahman, Anisa Schardl & Martin Walkow (eds), 1–14. Amherst MA: GLSA.

PART II

Monoclausal/biclausal analyses

Clefts in Durban Zulu*

Lisa L.-S. Cheng & Laura J. Downing
Leiden University / Göteborg University

In this paper, we argue that clefts in Zulu have a bipartite structure: a copular sentence with an adjoined DP/clause. This structure accounts for the prosody of clefts. Each constituent is parsed into a separate Intonation Phrase by the independently motivated phrasing algorithm of Zulu. It also accounts for the syntactic properties of Zulu clefts. We further argue that the nature of agreement in Zulu copular sentences support a pronominal predicate analysis.

Keywords: Prosody of clefts; copular sentences; pronominal predicate

1. Background

Cleft sentences in Durban Zulu (such as the example in (1)) look on the surface rather similar to their English counterparts. As we can see from the translation in English, the cleft sentence in Zulu in (1) also involves an optional copula (see Section 2, below), a pivot, followed by a clause which looks on the surface like a relative clause.

(1) *ng-ùm-fú:ndi ó-phéké ín-ku:kh' ízo:lo*
COP-1-student REL.1-cook 9-chicken 5.yesterday
'It is the student who cooked chicken yesterday.'

In this paper, we show that this similarity is only superficial. We provide both prosodic and syntactic evidence to show that (a) the cleft sentence involves a copular sentence with an adjoined phrase/clause; (b) the pivot and the clause following the pivot do not belong to the same clause; (c) the element following the pivot can be a

* We would like to thank, first of all, Meritta Xaba, our Zulu language informant, for her patience and thoughtfulness in helping us learn about her language. We also thank Leston Buell and Thilo Schadeberg for discussion of some aspects of the data and analysis. We are grateful to audience members at the Clefts Workshop and two anonymous reviewers for helpful comments.

DP (with a relative clause in it), or an adverbial clause, depending on the nature of the pivot; and (d) the copular sentence in cleft sentences involves a pronominal predicate.

The paper is organized as follows. In Section 2, we provide the core set of data and generalizations that need to be accounted for. In Section 3, we present the basic prosodic phrasing algorithm for Zulu in other constructions, and show that the prosodic phrasing of clefts provides a first argument for their bi-clausal structure. In Section 4, we provide syntactic arguments supporting the bi-clausal structure, and further discuss clefts involving temporal/locative elements. In Section 5, we discuss the copular sentence in the clefts, arguing for the presence of a pronominal predicate. Further, we examine how the post-pivot phrase/clause is interpreted in relation to the pivot.

2. Structure of clefts: Data and generalizations

The first step towards understanding the structure of clefts is to notice that clefts contain a copular clause. In Zulu, the copula is expressed by a depressor low tone and an optional segmental prefix, either *ng-*, *y(i)-*, or *w(u)*. (See Buell 2009; Doke 1961, and Poulos & Msimang 1998.) This can be seen in the identificational sentences in (2), where the syllable following the copular prefix is low-toned:[1]

(2) a. *(ú-Si:pho) (ng-ù'm-phe:ki).*
1-Sipho cop-1-cook
'Sipho is the cook.'

b. *(ú'm-phe:ki) (ng-ù-Sî:pho).*
1-cook cop-1-Sipho
'The cook is Sipho.'

As can be seen by comparing (3a) with (3b), the cleft pivot also begins with a copula: the lexical high tone of *úm-* in *úm-fúndísi* 'teacher' (as in (3a), when this word heads a relative clause) is replaced by the copular low tone when the same word is a pivot in a cleft (as in (3c)):

1. In the glosses, numbers indicate nominal agreement classes; REL is 'relative subject marker'; OM is 'object marker' and TAM is 'tense aspect marker'. Note that high tones are marked with an acute accent, and low tones are typically not marked in the examples. We have particularly indicated copular low tones in examples like (2) and (3) for clarity. Parentheses indicate the prosodic phrasing; see Section 3, below, for more discussion. Square brackets indicate syntactic boundaries, mainly relative clause boundaries.

(3) a. *Subject relative clause*
(*úm-fúndísi* [*ó-thól-ê:* *ín-dánda:tho*)]
1-teacher REL1-find-TAM 9-ring
(*ú-zo-thóla* *úm-klóme:lo*).
1-FUT-get 3-reward
'The teacher who found the ring will get a reward.'

Clefted subjects – question-answer pair

b. (*ù-bá:n'*) ([*ó-thól-ê:* *ín-dándatho* *e-bí-kú-láhléké:le*])?
COP.1-who REL1-find-TAM 9-ring REL9-TAM-you.OM-lost
'Who is it that found the ring that got lost from you?'

c. (*ùm-fúndí:si*) ([*ó-thól-ê:* *ín-dándatho* *e-bí-ngi-láhléké:le*]).
COP.1-teacher REL1-find-TAM 9-ring REL9-TAM-I.OM-lost
'(It) is the teacher who found the ring that got lost from me.'

Another important difference between the subject relative in (3a) and the clefted subjects in (3b, c) is that each half of the cleft construction – pivot and relative clause – is always parsed into its own prosodic phrase. In contrast, relative heads in Zulu are generally phrased together with the rest of the relative clause, as shown in (3a), and the first phrase break falls at the right edge of the relative clause. The prosodic phrase boundaries can be easily identified in the data by the position of lengthened penult vowels. Vowel length is not contrastive, and long vowels are only found in the penult syllables of some words. Work since Doke (1961) analyzes penult length as a correlate of stress, and since Khumalo (1987) it is accepted that penult lengthening is a phrase level (not lexical) process.

This difference in prosodic phrasing is striking, as there is no segmental difference distinguishing the clauses marked as relative in (3). All contain a participial verb, with relative subject morphology. (See e.g. Doke 1961 for more detailed discussion of this morphology.) In all cases in (3), the relative verb is marked for (subject) agreement with what appears to be its head.

The independent prosodic phrasing of each half of the cleft is mirrored in the syntactic independence of the two halves. As shown in (4), the two halves of the cleft can appear in either order. However, restrictive relative clauses occur in a strict order, following their heads. (See also Section 4.2, below.)

(4) a.1 [In answer to, 'Who is carrying the basket?]
(*ù-Nhlâ:nhla*) (*ó-thwél'* *ú-bhasikí:di*).
COP.1-Nhlanhla REL.1-carry 1-basket
'It is Nhlanhla who is carrying the basket.'

OR

a.2 (*Ó-thwél'* *ú-bhasikí:di*) (*ù-Nhlâ:nhla*).
REL.1-carry 1-basket COP.1-Nhlanhla
'The one who is carrying the basket is Nhlanhla.'

b.1 (*ù-Sî:phó*) (*ó-phéka:-yo*).
COP.1-Sipho REL.1-cook-REL
'It is Sipho who cooks/is cooking.'

OR

b.2 (*ó-phéka:-yo*) (*ng-ù-Sî:pho*).
REL.1-cook-REL COP-1-Sipho
'The one who cooks/is cooking is Sipho.'

Note that restrictive relative clauses and the relative clause half of a cleft in Zulu are morpho-syntactically indistinguishable from a headless relative, as shown in (5a–c). We conclude from this, together with the data in (4), that the relative clause following these clefts is a headless relative (DP).

(5) a. *Headed relative clause*
(*úm-fúnd`ísi* <u>ó-thól-ê:</u> <u>ín-dánda:tho</u>)
1-teacher REL.1-find-TAM 9-ring
(*ú-zo-thóla úm-klóme:lo*).
1-FUT-get 3-reward
'The teacher who found the ring will get a reward.'

b. *Headless relative*
(<u>Ó-thól-ê:</u> <u>ín-dánda:tho</u>) (*ú-zo-thóla úm-klóme:lo*).
REL.1-find-TAM 9-ring 1-FUT-get 3-reward
'The one who found the ring, s/he will get a reward.'

c. *Cleft*
(*ùm-fúndí:si*) (<u>ó-thól-ê:</u> <u>ín-dándatho</u> *e-bí-ngi-láhléké:le*).
COP.1-teacher REL.1-find-TAM 9-ring REL.9-TAM-me.OM-lost
'(It) is the teacher who found the ring that got lost from me.'

A headless relative can be analyzed as a relative clause containing a null head; in other words, it is a DP. As we shall see shortly, headless relative clauses are not the only kind of complex DP which can occur as a dependent clause in a cleft construction.[2]

In all the examples of clefts so far, the pivot of the cleft corresponds to the subject of the dependent clause. Indeed, clefts are obligatory in Durban Zulu, as in many other Bantu languages, when questioning the subject and when answering

2. Despite their DP status, copulas cannot be attached to headless relatives. This is probably due to a morphological requirement on the copulas, that they attach to an overt nominal element. However, this topic requires further research.

questions on the subject.[3] Non-subject clefts commonly indicate contrastive or identificational focus. Examples of non-subject argument clefts are given below. Notice in these examples that the relative clause contains a resumptive object prefix in the verb or absolute pronoun (non-italicized) agreeing with the pivot:

(6) a.1 (*ng-àbá-ntwa:na*) (*éngi-zo-khúlúma* na:-bo).
COP.2-child REL.I-FUT-talk with-2
OR – reversed

a.2 (*éngi-zo-khúlúma* na:bo) (*ng-àbá-ntwa:na*).
REL.I-FUT-talk with-2 COP-2-child
'It's the children who I will talk with.'

b.1 Q. (*Yî:-n'*) (*ó-nga-yí-ník-áng-a* *mu:-ntu*)?
COP.9-what REL.you-NEG-9.OM-give-NEG-FV 1-anyone
'What is it that you didn't give to anyone?'

b.2 A. (*ìn-cwâ:d'*) (*éngi-nga-yí-ník-áng-a* *mu:-ntu*).
COP.9-book REL.I-NEG-9.OM-GIVE-NEG-FV 1-anyone
'It's a book that I didn't give to anyone.'

c. [Context: Did they send the bicycle to Thandi?]
A. (*châ:*). (*ù-Sî:ph'*) (*ábá-*m-*thúmélél* *í-bhayiséki:li*),
no COP.1-Sipho REL.2–1.OM-sent to 5-bicycle
(*hhá:y'* *ú-Tha:ndi*).
not 1-Thandi
'No. It's Sipho they sent the bicycle to, not Thandi.'

In Zulu, not only arguments can occur as the pivot of clefts, but also adverbials. In fact, any *wh*-question word or morpheme can be clefted for emphasis. These examples share with the clefts we have seen so far the following properties: the cleft contains a copular sentence, each half of the cleft construction is parsed into its own prosodic phrase, and the two halves can be reversed.

However, the examples below also reveal differences. When complex *wh*-phrases or non-nominals are clefted, the dependent clause is not always a headless relative clause. Instead we find the following other possibilities:

- a headed relative clause with clefted 'which' question (7);
- an adverbial *lapho...khona* clause with clefted temporal or locative adjuncts, including 'when' and 'where' (8);
- a bare participial clause with the clefted question word, 'why' (9).

3. See Downing (2010), Maxwell (1981), van der Wal (2009), Walusimbi (1996) and Zerbian (2006) for discussion of other Bantu languages where clefts are normally required to focus the subject.

The headed relatives in (7), contain a noun phrase, which agrees with the pivot of the cleft. The headed relative clause contains the typical relative subject prefix, resumptive object marker (for object relatives) or full pronoun, which agree with the pivot of the cleft.

(7) *Clefted 'which', plus headed relative*

a.1 (*yì-mû:-phi*) (*úm-fúndisi ó-sí-bingeléla:-yo*)?
COP-1-which 1-preacher REL.1-us.OM-welcome-REL
'Which preacher is welcoming us?'[4]
[lit. 'It is which one, the preacher who is welcoming us?']

OR – reversed

a.2 (*úm-fúndisi ó-sí-bingeléla:-yo*) (*ì-mû:-phi*)?
1-preacher REL.1-us.OM-welcome-REL COP-1-which
'Which preacher is welcoming us?'
[lit. 'The preacher who is welcoming us is which one?']

b.1 (*ín-cwád' ó-nga-yí-ník-á:nga mu:-nt'*) (*ì-yî:-phi*)?
9-book REL.you-NEG-9.OM-give-NEG 1-anyone COP-9.which

OR – reversed

b.2 (*ì-yî:-ph'*) (*ín-cwád' ó-nga-yí-ník-ánga mu:-ntu*)?
'Which book didn't you give to anyone?'

c.1 (*ì-yî:-phi*) (*ín-dlu ó-béké kú-yóna ízím-pháhla za:mi*)?
COP-9-which 9-room REL.you-put LOC-9 10-thing 10.my

OR – reversed

c.2 (*ín-dlu ó-béké kú-yóna ízim-pháhla za:m'*) (*ì-yî:phi*)?
'Which room did you place my things in?'

However, the clauses which accompany clefted adjuncts or clefted 'why' do not contain any agreeing morphology, as shown in (8) and (9), below:

(8) *Clefted temporal or locative, plus* ***lapho...khona*** *clause*

a. [Context: Did they put your things in my room?]
(*ku-s-e-kámélwéní lí-ká-Si:phó*) (*lapho bé-béké*
COP-LINKER-LOC-5.room.LOC 5-of.1-Sipho Adv PT2-put

kho:na) (*ízi-mphá:hla*) (*hhá:yí kwé-lá:kho*).
Adv 10-thing not LOC-5.your

'It is in Sipho's room where they put the things, not in yours.'

---

4. The attentive reader will note in these examples that the words for 'preacher' and 'teacher' in Zulu are segmentally identical, but tonally distinct.

b. (*yì-kusá:sa*) (*lapho ngí-zo-ya kho:n'*) (*é-Thékwí:ni*),
COP-tomorrow Adv PT.I-FUT-go Adv LOC-Durban.LOC
(*hhá:yí namhlâ:nje*).
not today
'It is tomorrow that I will leave for Durban, not today.

c. (*be-kú-y-ízo:lo*) (*laph' úm-fúnd' e-phékélé kho:n'*)
BE-17-COP-5.yesterday Adv 1-student PT.1-cook.for Adv
(*ú-Thánd' in-kû:khu*).
1-Thandi 9-chicken
'It was yesterday that the student cooked chicken for Thandi.'

d. (*yì-kwâ:mi*) (*laph' ízo:lo*) (*ú-Síph' é-phékélé kho:n'*)
COP-LOC.my Adv 5.yesterday 1-Sipho PT.1-cook.for Adv
(*ú-Thánd' in-kû:khu*).
1-Thandi 9-chicken

OR- reversed

e. (*laph' ízo:l'*) (*ú-Síph' é-phékélé kho:na*) (*ú-Thánd' in-kû:khu*) (*yì-kwâ:mi*).
'It is at my house that Sipho cooked chicken for Thandi yesterday.'

Moreover, the participial clause accompanying a clefted 'why' question does not contain any subordinate marking, other than the participial morphology on the verb (indicated as PT in the glosses):

(9) *Clefted question word, 'why', plus bare participial clause*
(*y-î:nga:n'*) (*ú-Síph' é-phuzî:l'*) *úkú-fí:ka*)?
COP-why 1-Sipho PT.1-be late INFINITIVE-arrive
'Why is it that Sipho arrived late?'
[lit. 'It is why, Sipho is late to arrive?']

These morpho-syntactic distinctions between the participial clauses and the relative clauses which occur in cleft constructions are highlighted in the examples below, which show that nouns with adverbial meaning can head either a restrictive relative clause or an adverbial *lapho…khona* clause in non-cleft constructions. In cleft constructions, when the pivot of the cleft is adverbial, the dependent clause can only be a *lapho…khona* clause. Note that we find different subject prefixes – participial vs. relative – in the two dependent clauses, and that only the relative clause contains a resumptive pronoun (non-italicized) agreeing with the head:

(10) *Minimal pairs, relative vs. adverbial clausal modifiers*
a.1 (*índa:wo*) (*laph' ú-Síph' é:-khandelé: khon' í-mo:t'*) (*í-shí:le*).
9.place Adv 1-Sipho PT.1-fix Adv 9-car 9-burn
OR – relative clause (*ku-yona* resumptive for *indawo*)

a.2 (*índaw' ú-Síph' â:-khandelá* kú-yón' *í-mo:t'*) (*í-shí:le.*)
9.place 1-Sipho REL.1-fix LOC-9 9-car 9-burn
'The place where Sipho fixed the car burned down.'

b.1 (*ú-su:kú*) (*lapho ú-Sípho é-phékélé é-mzi-ni wá:kho*)
11-day Adv 1-Sipho PT.1-cook LOC-3.home-LOC 3.your
(*kho:na*) (*lú-qalé ka:mbi*).
Adv 11-begin badly

OR – relative clause:

b.2 (*ú-súk' ú-Síph' á-phekelé* nga-l' *é-mzi-ni wá:kho*)
11-day 1-Sipho REL.1-cook Prep-11 LOC-3.home-LOC 3.your
(*lú-qalé ka:mbi*).
11-begin badly
'The day when Sipho cooked at your house began badly.'

Let us sum up the important generalizations about Zulu clefts which our analysis needs to account for. Clefts have a bipartite structure: a copular sentence and a dependent clause. The prosodic phrasing provides one clue to the independence of each half of the cleft construction, as the pivot of the cleft forms an independent prosodic phrase from the dependent clause. Another clue to their independence is the fact that they can occur in either order. Both nominals and non-nominals can occur in the pivot of the cleft, and the type of dependent clause found in the second half of the clefted structure is conditioned by the nature of the pivot. Clefted nominals are accompanied by headless relative clauses. Clefted 'which' questions are accompanied by headed relatives. Clefted adverbials are accompanied by participial clauses, and in the case of clefted 'why,' the participial clause is otherwise bare of subordinating morphology.

We develop our syntactic analysis of the structure of clefts in Section 4. First, we provide, as necessary background, the analysis of prosodic phrasing in Zulu.

3. Prosodic phrasing in Durban Zulu and the phrasing of clefts

We begin our analysis of the structure of clefts, by taking a closer look at the implications of the prosodic phrasing for their syntactic structure. Cheng and Downing's (2007, 2009, 2012) work on prosodic phrasing in a range of Zulu constructions demonstrates that the right edge of phases, vP and CP, systematically correlates with a prosodic phrase break, while the left edges of these constituents only variably condition phrase breaks.[5] Evidence for a prosodic phrase break at the

5. Following Chomsky (2001), we take CP to be a phase. See An (2007), Fox and Pesetsky (2005) and Ishihara (2007) for discussions of whether *v*P in a particular language is a phase or not.

right edge of CP comes from the fact that we find a break following, but not preceding, restrictive relative clauses and other embedded clause types – see (11c, d, e). Simple subjects are only variably followed by a prosodic phrase break, as we can see in (11a, b, c).

(11) a. ([$_{\text{CP}}$ *úm-fúndísi ú-fúndel-ê: ábá-zal' ín-cwa:di.*])
1-teacher 1-read to-TAM 2-parent 9-letter
'The teacher read to the parents a letter.'

b. (*ú-Si:pho*) (*ú-yí-phékéla ba:ni*) (*ín-ku:khu*)?
1-Sipho 1–9.OM-cook.for who 9-chicken
'Who is Sipho cooking the chicken for?'

c. ([$_{\text{CP}}$ *ú-Síph' ú-fún'* [$_{\text{CP}}$ *úkúth' ú-Thándi á-théng' í-bhayiséki:li.*]])
1-Sipho 1-want that 1-Thandi 1-buy 5-bicycle
'Sipho wants Thandi to buy a bicycle.'

d. ([$_{\text{CP}}$ [$_{\text{CP}}$ *Ín-dod' é-gqoke ísí-gqo:ko*]) (*í-bon-é ízi-vaká:shi.*])
9-man REL.9-wear 7-hat 9-see-TAM 8-visitor
'The man who is wearing a hat saw the visitors.'

e. ([$_{\text{CP}}$*si-phul'* [$_{\text{CP}}$*ím-baz' é-théngw-é námhlâ:nje.*]])
we-break 9-axe REL.9-be.bought-TAM today
'We broke the axe that has been bought today.'

Evidence for a prosodic phrase break at the right edge of vP comes from the phrasing of adjuncts. Arguments must precede locative and temporal adjuncts, in a broad focus context or VP focus context like that illustrated in (12). Locative and temporal adjuncts are also separated from the preceding arguments by a prosodic phrase boundary. Both these facts are consistent with adjoining locative and temporal adjuncts above the vP.

(12) Context: Q: What did Sipho do?
A: a. (*ú-Síph' ú-phék' ín-ku:khu*) (*kwám' ízo:lo*).
1-Sipho 1-cook 9-chicken LOC.my 5.yesterday
'Sipho cooked chicken at my place yesterday.'

b. (*bá-ník' ú-Síph' í-bhayiséki:li*) (*namhlâ:nje*).
2-gave 1-Sipho 5-bicycle today
'They gave Sipho a bicycle today.'

We account for these prosodic phrasing generalizations in Edge-based alignment theory. (See, e.g. Selkirk 1986, 1995, 2000; Truckenbrodt 1995, 1999, 2005.) The basic parsing algorithm in the Edge-based theory requires one edge of a major syntactic constituent to coincide with an edge of a prosodic constituent, Phonological

As Cheng and Downing (2009) argue, when subjects are followed by a prosodic phrase break, they are plausibly in Topic position.

Phrase or Intonation Phrase. Phonological Phrases coincide with lexical XPs, while Intonation Phrases coincide with functional XPs. We follow work like An (2007), Ishihara (2007), Kahnemuyipour (2009) and Kratzer and Selkirk (2007) in proposing that prosodic domains can also be conditioned by phases: vP and CP. The constraints below, relevant for Zulu prosodic phrasing in a broad focus context, together optimize a strict match between the right edge of syntactic phases and the right edge of Intonation Phrases:[6]

(13) ALIGNR[PHASE, INTPH]: Align the right edge of every phase (vP/CP) with the right edge of an Intonation Phrase (IntPh).

(14) ALIGNR[INTPH, PHASE]: Align the right edge of every Intonation Phrase (IntPh) with the right edge of a phase (vP/CP).

The analysis of broad focus phrasing is exemplified in the tableaux below. Parentheses continue to indicate prosodic phrase boundaries:

(15) Broad focus phrasing
(a) Two arguments

	ALIGNR-PHASE	ALIGNR-INTPH
☞i. S V IO DO$]_{VP}]_{vP}]_{CP}$)		
ii. S V IO) DO$]_{VP}]_{vP}]_{CP}$)		*!

(b) Argument plus Adjunct

	ALIGNR-PHASE	ALIGNR-INTPH
☞i. S V DO$]_{VP}]_{vP}$) Adj$]_{IP}]_{CP}$)		
ii. S V DO$]_{VP}]_{vP}$ Adj$]_{IP}]_{CP}$)	*!	

In tableau (15a), with two arguments following the verb in a broad focus context, it is optimal to parse both arguments with the verb in a single Intonation Phrase. Phrasing the arguments separately from each other, as in (15a.ii), violates the alignment constraint in (14): the phrase breaks are not both at a phase edge. In contrast, in sentences with an argument and an adjunct following the verb in a broad focus context, it is optimal for a phrase break to fall between the argument and the adjunct, as in candidate (15b.i). Phrasing the argument and adjunct together, as in candidate (15b.ii), violates the constraint in (13): the right edge of the vP phase is not aligned with an Intonation Phrase break.

6. See Cheng and Downing (2009, 2012) for detailed motivation of these two phase-phrase alignment constraints in Zulu.

The prosodic phrasing we find in broad focus contexts has clear implications for the syntactic analysis of clefts in Zulu. Since the clefted head is phrased separately from the dependent clause, whatever order the two occur in, each half of the cleft structure must be separated by a phase edge – vP or CP – from the other half. The next sections develop syntactic arguments supporting this proposal.

4. Zulu clefts: Analysis

In this section, we first briefly discuss why a monoclausal structure for clefts cannot account for the data in Zulu. In 4.2, we present arguments supporting a bi-clausal analysis for both nominal and temporal/locative clefted elements.

4.1 Arguments against a monoclausal embedding structure

The prosodic phrasing of clefts provides our first argument against a monoclausal structure for cleft sentences. A typical monoclausal analysis can have the structures schematized in (16a,b), with the pivot of the cleft either in SpecCP or in SpecFocusP. (See É. Kiss 1998 for such an analysis of clefts in English and some other languages):

(16) a. [$_{IP}$ — copula [$_{CP}$ clefted-phrase [$_{C'}$ clausal predicate/RC]]]
b. [$_{IP}$ — copula [$_{FP}$ clefted-phrase [$_{CP}$ clausal predicate/RC]]]

Regardless of whether we are dealing with SpecCP or SpecFocusP, the prosodic phrasing of clefted sentences cannot be accounted for by this kind of analysis, nor can it account for the difference in prosodic phrasing between relative clauses and cleft sentences. As we have argued above, in Zulu, the right edge of a phase (vP or CP) is privileged in its alignment with the right edge of an Intonation Phrase. Given the structures in (16a, b), no prosodic break between the pivot and the clause following the pivot is expected because a right phase edge does not follow the clefted phrase. This means that clefts and restrictive relative clauses are expected to have the same prosodic phrasing, contrary to fact.

Given a structure such as (16a, b), the assumption is that what is clefted is an XP constituent, and what follows the pivot is either part of a CP or a whole CP. However, as we have shown above in (7a) (repeated here as (17)), when the cleft involves a *which*-phrase, what follows *which* is a noun phrase with a relative clause in it, not a clausal predicate:

(17) (*yì-mû:-phi*) (*úm-fúndisi ó-sí-bingeléla:-yo*)?
COP-1-which 1-preacher REL.1-US.OM-welcome-REL
'Which preacher is welcoming us?'

In other words, given (17), it appears that the pivot can be simply an element such as *muphi* 'which', and what follows is a noun phrase with a relative clause in it. In other words, neither the prosodic break following the pivot nor the type of phrase following the pivot can be accounted for, if the pivot is in SpecCP or SpecFocusP rather than at a right CP edge. (See also Wedgwood 2007.)

Note that a Kaynian relative clause structure does not rescue the monoclausal structure because the prosodic phrasing of (17) is still unexpected: the left edge of a CP does not align with an edge of the Intonation Phrase. An additional problem for a structure such as (16b), which involves a FocusP above the CP, is that Zulu does not have a high FocusP. (See Buell (2009), Cheng and Downing (2009, 2012), and Hyman and Polinsky (2010) for detailed discussion.)

4.2 A bi-clausal structure

We propose that both nominal and non-nominal clefts involve a copular sentence (an identificational sentence), with an appositive phrase/clause adjoined to the sentence. Consider first argument clefts, such as the sentence with a subject cleft in (3b), repeated here as (18a). We suggest that it has the structure in (18b).

(18) a. (ùm-fúndí:si) [(ó-thól-ê: *ín-dándatho e-bí-ngi-láhléké:le*)].
COP.1-teacher REL.1-find-TAM 9-ring REL.9-TAM-me.OM-lost
'(It) is the teacher who found the ring that got lost from me.'

b. $[_{CP}$ $[_{IP}$ ùm-fúndí:si]] $[_{DP}$ ø $[_{CP}$ ó-thól-ê: ín-dándatho e-bí-ngi-láhléké:le]]

In this structure, the pivot of the cleft is in a copular sentence, and the headless DP with the relative clause is adjoined to the copular sentence. This structure is similar to the structure of French cleft sentences proposed by Clech-Darbon et al. (1999). (See also Koch 2008 for a similar analysis of clefts in Thompson River Salish.)

Given this structure, the pivot of the cleft will be at the right edge of a CP. As the right edge of CP consistently conditions a prosodic phrase break in Zulu, this structure correctly accounts for the prosodic parse of clefts.

4.3 Headed relatives

The structure in (18b) not only accommodates headless relatives like the one given in (18a), but also cases involving headed relatives, like those discussed above with *which*-phrases. In (19) we repeat (7c), above, to illustrate this:

(19) ($[_{CP}$ $[_{IP}$ *ì-yî:-phi*]]) ($[_{DP}$$[_{CP}$ *ín-dlu* *ó-béké* kú-yóna
COP-9-which 9-room REL.you-put LOC-9

ízím-pháhla za:mi]])?
10-thing 10.my

'Which room is it that you put my things in?'
[lit. 'It is which [one], the room that you put my things in?']

We suggest that *yiphi* in (19) constitutes, in fact, a full noun phrase, with a null head in it (i.e. it has the reading *which one*). The noun class 9 prefix further supports the proposal that *yi-phi* is a noun phrase.

It should be noted that aside from the clefted *which*-phrases such as the one in (19), we find other kinds of clefts with a headed relative following a copular sentence. In particular, in certain situations (as we see below), a pronoun associated with the head of the relative clause can appear in the copular sentence. To understand the structure of these clefts, one must first consider copular sentences involving predicate nominals, as in (20a) and its negative counterpart in (20b):

(20) a. *ng-ùmû:-ntu lo:ná.*
COP-1-person 1.that
'That's a person.'

b. *a-kú-ye:n'* *úmú:-ntu lo:ná.* (adapted from Buell 2008)
NEG.COP-17-1PRO 1-person 1.that
'That's not a person.'

In the negative form in (20b), not only do we see the class 17 subject marker in the copular sentence, there is also a pronoun, *yena*, which accords with the noun class of the following noun, *umuntu*. These pronouns (non-italicized) also show up in negative clefts, as shown in (21):

(21) a. (*a-kú*-bo:na) (*ábá-fána kuphê:la*) (*áb-enzá lo:kho*).
NEG.COP-17-2PRO 2-boy only REL.2-do 17.that
'It's not just the boys who did that.'

b. (*a-kú*-ye:n') (*ú-tíshá éngi-m-ázi:-yo*) (*lona*
NEG.COP-17-1PRO 1-teacher REL.I-1.OM-know-REL 1.PRO
ó-bónwe u-Sî:pho).
REL.1-be seen by.1-Sipho
'It's not the teacher that I know [the one] that was seen by Sipho.'

Aside from negation contexts, we also see the pronoun showing up when there is an additional emphasis on the copular sentence (similar to verum focus), as in (22):

(22) a. (*ngù*-yê:n') (*ú-Síph' ow-énza lo:kho*).
COP-1PRO 1-Sipho REL.1-do 17.that
'It IS Sipho who does that.'

b. (*kwá-kú-yi*-bô:na) (*ábá-fán' áb-enzá lo:kho*).
17.PAST-17-COP-2PRO 2-boy REL.2-do 17.that
'It WAS the boys who did that.'

In all these cases, there is a prosodic phrase break right after the pronoun. This follows from our analysis – the copular sentence here ends with the pronoun, and it is thus at the right edge of a prosodic phrasal boundary, and the DP following the copular sentence is a headed relative clause.[7] The literal translation of (22b), for instance, is: 'It WAS them, the boys who did that'. These sentences show that a headed relative clause following the pivot of the cleft is actually not an option limited to *which*-phrases, but can be found in other constructions involving clefted pronouns.

4.4 Non-nominal clefts

We have shown in examples in (10) that non-argument clefts are followed by a non-relative participial clause. With temporal and locative elements, the participial clause is headed by *lapho*, which may indicate time or place, and the adverbial *khona* appears in the clause. In the case of a clefted *why*-question, the clause that follows it is also a participial clause, though it is not headed by an overt marker. Below, we first provide further examples to show that these participial clauses are not relative clauses. Note in the examples below that it is ungrammatical to use the relative subject prefix *a*-, rather than the participial subject prefix *e*-. The occurrence of a resumptive element (non-italicized) is also ungrammatical in these sentences but required in a relative clause:

Temporal/locative elements – *sentences have relative morphology

(23) a. *(yì-kû:phi) (laph' ú-Síph' é-yí-thénge: kho:n') ímí-fi:no)*
COP-where Adv 1-Sipho PT.1–4.OM-buy Adv 4-vegetables

b. **yì-kû:phi ú-Síph' a-yi-thengá* ku-yo:na *ímí-fi:no?*
COP-where 1-Sipho REL.1–4.OM-buy 17-PRO 4-vegetables
'Where did Sipho buy the vegetables?'

(24) a. *(yì-kwâ:mi) (laph' ú-Síph' ízo:l') (é-phékélé khon'*
COP-LOC.my Adv 1-Sipho 5.yesterday PT.1-cook.for Adv
ín-kúkhú ká-Tha:ndi).
9-chicken of.1-Thandi

b. **yì-kwâ:mi ízo:lo ú-Síph' á-yí-phékelé* ku-yo:na
COP- LOC.my 5.yesterday 1-Sipho REL.1–9.OM-cook.for 17-pro
ú-Tha:nd' in-kû:khu.
1-Thandi 9-chicken
'It is at my place that Sipho yesterday cooked chicken for Thandi.'

(25) a. *(yízo:lo) (laph' úm-fúnd' e-phékélé kho:n')*
COP.5.yesterday Adv 1-student PT.1-cook.for Adv
(ú-Ja:bu) (ín-ku:khu).
1-Jabu 9-chicken

---

7. We will not discuss here why the pronoun particularly shows up in negative or emphasis contexts. In the case of negation, we speculate that a X^0 element (such as a pronominal element) can be used to support a negative head.

b. **yízo:lo* *úm-fúnd'* *a-phékélé* ngayo
COP.5.yesterday 1-student REL.1-cook.for prep.5PRO
úJab' *in-kû:khu.*
1-Jabu 9-chicken
'It is yesterday that the student cooked chicken for Jabu.'

(26) a. (*y-î:nga:n'*) (*ú-Síph'* *é-phuzî:l'*) (*úkú-fí:ka*)?
COP-why 1-Sipho PT.1-be.late INFINITIVE-arrive
b. *y-*ingani* *u-Sipho* *a-phuzile* *uku-fika*?
COP-why 1-Sipho REL.1-be.late INFINITIVE-arrive
'Why did Sipho arrive LATE?'

It should be noted that *lapho* clauses also occur in non-cleft contexts, as shown in (27), cited from Doke (1961), who unfortunately does not mark tone or phrase penult lengthening:

(27) a. Lapho *usu-qed-ile,* *ma-wu-buye.*
when you.PRT-finish-PERF HORT-you-return.SUBJUNCTIVE
'*When* you have finished, come back.'
b. *Yi-beke* *in-cwadi* lapho *kade* *i-khona.*
9.OM-put.SUBJUNCTIVE 9-book *where* before COP-there
'Put the book *where* it was before.'

These examples illustrate that the *lapho* clauses are adverbial clauses.

We suggest that non-nominal clefts share with nominal clefts a structural property, namely, a copular sentence is involved. Instead of having a DP adjoined to the copular sentence as in the nominal clefts, however, we propose that an adverbial clause is adjoined to the copular sentence when it also contains an adverbial.[8] This is illustrated with the structure of (25a), given in (28):

(28) [$_{CP}$ [$_{IP}$ yízo:lo]] [$_{CP}$ laph' úmfúnd' e-phékélé kho:n' úJa:b' ínku:khu]

In the next sections, we motivate this structure in more detail. First we show the dependent clause does not result from extraposition. Then we develop a proposal arguing that the Zulu cleft structure involves a pronominal predicate (cf. Moro (1997) and Adger and Ramchand (2003)).

8. In *lapho…khona* clauses one fairly consistently finds a prosodic phrase break following *khona*. This suggests, as we showed in Section 3, that *khona* is at the right edge of vP. However, an object following *khona* is not resumed with object marking on the verb, as we would expect if it were external to vP. These constructions obviously require more study in order to better understand these seemingly contradictory properties. Such an analysis is, though, outside the scope of this paper. What is crucial to the analysis developed here is that a *lapho…khona* clause is an adverbial, and occurs when the clefted pivot is also adverbial.

5. Motivating the structure

5.1 The post-pivot phrase/clause is not extraposed

We begin by developing our argument that the post-pivot clause is not extraposed. Given the structure in (18b), one might consider the post-pivot clause on a par with a right-dislocated relative clause (under the assumption that it is not really a DP, but a CP). In other words, it might have the derivation suggested by Percus (1997) for English clefts. This is shown in (29). For the cleft sentence in (29), the base sentence starts out as a copular sentence with a subject containing a definite determiner and a null head (with a relative clause (CP) following the null head).

(29) a. It is John that Mary saw.
b. $[_{IP}$ $[_{DP}$ the 0 $[_{CP}$ OP_i that Mary saw t_i $]]_j$ $[_{VP}$ t_j is John]]
c. *Extraposition*
$[_{IP}$ $[_{DP}$ the 0 $t_k]_j$ $[_{VP}$ t_j is John]] $[_{CP}$ OP_i that Mary saw t_i $]_k$]

The relative clause is then extraposed, yielding the surface structure of a cleft (with the definite determiner and the null head subsequently spelled out as *it*). The structure in (29c) appears similar to the structure that we have in (18b).

However, we argue that no right-dislocation is involved in Zulu clefts. First, there is no comparable right-dislocation possibility for relative clauses in non-clefted contexts in Zulu. The data in (30b) and (31b) show very clearly that relative clauses cannot be right dislocated:

(30) a. $[_{DP}$ *(Ábá-ntwán'* $[_{CP}$ *ábá-jah'* *ím-bû:zi)*]] *(ba-yá-hle:ka).*
2-child REL.2-chase 9-goat 2-DJ-laugh
'The children who are chasing the goat are laughing.'
b. **aba-ntwana ba-ya-hleka* $[_{CP}$ *aba-jah' im-buzi*]

(31) a. $[_{DP}$ *(ú-thí:sha)* $[_{CP}$ *ó-si-fundél'* *ín-cwa:di)*]]
1-teacher REL.1-us.OM-read.to 9-letter
(ú-yá-si-thukuthéli:sa).
1-DJ-us.OM-make.angry
'The teacher who is reading us a letter makes us angry.'
b. **uthisha uyasithukuthelisa* $[_{CP}$ *ó-si-fundél' ín-cwa:di*]

If normally relative clauses cannot be right dislocated, it is very difficult to motivate a right-dislocation analysis just in the case of the clefts. Further, as we have already pointed out for the cases in which we have a headed relative (i.e. involving a *which*-phrase), it cannot be the case that it is the relative clause (CP) alone that is right dislocated.

5.2 The copular sentence

The next step in motivating the structure we argue for (i.e. (18b)) requires understanding the relation between the adjoined DP (in the case of a nominal DP pivot) or the adjoined adverbial clause (in the case of a non-nominal pivot), on the one hand, and the pivot on the other. To do this, we must take a closer look at the structure of the copular sentence. As we briefly mentioned above, in the case of nominal predication, the copula has three main segmental forms, *ng(a)-*, *y(i)-*, and *w(u)*. In (32a–c), we see that the subject agreement marker (non-italicized in these data) normally precedes the copula:

(32) a. *Mina* ngi-*ng-úm-ngane* *wá:kho.*
I.PRO I-COP-1-friend 1.your
'I am your friend.'

b. *uSipho* u-*ng-u-thisha.* (Buell 2008)
1.Sipho 1-COP-1-teacher
'Sipho is a teacher.'

c. *izi-nkomo* zi-*yi-ngcosana.* (adapted from Doke 1961)
10-cattle 10-COP-10.few
'The cattle are few.'

The subject marker on the copula agrees with the subject of the copular sentence, just as the subject marker of a verbal sequence in a typical sentence reflects the noun class of the subject. However, the subject marker in (32b) is optional. This is the case if the subject is a third person (e.g. belongs to class 1), and the verbal form is in the principal (i.e. non-participial) mood. Compare, though, (32b) with (33) which illustrates the copular verbal form in a participial clause:

(33) *uma* *u-Sipho* *e-ng-u-thisha, …* (Buell, p.c.)
if 1-Sipho PT1-COP-1-teacher
'If Sipho is a teacher, …'

Here, the copular sentence is in an *if*-clause, which requires that the verb be in the participial form, and the subject marker cannot be omitted.

Consider now subject agreement in clefts. None of the cleft sentences up to now show any subject marker in the pivot of the cleft. This makes the clefts look like they might contain a third person subject with a verbal form in the principal mood, just like (32b). The obvious way to test for the subject of the cleft is to put it in an *if*-clause, where the copula will be in the participial form and require subject marking (non-italicized). From comparing (34a) with (34b), we see that when the copula is in a participial clause, the subject marker is class 17, and not class 1 (third person human), as the ungrammatical (34c) shows.

(34) a. *(ng)-ù-Sî:pho ó-phék' úku:-dl' ízol' ébúsú:ku.*
cop-1-Sipho rel.1-cook 15-food 5.yesterday night
'It is Sipho who cooked dinner last night.'

b. *úmá* kú-*ng-ù-Sî:pho ó-phék' úku:-dl' ízol'*
if 17-cop-1-Sipho rel.1-cook 15-food 5.yesterday
ébúsú:ku ngeké kú-dlè:ké.
night be.unable 15-be.eaten
'If it is Sipho who cooked dinner last night, it wouldn't be eatable.'

c. **uma e-ng-ù-Sî:pho ó-phék' úku:-dl' ízol'*
if 1-COP-1-Sipho REL1-cook 15-food 5.yesterday
ébúsú:ku ngéké kú-dle:ké.
night be.unable 15-be.eaten

The class 17 subject agreement marker can also be found in sentences comparable to the expletive construction in English, as shown in (35):

(35) *ku-fik-e izingane* (adapted from Buell 2008)
17-arrive-PERF.CJ 10.children
'There arrived some children.'

Buell (2006, 2008) has argued that in cases such as (35), the logical subject *izingane* 'children' stays internal to the verb phrase (thus explaining the conjoint form of the verb).[9] *Ku* appears as a default subject marker.

Turning back to the copular clause in cleft sentences, the class 17 subject marking we find also illustrates default agreement. Note that class 17 agreement prefix *ku-* (non-italicized) not only appears with the participial mood, it also appears when the verb is in the past tense, as shown in (36a) or under negation, as shown in (36b, c):

(36) a. *bé-*kú-*yî:ni) ú-Síphó á-bé-yí-phe:ka)*
BE-17-COP:what.9 1-Sipho REL.1-be.past-9.OM-cook
é-mzi-ni wá:kho)?
LOC-3.home-LOC 3.your
'What was it that Sipho cooked at your house (this morning)?'

9. Zulu verbal forms distinguish between a *conjoint* (CJ) form and a *disjoint* (DJ) form. (See work like Buell 2005; Doke 1961; Poulous & Msimang 1998, and van der Spuy 1993 for detailed discussion.) Simplifying a bit, the *conjoint* form is used when there is something following the verb in the verb phrase. In (35), the verb is *conjoint*, indicating that aside from the verb, something else, in this case the logical subject, is also in the verb phrase.

b. *a-kú-mi:n')* *ów-enza* *lo:kho).*
NEG.COP-17-me.PRO REL.1-do 17.that
'It wasn't me who did that.'

c. *a-kú-ye:na)* *ú-Sípho* *ó-phéké:* *úku:-dl')*
NEG.COP-17-1PRO 1-Sipho REL.1-cook 15-food
ízol' *ébúsú:ku).*
5.yesterday night
'It is not Sipho who cooked dinner last night.'

We conclude from these data that we have class 17 agreement in the copular sentence in the case of clefts.

Following Adger and Ramchand (2003), we assume that the copula is a manifestation of the Predicate head (cf. den Dikken 2006):

(37)

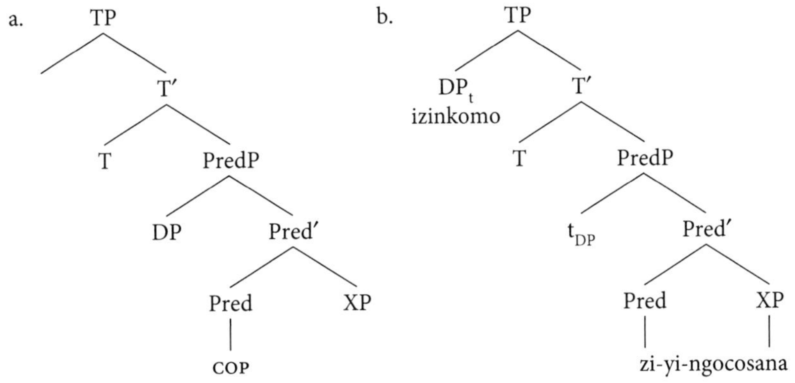

The XP can be a predicate nominal as in the case of (32a–c), with the subject DP in SpecPredP. When the subject DP moves to TP, subject agreement is realized (as in (32a–c)). The tree in (37b) illustrates the structure for (32c). This is the same as when we have a verbal predicate, with subject marking reflected in the verb.

In the case of clefts, we suggest, along the lines of Moro (1997) as well as Adger and Ramchand (2003) for similar sentences, that the predicate is a null pronominal element.[10,11] Following Adger and Ramchand (2003), we suggest

10. Buell (2008) suggests that the class 17 subject agreement reflects agreement with a silent demonstrative similar to the French *ce*.

11. Class 17 agreement in Zulu does not entail that we have locative agreement. Zulu does not really have a locative class in comparison with other Bantu languages. We thank Thilo Schadeberg for pointing this out to us.

that the structure we find in the cleft sentences involves predicate inversion, with the predicate raising to the subject position (and thus also blocking the subject DP from raising and triggering regular agreement; see Carstens 2005 for the argument that movement is required for agreement in Bantu). Since the copula appears to precede the pivot, this may in fact involve the movement of the Pred' to the SpecTP (similar to the Scottish Gaelic augmented copular sentences discussed in Adger & Ramchand 2003). Due to the fact that there is no element which can trigger agreement, a default (Class 17) agreement is used (see (40) for the structure).

5.3 The post-pivot phrase/clause

With the structure of the copular sentence in place, let us consider now the role and the interpretation of the post-pivot DP phrase/adverbial clause. Adger and Ramchand (2003) discusses a special case of copular sentences, the augmented copular construction, illustrated by the Scottish Gaelic examples in (38a, b):

(38) a. *'S e Calum.*
COP-PRES AUG Calum
'It's Calum.'

b. *'S e Calum Hamlet.*
COP-PRES AUG Calum Hamlet
'Calum is Hamlet.'

Adger & Ramchand proposes that the copula used in augmented copular constructions is a defective copula. It predicates the property denoted by its complement, that is, the pronominal predicate (i.e. the augment), directly of its subject. In the case of (38b), they suggest that *Hamlet* in (38b) is adjoined (to TP). This right-adjoined DP has a function of explicitly identifying the 'contextually given individual' in the semantics of the pronominal augment with overt linguistic material. For (38b), this yields the interpretation given in (39):

(39) 'The relevant distinguishing property associated with *x' holds of* 'Calum', where *x* is described/replaced by the definite description 'Hamlet'.
(Adger & Ramchand 2003: 353, (102))

Essentially, the semantic value of the pronoun is replaced by a definite description. That is, the adjoined DP provides a definite description for the interpretation of the variable in the semantic representation of the pronominal predicate. The interpretation they provide for the augmented copular construction is similar to the interpretation that Clech-Darbon et al. (1999) provide for French clefts, where the adjoined clause specifies the interpretation of *ce*.

We propose to extend this analysis to Zulu. Consider again the structure of Zulu clefts. The tree in (40) illustrates the structure of (34a), with predicate inversion, as well as the DP adjoining to CP.

(40)

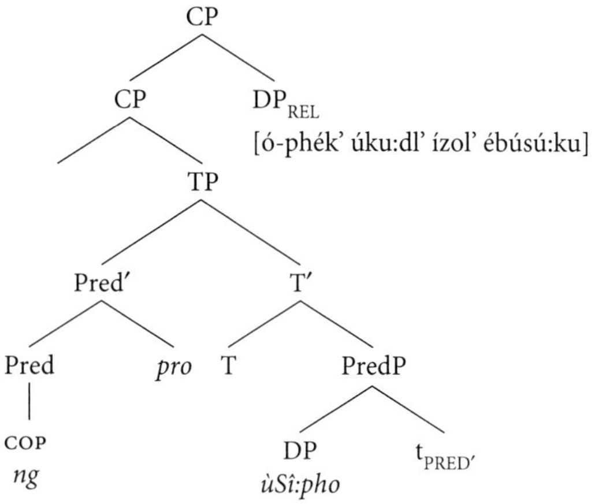

We assume that the DP phrase or adverbial clause is adjoined to CP, yielding the correct prosodic phrasing: this CP is optimally parsed into a separate Intonation Phrase from the adjoined DP phrase or adverbial clause by the alignment constraints in (13), (14), above. Further, the adjoined DP, for instance, serves to specify the semantic value of the pronominal. Similarly, when the adjoined element is an adverbial clause, it essentially states that the property which holds of a temporal/locative element is specified by the adverbial clause.

6. Conclusion

In sum, we have shown that clefts in Zulu involve a copular sentence with an adjoined DP/CP, depending on the nature of the pivot. This analysis accounts for the prosodic properties, as the copular sentence is a CP, parsed into a separate Intonation Phrase from the adjoined DP/CP by the independently-motivated prosodic phrasing algorithm for Zulu. This analysis is the only account which is consistent with the syntactic properties of Zulu clefts. Furthermore, the nature of agreement in Zulu copular sentences supports a pronominal predicate analysis. We expect that clefts which are parsed into two prosodic phrases in other Bantu languages – e.g. Luganda (Hyman & Katamba, 2010), Chewa, and Tumbuka (Downing, 2012) – will yield to a similar syntactic analysis.

References

Adger, David & Ramchand, Gillian. 2003. Predication and equation. *Linguistic Inquiry* 34: 325–359.

An, Duk-Ho. 2007. Clauses in noncanonical positions at the syntax-phonology interface. *Syntax* 10: 38–79.

Buell, Leston. 2005. Issues in Zulu Verbal Morphosyntax. Ph.D. dissertation, UCLA.

Buell, Leston. 2006. The Zulu conjoint/disjoint verb alternation: Focus or constituency? *ZAS Papers in Linguistics* 43: 9–30.

Buell, Leston. 2008. Predication types and predicate-internal arguments in Zulu. Ms, University of Leiden.

Buell, Leston. 2009. Evaluating the immediate postverbal position as a focus position in Zulu. *Selected proceedings of ACAL 38*, 166–172. Somerville MA: Cascadilla Proceedings Project.

Carstens, Vicki. 2005. Agree and EPP in Bantu. *Natural Language and Linguistic Theory* 23: 219–279.

Cheng, Lisa & Downing, Laura J. 2007. The prosody and syntax of Zulu relative clauses. In *SOAS WPL* 15: *Bantu in Bloomsbury*, Nancy Kula & Lutz Marten (eds), 51–63. London: SOAS.

Cheng, Lisa & Downing, Laura J. 2009. Where's the topic in Zulu? In *Topics Cross-linguistically*, Helen de Hoop & Geertje van Bergen (eds). Special issue of *The Linguistic Review* 26: 207–238.

Cheng, Lisa & Downing, Laura J. 2012. Against FocusP: Evidence from Durban Zulu. In *Information Structure: Contrasts and Positions*, Ivona Kucerova & Ad Neeleman (eds). 247–266. Cambridge: CUP.

Chomsky, Noam. 2001. Derivation by phase. In *Ken Hale, A Life in Language*, Michael Kenstowicz (ed.), 1–52. Cambridge MA: The MIT Press.

Clech-Darbon, Anne, Rebuschi, Georges & Rialland, Annie. 1999. Are there cleft sentences in French? In *The Grammar of Focus* [Linguistik Aktuell/Linguistics Today 24], Georges Rebuschi & Laurice Tuller (eds), 83–118. Amsterdam: John Benjamins.

den Dikken, Marcel. 2006. *Relators and Linkers: The Syntax of Predication, Predicate Inversion and Copulas*. Cambridge MA: The MIT Press.

Doke, Clement M. 1961. *Textbook of Zulu Grammar*, 6th edn. London: Longmans.

Downing, Laura J. 2010. Prosodic phrasing in relative clauses: A comparative look at Zulu, Chewa and Tumbuka. In *Bantu Languages: Analyses, Description and Theory* [East African Languages and Dialects 20], Karsten Legère & Christina Thornell (eds), 17–29. Köln: Rüdiger Köppe.

Fox, Danny & Pesetsky, David. 2005. Cyclic linearization of syntactic structure. *Theoretical Linguistics* 31: 1–45.

Hyman, Larry M. & Katamba, Francis. 2010. Tone, syntax, and prosodic domains in Luganda. *ZAS Papers in Linguistics* 63: 69–98.

Hyman, Larry M. & Polinsky, Maria. 2010. Focus in Aghem. In *Information Structure: Theoretical, Typological, and Experimental Perspectives*, Malte Zimmermann & Caroline Féry (eds), 206–233. Oxford: OUP.

Ishihara, Shinichiro. 2007. Major phrase, focus intonation, multiple spell-out (MaP, FI, MSO). *The Linguistic Review* 24: 137–167.

Kahnemuyipour, Arsalan. 2009. *The Syntax of Sentential Stress*. Oxford: OUP.

Khumalo, James S.M. 1987. An Autosegmental Account of Zulu Phonology. Ph.D. dissertation, University of the Witwatersrand.

É. Kiss, Katalin. 1998. Identificational focus versus information focus. *Language* 74: 245–273.
Koch, Karsten. 2008. Intonation and Focus in Nleʔkepmxcin (Thompson River Salish). Ph.D. dissertation, University of British Columbia.
Kratzer, Angelika & Selkirk, Elisabeth. 2007. Phase theory and prosodic spellout: The case of verbs. *The Linguistic Review* 24: 93–135.
Maxwell, Edith M. 1981. Question strategies and hierarchies of grammatical relations in Kinyarwanda. *BLS* 7: 166–177.
Moro, Andrea. 1997. *The Raising of Predicates: Predicative Noun Phrases and the Theory of Clause Structure* [Cambridge Studies in Linguistics]. Cambridge: CUP.
Percus, Orin. 1997. Prying open the cleft. *Proceedings of NELS* 27: 337–351.
Poulous, George & Msimang, Christian T. 1998. *A Linguistic Analysis of Zulu*. Cape Town: Via Afrika.
Selkirk, Elisabeth. 1986. On derived domains in sentence phonology. *Phonology Yearbook* 3: 371–405.
Selkirk, Elisabeth. 1995. The prosodic structure of function words. *UMOP 18: Papers in Optimality Theory*: 439–470.
Selkirk, Elisabeth. 2000. The interaction of constraints on prosodic phrasing. In *Prosody: Theory and Experiment*, Merle Horne (ed.), 231–261. Dordrecht: Kluwer.
Truckenbrodt, Hubert. 1995. Phonological Phrases: Their Relation to Syntax, Focus and Prominence. Ph.D. dissertation, MIT.
Truckenbrodt, Hubert. 1999. On the relation between syntactic phrases and phonological phrases. *Linguistic Inquiry* 30: 219–255.
Truckenbrodt, Hubert. 2005. A short report on intonation phrase boundaries in German. *Linguistische Berichte* 203: 273–296.
van der Spuy, Andrew. 1993. Dislocated noun phrases in Nguni. *Lingua* 90: 335–355.
van der Wal, Jenneke. 2009. Word Order and Information Structure in Makhuwa-Enahara. Ph.D. dissertation, University of Leiden. Utrecht: LOT.
Walusimbi, Livingstone. 1996. *Relative Clauses in Luganda*. Köln: Rüdiger Köppe.
Wedgwood, Daniel. 2007. Identifying inferences in focus. In *On Information Structure, Meaning and Form* [Linguistik Aktuell/Linguistics Today 100], Kerstin Schwabe & Susanne Winkler (eds), 207–228. Amsterdam: John Benjamins.
Zerbian, Sabine. 2006. Expression of Information Structure in the Bantu Language Northern Sotho. *ZAS Papers in Linguistics* 45.

The cleft pronoun and cleft clause in English

Matthew Reeve
University College London

In this paper I argue against both 'specificational' and 'expletive' analyses of English clefts. I provide new evidence that the cleft pronoun *it* is non-expletive, and that the cleft clause is interpreted as a discontinuous definite description with *it*, as under specificational analyses. On the other hand, I argue that specificational analyses are mistaken in positing a *syntactic* modification relationship between the cleft clause and *it*. Rather, the evidence shows that the cleft clause behaves in all relevant ways as if it is a syntactic modifier of the clefted XP.

Keywords: cleft constructions; relative clauses; copular sentences; definite descriptions.

1. Introduction

The English cleft construction is illustrated in (1a), and terminologically analysed in (1b):

(1) a. [It] [was] [John] [that Mary saw].
    b. pronoun – copula – clefted XP – cleft clause

In the generative literature, clefts have received two main types of analysis. One approach, which I will call the *specificational* approach, takes the cleft pronoun and the cleft clause to form a discontinuous definite description, and thus claims that clefts are syntactically equivalent in some sense to specificational sentences (in the sense of Higgins 1973) such as (2) (e.g. Akmajian 1970; Wirth 1978; Percus 1997):

(2) The one that Mary saw was John.

The second approach, which I will call the *expletive* approach, takes the cleft pronoun to have no semantic content, and thus takes the cleft clause to be directly combined syntactically and/or semantically with the clefted XP (e.g. Chomsky 1977; Delahunty 1982; É. Kiss 1998).

In this paper, I will present new evidence for an analysis essentially parallel to that of Hedberg (2000), and illustrated in (3):[1]

(3)

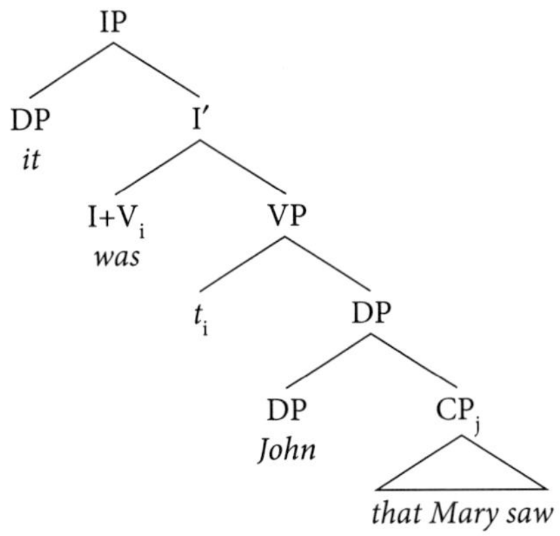

Under this analysis, the cleft clause is a relative clause adjoined to the maximal projection of the clefted XP. Thus, the analysis differs from other specificational analyses in that the cleft clause is a syntactic modifier of the clefted XP rather than of the cleft pronoun. On the other hand, in Section 2 I will provide evidence that the cleft pronoun *it* is non-expletive, which suggests that clefts are in fact semantically equivalent to specificational sentences such as (2), as proposed by analysts such as Percus (1997).[2] In Section 3, I will argue that previous specificational analyses are incorrect in treating the cleft clause as a relative extraposed from the surface subject, whether the extraposition relation is derived by movement (as in Percus) or licensed via some interpretive principle applying at LF (as suggested by Hedberg 1990).

1. In fact I argue in Reeve (2010) that the cleft clause undergoes obligatory extraposition to VP, which makes the present analysis closer to Hedberg's earlier analysis (Hedberg 1990). However, since the question of whether the cleft clause extraposes is not crucial to the arguments in this paper, I omit further discussion of it here.

2. A reviewer raises an important question which I cannot deal with in detail here for reasons of space: namely, whether, if the cleft pronoun is non-expletive, it is referential (individual-denoting) or predicative (property-denoting). In principle, a specificational analysis of clefts could adopt either of these positions, though in the recent literature it seems to be more common to treat *it* as an inverted predicate (e.g. Percus 1997; Adger & Ramchand 2003; Den Dikken 2006). In Reeve (2012), on the other hand, I follow Heycock and Kroch (1999) in taking specificational sentences to be a kind of equative, which means that cleft *it* must be referential. I refer the reader to the above sources for arguments for this position.

2. What specificational analyses get right: The non-expletive status of *it*

2.1 Syntactic arguments

It has often been noted that cleft *it* may alternate with demonstrative pronouns, as in (4a). This is not possible with other uses of *it*, such as raising *it*, 'weather' *it* and extraposition *it*, as in (4b–d) respectively (e.g. Bolinger 1972; Hedberg 1990, 2000):

(4) a. It/this/that was John that I saw.
b. It/*this/*that seems to me that you're wrong.
c. It/*this/*that is snowing.
d. It/*this/*that was clear that we were wrong.

This is a strong argument in favour of treating cleft pronouns as non-expletive: if demonstrative pronouns could be expletives, then we would expect them to be possible in (4b–d) as well as (4a). There are several further arguments in favour of treating cleft pronouns as non-expletive. First, they may control PRO, as in (5a).[3] This is also possible with 'weather' and extraposition *it*, as in (5b–c), but not with raising *it* and existential expletive *there*, as in (5d–e) (e.g. Chomsky 1981:323; Bennis 1986):

(5) a. It_i was the furniture that annoyed John on Sunday [despite PRO_i being the décor the day before].
b. It_i sometimes rains [after PRO_i snowing].
c. It_i was clear [after PRO_i having been explained to us] that we were wrong.
d. It_i seemed that John was wrong [without it/*PRO_i seeming that Mary was right].
e. $There_i$ were three men in the garden [without there/*PRO_i being any reason why].

---

3. Huber (2002), cited by den Dikken (this volume), claims that cleft *it* cannot control PRO, providing examples such as the following:

(i) ???It_i is Peter who is coming without PRO_i being a nice man.
(ii) ???[The murderer]$_i$ is the butler without PRO_i being a bad guy.
(iii) ???[Who murdered John]$_i$ was the butler without PRO_i being a bad guy.

But these do not show that *it* cannot control, since the corresponding sentences with *it* instead of PRO are also ill-formed, as shown in (iv–vi):

(iv) *It is Peter who is coming without it being a nice man.
(v) *[The murderer] is the butler without it being a bad guy.
(vi) *[Who murdered John] was the butler without it being a bad guy.

Since *without*-gerunds can generally have either a PRO or an overt DP subject, this suggests that the clefts in (i–iii) are ill-formed for reasons independent of whether *it* can control PRO.

Chomsky takes the possibility of (5b) to indicate that 'weather' *it* is in fact a 'quasi-argument' rather than an expletive. Bennis, noting the possibility of sentences like (5c) in Dutch, argues that extraposition pronouns are referential. Thus, since clefts pattern with referential DPs and quasi-arguments rather than with expletives, the data in (5) are further evidence for treating cleft pronouns as non-expletive.

A third argument for the non-expletive status of cleft pronouns comes from V2 Germanic languages, which in some cases allow *it*-like pronouns to be dropped if they are not in initial position. Thus, Vikner (1995) notes that in German, 'weather' and extraposition *es* are obligatory if they appear initially, as in (6a, c), but extraposition *es* is optional for many speakers if it does not appear initially, as in (6d):

(6) a. *Es regnete.*
it rained

b. *Gestern regnete *(es).*
yesterday rained it

c. *Es ist gut, dass du gekommen bist.*
it is good that you come are

d. *Natürlich ist (es) gut, dass du gekommen bist.*
of-course is it good that you come are

Icelandic is more liberal: although it requires 'weather' and extraposition *það* initially, the extraposition pronoun is optional under inversion, while the 'weather' pronoun must be omitted:

(7) a. *Það rigndi.* (Icelandic)
it rained

a′. *Í gær rigndi (*það).*
yesterday rained it

b. *Það er gott að þú ert kominn.*
it is good that you are come

b′. *Að sjálfsögðu er (það) gott að þú ert kominn.*
of-course is it good that you are come

Interestingly, in both languages cleft pronouns are obligatory whether or not they appear initially, as shown in (8a–b) for German and (8c–d) for Icelandic:

(8) a. *Es war* DIESER WAGEN, *den sie kaufen wollte.*
it was this car which she to-buy wanted
'It was THIS CAR that she wanted to buy.'

b. *Gestern war *(es)* DIESER WAGEN, *den sie kaufen wollte.*
yesterday was it this car which she to-buy wanted

c. *Það var* JÓN *sem ég hitti í bænum.*
it was Jón that I saw in the-town
'It was JÓN that I saw in town.'

d. *Í gær var *(það)* JÓN *sem ég hitti í bænum.*
yesterday was it Jón that I saw in the-town
(Peter Svenonius, p.c.)

Rizzi (1986: 541) identifies German as a language which allows *pro* only for non-arguments, and Icelandic as a language which allows *pro* for both non-arguments and quasi-arguments; neither language allows *pro* for referential DPs. If Vikner is correct in claiming that *pro* appears in all those cases in which the pronoun is apparently optional, then the data in (7–8) show that cleft pronouns pattern with referential DPs.

Italian clefts provide further evidence for the non-expletive status of cleft pronouns. Rizzi (1986) identifies Italian as a language which allows *pro* for all types of DP: thus, the fact that *pro* appears in clefts does not say anything about whether it is an expletive or not:

(9) *È Gianni che a rotto il vaso.*
is Gianni that has broken the vase
'It is Gianni that has broken the vase.'

There is a construction, however, which disallows referential *pro* but allows non-argument and quasi-argument *pro*: namely, the so-called 'Aux-to-Comp' construction illustrated in (10a). As (10b–d) show, *pro* may appear in the subject position of the embedded clause, but only if it is not a true referential DP:

(10) a. *Ritengo [aver Ria risolto molti problemi].*
believe.1.SG to-have Ria solved many problems
'I believe Ria to have solved many problems.'

b. *Ritengo essere* pro *probabile che S.*
believe.1.SG to-be *pro* likely that S.
'I believe it to be likely that S.'

c. *Ritengo essere* pro *troppo tardi per S.*
believe.1.SG to-be *pro* too late for S.
'I believe it to be too late for S.'

d. **Ritengo essere* pro *simpatico.*
believe.1.SG to-be *pro* nice
'I believe him to be nice.'

As expected if cleft pronouns are referential, they also cannot easily appear in this construction (Vieri Samek-Lodovici, p.c.):

(11) ??*Ritengo essere* pro *Gianni che ha rotto il vaso.*
believe.1.SG to-be *pro* Gianni that has broken the vase
'I believe it to be Gianni that broke the vase.'

A final piece of evidence for the non-expletive status of cleft pronouns, suggested by an anonymous *Lingua* reviewer, concerns 'experiencer blocking' in French, illustrated in (12) (e.g. Chomsky 1995: 305). (12b) shows that a referential DP may not raise across an experiencer; on the other hand, Bošković (2002: 196–7) notes that 'raising' *il* may do so, as shown in (12c):

(12) a. *Deux soldats semblent manquer à la caserne.*
two soldiers seem to-miss at the barracks
'Two soldiers seem to be missing at the barracks.'

b. **Deux soldats semblent au général manquer à la* caserne.
two soldiers seem to-the general to-miss at the barracks
'Two soldiers seem to the general to be missing at the barracks.'

c. *Il semble au général y avoir deux soldats manquants*
it seem to-the general there to-have two soldiers missing
à la caserne.
at the barracks
'There seem to the general to be two soldiers missing at the barracks.'

Once again, cleft pronouns pattern with referential DPs: cleft *ce* may not raise across an experiencer (Nausicaa Pouscoulous, p.c.):

(13) a. *Ce semble être Jean que Marie a vu.*
it seems to-be Jean that Marie has seen
'It seems to be Jean that Marie saw.'

b. **Ce semble au général être Jean que Marie a vu.*
it seems to-the general to-be Jean that Marie has seen
'It seems to the general to be Jean that Marie saw.'

Thus, there are several pieces of syntactic evidence suggesting that cleft pronouns are non-expletive, as claimed by specificational analyses. Such evidence argues against analyses such as that of É. Kiss (1998), for whom the expletivehood of cleft *it* is crucial.

2.2 Interpretative arguments

As many authors have noted (e.g. Akmajian 1970; Wirth 1978; Percus 1997), the claim made by specificational analyses that the cleft pronoun and the cleft clause make up a discontinuous definite description correctly predicts that they will show the same presuppositional effects as specificational sentences with a definite description subject. Thus, both types of sentences give rise to an existential presupposition, as shown by the fact that they may not focus a bare negative quantifier (e.g. Percus 1997; Rooth 1999), and an exhaustive interpretation of the focus, as shown by the fact that they disallow particles such as *even* in the matrix clause (e.g. É. Kiss 1998). In this respect they contrast with their non-copular equivalents, whether the focus is moved or not:[4]

(14) a. *It was NOTHING that he drank.
b. *The thing that he drank was nothing.
c. He drank NOTHING.
d. NOTHING, he drank.

(15) a. It was ??also/*even THE SHERRY that John drank.
b. The thing that John drank was *also/*even the sherry.
c. John also/even drank THE SHERRY.
d. Also/even THE SHERRY, John drank.

Under specificational analyses, the presuppositions of clefts thus reduce to the definiteness of the subject, since definite descriptions give rise to existential presuppositions, and, in combination with the semantics of specificational sentences, exhaustivity of the focus.

Expletive analyses face more difficulty in capturing the presuppositions of clefts. There have, however, been several proposals. Halvorsen (1978) and Delahunty (1982) argue that the presuppositions are in fact implicatures, but essentially stipulate them as properties of clefts. Similarly, Rochemont's (1986: 133) Cleft Focus Principle simply stipulates that a cleft focus has presuppositional properties. É. Kiss (1998), on the other hand, proposes an analysis which attempts to relate certain presuppositional effects (specifically, exhaustivity) to the properties of a focus-related functional head F in the left periphery. Under her analysis of clefts, the clefted XP moves to the specifier of F. F bears

4. A reviewer finds (14d) 'totally ungrammatical' and (15d) 'very unnatural'. As regards (14d), I accept that bare negative quantifiers seem worse in fronted position than, for example, referential DPs, but I think their acceptability increases if the context in which the sentence is uttered contains a sentence which is parallel in form; for example:

(i) A: Sue drank the vodka.
B: No, THE WATER, she drank.
C: No, NOTHING, she drank!

As for (15d), I agree that the version with *also* is somewhat unnatural (though once again improved by putting it in an appropriate context), but the example with *even* seems perfectly fine, which provides the required contrast with (15a).

the features [±contrastive] and [±exhaustive], whose settings vary according to the head selecting F. É. Kiss argues that F in clefts is specified as [±contrastive, +exhaustive], whereas in other environments F is [±exhaustive]. This accounts for the obligatory exhaustivity property of clefts, as well as the fact that clefts may generally be used to express either new information focus or contrastive focus. Although É. Kiss's approach can capture the differences between clefts and non-clefts with respect to exhaustivity and contrastivity, it does not explain why clefts should share all of the relevant properties with specificational sentences. Although she does not provide an analysis of specificational sentences, it seems undesirable to account for their interpretative properties by assigning F particular feature values. First, it is clear that obligatory exhaustivity in specificational sentences is tied to the particular choice of surface subject. Thus, a definite subject, as in (16a), gives rise to exhaustivity of the focus. On the other hand, if an indefinite subject is used, as in (16b), an exhaustive interpretation is not required (e.g. Den Dikken 2006: 82):

(16) a. The one that Mary hit was Bill.
b. One person that Mary hit was Bill.

Tying exhaustivity in (16a) to a property of a focus head would therefore not only duplicate information already derivable from the definiteness of the subject, it would not distinguish correctly between (16a) and (16b) without stipulation. This problem for É. Kiss's analysis is even more serious given that exhaustivity is dependent on the type of subject even in clefts. As noted by Davidse (2000), not only demonstratives but also 'existential' *there* may appear as the subject of clefts:

(17) There's JOHN who's causing us trouble.

Interestingly, unlike in *it*-clefts, the focus in *there*-clefts is not obligatorily exhaustive, as shown by the fact that *there*-clefts allow focus-sensitive particles:[5]

(18) There's also/even JOHN who's causing us trouble.

5. For (18) to be natural with *even*, it must be put in a context in which various people who are causing us trouble have already been listed; for example:

(i) Sue's causing us trouble, Bill's causing us trouble, and there's even JOHN who's causing us trouble!

Thus, clefts behave in a parallel fashion to specificational sentences in that the exhaustivity of the focus depends on the definiteness or otherwise of the surface subject. A specificational analysis is thus naturally equipped to handle these facts. Under É. Kiss's approach, on the other hand, exhaustivity is tied to the position occupied by the clefted XP. Since the properties of F are entirely determined by the category it is selected by (I in clefts), it is not clear how the dependence of presuppositions on the subject can be accounted for.

3. What specificational analyses get wrong: The behaviour of the cleft clause

3.1 Introduction

In this section I will show that previous specificational analyses of clefts are incorrect in positing an extraposition relation between the cleft clause and the cleft pronoun. There are two ways in which this has been implemented. Most authors claim that the extraposition relation is movement-derived: that is, the cleft clause originates inside the surface subject and moves rightwards, adjoining to some clausal projection (e.g. Akmajian 1970; Wirth 1978; Percus 1997). By contrast, Hedberg (1990) claims that the extraposition relation between the cleft clause and the cleft pronoun is mediated by Culicover and Rochemont's (1990) Complement Principle, which allows extraposed relative clauses to be base-generated in their surface positions, but which requires strict locality between them and their antecedents. The evidence I will present in this section shows that neither position can be correct. Rather, as expected under the analysis in (3), the cleft clause behaves as if its antecedent is the clefted XP rather than *it*.

3.2 The cleft clause as a restrictive relative clause

It will first be useful to establish that, contrary to expletive analyses, the cleft clause is a type of restrictive relative clause. (This is a position also taken by proponents of specificational analyses.) First, both cleft clauses and restrictive relatives feature an alternation between an overt relative operator, an overt complementiser *that*, and a null complementiser, an alternation which does not appear in other constructions involving A'-movement to SpecCP:

(19) a. It was THE VODKA which/that/0 Boris drank.
b. I bought the vodka which/that/0 Boris drank.
c. What/*that/*0 did Boris drink?
d. I drank what/*that/*0 Boris drank.
e. The vodka, *which/*that/0 Boris drank.

Also, the overt relative operators that can appear in restrictive (and non-restrictive) relatives can also appear in cleft clauses (with the exception of *why*), while the other constructions make use of a different set of *wh*-operators:[6]

(20) a. It was BORIS who bought the vodka.
b. I know the man who bought the vodka.
c. It was MOSCOW where Boris bought the vodka.
d I have been to the city where Boris bought the vodka.
e. It was TOMORROW MORNING when Boris was hoping to buy the vodka.
f. I remember the time when Boris bought the vodka.
g. *It was FROM A SHOT GLASS how Boris drank the vodka.
h. *I don't know the way how Boris drank the vodka.
i. *It was BECAUSE HE LIKED IT why Boris bought the vodka.
j. I know the reason why Boris bought the vodka.

In addition, cleft clauses, just like restrictive relatives, show 'anti-*that*-trace' effects, which are not found in complement CPs (Cottell 2002: 90):

(21) a. It was BORIS that *t* bought the vodka.
b. I know the man that *t* bought the vodka.
c. *Boris, you said that *t* bought the vodka.

Finally, clefts show the extraction properties that are expected if the cleft clause is a relative clause, rather than a selected clause containing an A′-moved XP in the left periphery, as in É. Kiss (1998). If the cleft clause is a relative clause, we expect it to act as a strong island (and hence to ban both argument and adjunct extraction), either because of (whatever is responsible for) the Complex NP Condition or the Adjunct Condition. Under É. Kiss's analysis, on the other hand, we expect the cleft clause to behave as a weak island (banning adjunct but not argument extraction), parallel to CPs in which *wh*-movement has taken place. As shown in (22), both argument and adjunct extraction from the cleft clause are ungrammatical; that is, the cleft clause behaves as a strong island, as expected if it is a relative clause:

(22) a. ?*Which drink$_i$ was it Boris [that bought t_i]?
b. *How$_i$ was it Boris [that bought the drink t_i]?

There are thus good reasons to treat cleft clauses as parallel to restrictive relatives.

6. As noted by a reviewer, the examples in (20g–i), which are labelled ungrammatical, are not necessarily bad if read as right-dislocation sentences (i.e. with comma intonation after the clefted XP). Such sentences, however, arguably have a quite different analysis. (See Reeve 2012 for some comments on this.)

3.3 The clefted XP as the antecedent of the cleft clause[7]

3.3.1 *Locality*

One well-known property of extraposed relative clauses is that they must surface locally to their antecedents (e.g. Ross 1967; Baltin 1981; Culicover & Rochemont 1990). For concreteness, I will adopt Culicover and Rochemont's (1990) Complement Principle as the relevant locality condition:[8]

(23) *Complement Principle* (ibid.: 41)
β is a *potential complement* of α ($\alpha, \beta = X^{max}$) [i.e. β is an extraposed phrase which can take α as its antecedent – MJR], only if α and β are in a government relation.

Importantly, the Complement Principle applies at 'S-Structure' (i.e. to overt rather than to underlying representations). This means that what is crucial for determining the antecedent of a relative is the surface position of the antecedent, and not its underlying position. Formulated as in (23), the Complement Principle requires relative clauses extraposed from surface objects (henceforth 'object relatives') to adjoin to VP, and allows relative clauses extraposed from surface subjects (henceforth 'subject relatives') to adjoin to IP or VP.

VP-ellipsis has often been used as a diagnostic for the surface position of extraposed clauses (e.g. Baltin 1981; Reinhart 1980; Culicover & Rochemont 1990). Baltin (1981) noted that there is an asymmetry between extraposed subject and object relatives in that subject relatives may be stranded by VP-ellipsis, while

7. Of course, on the face of it the cleft clause cannot be both restrictive and a modifier of the clefted XP, since (i) the clefted XP can be a proper name, and these cannot normally be restrictively modified, and (ii) the clefted XP can be a PP, CP, AP or AdvP (e.g. Heggie 1988), and these certainly cannot be restrictively modified. It is important to clarify that what I am claiming is that the cleft clause adjoins to the clefted XP, not that it modifies it semantically. As hinted by the parallel drawn with specificational sentences, I claim in Reeve (2012) that the cleft clause is a restrictive modifier of *it* (or rather its implied null nominal head) semantically.

8. The relevant ancillary definitions are given in (i–v):

(i) α *governs* β if α c-commands β and there is no δ, δ a barrier for β, that excludes α.

(ii) α *c-commands* β iff α does not dominate β and there is no δ that dominates α and not β.

(iii) δ is a *barrier* for α iff (i) δ is an X^{max} that dominates β and (ii) δ is not θ-governed (directly θ-marked).

(iv) δ ($\delta = X^{max}$) *excludes* α if no segment of δ dominates α.

(v) δ ($\delta = X^{max}$) *dominates* α only if every segment of δ contains α.

object relatives may not be. As shown in (24c), cleft clauses pattern with object relatives rather than subject relatives (e.g. Delahunty 1982):

(24) a. Although not many people would ride with Fred who knew just him, some would ___ who knew his brother.
b. *Although he didn't call people up who are from Boston, he did ___ who are from New York.
c. *Although it probably wasn't John who cooked the stew, it might have been ___ who baked the cake.

Another argument from locality comes from cases where a subject undergoes A-movement to a higher clause.[9] In this case the extraposed relative must surface in the same clause as the raised subject, as shown by the fact that the matrix passive *by*-phrase in (25) must precede the extraposed relative:

(25) a. A man was believed to have arrived that I had insulted.
b. ?A man was believed to have arrived by everybody that I had insulted.
c. *A man was believed to have arrived that I had insulted by everybody.

The same point can be made using binding: the Condition C violation in (26a) is obviated when the subject raises as in (26b), suggesting that the extraposed clause surfaces in the matrix clause, outside the c-command domain of the pronoun:

(26) a. ??It seemed to her_i that a man had arrived that $Mary_i$ knew from school.
b. A man seemed to her_i to have arrived that $Mary_i$ knew from school.

If the cleft clause is extraposed from *it*, then we expect it to pattern with the cases above. In fact, it does not: in (27) it must apparently remain in the embedded clause:

(27) a. ??It was believed to be John by everybody that Mary saw.
b. It was believed to be John that Mary saw by everybody.
c. ?*It seemed to her_i that it was John that $Mary_i$ saw.
d. ?*It seemed to her_i to be John that $Mary_i$ saw.

Finally, Culicover and Rochemont (1990) note that VP-fronting may take along extraposed object relatives but not extraposed subject relatives.

9. A reviewer disagrees with some of the judgements in (25–27), which potentially provides a serious argument against my analysis. I think the matter of potential speaker variation here deserves serious consideration, but unfortunately this cannot be provided within the confines of this paper, and I therefore leave it for future research.

(28) a. *They said that a man would come in who had lived in Boston, and come in who had lived in Boston a man did.
b. They said he would call people up who are from Boston, and call people up who are from Boston he did.

Once again, cleft clauses pattern with object relatives: as Hedberg (1990) notes, they may be taken along by VP-fronting;

(29) I said it'd be a conservative who'd win, and a conservative who won it certainly was.

3.3.2 *Restrictions on predicational clefts*
Under the analysis in (3), the cleft clause is a restrictive relative syntactically modifying the clefted XP. We thus expect the types of restrictions that hold between restrictive relatives and their head nouns to hold between the cleft clause and the clefted XP. One of these is that there must be a gap in the relative clause corresponding syntactically and semantically with the head NP. Thus (30b), unlike (30a) fails because the selectional restrictions imposed by *went* on the gap could not be satisfied by (*the*) *cat*:

(30) a. the cat that I saw ___
b. *the cat that I went ___

There is some evidence that clefts show restrictions of this type, which is not expected under specificational analyses such as Percus (1997), in which the cleft clause is a relative clause modifying *it*. It has been observed that as well as the 'specificational' function of clefts, in which the clefted XP provides a 'value' for a 'variable' in the cleft clause, it is also possible for clefts to have a predicational interpretation, in which the clefted XP is predicated of the subject *it* (see, e.g. Jespersen 1927; Declerck 1983; Hedberg 1990, 2000):

(31) a. It was an interesting meeting that I went to last night. (Declerck 1983)
b. It was a kid who beat John. (Han & Hedberg 2008)

Analyses such as Percus (1997) would correctly lead us to expect predicational interpretations of (31a, b) to be possible; however, they do not account for the fact that (32a) is impossible with the meaning in (32b):

(32) a. *It is feline that I am pointing at.
b. The thing that I am pointing at is feline.

Under Percus's analysis, we might expect (32a) to be derivable by cleft clause extraposition from the structure underlying (32b). Under the present analysis,

(32a) is ruled out, because the gap position in the cleft clause does not correspond in the relevant sense to the clefted XP. That is, (32a) is ill-formed for the same reason that (33) is:

(33) *I am pointing at feline.

3.3.3 *The features of the relative operator*

There is also evidence that the clefted XP restricts the possible *wh*-operators in the cleft clause, which is unexpected under Percus's (1997) analysis. As noted by Han and Hedberg (2008), the *wh*-operator must agree with the clefted XP for the features of number and humanness, as shown by the example in (34a). This is expected if the cleft clause is a relative modifying the clefted XP, since the same restrictions hold of relatives, as in (34b):

(34) a. It is THE TEACHERS who/*which are/*is tired.
b. The teachers who/*which are/*is tired will not be coming in.

On the other hand, it is clear that *it* is singular, since it triggers singular agreement on the copula. If the cleft clause were a modifier of *it*, then the *wh*-operator should always be singular. As for humanness, clefts differ from other specificational sentences, which allow a non-human *wh*-operator with a human postcopular DP, as shown in (35):

(35) a. The thing which/that bothers me is John.
b. What bothers me is John.
c. *the man which bothers me
d. *It is John which bothers me.

This therefore provides evidence that the cleft clause syntactically modifies the clefted XP, rather than *it* as would be expected under most specificational analyses.

3.3.4 *Reduced cleft clauses*

As expected if cleft clauses are relatives, they can be 'reduced':

(36) a. the man (who was) sitting outside
b. It was John (who was) sitting outside.

Subject relatives differ from object relatives, however, in that they do not tolerate reduction, as shown in (37) (e.g. Culicover & Rochemont 1990: 32 Footnote 23):

(37) a. *A man came into the room now sitting outside.
b. I saw a man yesterday now sitting outside.

Thus, clefts pattern once again with object relatives rather than subject relatives, as expected under the present analysis, but not under alternatives such as Hedberg (1990) and Percus (1997), under which the cleft clause is an extraposed subject relative.

3.3.5 *Evidence for a raising structure*

It is well known that specificational sentences, including clefts, show 'connectivity' effects: that is, the clefted XP behaves with respect to certain phenomena as if it is in the 'gap' position in the cleft clause. Thus, in (38a–d) the clefted XP shows connectivity for binding principles A–C, variable binding, intensionality and quantifier scope respectively:

(38) a. It is proud of himself$_i$/*him$_i$/*John$_i$ that he$_i$ seems to be.
b. It is his$_i$ finals that no student$_i$ enjoys.
c. It is a unicorn that John seeks. [can mean 'not a particular unicorn']
d. It was a chicken that every dog ate.

These effects are replicated in pseudoclefts, as shown in (39):

(39) a. What he$_i$ is is proud of himself$_i$/*him$_i$/*John$_i$.
b. What no student$_i$ enjoys is his$_i$ finals.
c. What John seeks is a unicorn.
d. What every dog ate was a chicken.

There are cases, however, in which clefts show connectivity effects but pseudoclefts do not. Thus, in (40a), *every dog* can take scope over *a chicken*, a reading which is not possible in (41a). This is also possible in (40b) with a distributive reading of *a different chicken* (i.e. no two dogs ate the same chicken), but not in (41b). Finally, the idiom *keep track of* can be split in (40c) but not in (41c):

(40) a. It was every dog that ate a chicken.
b. It was a different chicken that every dog ate.
c. It's careful track that she's keeping of her expenses.

(41) a. What ate a chicken was every dog.
b. What every dog ate was a different chicken.
c. *What she is keeping of her expenses is careful track.

Since it is generally agreed that connectivity effects in pseudoclefts are to be accounted for by means other than movement of the postcopular XP out of the surface subject, this suggests that the connectivity effects in clefts that do not hold in pseudoclefts are due to the possibility of movement of the clefted XP. This is expected if the cleft clause is a restrictive relative modifying the clefted XP, since it has been argued that restrictive relatives allow a 'raising' analysis under which the head NP originates inside the relative and moves to its surface position. Under Percus's analysis, however, it is not expected that the clefted XP can originate inside the cleft clause.

Another piece of evidence for raising comes from clefts in which the clefted XP receives an obligatorily contrastive reading. Thus, compare DP-clefts, which can either answer a *wh*-question or be used contrastively, with AP-clefts, which only allow the latter use (Heggie 1988):

(42) a. Who did Mary hit? It was John that Mary hit.
b. I think that Mary hit Bill. No, it was John that Mary hit.

(43) a. What colour are her eyes? #It's green that her eyes are.
b. Her eyes are green. No, it's blue that her eyes are, not green.

It is a well-known generalisation that in many languages, A'-moved foci differ from unmoved foci in that they receive an obligatory contrastive reading (e.g. É. Kiss 1998; Molnár 2006). Thus, this suggests that AP-clefts require a raising derivation, as has in fact already been argued by Pinkham and Hankamer (1975).

3.3.6 *Evidence that the clefted XP c-commands into the cleft clause*

In some cases, we find connectivity effects in pseudoclefts but not in the equivalent clefts. Thus, while a negative polarity item in postcopular position can be licensed by negation inside the subject in pseudoclefts, as in (42a), the equivalent cleft in (42b) is ungrammatical. Similarly, while a postcopular pronoun coreferential with an R-expression inside the subject is possible in pseudoclefts, the equivalent cleft requires a reflexive rather than a pronoun, as shown in (42c–d):

(42) a. What I don't have is any bread.
b. *It's any bread that I don't have.
c. (The one) who $Bill_i$ asked Sue to wash was $himself_i$/?him_i.
d. It was *him_i/$himself_i$ that $Bill_i$ asked Sue to wash.

Interestingly, as pointed out by Heycock and Kroch (2002) for NPIs, 'inverse pseudoclefts' and fronted topics contrast with canonical pseudoclefts in this way, as shown in (43a–b). (43c–d) show that the same is true of a pronoun coreferential with an R-expression:

(43) a. *Any bread is what I don't have.
b. *I bought lots of textbooks, but any novels, I didn't buy.
c. $Himself_i$/*he_i/*him_i was who $Bill_i$ asked Sue to wash.
d. $Himself_i$/*him_i, $Bill_i$ asked Sue to wash.

They attribute the unacceptability of (43a, b) to an anti-c-command requirement, noting that the effect disappears if the NPI does not c-command the licenser, as in (44a–b). The same effect is found with pronouns, as shown in (44c–d):

(44) a. A doctor with any real knowledge of acupuncture was what wasn't available.
b. We found various doctors, but a doctor who knew anything about acupuncture, we couldn't find.

c. A picture of him_i was what $Bill_i$ asked Sue to buy.
d. $Bill_i$ asked John to buy a book about him_i, but a picture of him_i, $Bill_i$ asked Sue to buy.

Clefts behave in exactly the same way as inverse pseudoclefts and topics, as shown in (45):

(45) a. It was a doctor with any real knowledge of acupuncture that wasn't available.
b. It was a picture of him_i that $Bill_i$ asked Sue to buy.

The contrast between (42b, d) and (45a, b) suggests that the clefted XP at some point c-commands into the cleft clause.

3.3.7 *Evidence for a 'matching' derivation*

It has been argued that restrictive relatives are potentially ambiguous between a raising derivation and a derivation in which the head NP is base-generated in its surface position and associated with an operator in the relative clause (sometimes called a 'matching' derivation) (e.g. Carlson 1977; Sauerland 1998; Aoun & Li 2003). The evidence for this is based on 'anti-connectivity' effects which occur when the relative contains an overt relative operator as opposed to an overt complementiser:

(46) a. ?*The picture of $himself_i$ which $John_i$ painted is impressive.
b. ?*The picture of his_i mother which every boy_i painted *t* in art class was impressive.
c. I phoned the two patients who every doctor will examine.
d. ?*The careful track which she's keeping of her expenses pleases me.

These authors argue that the presence of the relative operator blocks the head NP from being able to originate in the relative clause.

Since the present analysis of clefts takes the cleft clause to be a restrictive relative whose antecedent is the clefted XP, we expect a matching derivation of clefts to be possible alongside a raising derivation. Indeed, the 'blocking' effect seen in (46) is also found in clefts: the relative operator *who* in (47a) blocks the inverse scope reading, and the relative operator *which* in (47b) blocks the idiomatic reading (compare the acceptable (40c)):

(47) a. It's two patients who every doctor will examine.
b. ?*It was careful track which she kept of her expenses.

The claim that clefts are derivationally ambiguous in this way has in fact already been made by Pinkham and Hankamer (1975), though they do not relate this to the corresponding ambiguity in restrictive relatives. However, they argue that only DP-clefts allow matching alongside raising; all other clefts require raising. The present analysis, however, makes a slightly different prediction, since the possibility of a matching derivation for a restrictive relative relies on the availability of an appropriate relative operator. Thus we only expect clefts to allow matching if the cleft clause could potentially contain an appropriate relative operator. This appears to be correct.

The main piece of evidence Pinkham and Hankamer present for a matching derivation in DP-clefts but not in other clefts involves subextraction. The logic is that if a proper subconstituent of a clefted XP can move, then the clefted XP cannot itself have moved previously, as this would violate the Freezing Principle (e.g. Wexler & Culicover 1980). Thus, they attribute the contrast between the DP-cleft in (48b) and the PP-cleft in (48d) to the fact that DP-clefts, but not PP-clefts, allow base-generation of the clefted XP in its surface position:

(48) a. It was a picture of Marx that he decorated his door with.
b. ?Who was it a picture of that he decorated his door with?
c. It was with a picture of Marx that he decorated his door.
d. *Who was it with a picture of that he decorated his door?

The present analysis predicts, pace Pinkham and Hankamer, that subextraction should be possible from PP-clefts which allow a *wh*-operator in the cleft clause, since this forces a matching derivation. Although PP-clefts with *wh*-operators are somewhat awkward, some prepositions allow them more easily than others, as shown in (49):

(49) a. ?It was in Paris where she stayed.
b. ?It was on this shelf where he put his trophies.
c. *It was with John which/who/where she went to Paris.
d. *It was to the restaurant where she wanted to go.

As expected, those PP-clefts in which *wh*-operators are relatively acceptable also allow extraction of the DP complement of the preposition, in contrast to those in which *wh*-operators are unacceptable:

(50) a. Which city was it in that she first met John?
b. Which shelf was it on that he put his trophies?
c. ??Who was it with that she went to the cinema?
d. *Where was it to that she wanted to go?

The present analysis also predicts, along with Pinkham and Hankamer's does, that AP-clefts disallow subextraction, since no overt relative operator is possible in AP-clefts:

(51) a. It was drunk on vodka *which/that he was, not drunk on slivovitz.
b. *What was it drunk on that John was?

Thus, the present analysis makes better predictions than Pinkham and Hankamer's about the types of clefts that can have matching derivations.

To summarise Sections 3.3.5–3.3.7, the evidence argues that DP-clefts, and some PP-clefts, are derivationally ambiguous in that they allow both a structure in which the clefted XP is base-generated in postcopular position, as in (52a), and a structure in which it is raised from inside the cleft clause. As discussed further in Chapter 5 of Reeve (2010), I adopt the structure in (52b), in which the clefted XP adjoins to the cleft clause CP, for the raising derivation:

(52) a.

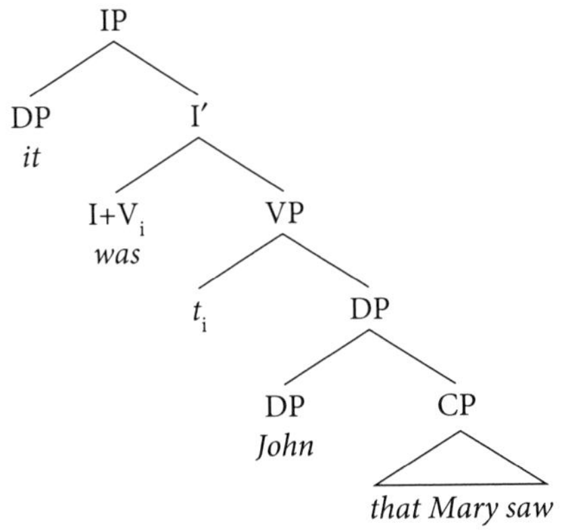

b.

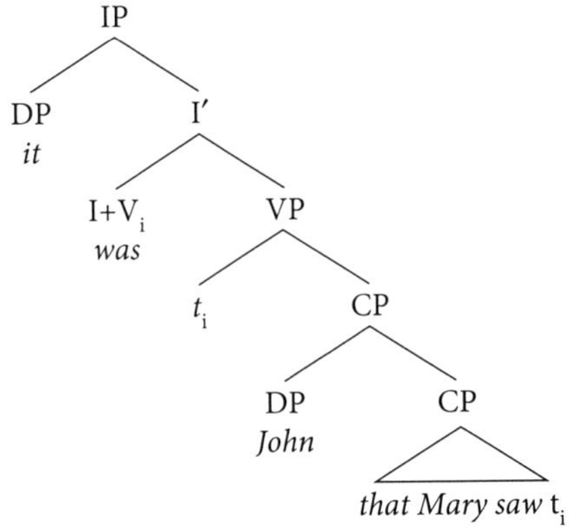

4. Conclusion

I have argued for an analysis essentially parallel to that of Hedberg (2000), on which the cleft pronoun is non-expletive and the cleft clause is a restrictive relative clause adjoined to the clefted XP. Assuming, as I argue in Reeve (2012), that the cleft is to be interpreted as a type of specificational copular sentence, this conclusion leads to an apparent problem: since the cleft clause is not underlyingly adjoined to *it*, nor is it licensed as a modifier of *it* by the Complement Principle, the question arises how it can be interpreted as restricting the reference of *it*, as would be required under a specificational interpretation. I propose a solution to this problem in Reeve (2012), in which I argue that relative clauses in general put two kinds of locality requirements on what they modify: a syntactic requirement which allows the relative to be inserted into the structure, and a thematic requirement which determines the semantic modification relation. In most cases of modification by relative clauses, these two requirements are satisfied by the same DP, but in clefts (and certain other types of sentences) they are satisfied by distinct XPs. In this paper, however, I merely leave the evidence discussed as a challenge both to proponents of specificational analyses such as Percus (1997), which correctly capture the non-expletive status of the cleft pronoun but do not capture the relation between the cleft clause and the clefted XP, and proponents of expletive analyses such as É. Kiss (1998), which are correct in claiming that the cleft clause is 'low' in the structure, but which do not capture the properties of the cleft pronoun.

References

Akmajian, Adrian. 1970. On deriving cleft sentences from pseudo-cleft sentences. *Linguistic Inquiry* 1(2): 149–168.

Aoun, Joseph & Li, Yen-hui Audrey. 2003. *Essays on the Representational and Derivational Nature of Grammar: The Diversity of Wh-Constructions*. Cambridge MA: The MIT Press.

Baltin, Mark. 1981. Strict bounding. In *The Logical Problem of Language Acquisition*, Carl Lee Baker & John J. McCarthy (eds), 257–295. Cambridge MA: The MIT Press.

Bennis, Hans. 1986. *Gaps and Dummies*. Dordrecht: Foris.

Bolinger, Dwight. 1972. A look at equations and cleft sentences. In *Studies for Einar Haugen Presented by his Friends and Colleagues*, Evelyn Scherabon Firchow, Kaaren Grimstad, Nils Hasselmo & Wayne O'Neill (eds), 96–114. The Hague: Mouton.

Bošković, Željko. 2002. A-movement and the EPP. *Syntax* 5(3): 167–218.

Chomsky, Noam. 1977. On *wh*-movement. In *Formal Syntax*, Peter Culicover, Thomas Wasow & Adrian Akmajian (eds), 71–132. New York NY: Academic Press.

Carlson, Greg N. 1977. Amount relatives. *Language* 53(3): 520–542.

Chomsky, Noam. 1981. *Lectures on Government and Binding*. Dordrecht: Foris.

Chomsky, Noam. 1995. *The Minimalist Program*. Cambridge MA: The MIT Press.

Cottell, Siobhán. 2002. The Comparative Syntax of Cleft Constructions. Ph.D. dissertation, University of Wales, Bangor.

Culicover, Peter & Rochemont, Michael. 1990. Extraposition and the complement principle. *Linguistic Inquiry* 21(1): 23–47.

Davidse, Kristin. 2000. A constructional approach to clefts. *Linguistics* 38(6): 1101–1131.

Declerck, Renaat. 1983. Predicational clefts. *Lingua* 61(1): 9–45.

Delahunty, Gerald. 1982. Topics in the synatx and semantics of English cleft sentences. Ph.D. dissertation, University of California, Irvine.
den Dikken, Marcel. 2006. *Relators and Linkers: The Syntax of Predication, Predicate Inversion, and Copulas*. Cambridge MA: The MIT Press.
den Dikken, Marcel. 2008. A cleft palette: On the landscape of cleft constructions and their syntactic derivations. Presentation at the Cleft Workshop 2008, ZAS, Berlin, 29 November 2008.
É. Kiss, Katalin. 1998. Identificational focus versus information focus. *Language* 74(2): 245–273.
Halvorsen, Per-Kristian. 1978. The Syntax and Semantics of Cleft Sentences. Ph.D. dissertation, University of Texas at Austin.
Han, Chung-hye & Hedberg, Nancy. 2008. Syntax and semantics of *it*-clefts: A Tree Adjoining Grammar analysis. *Journal of Semantics* 25(4): 345–380.
Hedberg, Nancy. 1990. The Discourse Function of Cleft Sentences in English. Ph.D. dissertation, University of Minnesota.
Hedberg, Nancy. 2000. On the referential status of clefts. *Language* 76(4): 891–920.
Heggie, Lorie. 1988. The Syntax of Copular Structures. Ph.D. dissertation, University of Southern California.
Heycock, Caroline & Kroch, Anthony. 1999. Pseudocleft connectedness: Implications for the LF interface. *Linguistic Inquiry* 30(3): 365–397.
Heycock, Caroline & Kroch, Anthony. 2002. Topic, focus, and syntactic representations. *Proceedings of WCCFL* 21: 101–125.
Higgins, Roger. 1973. The Pseudo-Cleft Construction in English. Ph.D. dissertation, MIT.
Huber, Stefan. 2002. *Es-clefts und Det-clefts: Zur Syntax, Semantik und Informationsstruktur von Spaltsätzen im Deutschen und Schwedischen*. Stockholm: Almqvist & Wiksell International.
Jespersen, Otto. 1927. *A Modern English Grammar on Historical Principles. Part III: Syntax*. Heidelberg: C. Winter.
Molnár, Valéria. 2006. On different kinds of contrast. In *The Architecture of Focus*, Valéria Molnár & Susanne Winkler (eds), 197–233. Berlin: Mouton de Gruyter.
Percus, Orin. 1997. Prying open the cleft. *Proceedings of NELS* 27: 337–351.
Pinkham, Jessie & Hankamer, Jorge. 1975. Deep and shallow clefts. *Papers from the Eleventh Regional Meeting of the Chicago Linguistic Society*, 429–450.
Reeve, Matthew. 2012. *Clefts and their Relatives*. Amsterdam. John Benjamins.
Reinhart, Tanya. 1980. The position of extraposed clauses. *Linguistic Inquiry* 11(3): 621–624.
Rizzi, Luigi. 1986. Null objects in Italian and the theory of *pro*. *Linguistic Inquiry* 17(3): 501–557.
Rochemont, Michael. 1986. *Focus in Generative Grammar* [Studies in Generative Linguistic Analysis Amsterdam: John Benjamins.
Rooth, Mats. 1999. Association with focus or association with presupposition? In *Focus: Linguistic, Cognitive, and Computational Perspectives*, Peter Bosch & Rob van der Sandt (eds), 232–244. Cambridge: Cambridge University Press.
Ross, John R. 1967. Constraints on Variables in Syntax. Ph.D. dissertation, MIT.
Sauerland, Uli. 1998. The Meaning of Chains. Ph.D. dissertation, MIT.
Svenonius, Peter. 1998. Clefts in Scandinavian. *ZAS Working Papers* 10: 163–190.
Vikner, Sten. 1995. *Verb Movement and Expletive Subjects in the Germanic Languages*. Oxford: OUP.
Wexler, Kenneth & Culicover, Peter. 1980. *Formal Principles of Language Acquisition*. Cambridge MA: The MIT Press.
Wirth, Jessica. 1978. The derivation of cleft sentences in English. *Glossa* 12: 58–81.

The morphosyntax of wolof clefts

Structure and movement

Harold Torrence
University of Kansas

This paper examines the structure and derivation of cleft clauses in the Atlantic language Wolof, which possesses distinct clefts for subjects and non-subjects. I argue that the clefts are based on two syntactically distinct copular constructions. In the subject cleft, the copula occurs with a TP-structure. In the non-subject cleft, the copula occurs with a CP-like structure. In terms of derivation, I argue that Wolof clefts involve overt movement of the clefted constituent, not base generation. I show that Wolof clefts are island-sensitive using general and Wolof-specific tests. I then present evidence from a number of reconstruction tests that converge on the conclusion that clefted items in Wolof undergo A'-movement.

Keywords: A'- movement; wh-movement; reconstruction; copula; cleft; focus; left periphery; Niger-Congo; Atlantic

1. Introduction

This paper investigates the morphosyntax and movement properties of cleft clauses in the St. Louis and Dakar varieties of Wolof, an Atlantic language of Senegal and the Gambia.[1] Wolof is of interest for the study of clefts because it possesses morphosyntactically distinct cleft clauses for subjects and non-subjects (as known from the work of Sauvageot 1965; Church 1981; Njie 1982; Robert 1986; and Kihm 1999):

---

1. Many thanks to my Wolof native speaker consultants: Mariame Sy, Khady Tamba, Mustapha Djigo, and Seynabou Ndoye, two anonymous reviewers, and to the audience at the Berlin Clefts Conference for their feedback.

(1) a. Subject Cleft[2]
Jigéén ji (mu) a lekk gato bi
woman the 3SG COP eat cake the
"It's the woman (she) who ate the cake"

b. Non-Subject Cleft
Gato bi l–a jigéen ji lekk
cake the XPL-COP woman the eat
"It's the cake that the woman ate"

In the subject cleft (1)a, the clefted subject (or the optional subject marker) immediately precedes the copula *-a*. In the non-subject cleft (1)b, an invariant expletive *l-* (Sauvageot 1965) immediately precedes the copular *-a*. The clefted constituent, *gato bi*, precedes the expletive.

The goals of this paper are twofold. First, I present a morpho-syntactic analysis of the subject and non-subject clefts and show that they have a common core. Specifically, I argue that a non-subject cleft like (1)b is a larger syntactic structure than the subject cleft in (1)a. Second, I argue that Wolof clefts are derived by overt A'-movement or 'promotion' of the clefted constitutent, roughly:

(2) [clefted XP]$_k$.....(l)-*a*..[$_{TP}$ t$_k$]

The main evidence for the analysis in (2) comes from examination of a number of reconstruction effects in Wolof clefts, which provide strong evidence that (2) is on the right track.

The paper is structured as follows. Section 2 provides background on Wolof and the relevant Wolof clause structures. In Section 2, I present some of the basic properties of Wolof clefts. Section 3 focuses on the syntactic structure of cleft clauses. I argue that Wolof cleft clauses are built from copular clauses. Thus, Section 3 introduces the copulas found in Wolof predicate nominal constructions and discusses how these are related to cleft constructions. Section 3.4 in particular details the relation between the two constructions. Section 4 presents the argumentation for the promotion analysis of Wolof clefts. I do this by discussing islandhood (Section 4.1), cross-linguistically applicable reconstruction tests (Section 4.2) and language-specific reconstruction tests for Wolof (4.3). Section 5 presents a summary of results.

2. I will translate these as English clefts for the most part, unless it yields a very unnatural English sentence.

2. Background on wolof and cleft structures

This section introduces basic properties of Wolof and the distribution of Wolof clefts. Wolof is an SVO noun class language with approximately 15 noun classes:

(3) neutral *na*-clause
Xale yi dàq-na-ñu góór ñi
child the.PL steal-FIN-3PL man the.PL
"The children chased the men"

Noun class membership in Wolof is typically indicated on dependents of the noun, such as articles and demonstratives. In (3), it can be seen that the nouns *xale* 'child' and *góór* 'man' belong to different noun classes because of the different definite articles that they occur with. The clause in (3) is a 'neutral' *na*-clause, in which no single constituent is in focus. Following Zribi-Hertz and Diagne (2002) and Koopman (2006), I take *-na* to be an instantiation of a low head in the complementizer field, FIN (Rizzi 1997), which introduces a subclass of finite clauses. I follow Torrence (2003) who argues that *na*-clauses involve remnant VP movement into the left periphery of the clause. In fact, *na*-clauses indicate that large-scale pied piping is involved in the derivation of Wolof clauses. This can be seen in cross-dialectal variation in TP pied piping:

(4) a. *Lekk-**oon**-na-a* ✓St. Louis, ✓Dakar
eat-PAST-FIN-1SG
"I ate"

a′. $[_{\text{FinP}}\ [_{\text{TP}}\ [_{\text{VP}}\ \underline{\text{lekk}}]\ \underline{\text{oon}}\ ]_k\ \text{na}\ [_{\text{AgrSP}}\ \text{a}\ \mathbf{t}_k\ ]\ ]$

b. *%Lekk-na-a **woon*** *St. Louis, ✓Dakar
eat-FIN-1SG PAST
"I ate"

b′. $[_{\text{FinP}}\ [_{\text{VP}}\ \underline{\text{lekk}}\ ]\ \text{na}\ [_{\text{AgrSP}}\ \text{a}\ [_{\text{TP}}\ \mathbf{t}_k\ \text{woon}\ ]]]$

In (4)a, as shown in (4)a′, VP has pied piped the (underlined) TP to SpecFinP, headed by *-na*. (4)b shows that in the Dakar variety, TP can be stranded, the result being that only (the underlined) VP ends up in SpecFinP ((4)b′). The paradigm in (4) is useful because of what it reveals about VPs in Wolof. First, if the VP is in a left peripheral specifier position in *na*-clauses, we might expect that it could interfere with A'-movement. This is shown to be correct in Section 4.1, where I show that *na*-clauses are islands. Second, the paradigm shows that a TP can be stranded or pied piped, like other XPs in a syntactic structure. This will have consequences in Section 4.3 (Example (71)b), where I show that it is not only verbs that can pied pipe TPs in Wolof.

In the cleft clauses in (1), the clefted constituent occurs on the left edge of the clause, which is a first hint of structural similarity between the two cleft types. That there is a close connection between the subject and non-subject clefts is also indicated by the fact that non-subject clitics occur between the *a*- and the main verb in both clause types:[3]

(5) a. Subject Cleft
Jigéén ji mu a **ko** *fa lekk-oon*
woman the 3SG COP $3SG_{Obj}$ LOC eat-PAST
"It is the woman who ate it there"

b. Non-Subject Cleft
Gato l–a fa lekk-oon
cake XPL-COP LOC eat-PAST
"It is a cake that he ate there"

Abstracting away from the individual examples, subject and non-subject clefts in Wolof are extremely similar in terms of linear order:

(6) Wolof cleft Constructions
a. Subject Cleft
[DP] (SM) *a* (O_{clt}-Loc_{clt}) [$_{TP}$ V]
b. Non-Subject Cleft
[XP] XPL *a* (O_{clt}-Loc_{clt}) [$_{TP}$ V]

In the two types of clefts, the copula -*a*- is preceded by a DP (subject cleft), an optional subject marker (subject cleft), or an expletive DP (*l*- in the non-subject cleft). The object and locative clitics immediately follow the copular -*a*. These are followed by TP. Put differently, the copular *a*- is always immediately preceded by either a nominal or an expletive D.

Cleft clauses in Wolof are associated with the expression of focus, as in (1) a–b, and Wh question formation.[4] As the question/answer pairs below show, cleft questions are answered with cleft responses:

(7) a. Subject Cleft Question
Ñan (ñu) a sàcc cin li
who.PL 3PL COP steal pot the
"Who(pl) is it that stole the pot?"

3. See Section 4.3 for further discussion of clitic phenomena.

4. There are two basic wh-question constructions in Wolof, the cleft construction and a relative clause-like construction (Torrence 2005). I leave aside discussion of the relative- ere.

b. Subject Cleft Answer
Xale yi (ñu) a sàcc cin li
chld the.PL 3PL COP steal pot the
'It's the children who stole the pot'

c. Non-subject Cleft Question
Lan l-a-ñu sàcc
what XPL-COP-3PL steal
"What is it that they stole?"

d. Non-subject Cleft Answer
Cin li l-a-ñu sàcc
pot the XPL-COP-3PL steal
"It is the pot that they stole?"

Wolof clefts can be used to indicate new information focus, correction, constrastive focus, and emphasis, as with focusing particles (Robert 1986; Torrence 2005):

(8) a. [*Cin li* rekk] *l-a-ñu sàcc*
pot the only XPL-COP-3PL steal
"It's only the pot that they stole"

b. [*Cin li* gaa] *l-a-ñu sàcc*
pot the indeed XPL-COP-3PL steal
"It's the pot indeed that they stole"

In addition, cleft structures are employed in various constructions, such as comparatives:

(9) Comparative Subject Cleft
Ma a la gën a njool
1SG *a* 2SG surpass COP tall
"I am taller than you"

Several syntactic categories can be clefted in Wolof:

(10) a. DP
Xale bi l-a-a gis
child the XPL-COP-1SG see
"It's the child that I saw"

b. PP
Ca lekkool ba l-a-a gis-e Isaa
P school the XPL-COP-1SG see-LOC isaa
"It's at school that I saw Isaa"

c. VP
*Suub simis bi l-a-a *(def)*
dye shirt the XPL-COP-1SG do
"Dye the shirt is what I did"

d. *na*-Clause
[Suub-na-a simis bi] l-a-ñu foog
dye-FIN-1SG shirt the XPL-COP-3PL think
"That I dyed the shirt is what they think"

Wolof also allows clefting of expressions that are either awkward or ungrammatical in English clefts, like *even* and indefinite pronouns:

(11) a. [*Ab taalif* sax] *l-a-a jàng*
a poem even XPL-COP-1SG read
"I read even a poem"
(Literally, *"It's even a poem that I read")

b. *Lenn l-a-a jàng*
something XPL-COP-1SG read
"I read SOMETHING"
(Literally, *"It's something that I read")

Data like (11) immediately raise the question of exactly how Wolof clefts parallel clefts in other languages.

Clefting in Wolof is unbounded and, as will be seen, shows the hallmarks of an A'-movement construction. In (12) below, a non-subject, *kan* 'who', has been clefted from a deeply embedded clause:

(12) Non-Local Non-Subject
Kan$_i$ *l-a taalibe bi foog ne* ***t***$_i$ *l-a-a wax ne*
who XPL-COP student the think *ne* XPL-COP-1SG say *ne*
t$_i$ *l-a sa yaay gëm ne* ***t***$_i$ *l-a-ñu bëgg* ***t***$_i$
XPL-COP your mother believe *ne* XPL-COP-3PL love
"Who does the student think that I said that your mother believes that they love?"
(Literally, "Who is it that the student thinks that it is that I said that it is that your mother believes that it is that they love?")

(12) shows that when a non-subject undergoes non-local extraction, a non-subject cleft occurs in all clauses (indicated by the underlined *l–a* strings).

Non-local extraction of subjects involves a subject cleft and obligatory subject marker (in bold below) in the clause of origin and non-subject clefts in higher clauses:

(13) Non-Local Subject
Kan$_i$ *l-a* *taalibe bi foog ne* t_i *l-a-a wax ne*
who XPL-COP student the think *ne* XPL-COP-1sg say *ne*
t_i *l-a sa yaay gëm ne* t_i ***(mu)** *a jàng taalif bi*
XPL-COP your mother believe *ne* 3SG COP read poem the
"Who does the student think that I said that your mother believes that read the poem?"
(Literally "Who is it that the student thinks that it is that I said that it is that your mother believes that it is that read the poem?")

That each clause higher than the clause of origin is marked by a cleft makes similar to Irish (McCloskey 2001) in that Wolof overtly marks successive cyclic A'-movement.

3. Copulas and predicates

The subject and non-subejct clefts in (1)a–b are related to copular constructions:

(14) Copulas and Clefts
Clefts
a. *Gàllaay* ***a*** *dem fale*
gallaay COP go there
"It's Gallaay who went there"
b. *Gàllaay* ***l-a*** *Ayda gis*
gallaay XPL-COP ayda see
"It's Gallaay that Ayda saw"

Copulas
c. *Gàllaay* ***a***
gallaay COP
"It's Gallaay"
d. *Gàllaay* ***l-a***
gallaay XPL-COP
"It's Gallaay"

Copular constructions like (14)c instantiate the '*a*-copula', while those like (14)d represent the '*l*-copula'. The non-subject cleft in (14)b, like the *l*-copula in (14)d, contains the expletive *l*- that precedes the copula (Torrence 2005). The subject cleft in (14)a, like the *a*-copula in (14)c, obligatorily lacks the expletive. These similarities suggest that the subject cleft is related to the *a*-copula, while the non-subject cleft is related to the *l*-copula. Thus, an understanding of these copular constructions is a prerequisite for understanding how cleft constructions work.

The basic analytical claim in this section is that the *-a-* that appears in the *a*-copula and *l*-copula is a semantically empty predicate that embeds clausal complements of different sizes. I will argue that copula *-a* can take small (TP-like) complements, big (TP) complements, and full CP complements.

3.1 Decomposing copular structures

In this section, I present an analysis of the *a*- and *l*-copulas.[5] Specifically, I focus on the expletive *l*- and the syntax of the copula *-a*.

I have assumed that the *l*- that appears in the non-subject cleft and the *l*-copula is an expletive. Here, I briefly lay out the evidence that this is correct. First, *l*- is in complementary distribution with subject markers in subject clefts:

(15) **Ñu* *l–a* *lekk* *gato* *bi*
3PL XPL-COP eat cake the
Intended: "It's them who ate the cake

This suggests that *l*- is a pronominal element. The positional complementary distribution between the expletive *l*- and subject markers follows straightforwardly if the subject marker and expletive occupy the same pre-*a* position.

Second, the *li*-class is one of the default non-human noun classes in Wolof.[6] The *li*-class is characterized by the prsesence of an *l*-. The *li*-class forms are used, for example, when the class of an object is not known:

(16) *L-ii* *l-an* *l–a*?
CL-this CL-*wh* XPL-COP
"What is this?"

This indicates that *l*- is equivalent to an expletive, like *it*. Note that in non-subject clefts (and in the *l*-copula) it is always *l*- that appears, irrespective of the class of the NP/DP which precedes it. This is especially telling in cases where Wolof has a dedicated semantic class. For example, the default human class is the *ki*-class, as in (17)a:

(17) a. *Nit* *k-ii* *l-a-a* *dóór*
person CL-this XPL-COP-1SG hit
"It's this person that I hit"

5. The discussion is based on Torrence (2005). See it for details.

6. There is also a *bi*-class which is a default class and which is used for new loanwords, for example. Terms like '*li*-class' refer to the fact that the definite article for nouns of this class is *li*.

b. **Nit* *k-ii* *k-a-a* *dóór*
person CL-this CL-COP-1SG hit
Intended: "It's this person that I hit"

(17)b shows that the *l*- is invariable. Thus, the *l*- is probably not a pronoun linked to the clefted element, but it does seem to occupy a subject position.

I follow Stowell (1981) and Moro (1997) and assume that nominal predication involves the presence of a small clause (which occurs lower than the copula itself). This means that the cases in (18), where both predicate and subject precede the copula, involve raising of the nominals:

(18) a. *a*-copula
Maryam jàngalekat ***a***
maryam teacher COP
"Maryam is a teacher"

b. *l*-copula
Maryam jàngalekat ***l-a***
maryam teacher XPL-COP
"Maryam is a teacher"

One piece of evidence that (at least) the *l*-copula involves raising is that either the subject or predicate can remain downstairs:[7]

(19) a. *Tey* ***Alxamis*** *l-a*
today Thursday XPL-COP
"Today is Thursday"

b. *Tey* *l-a* ***Alxamis***
today XPL-COP Thursday
"Today is Thursday"

The idea that the copula -*a* is a raising predicate meshes with the fact that it can take an expletive subject, as in non-subject clefts. This makes the Wolof copula -*a* look very much like English *seem*, which occurs with *there* or *it* as expletive subjects. From this perspective, it is unsurprising that -*a*, always occurs with a preceding nominal (subject) of some kind. In the *l*-copula, the subject of -*a* is an expletive, while in the *a*-copula, the subject is a (contentful) DP. That -*a* always has a subject indicates that -*a* has an EPP feature and therefore must have a subject (at some point in the derivation).

7. The conditions that make this possible are poorly understood. In fact, it is only nouns of time and days of the week for which this is possible. I leave analysis of this restriction for future research.

Taking -*a* as a raising category, I analyze (18)a–b as in (20) underlyingly:

(20) a. *a*-Copula b. *l*-Copula

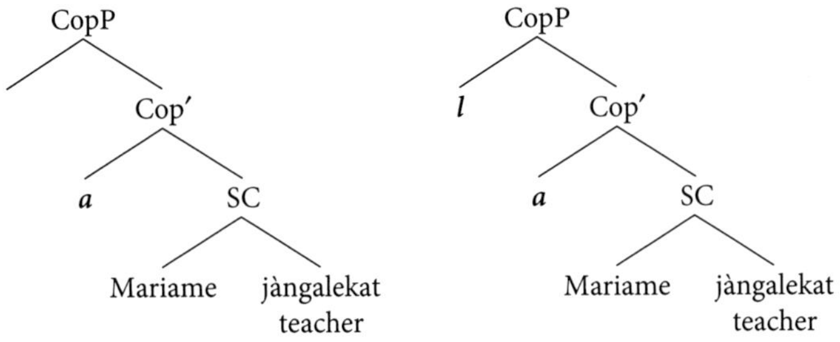

I take -*a* as the head of 'CopP' (since it is involved in nominal predication). In the trees in (20), I label the complement of -*a* as simply a small clause ('SC'). However, this is an oversimplification, as these small clauses contain quite a bit of structure. In the next section, I flesh out the complements of -*a* in the two copular construtions.

3.2 The size of the *a*- and *l*-copulas

While the *a*-copula and *l*-copula are clearly morphologically related, they are nevertheless distinct morpho-syntactically. This can be seen by investigating the range of functional heads available in each copular construction. Taking the available heads as a gauge of size, I argue that the 'SC' structure embedded by -*a*- in the *a*-copula and by extension subject clefts, is smaller than the structure embedded by -*a*- in the *l*-copula and non-subject clefts.

The tree in (21) gives the basic clausal functional hierarchy in Wolof, based on Torrence 2003, 2005. (AgrSP hosts a set of subject markers):

(21)

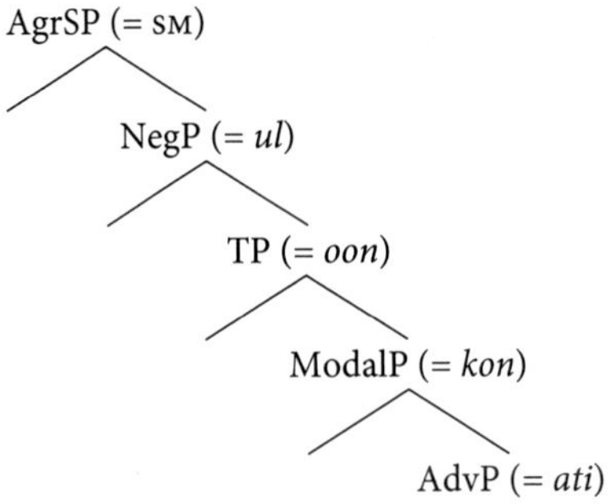

Proceeding along the hierarchy from the bottom up, (22) that the low repetitive adverbial *ati* 'again' occurs in both the *a*-copula and the *l*-copula:

(22) a. *a*-copula + *-ati*[8]
*Gàllaay-a-**ati***
gallaay-COP-REP
"It's Gallaay again"

b. *l*-copula + *-ati*
*Gàllaay l-a-**ati***
gallaay XPL-COP-REP
"It's Gallaay again"

The conditional particle *kon*, which is the head of ModalP, occurs in both copulas:

(23) a. *a*-copula + conditional
*Gàllaay-a **kon***
gallaay-COP COND
"It must be Gallaay"

b. *l*-copula + conditional
*Gàllaay l–a **kon***
gallaay XPL-COP COND
"It must be Gallaay"

As the translations indicate, the copular clauses in (23) are interpreted with type of epistemic modality. Torrence (2005) argues, on the basis of verbal complex structure and the distribution of negation, that *kon* can merger lower than (anterior) past tense, *-oon*. In Cinque (1999) epistemic and alethic modals merge (much) higher in the structure than anterior past tense. Therefore, *kon* may correspond more closely to an obligation (must/need) modal, which is merged lower.

Both the *l*- and *a*-copulas can occur with past tense:

(24) a. *a*-copula + past
*Sidi a **woon***
sidi COP PAST
"It was Sidi"

b. *l*-copula + past
*Sidi l–a **woon***
sidi XPL-COP PAST
"It was Sidi"

8. (22)a is pronounced with a short [a], i.e. [gallaaj-ati], not the expected long vowel, [aa].

Thus, both the *a*- and *l*-copulas contain at least the following structure:

(25)

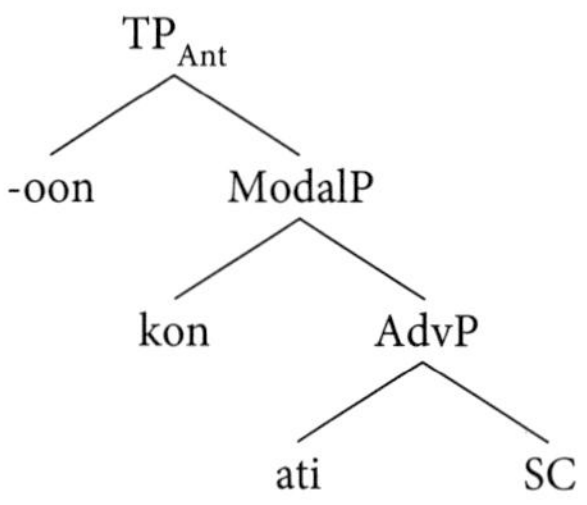

The *a*- and *l*-copulas differ however, regarding the higher functional projections (NegP and AgrSP). In a nutshell, the *a*-copula is systematically smaller than the *l*-copula in terms of functional structure. For example, the negative marker, -*ul*-, cannot occur in the *a*-copula, but it does occur in the *l*-copula (with an obligatory dummy auxiliary, *di*):

(26) a. **a*-copula + *ul*-negative
Gàllaay*-*a*-*wul***
gallaay-COP-NEG
Intended: "It's not Gallaay"

b. *l*-copula + *ul*-negative[9]
Jàngalekat l–a Gàllaay doon-***ul***
teacher XPL-COP gallaay AUX-NEG
"Gallaay is not a teacher"

The data in (26)a–b indicate that the negative head can not be present in the *a*-copula, while it is present in the *l*-copula (but needs an auxililary to support it). That the affixal negative head is merged higher than anterior past tense (Neg > T_{ant} > $Modal_{kon}$). Thus, while both of the copulas contain anterior past tense and the lower functional heads, the *a*-copula lacks at least part of the structure higher than anterior past. Further support for this conclusion comes from the distribution of subject markers. The (clitic) subject markers do not occur in the *a*-copula, but they do occur in the *l*-copula:

(27) a. *a*-copula
****Ñu***-*a*
3PL-COP
Intended: "It's them"

9. I treat *doon* as a single auxiliary here although it may in fact be morphologically complex. If *doon* is (26)a, it remains ungrammatical.

b. *a*-copula
Jàngalekat* ***ñu-a*
teacher 3PL$_{Clt}$-COP
Intended: "They are teachers"

c. *l*-copula
*Jàngalekat l-a-**ñu***
teacher XPL-COP-3PL
"They are teachers"

In the analysis in Torrence (2003), the subject markers are merged higher than negation. Their non-occurrence in the *a*-copula follows if the *a*-copula does not contain functional heads as high as or higher than (affixal) negation.

Finally, the *a*-copula and *l*-copulas differ in the possibility of stranding material to the right of *-a-*. For example, the *l*-copula allows a relative clause to be stranded to the right of *-a-*, but, the *a*-copula does not:

(28) a. *l*-copula + RC pied piping
Senegaal [réew [m–u ma neex lool]] l–a
senegal country CL-C$_{REL}$ 1SG be.pleasing very XPL-COP
"Senegal is a country I like a lot"

b. *l*-copula + RC stranding
Senegaal [réew$_i$] l–a [m–u ma neex lool]$_i$
senegal country XPL-COP CL-C$_{REL}$ 1SG be.pleasing very
"Senegal is a country I like a lot"

c. *a*-copula + RC pied piping
Senegaal [réew [m–u ma neex lool]]-a
senegal country CL-C$_{REL}$ 1SG be.pleasing very-COP
"Senegal is a country I like a lot"

d. **a*-copula + RC stranding
**Senegaal [réew] a [m–u ma neex lool]*
senegal country COP CL-C$_{REL}$ 1SG be.pleasing very
"Senegal is a country I like a lot"

The examples show that a relative clause modifier can be pied piped ((28)a/(28)c) or stranded ((28)b), so that it follows *-a-* (Incidentally, that fact that the relative clause can be stranded in this position provides evidence that the XP to the left of *l–a* has moved to that position from lower down.) With the *a*-copula, the relative clause must be pied piped ((28)c), as stranding is not possible ((28)d). Torrence (2005) takes the stranding to be a form of relative clause extraposition. Kayne (1994) argues that extraposition is not rightward movement, but leftward movement of the extraposed constituent followed by further movement of lower material to a position higher than the extraposed XP. Under this analysis, the possibility of extraposition is dependent upon the availability of higher stranding positions, i.e. the size of the clause. That is, stranding/extraposition is only possible if there is a position available for something to be stranded in. For the data above, this indicates that there is a stranding position in the *l*-copula, but there is no such position in the *a*-copula. That is, the *a*-copula is 'smaller' than the *l*-copula.

Drawing together these strands, I conclude that in the *a*-copula, -*a*- combines with a small part of the clausal structure, no bigger than TP, while in the *l*-copula, -*a*- selects for at least AgrSP:

(29)

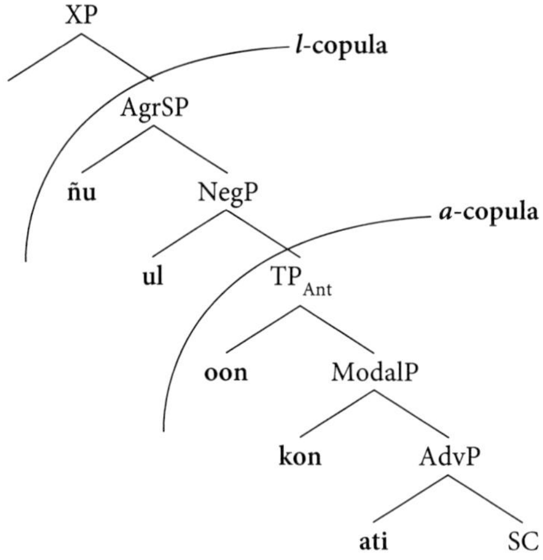

The tree in (29) essentially says that -*a*- selects for complements of different sizes. This analysis makes Wolof -*a* similar to raising predicates like English *seem*, which occur with complements of different sizes, such as small clauses, non-finite TPs, and full CPs:

(30) a. *seem* + SC
Greg$_i$ seems [$_{SC}$ t$_i$ happy]

b. *seem* + TP
Greg$_i$ seems [$_{TP}$ to be t$_i$ happy]

c. *seem* + CP
It seems [$_{CP}$ that Greg is happy]

While the (θ-marked) DP subject *Greg* occurs in all three constructions, the expletive subject *it* only occurs in one, namely when it is associated with a full CP:

(31) a. *xpl *seem* + small clause
*It seems [$_{SC}$ Bill happy]

b. *xpl *seem* + TP
*It seems [$_{TP}$ Bill to be happy]

Thus, as with English *seem*, the presence or absence of the expletive in Wolof is a diagnostic for the presence or absence of a CP-like structure. We can now reframe the discussion of the complement small clause category of -*a* in somewhat more precise terms. The *a*-copula involves a "little" clause, which is roughly like a TP. The *l*-copula involves a "big" clause, which is more like a CP. The relevant "extra" structure in the *l*-copula is given in bold:

(32) a. *a*-Copula

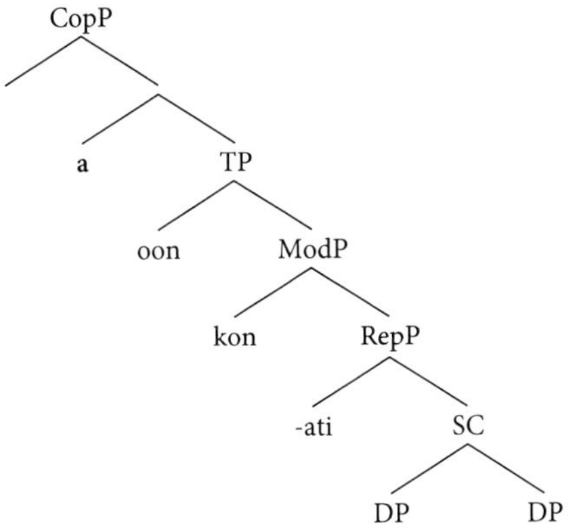

b. *l*-Copula

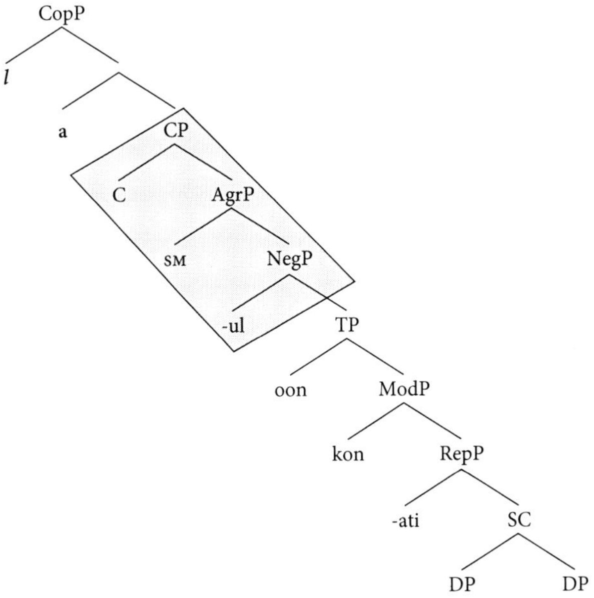

Given that -*a* is a raising predicate, its specifier is an A-position. This is again consistent with the fact that it can take an expletive subject in the *l*-copula. Movement of a DP from the small clause to SpecCopP is therefore an instance of A-movement.

With the analysis in (32) in mind, consider the *a*- and *l*-copula clauses below:[10]

(33) a. *a*-Copula
Gàllaay a woon
gallaay COP PAST
"It was Gallaay"

b. *l*-Copula
Gàllaay l–a woon
gallaay XPL-COP PAST
"It was Gallaay"

In analyzing clauses like (33)a–b, I will assume the presence of a silent 'it', which is the subject of predication.

(34) *a*-Copula
a.
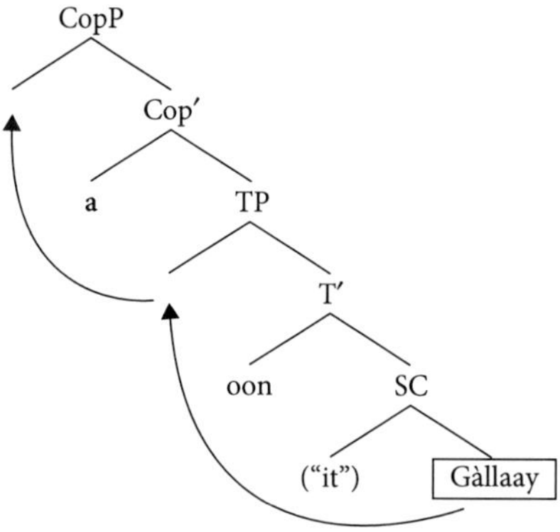

l-Copula
b.
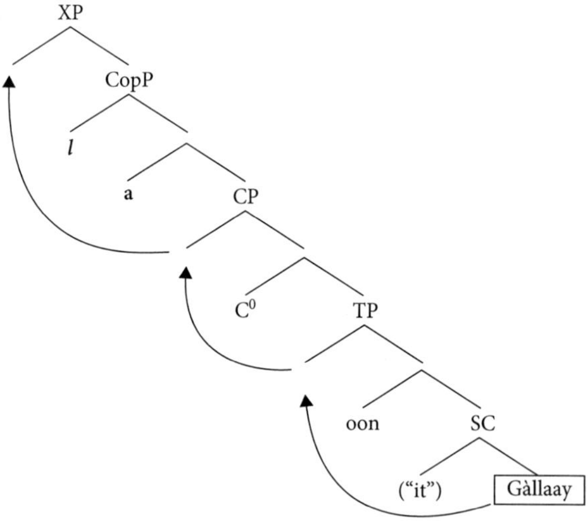

10. See Torrence (2005) for more complex examples.

In the *a*-copula in (34)a, the DP *Gàllaay* moves from the small clause, through TP, etc. and reaches SpecCopP. Since the predicate nominal *Gàllaay* must surface to the left of -*a*, this movement is obligatory. (For the sake of simplicity, I will assume that *Gàllaay* remains in SpecCopP, although it may be higher.) In the *l*-copula in (34)b, movement of the DP *Gàllaay* so that it surfaces to the left of -*a* must be an instance of A'-movement because this is movement out of a CP (presumably through SpecCP). This entails that a DP raised out of an *l*-copula cannot transit SpecCopP, which is an A-position. This also means that such a DP cannot satisfy the EPP feature of -*a* and an expletive, *l*-, is inserted as a last resort. In addition, the *l*-copula must involve a position higher than CopP, to serve as the landing site for the A'-moved DP.

3.3 On copulas and clefts

In this section, I take the analyses of the *a*- and *l*-copulas from the previous section and sketch out how these can be extended to the analysis of clefts in Wolof. I also briefly discuss crosslinguistic implications.

Unlike many other West African languages, for example those of the Gbe cluster (Aboh 2004), there is no overt marker of focus in Wolof. We have seen that cleft focus in Wolof involves the copula -*a*. However, the copula -*a* occurs independently, in nominal predication constructions for example, with no necessary focus interpretation. This pattern suggests that cleft constructions are quite literally built on top of copular constructions. Extending Rizzi (1997) to Wolof, I assume that the left periphery of Wolof contains a silent focus head, Foc^0, that attracts focused material to its specifier. Given that focus in Wolof always coincides with the presence of the copula -*a*-, Foc^0 must select for a CopP complement. This accounts for the fact that the focus clefted XP always precedes copula -*a*:

(35)

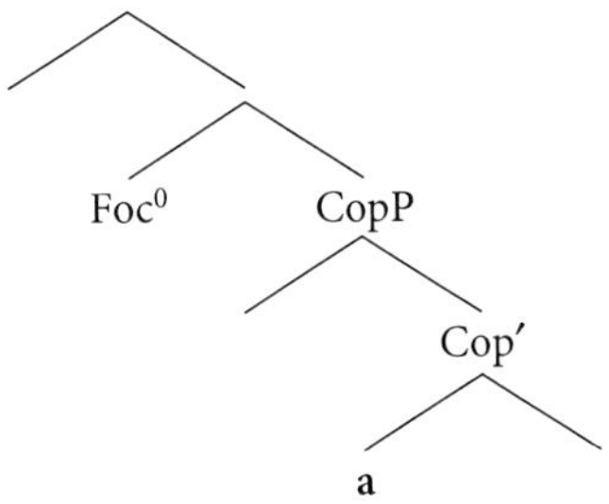

Taking concrete examples, recall cases of subject and non-subject clefts:

(36) a. Subject Cleft
Leston a bind léeb bi
leston COP write story the
"It's Leston who wrote the story"

b. Non-Subject Cleft
Lééb bi l–a Leston bind
story the XPL-COP leston write
"It's the story that Leston wrote"

I have argued that the Wolof *a*- and *l*-copulas involve two distinct structures lower than *a*-. The fact that subject clefts have -*a*, but obligatorily lack the expletive *l*- suggests that subject clefts are based on or closely related to *a*-copular clauses. Non-subject clefts, which have both *a*- and the expletive, seem to be based on the *l*-copula. If analysis is on the right track, subject clefts are "smaller" than non-subject clefts and subject clefts involve a step of A-movement through SpecCopP, while non-subject clefting involves A'-movement.

The copular sub-structure of a subject cleft, which has an ordinary lexical predicate, cannot literally be an *a*-copula because subject clefts can take both negation and subject markers:

(37) a. Subject Cleft
Xale ***mu*** *a sàcc-**ul** woon gato bi*
child 3SG COP steal-NEG PAST cake the
"It's not a child that stole the cake"

b. *a*-Copula
Golo* ***mu* *a* ***wul*** *woon*
monkey 3SG *a* NEG PAST
Intended: "It wasn't a monkey"

The grammaticality of (37)a indicates that in the subject cleft, -*a*- selects for an AgrSP, something still smaller than a full CP, but larger than a TP, roughly, a "big" TP. Taking a cue from the analysis of copulas, the subject and non-subject cleft foci originate in two different structures:

(38) a. Subject cleft

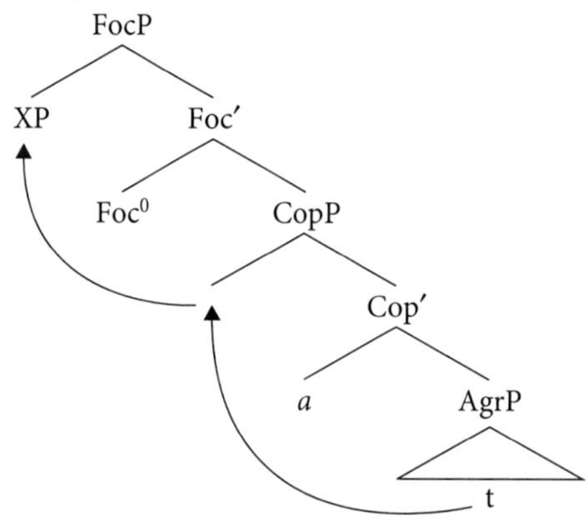

b. Non-subject cleft

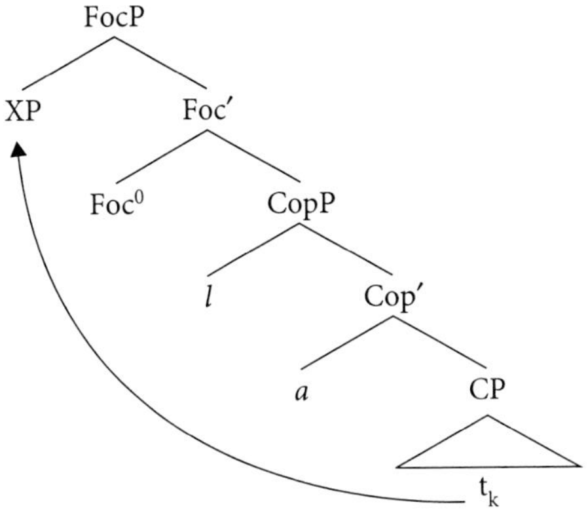

The clefts in (36) are then derived as below:

(39)

a. Subject cleft (= (36)a)

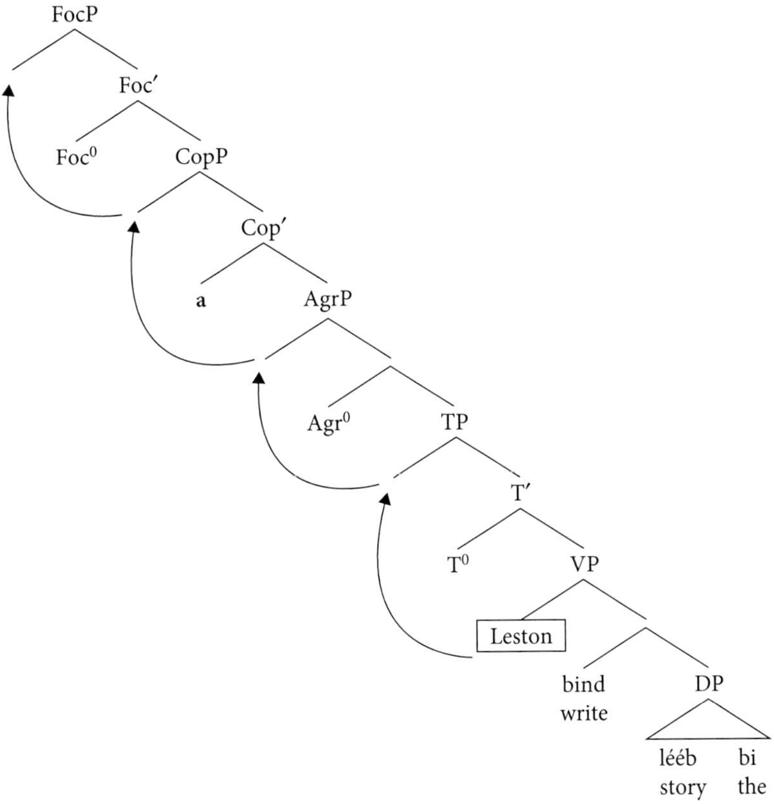

b. Non-subject cleft (= (36)b)

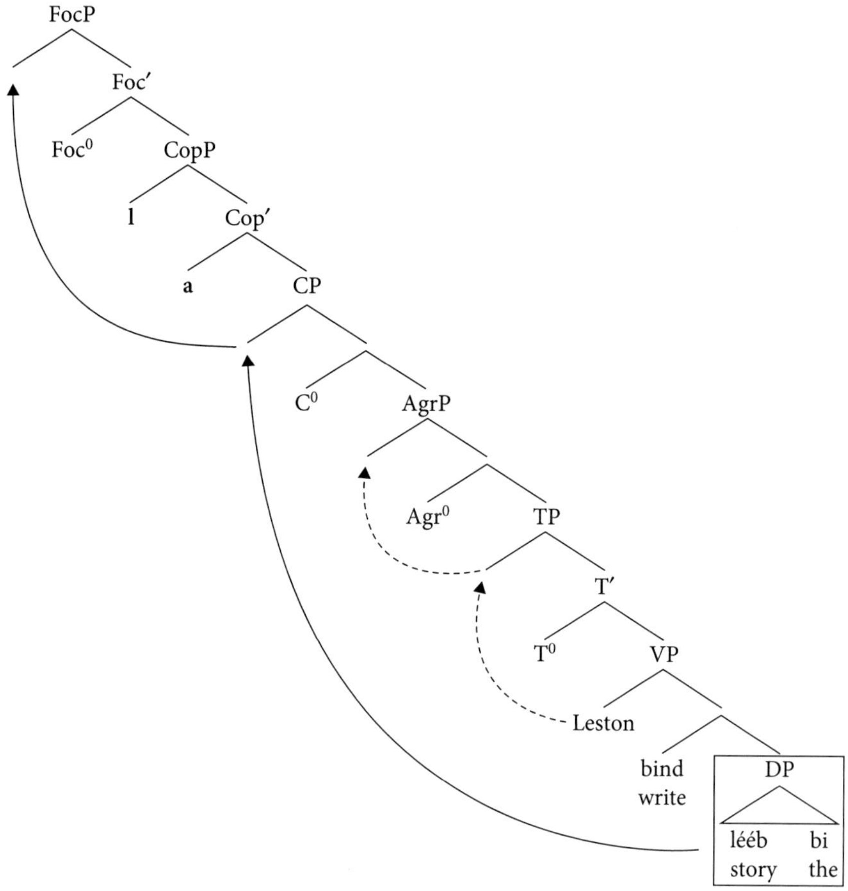

In the subject cleft in (39)a, the +focus subject, *Leston*, originates VP-internally and raises through SpecTP, SpecAgrP, and then to SpecCopP to satisfy the EPP feature of *-a*. The focused subject then undergoes A'–movement to SpecFocP. In the non-subject cleft in (39)b, which contains a full CP, the +focus object A'–moves through SpecCP and then moves to SpecFocP, skipping SpecCopP.

The analyses for Wolof subject and non-subject clefts bring to light several issues for comparative syntax of clefts. One immediate question that arises from my analysis is why Wolof uses different strategies for clefting subjects and non-subjects. From the perspective of English, the Wolof paradigms are unexpected since English does not display subject/non-subject morphological distinctions in clefts. However, looking across Atlantic languages, Wolof is not alone in possessing morpho-syntactically distinct subject and non-subject clefting or focussing constructions. This is true for closely related languages like Seereer and more distantly related Atlantic languages like (some of) those of the Joola group (Bassène 2007 for Joola Banjal). In languages like Wolof, the morphological differences between subject and non-subject clefts are not limited to the presence of an expletive, but include distinct subject markers that occur in different linear positions for example (See Church 1981; Njie 1982; Torrence 2005 for other differences). This suggests that the difference between the cleft types is not superficial. On the contrary, languages like Wolof present overt evidence for the presence of distinct syntactic structures. Beyond Atlantic, Fiedler et al. (2010) outline a number of syntactic differences between subject and non-subject focusing constructions in several Chadic, Kwa (<Niger-Congo), and Gur (<Niger-Congo) languages, which are only distantly related to Wolof. This suggests that such asymmetries are widespread. Syntactically distinct subject and non-subject clefts are not limited to African languages. The Wolof morpho-syntactic asymmetries are reminiscent of what is found in languages like French, which does not manifest distinct morphology for subject versus non-subject clefts, but nonetheless strongly hints at syntactic differences. For example, French does not permit subject *which* phrases to be clefted:

(40) a. Bare *wh*-Subj
Qui est-ce qui a embrassé Jean
who is-it that.agr has hugged jean
"Who is it that hugged Jean?"

b. *which* Subj
**Quelle homme est-ce qui a embrassé Jean*
which man is-it that.agr has hugged jean
"Which man hugged Jean?"

c. *which* DO
Quelle homme est-ce que Marie a embrassé
which man is-it that marie has hugged
"Which man is it that Marie hugged?"

(40)a shows that clefting of a bare wh subject is fine, while (40)b shows that clefting of a subject *which*-phrase subject is ungrammatical.[11] In contrast, clefting of an object *which*-phrase is fine, as (40) shows. I do not offer an analysis for this contrast in French, but give it here to show that the subject/non-subject asymmetry in clefting may be widespread, but more difficult to detect in other languages.

The analyses in (38) express the idea that a FocP that occurs with clefted subjects sits on top of a smaller piece of syntactic structure than the FocP that occurs with clefted non-subjects. The structural asymmetry in (38) is strongly

11. Philippe Schlenker (p.c.) (40)a, b are reported independently in Munaro and Pollock (2005).

reminiscent of recent proposals in Belletti (2008a, b). Working from Italian and French, Belletti argues that the basic structure of clefts consists of a copula *be* whose complement is a CP:

(41) ....*Be* [$_{\text{CP}}$............] (= Belletti 2008b, #2)

In her analysis, focused/clefted subjects occur in a low *v*P periphery.[12] In a cleft, it is the *v*P periphery of the copula *be* that contains the focus and topic heads. A French cleft like (42)a is analyzed as in (42)b:

(42) a. *C'est Jean (qui a parlé)* (= Belletti 2008b, #3b)
it is Jean (who spoke)

b. [$_{\text{TP}}$ Ce....[$_{\text{FocP}}$ [......[$_{v\text{P}}$ être [$_{\text{CP}}$ Jean [$_{\text{CP}}$ ~~qui a parlé~~]]]]]]
(= Belletti 2008b, #5')

The higher CP in (42)b is a CP that has an EPP feature, which she refers to as a "small CP", whose highest head is a projection lower than Force. That is, the CP of a subject cleft is a type of reduced CP. The lower CP is equivalent to FinP (Rizzi 1997). In (42)b the +focus subject raises to SpecFocP, while *be* raises into the TP domain. With respect to the subject *Jean*, Belletti argues that it is in the specifier of the small CP, which she takes to be an A-position. She analyzes non-subject clefts as involving a high left peripheral focus position, crucially, "within a full CP complement to the copula." (Belletti 2008a, page 17):

(43) ...*be* [~~$_{\text{CP}}$ Force~~...[$_{\text{FocP}}$... [che [$_{\text{TP}}$ S...O/PP]]]] (= Belletti 2008b, #35c)

Belletti is careful to note that the CP complement of the copula is still not like a complete declarative CP. Summarizing, Belletti's argument that subject clefts in French and Italian involve a reduced clausal structure (the *v*P focus position), while non-subject clefts involve something much more like a CP. I leave a precise comparison of Wolof and Italian/French clefts for future research. Given that an unrelated Atlantic language like Wolof patterns similarly to Italian and French suggests that the analyses are broadly on the right track. Having established a basic analysis of Wolof copulas and their relationship to clefts, I turn to derivational issues.

---

12. The low *v*P focus area is for new information focus. I abstract away from this here. See also Aboh (2007), who argues for high and low focus positions.

4. A'-Properties of clefts

The remainder of this paper addresses the movement properties of clefts. I argue for two points here. First, I present evidence that clefting in Wolof involves movement. Second, I argue that it is the clefted item that undergoes movement into the left periphery of a cleft clause. That is, I argue for a "promotion" analysis of Wolof clefts. This entails that Wolof clefting does not involve the presence of a silent operator which is bound by the base-generated clefted item.

One line of analysis of cleft clauses in English originates with Chomsky (1977), who posits the base-generation of the clefted item. The clefted constituent is interpreted by entering into a relation with the A'-chain, {OP, t_i} in (44) below. The relation between the clefted item and the operator is established by the clefted constituent's binding of the operator in the clause which has undergone movement from a case position. The movement of the operator is responsible for the A'-movement characteristics:

(44) it's **Bill**$_i$ [$_{CP}$ **OP**$_i$ that I think **t**$_i$ you saw **t**$_i$]

The standard analysis makes two predictions. First, clefts will display movement diagnostics, because of the movement of the silent operator, OP_i. Second, the clefted item, *Bill*, will not be able to reconstruct into the embedded CP for the simple reason that it is never in the embedded CP. However, examination of the reconstruction properties of Wolof cleft provide strong evidence for the Promotion analysis.

4.1 Island sensitivity

Clefting in Wolof is sensitive to both strong islands, as exemplified by the adjunct island in (45), and weak islands, as the Wh island in (46) shows:[13]

(45) Adjunct Island

a. *Xale bi dem-na* [*laata Bintë togg* ***laax***]
child the go-FIN before bintë cook laax
"The child left before Binta cooked laax"

b. ****Lan***$_i$ *l-a xale bi dem* [*laata Binta togg* t_i]
what XPL-COP child the go before binta, cook
"What did the child go before Binte cooked?"

13. Island sensitivity is also found for complex NPs and coordinate structures. For space reasons, I do not include examples here (but see Torrence 2005, pages 233–235).

(46) Wh Island

a. ****Lan***$_i$ *l-a Dudu xam [ndax* ***t***$_i$ *l-a-a jënd]*
what l-*a* dudu know whether XPL-COP-1SG buy
"What does Dudu know whether I bought?"

b. *Xam-na-a [**lan** l-a-ñu jox Ayda]*
know-FIN-1SG what XPL-COP-3PL give ayda
"I know what they gave Ayda"

c. *[***Ayda***]$_k$ *l-a-a xam [**lan**$_j$ l-a-ñu jox* ***t***$_k$ ***t***$_i$]
ayda XPL-COP-1SG know what XPL-COP-3PL give
"It's to Ayda that I know what they gave"

(46)a is an attempt to extract the Wh expression *lan* 'what' out of the (bracketed) embedded question. (46)b shows that an embedded cleft question, by itself, is fine. Thus, the problem with (46)c is the clefted *jigéén ji* 'the woman', which has moved out of the wh-island.[14]

Further evidence for A'-movement comes from the interaction of clefting and a Wolof-specific island. If a Wh word is substituted for the object (or subject) in (47)a, the resulting (47)b can only be interpreted as an echo question. A Wh word cannot be clefted out of a *na*-clause leaving only a gap. Instead, a resumptive clitic must be present ((47)c). In that case, the question can be interpreted as non-echo:[15]

(47) a. *na*-Clause
Lekk-nga
eat-FIN+2SG kola.nut
"You ate a kola nut"

b. *na*-Clause
Lekk-nga ***lan***
eat-FIN+2SG what
"You ate what?" echo question
*"What did you eat?"

14. Typically, both weak and strong island violations can be saved by the insertion of resumptive pronouns, in boldface in (i):

(i) *[Jigéén ji]*$_i$ *l-a-a xam [lan l-a-ñu-**ko**$_i$* jox] Wh Island
woman the XPL-COP-1SG know what XPL-COP-3PL-3SG give
"It's the woman that I know what they gave"

It is unclear exactly why resumption saves the structure in (i). As pointed out by a reviewer, resumption in an English cleft like (i) does not result in full grammaticality:

(ii) ??It's the woman that/who I know what they gave her.

I leave these contrasts here for future discussion and do not discuss them further in this paper.

15. In fact, the wh-expression in this case must be D-linked.

c. Real Question
Lan *l–a* *Sàmba* *wax* *ne* [*Dudu* *sàcc-na-∅-*(**ko**)*]
what XPL-COP samba say that dudu steal-FIN-3SG-3SG
"What is it that Samba said that Dudu stole it?"

The fact that a resumptive clitic is obligatory suggests that *na*-clauses are islands for extraction. This is consistent with the analysis from Torrence (2003) that *na*-clauses involve a left peripheral fronted VP remnant. I assume that the fronted VP occupies a (low) escape hatch in the left periphery, blocking extraction. It is therefore significant that clefting cannot span a *na*-clause:

(48) [non-subject cleft [*na*-
Lan_i *l–a* *Sàmba* *wax* *ne* [*Bintë* *foog-***na** *ne*
what XPL-COP samba say that binta think-FIN that
[non-subject cleft]]]
[t_i *l–a* *xale* *yi* *sàcc* t_i]]
XPL-COP child the steal
Intended: "What did Samba say that Binta thinks that the children stole?"

If *na*-clauses are indeed islands for movement and clefting involves movement, then the ungrammticality of (48) is expected. The wh-expression from the most embedded clause simply cannot escape the intermediate clause island by moving successive cyclically through it.

For completeness, an intervening subject cleft also blocks cleft formation from spanning over it:

(49) [non-subject cleft [subject cleft
Kan_i *l–a* *Bintë* *wax* *ne* [*Isaa* *mo-o* *foog* *ne*
who XPL-COP binta say that isaa 3SG-*a* think that
[non-subject cleft]]]
[t_i l-a-a dóór t_i]]
XPL-COP-1SG hit
"It's the child that Binta said that it's Isaa who thinks that I hit"

I showed earlier (in (12)) that clefting is unbounded, and this section has presented evidence that clefting involves movement. That the movement is successive cyclic is indicated by the fact that a cleft clause can itself be pied piped when the focus/Wh occurs on the left edge:

(50) a. CP stranding
Lan_i *l–a* *Bintë* *foog* [$_{CP}$ *ne* t_i *l-a-ñu* *jënd* t_i]
what XPL-COP binta think that XPL-COP-3PL buy
"what does Binta think that they bought?"
(Literally, "What is it that Binta thinks that it is that they bought?")

b. CP pied piping
[$_{CP}$ *Lan l-a-ñu jënd*]$_i$ *l-a Bintë foog* t_i
what XPL-COP-3PL buy XPL-COP binta think
"What does Binta think that they bought?"
(Literally, "What is it that they bought that it is that Binta thinks?"

In (50)a, the Wh word strands the embedded cleft clause. In (50)b the Wh occurs on the left edge of the embedded cleft clause and the entire embedded cleft CP appears on the left edge of the matrix clause. This follows if the Wh first transits the left periphery of the embedded clause and then pied pipes the embedded cleft when it raises to the matrix cleft position.

The island sensitivity and the interaction of islands and cyclicity all point to the conclusion that clefting in Wolof involves A'-movement of *something*. However, these data do not tell us *what* has undergone movement. Determining this is the goal of the next section.

4.2 General reconstruction effects

In this section, I present several pieces of evidence from reconstruction that clefted items are not base-generated in the cleft position, but undergo movement to the cleft position. I follow Sportiche 2005 and take reconstruction as a diagnostic for movement.

The first reconstruction effect is manifested by idiom chunks, which can be clefted (Vergnaud 1974). I discuss two types of idiomatic constructions: phrasal idioms and idiomatic adverbs.

Consider the non-clefted versions of two idioms, in neutral *na*-clauses:

(51) a. Idiom + *na*-clause
Sa jaan wàcc-na
your snake descend-FIN
"You have finished your work"

b. Idiom + *na*-clause
Def-na-a téeré Senegaal
make-FIN-1SG amulet senegal
"I am dedicated to Senegal"

The first observation is that phrasal idioms can be split in both subject and non-subject clefts.

(52) a. Subject Cleft
<u>Sa</u> <u>jaan</u> mu a wàcc
your snake 3sg COP descend
"YOU have finished your work"
(Literally, "It is your snake that has descended")

b. Subject Cleft
Sa jaan l-a-a foog ne mu a wàcc
your snake XPL-COP-1SG think that 3SG COP descend
"I think YOU have finished your work"

c. Non-Subject Cleft
Tééré l-a-a def Senegaal
amulet XPL-COP-1SG make senegal
"I do believe in Senegal"
(Literally, "It's an amulet that I made Senegal")

d. Non-Subject Cleft
Tééré l-a-ñu foog nel-a-a def Senegal
amulet XPL-COP-3PL think thatXPL-COP-1SG make senegal
"I am indeed dedicated to Senegal"
(Literally, "It's an amulet that they think that I made Senegal")

In (52)a–b, subject clefts, the idiom consists of a verb *wàcc* 'descend' and a possessed subject *sa jaan* 'your snake'. These examples show that in both local and long distance clefting, the subject portion of the idiom can be split from the idiomatic VP. The same generalizations hold for the non-subject clefts in (52), where the idiom consists of the verb *def* 'do' and an object *tééré* 'amulet'. The fact that idiom chunks can be clefted follows straightforwardly from the promotion analysis. This is because the phrasal idiom is a type of complex lexical item and underlyingly forms a constituent. Under a movement analysis, there is subsequent raising of a subpart of the idiom, e.g. [*s–a jaan*] to the cleft position.

Turning to adverbs, like the great majority of Niger-Congo languages, Wolof has a large class of idiomatic adverbs (Welmers 1973; Dialo 1985), so-called 'ideophones', that select for particular verbs or semantic verb classes. These types of idiomatic adverbs usually add emphasis, intensity, or indicate manner or extent:

(53) a. verb
Xam-na-a-ko
know-FIN-1SG-3SG
"I know it"

b. *know + xell*
Xam-na-a-ko ***xell***
know-FIN-1SG-3SG IDEO
"I am really sure of it"

c. **be sure + xell*
Wóór-na-ma* ***xell*
be.sure-FIN-1SG IDEO
"I am really sure"

d. ideophone
*__Xell__-na-a-ko
IDEO-FIN-1SG-3SG
"I am really sure of it"

(53)a–d show that the adverb *xell* occurs with the verb *xam* 'know' and adds emphasis. Semantically similar predicates like *wóór* 'be sure' are ungrammatical when they occur with *xell*, as shown by (53)c–d.

The distribution of ideophones suggests a *selectional* relation between the ideophone and the predicate.[16] I assume that this relation is structurally instantiated by the adverb taking the verb as its complement (with subsequent verb movement obscuring the underlying order). That is, the ideophone must occur with the particular verb because the ideophone selects for it:

(54)

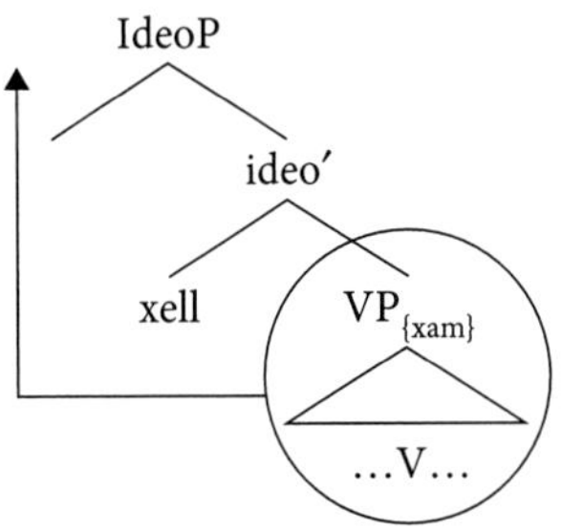

Given the very tight syntactic and semantic relation between idiomatic adverbs and the verbs they select for, it is significant that ideophones can be clefted, stranding the verb:

(55) a. *na*-Clause
Tëj-na-a ***ràpp*** *bunt bi*
close-FIN-1SG IDEO door the
"I closed the door completely shut"

b. IDEO + Verb
Bunt bi l-a-a ***tëj ràpp***
door the XPL-COP-1SG close IDEO
"it's the door that I closed completely shut"

c. Clefted IDEO
Ràpp *l-a-a* ***tëj*** *bunt bi*
IDEO XPL-COP-1sg close door the
"I closed the door COMPLETELY SHUT"

16. This is a rather rough characterization of these interesting adverbs. A thorough description of their properties is beyond the scope of this paper.

In (55)a, the verb and ideophone cooccur in a *na*-clause. In (55)b, the object has been clefted, while the verb and ideophone remain downstairs in TP. (55)c shows that the ideophone can be clefted and therefore split from the verb that it selects for.

A second case of reconstruction involves the negative polarity item (NPI) *dara*:

(56) a. **Togg-na-a* ***dara***
cook-FIN-1sg anything
"I cooked anything"

b. *Togg-**u**-ma* ***dara***
cook-neg-1sg anything
"I did not cook anything"

c. *Togg-na-a* ***lenn***
cook-FIN-1SG something
"I cooked something"

Comparing (56)a–b, it can be seen that *dara* must appear in a clause with negation.[17] In order to obtain a simple existentially quantified reading, a distinct form, *lenn*, is used ((56)c). What is significant here is that *dara* can be clefted, even if it is associated with negation in an embedded clause:

(57) a. ***Dara*** *l-a-a* *togg-*(**ul**)*
anything XPL-COP-1SG cook-NEG
"It's anything that I didn't cook"
"I didn't cook ANYTHING"

b. ***Dara*** *nga* *foog* *ne* *l-a-a* *togg-*(**ul**)*
anything 2SG+XPL+COP think that XPL-COP-1SG cook-NEG
"It's anything that you think I didn't cook"
"You think that I didn't cook ANYTHING"

(57)a–b show that the clefted NPI reconstructs into the scope of negation in matrix clauses and into embedded clauses. Under the movement analysis, this distribution is unsurprising: the clefted NPI originates in the embedded clause with its licensing negation and subsequently moves into the matrix clause. The grammaticality of NPI clefting is mysterious under a base-generation approach, since in (57)b, for example, the NPI appears quite far from the negation that licenses it.

17. In some dialects, for example, the Dakar variety, the word *dara* is ambiguous between an NPI and a simple existentially quantified indefinite meaning *something*. Thus, in the Dakar dialect, (56)a could mean, "I cooked something". However, the force of the argument is retained because in the Dakar dialect, for example, the indefinite *dara* can still reconstruct under the scope of negation. The difference then is whether *only* the NPI interpretation is possible.

An NPI like *dara* can also be clefted as a subject:

(58)

Dara	*(mu)*	*a*	*dàq-ul*	*xaj*	*yi*
anything	3SG	COP	chase-neg	dog	the.PL

"NOTHING chased the dogs"

In (58), the subject NPI can reconstruct into the c-command domain of negation. I take this as evidence that the clefted subject originates from within the scope of negation.

Wolof clefts display reconstruction effects for Principle A and Principle C of the Binding Theory. Wolof lacks a distinct *self* reflexive pronoun. Instead, a genitive collocation with *bopp* 'head' is used:

(59)

Dóór-na-a	***sama***	***bopp***
hit-*na*-1sg	my	head

"I hit myself" ✓Reflexive Reading
"I hit my head" ✓Literal Reading

(59) can be truthfully uttered in a situation in which I punched myself in the stomach, not the head. Of course, it could also be used if I punch my own head. Thus, (59) has a literal and a reflexive reading. The reflexive interpretation is unavailable if there is no appropriate, local, c-commanding antecedent. In that case, only the literal interpretation obtains, as in (60):

(60)

Binta$_k$	*foog-na*	*ne*	*dóór-na-a*	***bopp-am***$_k$
binta	think-FIN	that	hit-FIN-1SG	head-her

"Binta$_k$ thinks that I hit her$_{k/j}$ head" ✓Literal Reading
*"Binta$_k$ thinks that I hit her$_k$" *Reflexive Reading

In (60), the reflexive interpretation is impossible because the 1sg subject *-a* intervenes between the reflexive and its antecedent *Binta*.

Siginificantly, under clefting, the reflexive interpretation is possible:

(61)

[*Sama*	***bopp***]	*l-a-ñu*	*foog*	*ne*	***l-a-a***	*dóór*
my	head	XPL-COP-3PL	think	that	XPL-COP-1SG	hit

"It's myself that they think that I hit" ✓reflexive
"It's my head that they think that I hit" ✓literal

The significance of (61) is that the clefted reflexive, although in the matrix clause, can be bound by the embedded subject. Under the promotion analysis, this follows from the reflexive originating in the embedded clause, where it is bound by the embedded subject, satisfying Principle A. Movement subsequently takes the reflexive out of the domain of its antecedent.

Reconstruction also takes place for Principle C:

(62) a. **Nataal u* ***Isaa***$_i$ *l-a-a foog ne* ***t***$_i$ *l-a-∅*$_i$ *bëgg* ***t***$_i$
picture *u* isaa XPL-COP-1SG think that XPL-COP-3SG love
"It's a picture of Isaa$_i$ that I think that he$_{*i/j}$ loves"
(i.e., "Isaa$_i$ has the property that I think that he$_i$ loves the picture of himself$_i$.")

b. **Nataal u* ***kan***$_i$ *l–a xale yi wax ne* ***t***$_i$
picture *u* who XPL-COP child the.pl say that
l-a-∅$_i$ *bëgg* ***t***$_i$
XPL-COP-3SG love
"Whose$_i$ picture is it that the children say that he$_{*i/j}$ loves?"
(i.e., "Which person's picture has the property that the children said that person loves that picture of himself")

In (62)a, reconstruction of *Isaa* into it's base position triggers a Principle C violation, for *Isaa*, as an R-expresssion, would be bound by the embedded 3sg subject. If *Isaa* were base-generated in the matrix cleft position, we would expect coreference to be possible between *Isaa* and the embedded 3sg subject. The strong crossover effect in (62)b is reducible to a Principle C violation. As a Wh-trace is an R-expression, (62)b is expected to be ungrammatical under the promotion analysis because the Wh-trace is bound by the embedded 3sg subject. If the Wh element were generated in the cleft position in the matrix clause, there would be no Wh-trace to trigger the Principle C violation. Thus, there could not be a strong crossover effect.

Reconstruction effects in clefting are also manifested for quantifier binding:

(63) a. *Lan l–a [xale b–u nekk] bëgg*
what XPL-COP child CL-*u* exist love
"Who does every child love?"
Wh > ∀, ∀ > Wh

b. *Kan nga foog l–a [xale b–u nekk] bëgg*
who 2SG+*a*+XPL think XPL-COP child CL-*u* exist love
"Who do you think that every child loves?"
Wh > ∀, ∀ > Wh

c. **[l-an]**$_j$ l–a [xale b–u nekk]$_i$ bëgg **t**$_j$

d. **[k-an]**$_j$ nga foog [$_{CP}$ **t**$_j$ l–a [xale b–u nekk] bëgg **t**$_j$

(63)a–b show that a clefted Wh expression can be interpreted with wide or narrow scope with respect to a quantified subject (*xale bu nekk* 'every child') in a matrix clause ((63)a) or an embedded clause ((63)b). Under the promotion analysis, the narrow scope reading of the Wh word follows from reconstruction into its base position. Under a base-generation analysis, it is unclear how the wh word could scope lower than the universal quantifier, as the Wh word is never in the embedded clause.

4.3 Wolof-specific reconstruction diagnostics

In addition to the crosslinguistic reconstruction tests already discussed, Wolof-specific diagnostics also provide support for the promotion analysis. In Wolof, a verb like *bëgg* 'want' typically takes a subjunctive-like clause complement:

(64) *Bëgg-në-ñu Gàllaay jàng taalif bi*
want-FIN-3PL gallaay read poem the
"They want Gallaay to read the poem"

Subjunctive clauses have the restriction that the verb cannot carry past tense unless the higher verb carries overt tense marking:

(65) a. *Bëgg-*(**óón**)-në-ñu [Gàllaay jàng-**oon** taalif bi]*
want-past-FIN-3PL gallaay read-past poem the
"They had wanted Gallaay to read the poem"

b. *Bëgg-**óón**-në-ñu [Gàllaay jàng taalif bi]*
want-past-FIN-3pl gallaay read poem the
"They had wanted Gallaay to read the poem"

The examples in (65) show that the dependency goes one-way. If the subjunctive clause has past tense, then the higher clause must have a past tense, as in (65)a. However, if the higher clause has past tense, then the subjunctive clause may or may not have it as in (65)b. If the embedded subjunctive clause is clefted, the same restriction holds:

(66) *[Gàllaay jàng-**oon** taalif bi] l-a-ñu bëgg-*(**óón**)*
gallaay read-past poem the XPL-COP-3PL want-past
"For Gallaay toread the poem is what they wanted"

In other words, the (bracketed) subjunctive clause in (66) acts as if it were embedded under *bëgg* 'want'. That overt past tense is required on *bëgg* follows if the embedded subjunctive clause has been raised from its underlying complement position. Under a base generation approach to clefting, this is mysterious. If tense marking is absent in the subjunctive clause, then it is optional in the matrix *bëgg* clause under clefting:

(67) *[Gàllaay jàng taalif bi] l-a-ñu bëgg-(**óón**)*
gallaay read poem the XPL-COP-3PL want-past
"For Gallaay read the poem is what they want/ed"

This is exactly the same distribution as when the subjunctive is overtly embedded under *bëgg*. It is clear that the requirement on tense in the higher clause is not generally applicable across clause types, in (68), where the matrix verb *wax* may or may not carry past tense independent of the embedded clause:

(68) [*Gàllaay jàng-***oon** *taalif bi*] *l-a-ñu wax-*(**oon**)
gallaay read-past poem the XPL-COP-3PL say-past
"That Gallaay read the poem is what they said"

Because the clefted string behaves as if it were literally the complement of *bëgg*, I take this as support for the promotion analysis.

Certain facts concerning VP clefting can be made sense of if a clefted VP moves from inside of TP to the cleft position. The first observation is that a definite DP can be stranded when a VP is clefted, as attested by (69)a, where the object *simis* 'shirt' bears the definite article *bi* 'the', but an indefinite cannot, as (69)c shows:

(69) a. DP_{def} stranded
$[_{VP}$ ***Suub***] *l-a-a def* ***simis bi***
dye XPL-COP-1SG do shirt the
"Dying is what I did to the shirt"

b. [V + DP_{indef}] clefted
$[_{VP}$ ***Suub simis***] *l-a-a def*
dye shirt XPL-COP-1SG do
"Dying a shirt is what I did"

c. *DP_{indef} stranded
*$[_{VP}$ *Suub* t_i] *l-a-a def* ***simis***$_i$
dye XPL-COP-1SG do shirt
"Dye is what I do to a shirt"

d. DP_{indef} clefted
Simis *l-a-a suub*
shirt XPL-COP-1SG dye
"It's a shirt that I dyed"

In fact, VP clefting looks like the so-called VP remnant topicalization construction attested in Continental Germanic (Müller 1998, among others). (69)d shows that an indefinite DP can be clefted by itself. Following Diesing (1992), I take indefinite DPs to be lower in the structure than definite DPs, which can scramble. Scrambling itself is difficult to observe directly in Wolof as a result of factors such as verb movement that may obscure the effect. The fact that the indefinite DP in (69)b–c must be clefted with VP follows because an indefinite cannot raise high enough to escape the fronting VP. On the other hand, if VP is simply generated in the cleft position in (69)a–b, it is unclear why an indefinite DP cannot be generated low, as in (69)c.

A second property of VP clefting in Wolof is that non-subject clitics can be fronted with VP or remain inside of TP:

(70) a. Clitic in VP
[$_{VP}$ ***Suub-léén***] *l-a-a* *def*
dye-3PL XPL-COP-1SG do
"Dye them is what I did"

b. Clitic outside of VP
[$_{VP}$ ***Suub***] *l-a-a-**léén*** *def*
dye XPL-COP-1SG-3PL do
"It's dying that I did to them"

c. *[$_{XP}$ ***Simis-léén***] *l-a-a-y* *suub-ël*
shirt-3PL XPL-COP-1SG-*di* dye-ben
"It's a shirt for them that I will dye"

This pattern of clitics follows if the clitics are merged as an argument in the object position in vP or VP. Under the promotion analysis, when the VP is clefted, it can carry the clitic along with it ((70)a) or the clitic can move out of VP first ((70)b), followed by VP fronting to the cleft position. The example in (70)c shows that the clitic distribution is directly tied to the presence of VP clefting, not clefting per se. That is, the distribution of the clitics falls out from the mechanics of VP movement under clefting.

A final piece of Wolof-specific evidence comes from the interaction of clefting and pied piping. Wolof allows for wh-expressions and past tense to be clefted together:

(71) a. ***Kan*** l-a-ñu y wax ne l-a-a dóór-***oon***
who XPL-COP-3PL IMPERF say that XPL-COP-1SG hit-PAST
"Who will they say that I hit?"

b. [***Kan oon***] *l-a-ñu* *y* *wax* *ne* *l-a-a* *dóór*
who PAST XPL-COP-3PL IMPERF say that XPL-COP-1SG hit
"Who will they say that I hit?"

In (71)a, the wh-expression *kan* 'who' has been clefted into the matrix clause, which is in the imperfective. In (71)b the wh-expression and past tense from the embedded clause surface in the matrix cleft position. The past tense (*-oon*) is interpreted with the embedded verb, which is a reconstruction effect. For the promotion analysis, (71)b results from pied piping of TP. Recall that in the discussion of *na*-clauses in (4), I showed that TP could be pied piped ((4)a) or stranded ((4)b. (71)b would arise when VP strands TP (leaving its trace in SpecTP) and if there is a wh-position above TP, roughly:

(72)

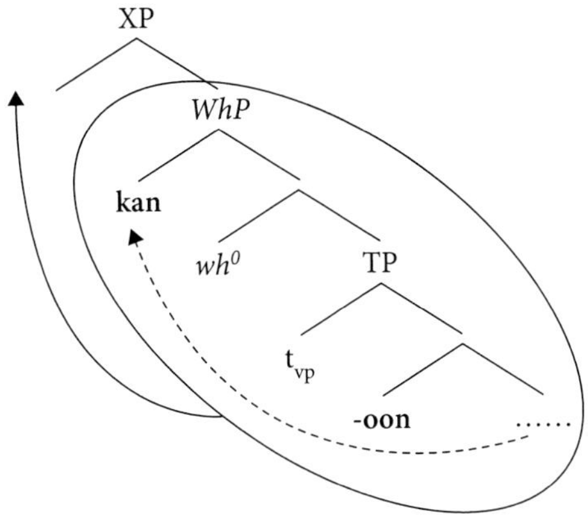

In (72), the wh-expression has an intermediate landing site above TP which I label '*WhP*'. From this position, the wh-can either pied pipe *WhP* and therefore TP, which is contained in *WhP*. Thus, there is no direct relation between the wh-expression and the clefted TP. The TP just happens to be inside of a pied piped constituent. I leave the precise nature of the constituent that is pied piped in (71) b and (72) as an open question. If something like (72) is correct, it suggests that the internal structure of non-subject (and subject clefts) is probably far richer than the representations I give in (39)a–b. Under this analysis, the fact that a Wh and tense can be clefted together indicates that the movement is not directly from object position to SpecCP, but involves other lower positions (Chomsky 1986; Rackowski & Richards 2005; Torrence 2010). I leave these too as open questions, but overall take cases like (71)b as support for the promotion analysis.

5. Summary

In this paper, I have argued for a morphosyntactic point, namely, that all Wolof clefts are constructed around a common core consisting of the copular predicate *-a*. The copular *-a* has the property that it is preceded by a nominal (subject, subject marker, non-subject DP) or an expletive/dummy element (the *l-*). The clefted item always occurs on the left edge of the cleft clause, preceding the copula *-a* and the expletives, if present. In looking at the copular structures, I determined that they come in different "sizes" and that subject clefts are smaller than non-subject clefts in Wolof. Syntactically, I have argued that in Wolof clefts, the clefted item undergoes A'-movement to the cleft position. Evidence for this comes from crosslinguistically applicable and Wolof-specific reconstruction tests. Wolof is important because it adds to the typology of cleft constructions. Specifically, Wolof contrasts with languages like English, for which clefting is argued to involve A'-movement of a silent operator. As has been shown, clefting in Wolof is different because clefting does not involve the presence of a silent operator. At the same time, the Wolof and English constructions are similar in that they both involve movement.

References

Aboh, Enoch. 2004. *The Morphosyntax of Complement-Head Sequences*. New York: Oxford University Press.

Aboh, Enoch Oladé. 2007. Focused versus non-focused wh-phrases. In *Focus Strategies in African Languages*, Enoch Oladé Aboh, Katharina Hartmann & Malte Zimmermann (eds), 287–314. New York NY: Mouton de Gruyter.

Bassène, Alain-Christian. 2007. *Morphosyntaxe du jóola banjal*. Köln: Rüdiger Köppe.

Belletti, Adriana. 2008a. Answering strategies: New information subjects and the nature of clefts. Ms.

Belletti, Adriana. 2008b. The CP of *clefts*. Studies in Linguistics [CISCL Working Papers 2].

Chomsky, Noam. 1977. On wh-movement. In *Formal Syntax*, Peter Culicover, Tom Wasow & Adrian Akmajian (eds). New York NY: Academic Press.

Chomsky, Noam. 1986. *Barriers*. Cambridge MA: The MIT Press.

Church, Eric. 1981. *Le Système Verbal du Wolof. Dakar* [Université de Dakar, Documents Linguistiques, N.27].

Cinque, Guglielmo. 1999. *Adverbs and Functional Heads*. Oxford: OUP.

Dialo Amadou. 1985. *Elements Expressifs du Wolof Contemporain* [Les Langues Nationales au Sénégal 27]. Dakar: Centre de Linguistique Appliquée de Dakar.

Diesing, Molly. 1992. *Indefinites*. Cambridge MA: The MIT Press.

Fiedler, Ines, Hartmann, Katharina, Reineke, Brigitte, Schwarz, Anne & Zimmermann, Malte. 2010. Subject focus in West African languages. In *Information Structure: Theoretical, Typological, and Experimental Perspectives*, Malte Zimmermann & Caroline Féry (eds), 234–257. Oxford: OUP.

Kayne, Richard. 1994. *The Antisymmetry of Syntax*. Cambridge MA: The MIT Press.

Kihm, Alain. 1999. Focus in Wolof: A study of what morphology may do to syntax. In *The Grammar of Focus* [Linguistik Aktuell/Linguistics Today 24], Georges Rebuschi & Laurice Tuller (eds), 245–274. Amsterdam: John Benjamins.

McCloskey, James. 2001. The morphosyntax of Wh-extraction in Irish. *Journal of Linguistics* 37: 67–100.

Koopman, Hilda. 2006. Word Formation in Syntax and Mirror Principle violations: Wolof and Japanese. Handout from talk at University College London, October.

Moro, Andrea. 1997. *The Raising of Predicates: Predicative Noun Phrases and the Theory of Clause Structure* [Cambridge Studies in Linguistics 80]. Cambridge: CUP.

Müller, Gereon. 1998. *Incomplete Category Fronting*. Dordrecht: Kluwer.

Munaro, Nicola and Jean-Yves Pollock. 2005. "Qu'est-ce-que (qu)-est-ce-que?". *The Oxford Handbook of Comparative Syntax*. Guglielmo Cinque and Richard S. Kayne (eds.), pp. 542–606. New York: Oxford University Press.

Njie, Codu Mbassy. 1982. *Description Syntaxique du Wolof de Gambie*. Dakar: Les Nouvelles Editions Africaines.

Rackowski, Andrea & Ric Rizzi, Luigi. 1997. The fine structure of the left periphery. In *Elements of Grammar*, Liliane Haegeman (ed.). Dordrecht: Kluwer.

Robert, Stéphane. 1986. Le Wolof: Un example d'expression morphologique de l'emphase. *Bulletin de la Société de Linguistique de Paris* LXXXI: 319–341.

Sauvageot, Serge. 1965. *Description synchronique d'un dialecte Wolof: Le parler du Dyolof*. Dakar: Institut Fondamental D'Afrique Noire.

Sportiche, Dominique. 2005. Reconstruction, binding, and scope. In *The Syntax Companion*, Vol. 4, Martin Everaert & Henk van Riemsdijk (eds), 35–93. Malden MA: Blackwell.

Stowell, Timothy Angus. 1981. Origins of Phrase Structure. Ph.D. dissertation, MIT.

Torrence, Harold. 2003. Verb movement in Wolof. In *Papers in African Linguistics 3* [UCLA Working Papers in Linguistics 9], Jason Kandybowicz (ed.), 85–115. Los Angeles CA: University of California, Los Angeles Linguistics Department.

Torrence, Harold. 2005. On the Distribution of Complementizers in Wolof. Ph.D. dissertation, University of California, Los Angeles.

Torrence, Harold. 2010. Successive Cyclic Stranding and Agreement in Wolof. Ms.

Vergnaud, J.R. 1974. French Relative Clauses. Ph.D. dissertation, MIT.

Welmers, William. 1973. *African Language Structures*. Los Angeles CA: University of California Press.

Zribi-Hertz, Anne & Diagne, Lamine. 2002. Clitic placement after syntax: Evidence from Wolof pronouns and person markers. *Natural Language & Linguistic Theory* 20(4): 823–884.

PART III

The focus potential of clefts

Multiple focus and cleft sentences

Nancy Hedberg
Simon Fraser University

The information structure of English cleft sentences is discussed. A cleft sentence divides a proposition into two parts, which are interpreted as an exhaustive focus and a pragmatic presupposition. These two semantic components can be flexibly mapped onto the information structure categories of topic and comment to arrive at comment-topic ('stressed focus') clefts and topic-comment ('informative presupposition') clefts. Clefts thus introduce a cleft focus or even a pair of foci constructionally. They also exhibit an assertive (comment) focus, which may or may not correspond to the cleft focus. While only exclusive focus particles can associate with the cleft focus, additive and scalar focus particles can associate with the assertive focus in the cleft clause, thus giving rise to additional cleft sentences containing multiple instances of focus.

Keywords: cleft; focus; presupposition; topic

1. Introduction

Cleft sentences have traditionally been viewed as divided into two parts, whereby the clefted constituent expresses a focus and the cleft clause expresses a presupposition. Prince (1978), in fact, uses the terms 'focus' and 'presupposition' to identify these two parts of a cleft sentence. An example illustrating a typical use of a cleft sentence is shown in (1).

(1) 'Then,' went on Evelyn with a subdued bitterness that grew more intense with every word, 'when I had done all they asked, and he had come to depend on me – as might have been expected – they <u>decided that this would never do</u>, either. Or rather **it was Ursula who decided**, and she talked Jim into it…' [Mary Fitt, Death and the Pleasant Voices, 1946/1984, p. 60]

In this section, I will argue that the structural meaning of a cleft sentence is precisely to express these two components: the clefted constituent inherently expresses a particular type of focus, namely an 'exhaustive' focus, and the cleft clause inherently expresses a pragmatic presupposition. In Section 2, I argue that these two syntactic and semantic parts of a cleft can map onto topic/comment structure in a flexible way, so that the cleft sentence as a whole can have a topic-comment as well as a comment-topic organization, with the consequence that the cleft clause as well as the clefted constituent can contain a prosodic focus when spoken aloud. In Section 3, I argue that it is fruitful to view each of these prosodic foci as expressing a semantic focus in the sense defined immediately below as expressing the presence of alternatives. This allows cleft sentences with more than one prosodic focus to be viewed as multiple focus constructions semantically, which in turn allows several interesting subtypes of cleft usage to be explicated. In Section 4, I briefly conclude.

1.1 Clefted constituent expresses an exhaustive focus

For 'focus', it is useful to adopt the definition given in (2) from Krifka (2007), which is based on the view of focus taken in Alternative Semantics (Rooth 1985, 1992).

(2) *Focus indicates the presence of alternatives that are relevant for the interpretation of linguistic expressions.*

Krifka (2007, p. 7) goes on to say,

> It might well be that different ways of focus marking signal different ways of how alternatives are exploited; e.g. focus marking by cleft sentences often signals an exhaustive interpretation that in-situ focus lacks. We can then talk about subtypes of focus, such as cleft focus and in-situ-focus, that may employ the alternatives in more specific ways.

It is clear that in (1), the speaker exhaustively picks out Ursula as the one who decided, excluding the alternative that it was Jim or, in particular, both Ursula and Jim. Focus can be used pragmatically to answer a question, to correct information, or to confirm information (Krifka 2007, p. 12). In (1), we have an example of the corrective use of cleft focus, as the speaker is correcting herself.

É. Kiss (1998) presents a test for the exhaustivity of cleft focus, which she attributes to Donka Farkas. Notice the contrast between the felicity of (3aB) adding to a cleft focus and the infelicity of (3bB) adding to an in situ focus:

(3) a. A: It was a HAT that Mary picked for herself.
B: No, she picked a COAT, too.
b. A: Mary picked a HAT for herself.
B: #No, she picked a COAT, too.[1]

1. Wedgewood (2007) points out that this dialogue is felicitous in some exhaustive in situ contexts, such as that in (i):

Hedberg (1990, 2000) argues that the cleft clause forms a discontinuous definite description with the cleft pronoun acting as a definite determiner, and this definite description being equated with the referent of the clefted constituent via the copula. Implementing this analysis formally in Tree-Adjoining Grammar, Han and Hedberg (2008) assign the semantics in (4b) to the 'equative' cleft in (4a). (4b) entails the Russellian predicate logic formula in (4c), which contains the exhaustive meaning associated with the clefted constituent.

(4) a. It was Ohno who won.
b. THEz [won(z)] [z = Ohno]
c. $\exists z\ [won(z) \wedge \forall y[won(y) \rightarrow y = z] \wedge z = Ohno]$

As Wedgewood (2007) argues, however, the cleft cannot be said to assert an exhaustive focus, with the semantics in (5) because, as Horn (1981) pointed out, it is infelicitous to use an otherwise unmodified cleft sentence to directly assert that this exhaustive meaning holds. Thus, (6a) is infelicitous. To assert exhaustiveness, a focus particle must be used, as in (6b).

(5) $\lambda x[\lambda P[P(x) \wedge \forall y[P(y) \rightarrow y{=}x]]]$

(6) a. # I know Mary ate a pizza but I've just discovered it was a pizza that she ate.

b. I know Mary ate a pizza but I've just discovered it was only a pizza that she ate.

Instead of encoding an exhaustive focus as part of the assertion, it is compatible with the data in (6) to analyze the cleft as encoding an identificational focus, with the semantics in (7), whereby the exhaustive meaning is conveyed as a presupposition.[2]

(7) $\lambda x[\lambda P[x = \iota y[P(y)]]]$

(i) C: I see that Jane picked herself a coat, a scarf and a pair of gloves.
A: Whereas Mary picked herself a HAT.
B: No, she picked a COAT, too.

2. Horn (1981) further argues that the exhaustiveness condition may in fact be a generalized conversational implicature, instead of an entailment or presupposition, because it can be cancelled, as in the examples in (i).

(i) a. It was in that article, among other places, that Bork expressed his support for California's anti-open-housing referendum and his belief that it was only 'political speech' which deserved First Amendment protection. [David S. Broder, 'The need to be sure on Bork', Minneapolis Star and Tribune, 9/20/87]

b. It's the ideas that count, not just the way we write them. [Richard Smaby, lecture; example provided by Ellen Prince and discussed in Horn 1981]

For more discussion and additional examples, see Horn (1981) and Hedberg (1990).

The syntax of the cleft transparently reflects this semantics, as Wedgewood further points out, if the cleft is given the syntactic and semantic analysis argued for in Hedberg (1990, 2000). The formal analysis in Han & Hedberg (2008) is compatible with this if the semantic account is elaborated to specify the exhaustiveness condition just discussed as well as the existential condition next to be discussed as presuppositions.

1.2 Cleft clause expresses a pragmatic presupposition

In addition to the exhaustiveness condition associated with the clefted constituent, the second part of the cleft, the cleft clause, expresses an existential presupposition, as can be seen by the fact that the corresponding existentially quantified proposition survives under negation, questioning, and in the antecedent of a conditional (Chierchia & McConnell-Ginet 1990). Thus a speaker of (8a–d) would normally believe (8e) and assume that the addressee shares this belief.

(8) a. It was Ursula who decided.
b. It wasn't Ursula who decided.
c. Was it Ursula who decided?
d. If it was Ursula who decided, then Jim is off the hook.
e. Someone decided.

The relevant notion of pragmatic presupposition was defined by Stalnaker (1974: 200) as shown in (9).

(9) *A proposition P is a pragmatic presupposition of a speaker in a given context just in case the speaker assumes or believes that P, assumes or believes that his addressee assumes or believes that P, and assumes or believes that his addressee recognizes that he is making these assumptions or has these beliefs.*

Dryer (1996) gives a number of examples supporting the thesis that the information expressed by the cleft clause is pragmatically presupposed, as shown in (10). In (a), B would be uttering a cleft sentences without believing the presupposition that someone saw John. In (b) and (c), B would be uttering a cleft sentence in a context where it is clear that it is not the case that A believes the presupposition. Since a presupposition must be mutually believed, the clefts in all three cases are infelicitous.

(10) a. A: Who saw John?
B: #It was NOBODY that saw John.

b. A: Who if anyone saw John?
B: #It was MARY that saw John.

c. A: Did anyone see John?
B: #It was MARY that saw John.

Crucially, Dryer shows that the non-focus information in a non-cleft sentence containing only a prosodic focus is not pragmatically presupposed. The simple sentence counterparts of the clefts in (10) are perfectly felicitous in (11).

(11) a. A: Who saw John?
B: NOBODY saw John.

b. A: Who if anyone saw John?
B: MARY saw John.

c. A: Did anyone see John?
B: MARY saw John.

Dryer argues that the non-focus in simple sentences is activated instead of presupposed, where activation is a cognitive notion meaning that the material conveyed is represented in short-term or working memory.[3] The main thesis of his paper is that a distinction needs to be drawn between pragmatic presupposition and activation. While some linguistic phenomena, like cleft clauses, involve true pragmatic presupposition (shared belief), others, like the non-focus of simple sentences, involve activation (presence in consciousness). The two notions are distinct: there can be presupposed propositions that are not activated, and activated propositions that are not presupposed.[4]

As a further argument against the idea that prosodically non-focused material and presupposition should be equated, Dryer shows that presupposed material can be prosodically focused. He illustrates with the example from Halliday (1967) in (12) in which prosodic focus occurs on a cleft clause:

(12) A: Have you told John that the window got broken?
B: It was John that BROKE the window.

---

3. Dryer deliberately does not attempt to formalize his notion of 'activation' because the nature of activation is an empirical matter under investigation by psychologists. Chafe (1974) perhaps was the first to introduce the psychological notion of activation (or 'consciousness') into linguistics, and 'activated' is the term used in Gundel, Hedberg and Zacharski (1993) for one of their cognitive statuses. An element is activated for a subject whenever it is represented in short-term or working memory, whether it was linguistically introduced, introduced in the physical context, arrived at by inference, or retrieved from long-term memory. It is thus a broader notion than some similar notions that linguists have formally defined, such as Rochemont's (1986) notion of 'c-construable' or Schwarzschild's (1999) notion of 'Givenness'.

4. An anonymous reviewer points out that Rooth's theory correctly predicts in a formal way that the background to a simple sentence with prosodic focus does not require existential closure. Thus Rooth (1992) uses a ~ operator to indicate that the background of the focus is anaphorically linked to an antecedent in the context.

This example shows that cleft focus and prosodic focus can diverge in a cleft sentence. The example also shows that cleft clause material need not always be activated, although in the examples in (1) the cleft clause material was both presupposed and activated. In (12B), it doesn't seem necessary to assume that A is necessarily consciously contemplating the proposition that someone or something broke the window, although this is something that he presumably believes.

A cleft presupposition can also be denied or suspended like other pragmatic presuppositions, as in the examples in (13) and (14):

(13) You believe that Mary kissed someone in this room. But *it wasn't Joe that she kissed*, and it wasn't Rita, and clearly it wasn't Bill, and there hasn't been anyone else here. Therefore, Mary didn't kiss anybody in this room. [Halvorsen 1978, variants in Keenan 1971; Gazdar 1979; Levinson 1983]

(14) If *it wasn't an apple that John ate*, then John ate nothing. [Delahunty 1982]

To sum up, a cleft sentence packages a proposition in such a way that the two principal semantic parts of a cleft – an exhaustive focus and a pragmatic presupposition – are mapped transparently onto two syntactic constituents – a clefted constituent and a cleft clause – and are equated with each other via a copula. In the following section, I examine clefts where the prosodic focus falls on the clefted constituent and those where the prosodic focus falls on the cleft clause, and discuss the extent to which such clefts can be analyzed as differing in the mapping between the different parts of the cleft and the information structural distinction between topic and comment. In Section 3, I present an analysis of clefts in which the primary sentence accent falls on the cleft clause as multiple focus structures.

2. Cleft sentences and the topic/comment mapping

In this section, I argue that the mapping of the two primary parts of a cleft sentence onto the information structure categories of topic and comment is flexible, so that cleft sentences can exhibit either comment-topic or topic-comment organization. These two organizations correspond to the distinction that Prince (1978) drew between 'stressed focus' and 'informative presupposition' it-clefts.

2.1 Comment-topic clefts

In prototypical clefts, like that in (1), the cleft clause expresses an activated presupposition and the clefted constituent, which does or at least could receive the primary sentence accent, expresses a focus that is used to make a correction as in (1), to answer a question or to present a contrast.

Example (15) shows a 'truncated' cleft that answers an indirect question, and where the content of the question is so strongly activated that it can be elided in the cleft. It is difficult to find examples of clefts directly answering a wh-question, probably because wh-questions are usually directly answered using a sentence fragment instead of a whole sentence.

(15) Haven't you been wondering who the dickens put them in that watermelon? Of course you have; but you might have known **it was Janet,** because no one else would have done it. [Rex Stout, The Hand in the Glove, 1936, p. 271]

Example (16) shows a cleft used to make a contrast. The material expressed by the cleft clause represents an inference by the speaker and could probably be pronounced with no accent on the cleft clause.

(16) 'His inheritance? Was he the eldest son, then?'
'No, Barnabas was the eldest, but he was killed at Waterloo and left no family. Then there was a second son, Roger, but he died of smallpox as a child. Simon was the third son.'
'Then it was the fourth son who took the estate?
'Yes, Frederick. He was Henry Dawson's father. They tried, of course, to find out what became of Simon, but in those days it was very difficult, you understand, to get information from foreign places, and Simon had quite disappeared. So they had to pass him over.'
[Dorothy Sayers, Unnatural Death, 1927, p. 127]

It is quite common for material in the cleft clause to be inferred instead of directly activated linguistically. Another example is shown in (17), which would most likely be pronounced with primary sentence accent on the clefted constituent, and again the cleft clause can be expressed with no accent.

(17) Beginning at the top of the list, I went along the landing and tapped at Ruskin's door. When it was opened, **it was Webber who stood there.** We stared at each other for a moment, both of us taken aback.
[Lucille Kallen, The Piano Bird, 1984, p. 95]

In all of these cases, the clefted constituent expresses an exhaustive focus and the cleft clause expresses an activated proposition or one that is easily inferable from activated information. Primary sentence accent falls on the clefted constituent and the cleft clause is or can be left unaccented or even not expressed at all. Prince (1978) calls such clefts 'stressed focus clefts'.

Following Gundel (1985), such clefts were analyzed as comment-topic (termed 'topic-clause') clefts in Hedberg (1990) because the cleft clause can be seen as expressing the topic of the utterance and predication of the clefted constituent as expressing the comment. The evidence is that primary sentence accent falls on the clefted constituent rather than the cleft clause, and that the cleft clause material passes topic tests better than the clefted constituent does. Thus, (18a) illustrates the 'question test' (Sgall et al. 1973; Gundel 1974; Reinhart 1982), whereby elements in the question eliciting a sentence are concluded to be part of the topic. Likewise, (18b) illustrates the '*as for* test' (Kuno 1972; Gundel 1974), and (18c) illustrates the '*said-about* test' (Reinhart 1982). According to all of these tests, elements singled out by 'as for' or 'said about' are concluded to be topics.

(18) a. Who decided? Actually, it was Ursula.
#What about Ursula? Actually, she decided.

b. Or rather, as for who decided, it was Ursula.
#Or rather, as for Ursula, she decided.

c. Then, Evelyn said about who decided that it was Ursula.
??Then Evelyn said about Ursula that she decided.

The cleft clause material in (15)–(17) also passes the topic tests, as (19) shows:[5]

(19) a. As for who put them in the watermelon, it was Janet.
b. As for who took the estate, was it the fourth son?
c. As for who stood there, it was Webber.

A potential problem with taking cleft clause material to be topical is that it may not be immediately clear how a clause can denote an entity. Hedberg (1990) followed Gundel's (1988) definition of 'topic', given in (20). This is very similar to Krifka's (2007) definition of topic, given in (21), which is based on Reinhart's (1982) definition. In addition to containing a set of propositions, the Common Ground here is understood as containing a set of entities.

(20) *An entity, E, is the topic of a sentence, S, iff, in using S, the speaker intends to increase the addressee's knowledge about, request information about or otherwise get the addressee to act with respect to E.*

5. These tests have sometimes been misunderstood as substitution tests, and rejected on that basis. However, the claim is not, for example, that an 'as-for' phrase can always be appended to the front of the sentence containing the purported topic, with the modified sentence then being felicitously substitutable for the original sentence in the original discourse context. Other adjustments almost always need to be made to the discourse. Thus, a discourse showing that (19c) is felicitous would be one like that shown in (i):

(i) I went along the landing and tapped at Ruskin's door. The door opened. [Pause.]
As for who stood there, it was Webber.

Similarly, the context for (18a) would have to be one that modifies the discourse in (1) into a dialogue, and then pronounces the question in (18a) as an echo question.

(21) *The topic constituent identifies the entity or set of entities under which the information expressed in the comment constituent should be stored in the CG [Common Ground] content.*

Gundel (1985) assumes that a cleft clause can express an entity in the same way that a free relative can. In this way the topic of (1) would be [the person(s)] who decided, and then this entity would be identified as Ursula by the cleft utterance. Such an analysis is made explicitly in the account of clefts of Hedberg (1990, 2000) and Han and Hedberg (2008), where (specificational) clefts are treated as equative constructions equating an entity or set of entities with the denotation of a discontinuous definite description.

Krifka's definition makes it clear that a topic constituent needs to identify a location for the information expressed in the comment constituent to be stored. With regard to the cleft in (1), we could perhaps assume that there is a temporary storage place, or file card, corresponding to the question, 'who decided?' In a mystery novel, for example, the detective can be seen as creating a set of cards sorted by questions, which are filled in when they are answered, and then the information on those cards is transferred to the cards corresponding to the entities referred to in the question and the answer. When the hearer of the utterance in (1) processes the cleft, perhaps he first accommodates a new card corresponding to the question 'who decided?', then completes it with the answer, Ursula. He then transfers the information that Ursula decided to the Ursula card, and deletes the information from the Ursula and Jim card that they decided, or perhaps more precisely deletes from the Ursula card the information that she decided with Jim and from the Jim card that he decided with Ursula.

Alternatively, following Dahl (1974), we could posit two information structure distinctions: Topic/Comment, to be used when the topic constituent denotes an entity; and Focus/Background, to be used when there is a focus+presupposition structure to the sentence, as in the case of stressed focus clefts.[6] However, this still leaves open the question as to where the information would be stored. Presumably, after processing the sentence, the information would be stored on the cards corresponding to the entities denoted by the DPs in

6. Alternatively, we could follow Vallduvi (1990) and identify a tripartite information structure, where 'focus' is opposed to 'background' and the latter is divided into two subparts. Valluduvi (1990) would oppose 'link' to 'focus' in the case of initial, entity-level topics, and 'tail' to 'focus' in the case of unaccented cleft clauses.

the sentence. I don't know of any substantive way to decide between these alternative approaches, and I will continue to use the Gundel-based terminology.[7]

2.2 Topic-comment clefts

Clefts with primary accent on the cleft clause were first discussed systematically by Prince (1978). She contrasted the previously more commonly discussed type of cleft, which she called a 'stressed focus' cleft, in which the clefted constituent presents contrastive information and the clause presents information that is given in the discourse, with clefts in which the information in the cleft clause is new and thus can appear discourse initially. One of her examples of such 'informative presupposition clefts' is shown in (22), where the writer does not seem to be expecting that readers already know that Henry Ford was responsible for introducing the weekend.

(22) [BEGINNING OF A NEWSPAPER ARTICLE]
It was just about 50 years ago that Henry Ford gave us the weekend. On September 25, 1926, in a somewhat shocking move for that time, he decided to establish a 40-hour work week, giving his employees two days off instead of one. [Philadelphia Bulletin, 1/3/76, p. 3L, cited in Prince 1978, p. 898]

According to Prince (1978, p. 899), informative presupposition clefts "mark a piece of information as fact, known to some people although not yet known to the intended hearer." Delin (1992, p. 302) characterizes such a presupposition as "non-negotiable in the discourse at the time at which it appears." In such uses of clefts, the speaker intends to convey information that is new to the hearer and thus not in fact already in the common ground. However, because the information is presented as a known fact, it is presented as easily accommodatable into the common ground (Lewis 1979). With this use, then, the speaker exploits the presuppositional structure of a cleft as a rhetorical device in order to effect a change in the common ground.[8] Such clefts thus can be used even discourse initially to begin a newspaper article, as in Example (22) or to dramatically begin a novel as in Example (23).

7. Huber (2006) objects to Hedberg's use of the term 'topic' in her 'topic-clause clefts' because for him a topic cannot follow a focus. However, a topic can follow a focus in Gundel's system if it is an 'activated topic'. Thus postverbal object pronouns often express the topic of an utterance, as do right-dislocated constituents. 'Topic' for Gundel (1985, 1988) really corresponds to Vallduvi's 'background' and thus topics can come in two flavors: that of Vallduvi's 'link' and that of his 'tail'.

8. Consistent with this analysis, Ball (1992) argues that the English informative presupposition cleft is historically newer than the stressed focus cleft, having emerged during the Late Middle English period (1300–1500), whereas stressed focus clefts were attested in the Old English period.

(23) [BEGINNING OF A MYSTERY NOVEL]
It was jealousy that kept David from sleeping, drove him from a tousled bed out of the dark and silent boardinghouse to walk the streets. He had so long lived with his jealousy, however, that the usual images and words, with their direct and obvious impact on the heart, no longer came to the surface of his mind. It was now just the Situation.
[Patricia Highsmith, This Sweet Sickness, 1961, p. 1]

As Hedberg (1990) points out, clefts with primary accent on the cleft clause can have familiar as well as informative presuppositions, as in (24). Such presuppositions are 'discourse new' but 'hearer old' in the terms introduced in Prince (1992), and thus are not actually informative to the hearer.

(24) '...And of course, we've only got his version of the niece and the nurse – and he obviously had what the Scotch call ta'en a scunner at the nurse. We musn't lose sight of her, by the way. She was the last person to be with the old lady before her death, and **it was she who administered that injection**.'
'Yes, yes – but the injection had nothing to do with it. If anything's clear that is'. [Dorothy Sayers, Unnatural Death, 1927, p. 17]

It was argued in Hedberg (1990) that clefts such as (24) map onto information structure in such a way that the clefted constituent expresses the topic and the cleft clause expresses the comment. Evidence in support of this analysis comes from the results of the topic tests shown in (25).

(25) a. As for the nurse, it was she who administered that injection.
b. A: What about the nurse?
B: It was she who administered that injection.
c. He said about the nurse that it was she who administered that injection.

Other pieces of evidence that the clefted constituent expresses the topic are that the material denoted by the clefted constituent is activated in the discourse and more activated than the material in the cleft clause, which is merely familiar; and that the main prosodic accent in the sentence falls on the cleft clause. Finally, Prince (1978) observes that the clefted constituent in informative presupposition clefts perhaps always represents the subject of the cleft clause proposition or a sentence adverbial. Such constituents are also widely believed to be the most typical sentence topics.

It is widely believed that topics in English are marked with a fall-rise prosodic accent, and it can be seen from the examples in (26) and (27), from Geluykens 1984, that the clefted constituent in clefts with two accents is at least sometimes marked with a fall-rise accent, while the cleft clause is marked with a falling accent. This accent pattern is consistent with such clefts having a topic-comment organization.[9]

(26) Well she must have known about it # and. it was "[[SHE$_{FR}$ who at'tempted to 'burn the BOOKS$_F$ #and de||stroy the EVIDENCE$_F$.
[Geluykens 1984, C19]

(27) It was "JOHNNY$_{FR}$ that 'stole her MONEY$_F$ while we were away in France, I think, wasn't it? [Geluykens 1984, C41]

Other examples from Geluykens' corpus exhibit a falling accent on the cleft clause and an unaccented clefted constituent:

(28) a. Did you meet Fuller?
b. Yes, # it was || he who INVITED$_F$ me #- and it was a very pleasant day.
[Geluykens 1984, C22]

(29) ... though Sir Garnet was marvelous that he'd done it all you see. So this was a mysterious phrase which I knew perfectly well what it meant, it meant that everything was tidy you see # but it was || he who EXPLAINED$_F$ #what it "MEANT$_F$#. [Geluykens, 1984, C12]

Despite the plausibility of this topic-comment analysis, one might equally well conclude that the cleft construction is used precisely to mark subjects and sentence adverbials as non-topics. Lambrecht (2001) criticizes Hedberg's analysis of some subject-extracted reverse pseudoclefts as topic-comment structures on the grounds that if the clefted constituent is a topic, why would a cleft construction be used at all when a non-clefted subject-predicate structure directly expressing a topic-comment structure could have been chosen for that function? I would say in response that the cleft, unlike a non-clefted sentence, allows the subject to be marked as an exhaustive focus and the material in the predicate to be marked as presupposed.

At this point I would like to leave this debate about whether or not the clefted constituent can express the topic of a cleft utterance, and concentrate on discussing some interesting types of clefts that contain a primary accent on the cleft clause. The definition of focus given above in (2), which says simply that foci present

9. For discussion and references on fall-rise accents as marking topics, see Hedberg and Sosa (2007). In that article we argue that the L+H*pitch accent can mark comments as easily as it can mark topics in English, but we concede that the entire fall rise tune (L+)H*LH% probably does have the function of marking 'contrastive topics' in the sense that has been recently developed in formal semantics, e.g. Büring (2003), Steedman (2007).

alternatives, is conveniently neutral with regard to whether the items so marked are topics or not. Clefts which are prosodically prominent on both subparts can then be seen as sentences containing multiple foci. In the next section, I hope to show that examining them from this perspective can shed light on the meaning and use of the cleft construction.

3. Multiple focus clefts

In this section, I examine three subtypes of clefts that contain prosodic prominence on both the clefted constituent and the cleft clause, and explore the consequences of viewing such clefts as multiple focus constructions in the sense of Krifka (1992, 2007).

3.1 Vice-versa clefts

Ball and Prince (1978) discuss the cleft example in (30). They point out that such clefts constitute an exception to the generalization that cleft clauses express presupposed information.

(30) *It's not John that shot Mary. It's Mary that shot John.*

The presupposition in the first cleft in (30) is not that 'someone shot Mary' (because the speaker does not believe this – the speaker is here most likely objecting to the addressee's assertion that John shot Mary) and in the second it-cleft the presupposition is not that 'someone shot John' (because the addressee does not believe this – the addressee just asserted that John shot Mary). Rather the background presupposition that is shared by speaker and addressee is that 'someone shot someone'.

Carlson (1983, p. 234) also mentions such clefts and concludes that the question eliciting such a cleft as its answer is a "double question with a unique pair presupposition, who has lost (and) what?". He gives the example in (31):

(31) It is not I who have lost the Athenians but the Athenians who have lost me. [Anaxagoras]

Two more recently attested examples are shown in (32) and (33). In (32), Robert assumes that Anna is taking it for granted that he called her. Thus it is not presupposed that someone called Robert. What is actually shared background knowledge is that someone called someone. In (34), it is established that Russell was with someone, and that someone else followed. The cleft sentences give two possible ways of pairing the two unknowns, and they are the reverse of each other.

(32) Anna: So, what's the case you're working on?
Robert: Nothing I need bother you with now. It's YOU who called ME, remember? [General Hospital, ABC, 6/21/89]

(33) 'He didn't go down to the river alone that night, did he?' In fact Lauren had every reason to suppose that Russell had gone down to the river with Sandy Grayson.
'No I don't think he did,' said Tracy.
'And someone else was following?' Laura suggested.
'Yes, perhaps,' said Tracy noncommittally.
Was it Tracy who followed Russell and Sandy? Or was it Sandy who followed Russell and Tracy? And how did Dora Carpenter fit in?
[Victoria Silver, Death of a Harvard Freshman, 1984, p.99]

Krifka (1992, 2007) discusses cases of 'complex focus' like the reading of the example in (34), where "the only pair of persons such that John introduced the first to the second is Bill and Sue." There are two foci related to one focus operator.

(34) John only introduced BILL to SUE.

Vice-versa clefts are a type of complex focus construction since there is one focus operator (the exhaustive focus operator associated structurally with the cleft) and two foci, one expressed in the clefted constituent and one in the cleft clause. Following Krifka, a schematic representation of this focus structure is shown in (35).

(35) It's not CLEFT_1 $[\text{JOHN}]_{F1}$ that shot $[\text{MARY}]_{F1}$. It's CLEFT_2 $[\text{MARY}]_{F2}$ that shot $[\text{JOHN}]_{F2}$.

Although according to Han and Hedberg's (2008) analysis of cleft structures, the cleft clause and the cleft pronoun are semantically composed together, as represented in the TAG derivation tree, the negation particle and the exhaustive operator can be seen as syntactically c-commanding both prosodic foci in the derived structure, in which the clefted constituent and the cleft clause form a constituent as elements of a functional projection (FP) that serves as the complement of the copula. The c-command requirement of focus operators with their focused associates, discussed in Krifka (1992), is thus met.

Krifka contrasts cases of complex focus with cases of multiple focus, where there are multiple foci but also multiple focus operators. In the next two subsections, I give examples of clefts exhibiting multiple foci.

3.2 Emphatic repetition clefts

Hedberg (1990) discusses a use of clefts that she calls 'emphatic repetition clefts'. Some examples are given in (36) and (37). These are typical 'informative presupposition' clefts in that the clefted constituent expresses either the subject of the cleft proposition as in (36) or a sentence adverbial, as in (37).

(36) The little woman in the blue trouser suit came into the restaurant car and hesitated for a moment before making for the table where the two married couples sat. The barrister jumped up and pulled out a chair for her. And then Wexford understood it was she he had seen. *It was she who had been coming down the corridor when he turned away from the window, she who, while his eyes were closed, had vanished into her own compartment.* She too was a small slight creature, she too was dressed in a dark-coloured pair of trousers and a jacket, and though her feet had certainly never been subjected to binding, they were not much bigger than a child's and they too were encased in the black Chinese slippers on sale everywhere....
[Ruth Rendall, Speaker of Mandarin, 1983]

(37) Just what is Canada?
It is a question that each traveler brings to this nation, and it is a question that has no single answer. Canada is a delightful labyrinth of cultures and customs, of peaceful coexistence and political squabbles....
It is here where the hearty French established a settlement along the frothy St. Lawrence River and survived the first relentless winter. It is here that the first bewildered European immigrants wondered how they would ever be able to thrive in such an unruly land; here where the British Loyalists fled from American revolutionaries; here where provinces separated by great distances and differences joined to form one nation. [Insight Guide to Canada, 1988, p. 15]

Such clefts can be seen as multiple focus constructions if an ASSERT operator is posited to bind the comment focus given in the cleft clause, as Krifka (1992) discusses, following Jacobs (1984). A schematic representation of the resulting focus structure is given in (38). Here the CLEFT focus operator binds the focus presented in the clefted constituent, and the ASSERT focus operator binds the focus presented in the cleft clause.

(38) ASSERT_1 It was CLEFT_2 $[\text{SHE}]_{F2}$ [who had been coming down the corridor when he turned away from the $\text{WINDOW}]_{F1}$

It is consistent with Krifka's framework, for a focus to also function as a topic in a different dimension, and the examples in (36) and (37) can be seen as expressing continuing topics in the clefted constituent. Contrastive topics are also possible, as in the example in (39) and (40).

(39) The women who went were almost all married. But *it was* *husbands* *who were captured by the glowing descriptions of the West,* *wives* *who were skeptical.* *Husbands* *who thought of what could be gained;* *wives* *who thought of what would be lost.*
[Ellen Goodman, 'the uprooted II', in Goodman 1985, p. 231]

(40) Not every community, courtroom, or jury today accepts this simple standard of justice. But ten years ago, five years ago, even three years ago, these women might not have pressed charges.
It was the change of climate which enabled, even encouraged, the women to come forward. It was the change of attitude which framed the arguments in the courtroom. It was the change of consciousness that infiltrated the jury chambers. [Ellen Goodman, 'If she says no', in Goodman 1985, p. 326]

I suggest that such examples can be given the semantic analysis sketched in (41) for (39). These examples differ from the cases exemplified in (38) only insofar as the clefted constituent expresses a contrastive topic as well as an alternative focus. Again the CLEFT focus operators binds the focus presented in the clefted constituent and the ASSERT focus operator binds the focus presented in the cleft clause.

(41) ASSERT_1 It was CLEFT_2 [$[\text{HUSBANDS}]_{F2}]_{CT}$ [who were captured by the glowing description of the $\text{WEST}]_{F1}$

3.3 *Also* and *even* clefts

The last subtype of cleft that I will discuss involves an additional focus operator binding a focus expressed in one of the two parts of a cleft sentence. If we continue to posit an ASSERT and a CLEFT focus operator in such sentences, then the additional focus particle contributes a second focus operator binding an already bound focus, so such examples represent an even more complex type of multiple focus construction, whereby there are multiple focus operators binding a single prosodic focus (see Krifka 2007 for non-cleft examples of this situation).

Krifka (1999) gives the relatively informal formulations of the meaning of the three major focus particles of English, *only*, *also*, and *even*, shown in (42). He labels these focus particles 'exclusive', 'additive' and 'scalar', respectively, and the logical formulas show the assertions and presuppositions of these three types of focus particles.

(42) $[\text{EXCL}_1 [\ldots F_1 \ldots]]$: $\neg\exists F' \neq F[\ldots F' \ldots]([\ldots F \ldots])$
$[\text{ADD}_1 [\ldots F_1 \ldots]]$: $[\ldots F \ldots](\exists F' \neq F[\ldots F' \ldots])$
$[\text{SCAL}_1 [\ldots F_1 \ldots]]$: $[\ldots F \ldots](\neg\exists F \neq F[[\ldots F \ldots] <_{likely}[\ldots F' \ldots]])$

It was argued above that the clefted constituent in a cleft inherently expresses exhaustiveness. It has often been pointed out that this exhaustive semantics is compatible with the exclusive focus adverb *only* but not with additive focus particles like *also* or scalar focus particles like *even*. Thus, Horn (1969, p. 106) makes the claim that "clefting, like *only*, specifies uniqueness, while *even* and *also* presuppose non-uniqueness and thus cannot be clefted", and gives the examples shown in (43).

(43) a. It's only Muriel who voted for Hubert.
b. *It's also Muriel who voted for Hubert.
c. *It's even Muriel who voted for Hubert.

In arguing that clefted constituents in it-clefts constitute identificational foci, É. Kiss (1998) reiterates this claim but points out that there are exceptional contexts that allow a clefted constitutent to be modified by *also*, citing the example in (44):

(44) A: Bill danced with Mary.
B: No, it was Sam that danced with Mary.
C: **It was also John that danced with her.**

She says (p. 252), "A cleft *also*-phrase appears to be acceptable precisely in a context where it can be understood to identify a member of a relevant set in addition to one or more members identified previously as such for which the predicate holds, with the rest of the set still excluded."[10] Note that the example in (44C) is a comment-topic cleft, since it can be paraphrased as shown in (45):

(45) As far as who danced with her is concerned, that was also John.

Nonetheless, it was pointed out in Hedberg (1990, 2000, 2006) and Hedberg and Fadden (2007) that attested exhaustive examples with *also* apparently syntactically adjoined to the clefted constituent in clefts can occasionally be found, for example the clefts in (46)–(48). Such examples do not fit the formula proposed by É. Kiss. In these examples, *also* apparently associates with a focus in the cleft clause, and this association of *also* does not lead to a contradiction to the meaning of the cleft.[11]

---

10. An attested example of É. Kiss's scenario is shown in (i). The focus particle *also* does not occur here, but it could:

(i) A: What is it about literature that you find so attractive?
B: Because literature is in some cases the product of the imagination isn't it and of men's minds, and it is the imagination and the mind of man that I'm interested in. I think one must know the mind of man....[5 intonation units]... Yes but it's not just imagination, *it's the character of men and the actions of men that I'm interested in.* [Geluykens 1984, C45]

11. I thank an anonymous reviewer for clarifying the introduction to these examples.

(46) It was the President, in a rare departure from the diplomacy of caution, who initiated the successful Panama invasion. *It was also Bush who came up with the ideas of having an early, informal Malta summit with Gorbachev and a second round of troop cuts in Europe after the fall of the Berlin wall.* But it was Baker who subtly turned the Malta summit from the informal, 'putting our feet up' chat initially envisaged by the President into a platform for the United States to demonstrate through a 16-point initiative that it was prepared to help Gorbachev. [M. Dowd and T.L. Friedman, 'The Fabulous Bush and Baker Boys', The New York Times Magazine, 5/6/90, p. 64].

(47) The rate of fatal heart attacks among middle-aged men increased steadily until the late 1960's, at which point it leveled off and soon began to decline. Not coincidentally, it was about that time that large numbers of men wised up to the harmfulness of cigarettes. *It was also in the late 60's that more healthful foods – specifically, foods low in cholesterol and saturated fat – began to invade American kitchens.* Since then, the average cholesterol level of adult males has fallen…. [Jane E. Brody, 'America's Health: An Assessment,' the New York Times Magazine, 10/8/89, p. 42]

(48) [12] These are the men who are hidden reefs in your love feasts when they feast with you without fear, caring for themselves; clouds without water, carried along by winds; autumn trees without fruit, doubly dead, uprooted; [13] wild waves of the sea, casting up their own shame like foam; wandering stars, for whom the black darkness has been reserved forever. [14] *It was also about these men that Enoch, in the seventh generation from Adam, prophesied,* saying, «Behold, the Lord came with many thousands of His holy ones, [15] to execute judgment upon all, and to convict all the ungodly of all their ungodly deeds which they have done in an ungodly way, and of all the harsh things which ungodly sinners have spoken against Him. [New American Standard Bible, the Epistle of St. Jude, Chapter 1]

Crucially, in such clefts, the primary sentence accent falls on the cleft clause, and I suggest that it is this prosodic focus that the additive focus particle associates with.

The clefted constituent seems to express the topic of the cleft sentence. The clefted constituent has just been mentioned and is relatively unstressed. Additional evidence for this conclusion comes from the 'speaking of' variant of the classical 'as for' topic test shown in (49).

(49) a. Speaking of the President, it was also Bush who came up with the ideas of having an early, informal Malta summit with Gorbachev…
  b. Speaking of the late 1960's, it was also in the late 1960's that more healthful foods began to invade American kitchens.
  c. Speaking of these men, it was also these men that Enoch prophesied about.

A schematic example illustrating the type of discourse context in which *also* clefts can be found is given in (50). Replacing *also* with *even*, as in (51), also results in a felicitous cleft.

(50) A: Why do you think that John is the murderer?
B: It was John who had the motive. It was John who had the opportunity. *It was also JOHN who found the BODY.*

(51) A: Why do you think that John is the murderer?
B: It was John who had the motive. It was John who had the opportunity. *It was even JOHN who found the BODY.*

Also- and *even*-marked clefts still exhibit exhaustiveness, as can be seen from the fact that the clefts in (50) and (51) can be paraphrased as shown in (52), where an exclusive focus particle *only* is added to bind the focus expressed in the clefted constituent:

(52) a. It was only John who had the motive. It was only John who had the opportunity. *It was also only JOHN who found the BODY.*
b. It was only John who had the motive. It was only John who had the opportunity. *It was even only JOHN who found the BODY.*

A Krifka-style schematic representation of the focus structure of the *also* cleft in (50) is shown in (53), and the more complicated example in (52a) is shown in (54). In the latter, both prosodic foci are bound by two focus operators.

(53) ASSERT_1 It was ALSO_2 CLEFT_3 $[\text{JOHN}]_{F3}$ [who found the $\text{BODY}]_{F1, F2}$

(54) ASSERT_1 It was ALSO_2 ONLY_3 CLEFT_4 $[\text{JOHN}]_{F3, F4}$ [who found the $\text{BODY}]_{F1, F2}$

My only attested example of an *even* cleft is shown in (55). Here *even* seems to have scope over the whole cleft proposition, as paraphrased in (56). 'Wexford' is activated information, although the cleft in this case does not seem to be 'about' Wexford in the sense of 'topic' defined above, which would mean that the information in the cleft would be intended to be stored in the common ground under the heading 'Wexford'.

(55) Wexford and Mr. Sung looked through the wooden grille at the great deep rectangular burial shaft and Mr. Sung quoted almost verbatim a considerable chunk from *Fodor's Guide to the People's Republic of China*. He had a retentive memory and seemed to believe that Wexford, because he couldn't decipher ideographs, was unable to read his own language. *It was even Wexford's* Fodor's *he was quoting from, artlessly borrowed the night before.* Wexford didn't listen. [Ruth Rendall, Speaker of Mandarin, 1983, p. 4]

(56) *It was even the case that it was Wexford's* Fodor's *he was quoting from.*

It seems that in this example, the Fodor's guide that Mr. Sung was quoting from is being said to have belonged to Wexford. This state of affairs is a very unlikely one, given that Mr. Sung thought Wexford couldn't read in his own language – but why would Wexford have brought the book to China if he couldn't read it? The proposition expressed in the cleft as a whole is thus at the low end of a scale of plausibility, so the scalar focus particle is appropriate. The schematic focus structure that seems to be involved is sketched in (57). Here the EVEN focus particle binds the entire cleft proposition.[12]

(57) ASSERT_1 It was EVEN_2 [CLEFT_3 [WEXFORD's]$_{F3}$ Fodor's he was QUOTING from]$_{F1,F2}$

Finally, we can consider the relative degree of prosodic prominence on the multiple foci that can occur in cleft sentences. In the examples given in this subsection, the highest degree of prominence falls on the focus in the cleft clause, which is bound by the ASSERT operator. The focus associated with the CLEFT operator and focus particle exhibits a lesser degree of prominence and even seems to lack prosodic prominence altogether. I suggest that rules of relative prosodic prominence associated with instances of second-occurrence focus, as detailed in Féry and Ishihara (2009), may apply in the clefts discussed here. One such rule is that 'focus boosts prominence', and this would apply to both foci. In the examples discussed in this subsection, I would suggest that the primary accent falls on the focus that takes the widest scope, which in the examples given here is the focus associated with the ASSERT operator, which again is the focus in the cleft clause. [13] A second rule is that 'givenness weakens prominence', and this would apply to the focus in the clefted constituent in the examples in §3.3 and most of the examples in §3.2. The end result would then be that the primary prominence falls on the focus in the cleft clause in those examples, and the focus in the clefted constituent is deaccented due to marking given information.[14] In the complex-focus, vice-versa clefts

12. In the Hedberg (1990, 2000) and Han and Hedberg (2008) syntactic analysis of clefts, the clefted constituent and the cleft clause together form a syntactic constituent, which is thus available to be the syntactic scope of a focus operator.

13. The prominence associated with a comment may also be inherently more prominent than a prominence associated with a topic. The comment would be the constituent in the scope of the ASSERT operator.

14. Possibly, the prominence on the clefted constituent in these examples is further reduced due to a prosodic prominence needing to appear on the focus particle itself. A reversal of weak and strong beats in a metrical structure, may thus take place, along the lines discussed by Ladd (1980) in his account at that time of deaccenting and default accent.

of §3.1, both foci apparently appear with equal prominence (and both would be associated with the same ASSERT operator), although perhaps the second focus receives a greater prominence than the first one, possibly due to a rule of end prominence.

4. Conclusion

In this paper I have argued that English cleft sentences divide a proposition into two parts both syntactically and semantically. The clefted constituent expresses an exhaustive focus, and the cleft clause expresses a pragmatic presupposition. This core semantic structure of the cleft construction can be exploited rhetorically to allow cleft presuppositions to be informative to the hearer. Both parts of the cleft can contain a prosodic focus. I argued that clefts can map variously onto topic/comment structure, so that the cleft as a whole can have topic-comment organization as well as comment-topic organization. Hedberg (1990, 2000) also argues that English clefts can have all-comment organization.[15]

What is most innovative about this paper is that I have argued that it is fruitful to view the prosodic foci that can be associated with the two parts of the cleft as both presenting a focus in the sense of Krifka (2007), who defines a focus as indicating the presence of alternatives. This allows us to view certain interesting subtypes of clefts as complex or multiple focus constructions. In this way, a focus on the clefted constituent can be seen as always associating with the structural CLEFT exhaustive focus operator and can associate in addition with an exclusive focus particle, ONLY, since ONLY and CLEFT focus have compatible semantics. A focus on the cleft clause in some examples associates with an ASSERT focus operator and thereby expresses the comment of the sentence, and can in addition associate with an additive focus particle ALSO or a scalar focus particle EVEN. A focus corresponding to the entire cleft proposition can also associate with a focus particle, and possibly with the ASSERT operator. With this analysis, I hope to have explicated some interesting subtypes of clefts as well to have contributed to an integration of discourse-pragmatic approaches and formal semantic approaches to focus, topic and cleft sentences.

15. This is also consistent with the conclusions of Huber (2006) concerning the information structure of clefts in English, German and Swedish.

References

Ball, Catherine N. 1992. The origins of the informative presupposition it-cleft. *Journal of Pragmatics* 22: 603–628.

Ball, Catherine N. & Prince, Ellen. 1978. A note on stress and presupposition. *Linguistic Inquiry* 8: 585.

Büring, Daniel. 2003. On D-trees, beans, and B-accents. *Linguistics and Philosophy* 26: 511–545.

Carlson, Lauri. 1983. *Dialogue Games: an Approach to Discourse Analysis*. Dordrecht: Reidel.

Chafe, Wallace. 1974. Language and consciousness. *Language* 50: 111–133.

Chierchia, Gennaro & McConnell-Ginet, Sally. 1990. *Meaning and Grammar*. Cambridge MA: The MIT Press.

Dahl, Östen. 1974. Topic-comment structure revisited. In *Topic and Comment, Contextual Boundness and Focus*, Östen Dahl (ed.), 1–24. Hamburg: Helmut Buske.

Delahunty, Gerald. 1982. *Topics in the Syntax and Semantics of English Cleft Sentences*. Bloomington IN: Indiana University Club.

Delin, Judy. 1992. Properties of it-cleft presupposition. *Journal of Semantics* 9: 289–306.

Dryer, Matthew. 1996. Focus, pragmatic presupposition and activated propositions. *Journal of Pragmatics* 26: 473–523.

É. Kiss, Katalin. 1998. Identificational focus versus information focus. *Language* 74: 245–273.

Féry, Caroline & Ishihara, Shinichiro. 2009. The phonology of second occurrence focus. *Journal of Linguistics* 45: 285–313.

Gazdar, Gerald. 1979. *Pragmatics: Implicature, Presupposition and Logical Form*. New York NY: Academic Press.

Geluykens, Ronald. 1984. Focus phenomena in English: An empirical investigation into cleft and pseudo-cleft sentences *Antwerp Papers in Linguistics* 36.

Goodman, Ellen. 1985. *Keeping in Touch*. New York NY: Fawcett.

Gundel, Jeanette K. 1988. Universals of topic-comment structure. In *Studies in Syntactic Typology* [Typological Studies in Language 17], Michael Hammond, Edith A. Morvacsik & Jessica R. Wirth (eds), 209–242. Amsterdam: John Benjamins.

Gundel, Jeanette K. 1985. 'Shared knowledge' and topicality. *Journal of Pragmatics* 9: 83–97.

Gundel, Jeanette K. 1974. The Role of Topic and Comment in Linguistic Theory. Ph.D. dissertation, University of Texas at Austin.

Gundel, Jeanette K., Hedberg, Nancy & Zacharski, Ron. 1993. Cognitive status and the form of referring expression in discourse. *Language* 69: 274–307.

Halliday, Michael A.K. 1967. Notes on transitivity and theme in English, Part 2. *Journal of Linguistics* 3: 199–244.

Halvorsen, Per-Kristian. 1978. The syntax and semantics of cleft constructions. *Texas Linguistics Forum* 11. Austin TX: Department of Linguistics, University of Texas.

Han, Chung-hye & Hedberg, Nancy. 2008. Syntax and the semantics of it-clefts: A Tree-Adjoining Grammar analysis. *Journal of Semantics* 25: 345–380.

Hedberg, Nancy. 2006. Topic-focus controversies. In *The Architecture of Focus*, Valéria Molnár & Susanne Winkler (eds), 373–397. Berlin Mouton de Gruyter.

Hedberg, Nancy. 2000. The referential status of clefts. *Language* 76: 891–920.

Hedberg, Nancy. 1990. Discourse Pragmatics and Cleft Sentences in English. Ph.D. dissertation, University of Minnesota.

Hedberg, Nancy & Fadden, Lorna. 2007. The information structure of it-clefts, wh-clefts and reverse wh-clefts in English. In *The Grammar-Pragmatics Interface: Essays in Honor of Jeanette K. Gundel* [Pragmatics & Beyond New Series 155], Nancy Hedberg & Ron Zacharski (eds), 49–76. Amsterdam: John Benjamins.

Hedberg, Nancy & Sosa, Juan M. 2007. The prosody of topic and focus in spontaneous English dialogue. In *Topic and Focus: Cross-linguistics Perspectives on Meaning and Intonation*, Chungmin Lee, Matthew Gordon & Daniel Büring, (eds) 101–120. Dordrecht: Springer.

Horn, Laurence R. 1981. Exhaustiveness and the semantics of clefts. *Proceedings of NELS* 14: 108–131.

Horn, Laurence R. 1969. A presuppositional analysis of *only* and *even*. *CLS 5: Papers from the Fifth Regional Meeting*, 98–107. Chicago IL: Chicago Linguistics Society.

Huber, Stefan. 2006. The complex function of it-clefts. In *The Architecture of Focus*, Valéria Molnár & Susanne Winkler (eds), 549–578. Berlin: Mouton de Gruyter.

Jacobs, J. 1984. Funktionale Satzperspektive und Illokutionssemantik. *Linguistische Berichte* 91: 25–28.

Keenan, Edward L. 1971. Two kinds of presupposition in natural language. In *Studies in Linguistic Semantics*, Charles J. Fillmore & D. Terrence Langendoen (eds), 45–54. New York NY: Holt, Rinehart and Winston.

Krifka, Manfred. 2007. Basic notions of information structure. In *Interdisciplinary Studies of Information Structure* 6, Carolyn Féry & Manfred Krifka (eds). Potsdam: University of Postdam.

Krifka, Manfred. 1999. Additive particles under stress. *Proceedings of SALT* 8, Devon Strolovitch & Aaron Lawson, 111–128. Ithaca NY: CLC Publications.

Krifka, Manfred. 1992. A compositional semantics for multiple focus constructions. In *Informationstruktur und Grammatik*, Joachim Jacobs (ed.), 17–53. Opladen: Westdeutscher Verlag.

Kuno, Susumo. 1972. Functional sentence perspective: A case study from Japanese and English. *Linguistic Inquiry* 2: 296–320.

Ladd, D. Robert. 1980. *The Structure of Intonational Meaning*. Bloomington IN: Indiana University Press.

Lambrecht, Kund. 2001. A framework for the analysis of cleft constructions. *Linguistics* 39: 463–516.

Levinson. Stephen. 1983. *Pragmatics*. Cambridge: CUP.

Lewis, David. 1979. Scorekeeping in a language game. *Journal of Philosophical Logic* 8: 339–359.

Prince, Ellen F. 1992. The ZPG letter: Subjects, definiteness and information status. In *Discourse Descriptions: Diverse Analyses of a Fund-Raising Text* [Pragmatics & Beyond New Series 16], Sandra Thompson & William C. Mann (eds), 295–325. Amsterdam: John Benjamins.

Prince, Ellen F. 1978. A comparison of wh-clefts and it-clefts in discourse. *Language* 54: 883–906.

Reinhart, Tanya. 1982. *Pragmatics and Linguistics: An Analysis of Sentence Topics*. Bloomington IN: Indiana University Linguistics Club.

Rochemont, Michael. 1986. *Focus in Generative Grammar* [Studies in Generative Linguistic Analysis 4]. Amsterdam: John Benjamins.

Rooth, Mats. 1992. A theory of focus interpretation. *Natural Language Semantics* 1: 75–116.

Rooth, Mats. 1985. Association with Focus. Ph.D. dissertation, University of Massachusetts at Amherst.

Schwarzschild, Roger. 1999. Givenness, AvoidF and other constraints on the placement of accent. *Natural Language Semantics* 7: 141–177.

Sgall, Petr, Hajičova, Eva & Benešová, Eva. 1973. *Topic, Focus and Generative Semantics.* Kronberg: Scriptor.

Stalnaker, Robert. 1974. Pragmatic presuppositions. In *Semantics and Philosophy*, Milton K. Munitz & Peter K. Unger (eds), 197–213. New York NY: New York University Press.

Steedman, Mark. 2007. Information-structural semantics for English intonation. In *Topic and Focus: Cross-linguistics Perspectives on Meaning and Intonation*, Chungmin Lee, Matthew Gordon & Daniel Büring (eds), 245–264. Dordrecht: Springer.

Vallduvi, Enric. 1990. The Informational Component. Ph.D. dissertation, University of Pennsylvania.

Wedgewood, Daniel. 2007. Identifying inferences in focus. In *On Information Structure, Meaning, and Form* [Linguistik Aktuell/Linguistics Today 100], Kerstin Schwabe & Susanne Winkler (eds), 207–227. Amsterdam: John Benjamins.

Recursion of FocP in Malayalam*

Rosmin Mathew
CASTL, Tromsø

This paper attempts to look into Malayalam where both Identificational Focus and Information Focus are overtly represented. With the help of diagnostic tests for exhaustivity the paper argues that clefts in the language encode Exhaustive Identificational Focus. It has been shown by Jayaseelan (2001) that there is a Focus position above vP and below IP. It is argued here that while the language encodes Information Focus in this preverbal lower Focus position, Exhaustive Focus involves a higher C- level Focus position, thus manifesting different types of Focus in different domains.

Keywords: Focus; recursion; exhaustivity; new information

1. Introduction

The term recursion is used in generative linguistics literature to denote various phenomena (Tomalin 2007). At least one of the contexts in which the term is used is in arguments about the nature of projections associated with the notion of Phases in the sense of Chomsky (2001 et seq), to argue that some projections like Focus appear recursively in every Phase.[1] Thus, in line with the articulated left periphery proposed by Rizzi (1997) for the CP domain, an articulated periphery had been proposed to the vP domain as well (see for eg Jayaseelan 2001; Poletto 2009). Belleti (2004) also argued for a FocPhrase above the vP which encodes new information. Though this proposal has been claimed to be useful in analysing Focus/Wh constructions in various languages (cf. Collins and Essizewa (2007) for Kabiye, Aboh (2007) for Kwa languages, Sinopoulou (2008) for Greek), it has not gone

---

* I thank Éva Dékany, P. Madhavan, K.A. Jayaseelan, Shin Ishihara, Marika Lekakou and Gillian Ramchand for comments and suggestions. Comments from two anonymous reviewers played a major role in making this paper better. Needless to say, all errors are mine. Thanks to Anup Sam Ninan for grammaticality judgements. Thanks Marianna!

1. see Horvath (2007) for an alternative approach.

unchallenged (for eg. Brunetti (2004) for Italian, Cheng (2008) for Zulu). In this paper we examine the manifestations of focus in Malayalam in an attempt to gain a better view of the proposed focus positions for two Phases, namely, CP and *v*P.

Malayalam is a SOV Dravidian language spoken in South India. The language does not exhibit any subject-verb agreement and has a Nom-Acc case system. It is conventionally described as a Wh-in-situ language. However, certain peculiarities in Malayalam with respect to the interrogative constructions along with other factors led Jayaseelan (2001) to propose a Focus Phrase immediately above vP in the language. He analysed the mandatory positioning of question words at an immediately preverbal position in interrogative constructions as movement. According to Jayaseelan, the Wh word moves to the FocP above the vP in these constructions. He, then, brings what is traditionally described as cleft constructions in Malayalam under the same preverbal FocP umbrella arguing that the clefted element utilises the same lower FocP position of the focus marker *a:nu*. He characterised *a:nu* as a copular verb which provides a lower preverbal focus position. Thus, from Jayaseelan (2001) it appears that only the lower focus position is available in the language.

However, a closer look at the nature of Focus in the focus constructions described as clefts and the non-cleft constructions prove that there is a marked difference in the nature of Focus encoded in these two constructions. The difference is in accordance with É. Kiss (1998) who argues that syntactic as well as semantic distinctions exist between Exhaustive Identificational Focus[2] and Information Focus. She explains that while Information Focus conveys non-presupposed information, Exhaustive Focus expresses exhaustive identification and syntactically acts as an operator, moving into a scope position and binding a variable. This distinction is evident in Malayalam in constructions that involve the focus marker *a:nu* (clefts) versus constructions that involve a preverbal Focus position; the movement is evidenced by the retention of case-morphology as well as restrictions on what can be moved to the cleft focus.

It is shown in this paper, drawing on the results of tests pertaining to exhaustivity, scope interaction, and distributional restrictions (cf. Szabolcsi 1981) that cleft constructions in Malayalam encode Exhaustive Focus. More over, the tests for Exhaustivity fail to produce positive results in the preverbal Focus position. The paper argues that the lower preverbal Focus position that Jayaseelan (2001) proposes is an instantiation of Information Focus. It is further shown that the cleft construction does not involve the preverbal Focus position as Jayaseelan argues, but rather involves a higher position at the left periphery of the CP (*à la*

2. Following the arguments of Kenesei (2006) that Focus is generally Identificational, what is termed as Identificational Focus in É. Kiss (1998) is called Exhaustive Focus in this paper.

Rizzi 1997) and encodes Exhaustive Focus (*à la* É. Kiss 1998). This neat division of labour w.r.t. Focus in Malayalam, thus, provides evidence for the argument that though FocP may appear both in the left periphery and in the lower IP area, there is a clear difference in the nature of the Focus invoked in these two positions; it is not mere recursion of the same FocP.

The paper is organised as follows: Section 2 provides an overview of the preverbal Focus position argued by Jayaseelan (2001). This Focus position is then tested for Exhaustivity and is shown that there is no reading of Exhaustivity associated with this position. Section 3 looks into the cleft constructions and shows that these constructions are always exhaustive. It is further shown that a biclausal analysis of these constructions does not do justice to the observed facts and a monoclausal analysis in the lines of Hiraiwa and Ishihara (2002) is adopted. Thus we get two domains for Focus in the language – the CP domain and *v*P domain. Section 4 concludes the paper by revisiting the core facts and bringing to fore the argument that though both the CP and *v*P left peripheries may have information structure related positions, these two domains differ in the nature of information encoded in them. Thus it is not merely a recursion of the same FocP that we get in these two domains in Malayalam.

2. Preverbal FocP

2.1 The position

Malayalam is a language with a clause-final complementiser and is traditionally described as a Wh-in-situ language. Being an SOV language, this leads us to expect a content question with a Wh word to appear in its presumed canonical position as in the following pair of sentences:

(1) a. *Paily enn-e kandu.*
Paily I-ACC saw
'Paily saw me.'

b. *Paily a:r–e kandu?*
Paily who-ACC saw
'Who did Paily see?'

However, we run into a problem when we look at Wh subjects. The predicted way is ungrammatical as shown in (2). The correct way to ask this question is one in which the Wh appears at a position immediately before the verb as in (3):

(2) **a:ru ninne kandu?*
who you-ACC saw
'Who saw you?'

(3) *ninne a:ru kandu?*
you-ACC who saw
'Who saw you?'

It was Madhavan (1987) who first noticed that in Malayalam all Wh words obligatorily appear immediately before the verb in content questions. This can be seen in the following examples.

(4) a. *Paily avanu panam*[3] *koduttu*
Paily he-DAT money gave
'Paily gave him money.'

b. **a:ru avanu panam koduttu?*
who he-DAT money gave
'Who gave him money?'

c. *avanu panam a:ru koduttu?*
he-DAT money who gave
'Who gave him money?'

(5) *Paily avan-e eppo:l kandu?*
Paily he-ACC when saw
'When did Paily see him?'

(6) *Paily avan-e entinu kandu?*
Paily he-ACC why saw
'Why did Paily see him?'

Assuming Cinque's (1999) hierarchy for adverbials, we can see that the Wh is below the TP by using a temporal adverb:

(7) *ninne innu a:ru kandu?*
you-ACC today who saw?
'Who saw you today?'

An analysis for this was proposed by Jayaseelan (2001) who argued that the question words in these cases move obligatorily to a Focus projection above the *v*P, *à la* the Focus projection at the left periphery of the CP proposed by Rizzi (1997). A tree diagram for (3) is given in Figure 1.

3. Inanimate objects don't show Accusative case in Malayalam.

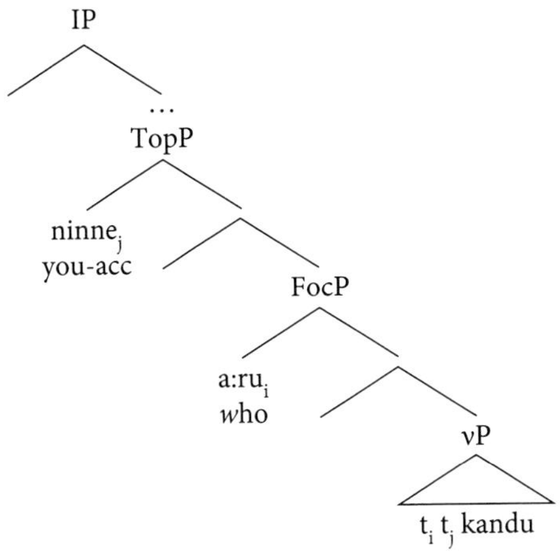

Figure 1. Focus movement in Malayalam

According to this analysis, in a sentence like (3), the Wh moves to the Specifier of this FocP above *v*P and the object, being definite, moves to the specifier of a Topic position above the FocP and we get the right word order.

2.2 Nature of preverbal FocP

The term Focus appears in the literature in many contexts. If we subscribe to the notion that there is a Focus projection in the syntax, we need to arrive at a refined understanding of the nature of the information encoded in this projection. In order to do that, I employ the distinction pointed out by É. Kiss (1998). She argues that there are two types of Focus – Exhaustive Identificational Focus and New Information Focus. While Information focus conveys non-presupposed information,[4] Identificational focus expresses exhaustive identification. This is not to be taken to mean that Exhaustive Focus cannot convey new information. Rather, an Exhaustive Identificational focus represents a subset of the set of contextually or situationally given elements for which the predicate phrase can potentially hold; it is identified as the exhaustive subset for which the predicate phrase actually holds.

4. É. Kiss (1998) suggests that Information focus is not associated with movement at all. This is in contradiction with Jayaseelan's (2001) arguments for a Focus Phrase above vP to which the focused element moves – though Jayaseelan does not distinguish between the two types of Focus. In any case, this is not of concern here as we borrow only her classification, and not the analysis.

It is this exhaustive character that sets Exhaustive Identification Focus apart from Information Focus. She further outlines certain tests based on Szabolcsi (1981) as diagnostic for Exhaustive[5] Focus.

Now, if there is a Focus position above the *v*P in Malayalam as Jayaseelan argues, we would expect the focused elements also to make use of this position, apart from Wh words. This is indeed the case as can be seen from the question answer pairs below:

(8) *ninne a:ru kandu?*
you-ACC who saw
'Who saw you?'

(9) *enne Paily kandu*
I-ACC Paily saw
'Paily saw me.'

As an answer to the question in (8), the felicitous answer is one in which the new information that the question seeks appear in the position immediately before the verb. Notice that an unmarked answer like (1) reproduced below where the subject and the object appear in their canonical position is infelicitous in this context.

(10) #[6]*Paily enn-e kandu.*
Paily I-ACC saw
'Paily saw me.'

The answer in (9) conveys information that is new and non-presupposed. Thus this position is a natural candidate for Information Focus. However, since Exhaustive Focus also can convey new information, we need to check if this position shows any exhaustivity effects. The main test for this is the co-ordination test that É. Kiss borrows from Szabolcsi (1981). This test involves a minimal pair where the first sentence has a co-ordinated phrase as the focus and the second sentence has only one of the co-ordinated phrase at the focus. The focus expresses exhaustive identification if the second sentence is not among the logical consequences of the first one. Reproducing the test for Malayalam, we get the sentences given in (11) and (12).

(11) *enn-e karambi-(y)*[7] *um Paily-um kandu*
I-ACC Karambi- and Paily-and saw
'Karambi and Paily saw me.'

5. See footnote (1) for an explanation of the terminology used here.

6. # is used to denote infelicitous sentences.

7. The marker for co-ordination is *-um*, the glide appearing here is a matter of phonology and not syntax.

(12) *enn-e Paily kandu*
I-ACC Paily saw
'Paily saw me.'

(12) is a logical consequence of (11) in Malayalam and thus we can conclude that the preverbal position is not exhaustive in nature. Probing further, É. Kiss also gives certain distributional restrictions that apply to Exhaustive Focus. She shows that this position is not available for universal quantifiers, 'also'-phrase, and 'even'-phrases.[8] We can see from the following examples that the preverbal Focus position is available for all these.

(13) *Paily-e ella:varum kandu*
Paily-ACC everyone saw
'Everyone saw Paily.' [universal quantifier]

(14) *Paily-e avan-um kandu*
Paily-ACC he-also saw
'He also saw Paily.' [also phrase]

(15) *Paily-e avan po:lum kandu*
Paily-ACC he even saw
'Even he saw Paily.' [even phrase]

Unlike the Exhaustive Focus constructions (which we will examine in the next section) the preverbal Focus position is amenable to adding information. So as an answer to the question in 16, it is felicitous to answer as in (17).

(16) *ninne a:ru kandu?*
you-ACC who saw
'Who saw you?'

(17) *enne Paily kandu; karambi-(y)um kandu.*
I-ACC Paily saw Karambi-and saw
'Paily saw me; and Karambi, too.'

So we can safely conclude that the preverbal Focus position encodes Information Focus and not Exhaustive Focus.

---

8. É. Kiss employs scope interactions as well in order to identify Exhaustive Focus. However, those tests are not reproduced here as Malyalam shows surface scope and makes use of scrambling – two factors which make the use of this test less than ideal. Furthermore, for É. Kiss, only the Exhaustive Focus undergoes movement, an assumption that we do not subscribe here. Since we buy the argument by Jayaseelan that the preverbal Focus position in Malayalam involves movement, this position also may be regarded as available for scope interactions.

3. Another focus construction

3.1 Exhaustive nature of clefts

There is another widely used focus construction in Malayalam which is conventionally termed clefts. These constructions involve the focus marker *a:nu*. An example is given in (18).

(18) *karambi-e a:nu Paily kand-aDu*
Karambi-ACC FM Paily saw-IIIP.SG.N.
'It is Karambi whom Paily saw.'

a:nu marks the focus in these constructions and any argument can be clefted. Apart from that, adverbs and adjuncts also can be focused in clefts.

(19) *innale a:nu Paily karambi-e kand-aDu*
yesterday FM Paily Karambi-ACC saw-IIIP.SG.N.
'It is yesterday that Paily saw Karambi.'

(20) *sankadam vann-ittu a:nu avan karanj-aDu*
sorrow came-perfective FM he cried-IIIP.SG.N.
'It is because (he) became sad that he cried.'

These constructions are amenable to scrambling:

(21) *Paily kand-aDu karambi-e a:nu*
Paily saw-IIIP.SG.N. Karambi-ACC FM
'It is Karambi whom Paily saw.'

(22) *Paily karambi-e a:nu kand-aDu*
Paily Karambi-ACC FM saw-IIIP.SG.N.
'It is Karambi whom Paily saw.'

The entire clause can be clefted as in the following sentence:

(23) *Paily karambi-e kand-aDu a:nu*
Paily Karambi-ACC saw-IIIP.SG.N. FM
'Paily did see Karambi.'

Now, applying the tests for Exhaustivity, we can see that clefts are obligatorily interpreted as encoding Exhaustive Focus. If we have a co-ordinated phrase at the cleft focus, it is interpreted as exhaustively identifying all the members of the set that holds true for the proposition in the cleft. Thus (25) is NOT a logical consequence of (24):

(24) *Paily-um Karambi-(y)um a:nu vann-aDu*
Paily-and Karambi-and FM came-IIIP.SG.N.
'It is Paily and Karambi who came.'

(25) *Paily a:nu vann-aDu*
Paily FM came-IIIP.SG.N.
'It is Paily who came.'

Gryllia (2008) shows that collective and distributive interpretations of the co-ordinated phrase in a minimal pair like in the above test is crucial in determining whether the second sentence with only one of the co-ordinated phrase at the focus is a logical entailment of the first or not. Recalling Gamut (1991) she points out that the entailment pattern for co-ordination test is similar to the entailment pattern of test for collectivity. Consider the following minimal pairs.

(26) Cheech and Chong are fun at parties

(27) Cheech is fun at parties

In the above pair, (27) can be a logical consequence of (26) under a distributive reading of (26) where Cheech and Chong are fun at parties independent of each other. However, notice that under a collective interpretation of the co-ordinates phrases, (27) is not entailed by (26). This is the interpretation that Cheech and Chong are fun only when they are together. Gryllia points out that in the test for exhaustivity, it is the exhaustive nature of the second sentence that blocks the entailment whereas in the test for collectivity, it is the collective nature of the first sentence with the coordinated phrases that blocks the entailment. An example that has a dominant collective reading of the coordinated phrases can bring out this point:

(28) Bread and butter is John's favorite food

(29) Bread is John's favorite food

'Bread and butter' is interpreted collectively and this results in (29) not being a logical consequence of (28). However, this does not mean that (28) and (29) are structures that obligatorily encode exhaustivity. This rather means that one should tease apart the instances of collectivity from exhaustivity. In order to do that, I employ a construction that has an obligatory distributive reading in Malayalam and use it in a cleft sentence.

(30) *Karambi Devi-kk-um Paily-kk-um o:ro:pustakam koduttu*
Karambi Devi-DAT-and Paily-DAT-and a book each gave
'Karambi gave a book each to Devi and Paily.'

Now using this in a cleft sentence we get the following:

(31) *Devi-kk-um Paily-kk-um a:nu Karambi*
Devi-DAT-and Paily-DAT-and FM Karambi
o:ro: pustakam kodutt-aDu
a book each gave-IIIP.SG.N.
'It is to Devi and Paily that Karambi gave a book each.'

Here we get the obligatory distributive interpretation where a total of two books have been given and Devi and Paily got a book each. However, (32) is still not a logical consequence of (31), showing that it is not a collective reading of the coordinated phrases that gives rise to the entailments.

(32) *Paily-kku a:nu Karambi oru pustakam kodutt-aDu*
Paily-DAT FM Karambi a book gave-IIIP.SG.N.
'It is to Paily that Karambi gave a book.'

Coming to the next major test that É. Kiss talks about – distributional restrictions – we see that Malayalam clefts show all the restrictions that É. Kiss associates with Exhaustivity.

(33) **ella:varum a:nu vann-aDu*
everyone FM came-IIIP.SG.N.
'It is everyone that came.' [quantificational elements]

(34) **Karambi-um a:nu Paily-e kand-aDu*
Karambi-also FM Paily-ACC saw-IIIP.SG.N.
'It is Karambi also that saw Paily.' [also phrase]

(35) **Karambi-po:lum a:nu Pailiy-e kand-aDu*
Karambi-even FM Paily-ACC saw-IIIP.SG.N.
'It is even Karambi who saw Paily.' [even phrase]

Thus all the distributional restrictions that É. Kiss associates with Exhaustive Focus are operational in Malayalam clefts, substantiating the point that it is Exhaustive in nature.

Another point to be noted is that the definition of É. Kiss (1998:245) implies a tight relation between contrastivity and exhaustivity as can be seen from the statement: "[identificational focus] represents a subset of the set of contextually or situationally given elements for which the predicate phrase can potentially hold; it is identified as the exhaustive subset for which the predicate phrase actually holds". Thus it appears that Exhaustive Focus is necessarily Contrastive as well. However, this is not the case in Malayalam. According to Horvath (2010) Contrast, as manifested in the case of Contrastive Focus, means the existence of a membership set of relevant elements that identification operates on, identifying a proper subset for which the predicate holds, while excluding other members of the set. That is, Contrastive Focus demands an alternative set of elements.[9] This is not a necessary condition for Malayalam clefts which do not have a reading that presupposes the existence of alternative set(s) as opposed to Contrastive Focus:

9. This is argued to be generally in line with Rooth (1992). However, for a different view, see Zimmerman (2008). For an overview see Repp (2010).

Context: A and B are talking about the selection of new Ph.D. Students where A says (36):

(36) *John-ine a:nu avar select ceyth-aDu*
John-DAT FM they select did-IIIP.SG.N.
'It is John whom they selected.'

B: Were there other applicants?
There might not have been any other applicants.

B has a very low opinion of John's academic calibre and B can felicitously ask the question *were there other applicants*? or give the statement *there might not have been any other applicants*. Notice that neither of these utterances are felicitous as response to Contrastive Focus as Contrastivity obligatorily presupposes the existence of an alternative set:

(37) *avar John-ine ma:tram select ceytu*
they John-DAT only select did
'They selected only John.'

B: #Were there other applicants?
#There might not have been any other applicants

In fact, Exhaustive Focus cannot go with a subset of the potential set. Consider the following context: Whether John is eligible for promotion – John needs 5 published articles to get promoted. It is infelicitous to make a statement like the following in this context:

(38) *#John 3 articles a:nu publish ceyt-aDu; so he can't be promoted*
John 3 articles FM publish did-IIIP.SG.N.
'It is 3 articles that John published, so he can't be promoted.'

The same can be seen in the following context as well:
Context: World Cup Football.

(39) *Quarter final-il Germany-um Brazil-um undo?*
Quarter final-LOC Germany-and Brazil-and be-Question
'Are Germany and Brazil in the Quarter Final?'

(40) *#illa, Brazil a:nu ull-aDu*
no, Brazil FM be-IIIP.SG.N.
'No, it is Brazil that made it to the quarter final.'

Further more, Contrastive Focus is incompatible with a unique single member set whereas Exhaustive Focus is the preferred option:
Context: talking about who won the last world cup

(41) *Italy a:nu jeyicc-aDu*
Italy FM won-IIIP.SG.N.
'It is Italy who won.'

(42) *#Italy ma:tram jeyiccu*
Italy only won
'Only Italy won.'

(43) *Mary a:nu Yesu-vinu janmam nalkiy-aDu*
Mary FM Jesus-DAT birth gave-IIIP.SG.N.
'It is Mary who gave birth to Jesus.'

(44) *#Yesu-vinu Mary ma:tram janmam nalki*
Jesus-DAT Mary only birth gave.
'Only Mary gave birth to Jesus.'

Thus, the clefts in Malayalam encode Exhaustive Focus without demanding the existence of an obligatory alternative set.

3.2 Structure of clefts

Jayaseelan (2001) argues that the above constructions are biclausal ones that make use of the preverbal Focus position. He analyses the focus marker *a:nu* as a copula and the focussed phrase as moving to the preverbal Focus position of that copula. However, as shown in the previous section, this particular Focus position is associated with Information Focus and none of the Exhaustivity effects are obtained in this position. First and foremost, Jayaseelan's analysis fails to capture this important distinction. Secondly, Jayaseelan's argument that *a:nu* is functioning as a verb in clefts is a contested idea. Mohanan (1982) analyses it essentially as a focus marker. Madhavan (2008) also points in this direction. A point which all seem to agree is that it is defective in various ways. Descriptive facts show that it does not have any other forms like past or future; no relative clause can be made out of it. In fact, there is no other attested form of *a:nu* in the language that makes it fit into a verbal paradigm.[10] At the very least, we can safely assume that *a:nu* functions as a focus marker in cleft constructions. Here we adopt a monoclausal analysis of clefts. Specifically, a structure on the lines of Hiraiwa and Ishihara (2002) is adopted where we treat *a:nu* as a focus marker.

Hiraiwa and Ishihara examines *in situ* focus constructions and *no-da* cleft constructions in Japanese:

(45) [*Naoya-ga* e_i *tabeta no*]-*wa ringo-o mit-tu*$_i$ *da*
N-NOM ate C-TOP apple-ACC 3-CL COP
'It was three apples that Naoya ate.' [cleft]

10. It is possible that *a:nu* is a focus marker grammaticalised from a copula, a tendency attested in many languages.

(46) [*Naoya-ga RINGO-O MIT-TU tabeta no*] (*da*)
N-NOM apple-ACC 3-CL ate C COP
'Naoya ate THREE APPLES.' [in situ focus]

The structure that Hiraiwa and Ishihara proposes for clefts is given in Figure 2:

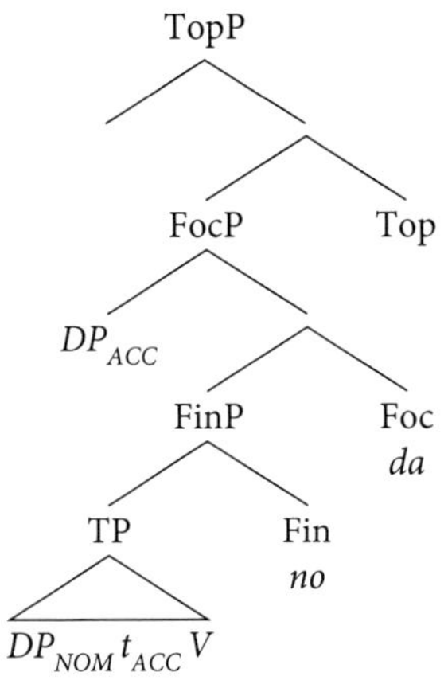

Figure 2. Japanese cleft structure

We can see the parallel structures in Malayalam in the following examples (see also examples 21 and 23):

(47) [*Paily tinn-aDu*] *3 apple a:nu*
Paily ate-IIIP.SG.N. 3 apple FM
'It is 3 apples that Paily ate.'
(Reading: What Paily ate is 3 apples)

(48) [*Paily 3 APPLE tinn-aDu*] *a:nu*
Paily 3 apple ate-IIIP.SG.N. FM
'Paily ate THREE APPLES.'

On the surface level, we can see a couple of differences between the Japanese constructions and the Malayalam ones. To begin with, Malayalam does not have an overt Topic marker unlike Japanese. However, the elements in the position before the focused element invariably receives Topic interpretation in all the scrambled sentences. In (48) above, *what Paily ate* is the topic of the sentence. In a sentence like the following, 'Paily' is the sentential topic, indicating that there is indeed a Topic position above the cleft Focus.

(49) *Paily 3 apple a:nu tinn-aDu*
Paily 3 apple FM ate-IIIP.SG.N.
'It is 3 apples that Paily ate.'
(Reading: Paily, it is 3 apples he ate)

Secondly, Hiraiwa and Ishihara analyse the copula *da* as functioning as a focus marker, placing it at the Focus head with the focused element moving to its specifier. In Malayalam, *a:nu* also functions as a focus marker in clefts, the focused phrase moving to the cleft focus rather than being base-generated there. This movement is evidenced by the case morphology on the moved phrase. For example, in (50) we have a verb that assigns Dative case to its subject, and in (51) we see that this case marking is retained in the cleft:

(50) *Paily-kku visannu*
Paily-DAT hunger
Meaning: Paily is hungry

(51) *Paily-kku a:nu visann-aDu*
Paily-DAT FM hungered-IIIP.SG.N.
'It is Paily who was hungry.'

Thirdly, the verb in Malayalam seems to carry a pronominal element whereas in Japanese, *no* is glossed as a complementiser. Nonetheless, Hiraiwa and Ishihara point out that this element is widely used as a substitutive pronoun in Japanese. The argument is that in clefts it occupies a position in the C-domain. In fact, in Dravidian languages, the same IIIP.SG.N. morphology can be employed in nominal-verb agreement contexts. Moreover, it has been argued that agreement is the means of indicating finiteness in Dravidian (Steever 1988).

Figure 3 represents the structure for Malayalam clefts, where *a:nu* appears as the head of the Focus projection, *-aDu* is at the Fin head, and the phrase carrying a Focus feature moves overtly to the specifier of the FocP:

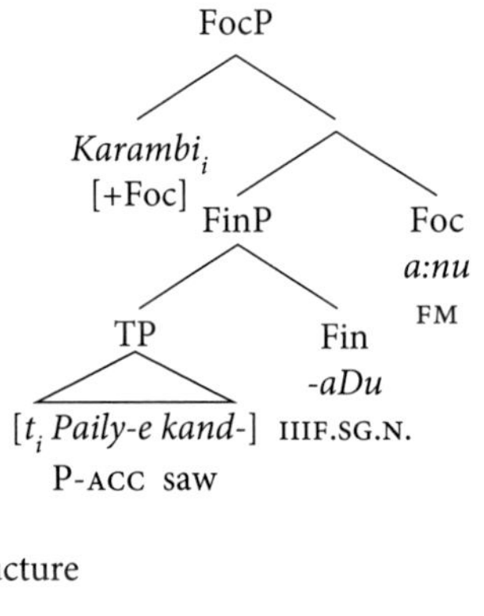

Figure 3. Malayalam cleft structure

In Malayalam, the background information may undergo right dislocation, and we get *Karambi a:nu Pailye kandaDu*.

(52) $[_{Foc}$ Karambi$_i$ t_{FinP} a:nu $[_{FinP}$ t_i Paily-e kanda-aDu]]
right dislocation
Karambi FM Paily-ACC saw-IIIP.SG.N.
'It is Karambi who saw Paily.'

Hiraiwa and Ishihara also talk about an option where the focused phrase does not move overtly: the in-situ focus constructions. As we saw in examples (23) and (48), these are possible in Malayalam in two contexts – in cases where the entire clause carries a Foc feature (example 23) and cases where the phrase carrying a Foc feature does not move (example 48). A representative tree diagram for (23) is shown in Figure 4:

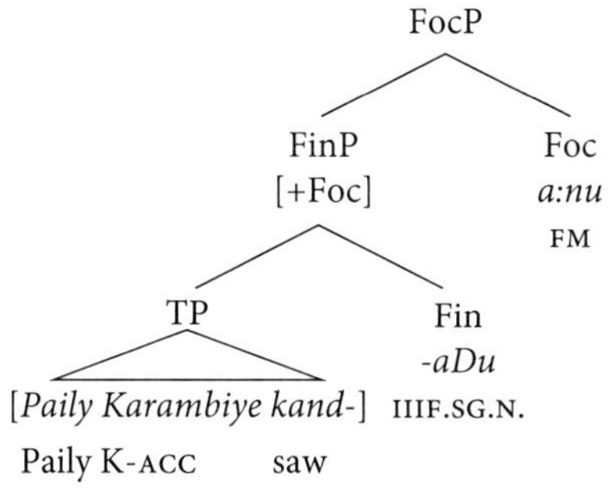

Figure 4. In situ focus in Malayalam

(23) is reproduced below, where the entire clause is focused:
Paily karambi-e kanda-aDu a:nu
Paily Karambi-ACC saw-IIIP.SG.N. FM
'Paily did see Karambi.'

(48) with in-situ Focus:
[*Paily 3 APPLE tinn-aDu*] *a:nu*
Paily 3 apple ate-IIIP.SG.N. FM
'Paily ate THREE APPLES.'

We also saw earlier that clefts are amenable to appearing in different word orders. This has been sometimes analysed as instances resulting from a floating focus marker, where *a:nu* was argued to be moving, attaching itself to the focused element like a clitic (Mohanan 1982). Under the analysis pursued here, these are instances when the Specifier of the TopP is filled by movement of the Topic; it is not free movement of the focus marker that results in scrambling constructions.

Thus, we get two word orders corresponding to the right dislocated and the non-right dislocated structures. Without right dislocation, we get the following:

(53) *Paily-e karambi kanda-aDu a:nu*
Paily-ACC Karambi saw-IIIP.SG.N. FM
Reading: Paily, Karambi did see him

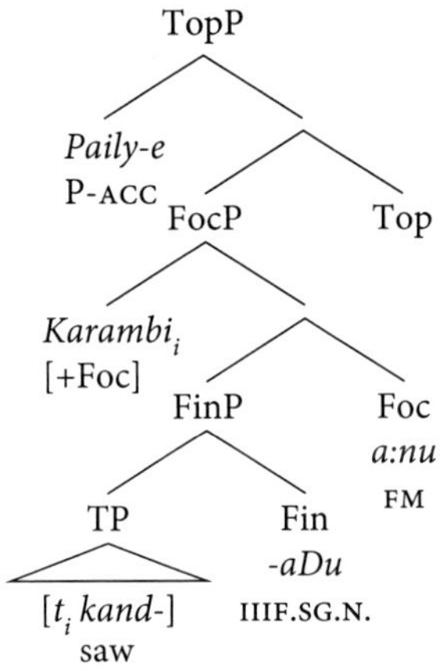

Figure 5. Topic-focus structure in Malayalam

Right dislocating the remnant FinP carrying the background information, we get (54):

(54) $[_{Top}$ Paily-e $[_{Foc}$ Karambi t_{FinP} a:nu $[_{Fin}$ kanda-aDu$]]]$
right dislocation

Paily-ACC Karambi FM saw-IIIP.SG.N.
Reading: Paily, it is Karambi who saw him.

We already saw that the cleft focus obligatorily encodes Exhaustive Focus. In other words, the domain of Exhaustive Focus in Malayalam is CP.

4. Different domains, different information

Once we subscribe to the monoclausal analysis of clefts we are in a position where we get two Focus projections contained in the same clause. As shown in the paper, the two projections exhibit different syntactic and semantic properties. What is traditionally known by the blanket term Focus finds two positions in the clause – at the vP level and the CP level respectively, giving rise to the impression that Focus

Projection could recursively appear at both these Phases. However, a closer look at the nature of these positions reveals that they exhibit different syntactic behaviour. With regard to Information Strucutre properties, the information encoded at these two levels are different. Apart from the historical accident of using the same label, there does not seem to be much else that is common to these two positions. Hence, it would be a fallacy to assume (on the basis of labels) that the same Information Structure related projection recursively appears at every Phase, at least for Malayalam. To say that Information Structurally, different information gets encoded at different Phases would be a better descriptive statement. Thus it turns out that this is not a mere recursion of the FocP at the phase levels. Rather, it would be more accurate to say that there are positions available at the edge of the phases that encode Information Structure (Chomsky 2004).

References

Aboh, Enoch Olade. 2007. Leftward focus versus rightward focus: The Kwa-Bantu conspiracy. *SOAS Working Papers in Linguistics*, Vol. 15.

Asher, Ronald E. & Kumari, T.C. 1996. *Malayalam*. London: Routledge.

Belletti, Adriana. 2004. Aspects of the low IP area. In *The Structure of CP and IP*, Luigi Rizzi (ed.). Oxford: OUP.

Brunetti, Lisa. 2004. Are there two distinct foci in Italian?. *Southwest Journal of Linguistics* 23(2).

Cheng, Lisa. 2008. Against FocP: Evidence from Zulu. *Must*. Utrecht University.

Chomsky, Noam. 2001. Derivation by phase. In *Ken Hale: A Life in Language*, Michael Kenstowicz (ed.). Cambridge MA: The MIT Press.

Chomsky, Noam. 2004. Beyond explanatory adequacy. In *The Cartography of Syntactic Structures*, Vol. 3: *Structures and Beyond*, Adriana Belletti (ed.). Oxford: OUP.

Cinque, Guglielmo. 1999. *Adverbs and Functional Heads*. Oxford: OUP.

Collins, Chris & Essizewa, Komlan E. 2007. The syntax of verb focus in Kabiye. In *Selected Proceedings of the* 37th *Annual Conference on African Linguistics*, Doris L. Payne & Jaime Pena (eds). Somerville MA: Cascadilla Proceedings Project.

É. Kiss, Katalin. 1998. Identificational focus versus information focus. *Language* 74(2): 245–273.

Gamut, L.T.F. 1991. *Logic, Language and Meaning*. Chicago IL: University Press of Chicago.

Gryllia, Styliani. 2008. On the Nature of Preverbal Focus in Greek: A Theoretical and Experimental Approach. Ph.D. dissertation, Universiteit Leiden.

Hiraiwa, Ken & Ishihara, Shinchiro. 2002. Missing links: Cleft, sluicing and 'no da' construction in Japanese. *MIT Working Papers in Linguistics* 43: 35–54.

Horvath, Julia. 2007. Seperating "focus movement" from focus. In *Phrasal and Clausal Architecture: Syntactic Derivation and Interpretation. In Honor of Joseph E. Emonds* [Linguistik Aktuell/Linguistics Today 101], Simin Karimi, Vida Samiian & Wendy K. Wilkins (eds). Amsterdam: John Benjamins.

Horvath, Julia. 2010. Discourse-features. Syntactic displacement and the status of contrast. *Lingua* 120: 1346–1369.

Jayaseelan, K.A. 2001. IP-internal topic and focus phrases. *Studia Linguistica* 55: 39–75.

Kenesei, István. 2006. Focus as identification. In *The Architecture of Focus,* Valeria Molnár & Susanne Winkler (eds). Berlin: Mouton de Gruyter.

Madhavan, Punnappurath. 1987. Clefts and Pseudoclefts in English and Malayalam: A Study in Comparative Syntax. Ph.D. dissertation, CIEFL, Hyderabad.

Madhavan, Punnappurath. 2008. Multiple Wh-questions and clefts in Malayalam: Agree or Move? Presentation at Cleft Workshop 2008. at ZAS Berlin.

Mohanan, K.P. 1982. Grammatical relations and clause structure in Malayalam. In *The Mental Representation of Grammatical Relations,* Joan Bresnan (ed.). Cambridge MA: The MIT Press.

Poletto, Cecilia. 2009. Limits to cartography. Talk delivered at University of Tromso 26 March 2009.

Repp, Sophie. 2010. Defining 'contrast' as an information-structural notion in grammar. *Lingua* 120(6): 1333–1345.

Rizzi, Luigi. 1997. The fine structure of the left periphery. In *Elements of Grammar,* Liliane Haegeman (ed.). Dordrecht: Kluwer.

Rooth, Mats. 1992. A theory of focus interpretation. In *Natural Language Semantics* 1: 75–116.

Sinopoulou, Ourania. 2008. Multiple questions and apparent Wh-in-situ: Evidence from Greek. *Proceedings of ConSOLE* XV: 223–246.

Steever, Sanford B. 1988. *The Serial Verb Formation in the Dravidian Languages.* Dehli: Motilal Banarassidass.

Szabolcsi, Anna. 1981. The semantics of topic-focus articulation. In *Formal Methods in the Study of Language,* Jan Groenendijk, Theo Janssen & Martin Stokhof (eds). Amsterdam: Matematisch Centrum.

Tomalin, Marcus. 2007. Recursion, computability, and syntactic theory. *Lingua* 117(10): 1784–1800.

Zimmerman, Malte. 2008. Contrastive focus and emphasis. *Acta Linguistica Hungarica* 55(3–4): 1–16.

Multiple Wh-questions and the cleft construction in Malayalam

Punnapurath Madhavan
The English and Foreign Languages University, Hyderabad

Wh-questions in Malayalam are usually clefts, with the wh-phrase occupying the cleft focus. An alternative to clefting the wh-element is to cleft the whole clause containing the wh. When there are multiple wh-phrases in the embedded clause, however, the only option is to cleft the embedded clause wholesale. Another interesting observation is that when there is potential scope ambiguity involving, say, a time adverbial like *eppooL* 'when', clefting of the whole clause versus clefting of the time adverbial is being resorted to as a means to disambiguate. The paper shows that a two-way distinction of languages, namely those which are wh-in-situ and those which are not, will not do justice to the array of facts, and that a more nuanced typological account is called for.

Keywords: Clefts; wh-in-situ; scope ambiguity; question interpretation

0. Introduction

In this paper, I examine multiple wh-questions in Malayalam. Malayalam is a head-final language and it is generally held that it is a wh-in-situ language. In simple, monoclausal sentences it is possible to have the object/adjunct wh-phrase in its original position. The interrogative interpretation in such cases is achieved by the question intonation, in much the same way it happens in English echo questions. Thus, (1) is a well-formed direct question in Malayalam.

(1) *nii entə marunnə kaziccu*
you what medicine eat past
'What medicine did you take?'
or 'You took WHAT MEDICINE?'

However, when there is embedding it is not possible to have an in-situ wh-phrase in the embedded clause, see (2).[1] (I am using capital letters for retroflex sounds.) The strategy the language employs is to cleft the clause containing the wh-phrase, as exemplified in (3):

(2) **awaL nii entə marunnə kaziccu ennə wicaariccu*
she you what medicine eat past that think past
'What medicine did she think that you took?'

(3) *nii entə marunnə kaziccu ennə aaNə awaL wicaariccatə*
you what medicine eat past that be she think past *atə* = (2)

In (3), the particle glossed as *atə* is a nominalizer which characteristically attaches to the inflected verb of the cleft clause. The cleft focus is indicated by *aaNə* 'be': whatever comes to the left of *aaNə* is the cleft focus.

An alternative to clefting the embedded clause is to cleft just the wh-constituent as shown in (4):

(4) *entə marunnə aaNə awaL nii kaziccu ennə wicaariccatə*
what medicine be she you eat past that think past atə
'What medicine was it that she thought you took?'

When there are multiple wh-phrases in the embedded clause, however, the only option is to cleft the embedded clause wholesale. For the sentence to receive a reading with a multiple wh-interrogation, the whs can neither be left in-situ nor can the whs alone be clefted. Another interesting observation is that when there is potential scope ambiguity involving a time adverbial (say, *eppooL* 'when') clefting of the whole clause versus clefting of the time adverbial is being resorted to as a means to disambiguate. This set of facts sheds light not only on the syntactic nature and function of the cleft construction, but it also tells us about the nature of wh-typology across languages. I show in this paper that a two-way distinction of languages, namely those which are wh-in-situ and those which are not, will not do justice to the array of facts, and that a more nuanced typological account is called for.

The paper is organized as follows. Section 1 presents the basic word order facts of Malyalam, followed by a preliminary formal account of clefts, based on my earlier work. Section 2 deals with the wh-typology and addresses the issue of where the Malayalam wh fits in. A plausible analysis of clefting as movement to Focus

1. Why the echo question strategy is not available with embedded questions is a puzzle. "English echo questions are notorious for allowing wh phrases in any position", as pointed out to me by an anonymous reviewer.

on the one hand and as an extraction out of a phase necessitated by scope bearing elements is discussed in Section 3. Section 4 discusses, following Jayaseelan (2001), an alternative to the received wisdom on the question interpretation. In the final section, Section 5, the relevance of PIC (Phase Impenetrability Condition) in wh-feature checking, especially in multiple wh-questions, is taken up in detail, highlighting the issues for Malayalam as well as English. It is shown that Agree of Chomsky (2000) is constrained by PIC.

1. Clefts: A preliminary account

Malayalam is a verb-final language. There is overt case marking on the DPs which allows for a high degree of freedom in constituent order. Though the normal word order is SOV, the object can precede the subject, and the adjuncts are free to occur in any preverbal position. A structure that is non-verb-final, though grammatical, will be highly marked. When there is embedding, the clausal complement is usually fronted, as shown below:

(5) *ellaawarum* [$_{CP}$ *awaL pariiksha paassawum ennə*] *wicaariccu*
all she exam pass future that think past
'Everyone expected her to pass the examination.'

(6) [$_{CP}$ awaL pariiksha paassaavum ennə] ellaawarum wicaaricccu

(6) is the preferred order. The complementizer is *ennə* which predictably occurs on the right periphery of the CP.

Clefting is a very productive strategy of giving prominence to constituents. The structure of the Malayalam cleft is quite similar to that of English clefts, as has been shown in my earlier work. In Madhavan (1987), I had offered a GB-theoretical analysis of the Malayalam cleft, in terms of an empty operator movement that links the element in the cleft focus to the gap in the cleft clause. I was essentially assuming a bi-clausal structure for a cleft as shown in (7):[2]

(7) a. *awaL aaNə ii kaaryam ennooTə paRanjatə*
she is this matter I Dat say past atə
'It was she who told me this.'

2. I had used S and S' in Madhavan (1987) which have been changed to IP and CP here.

b.

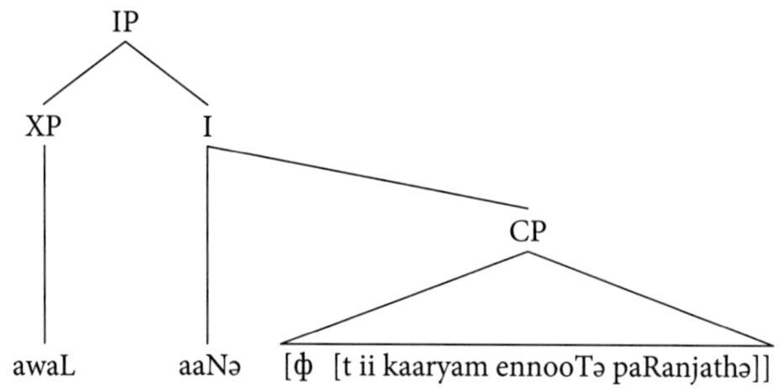

The position marked *t* in the clause is from where an empty operator ϕ is moved into the Spec of the CP, and *awaL* 'she' generated in the cleft focus will be co-indexed with it. (7) is the clefted version of (8):

(8) *awaL ii kaaryam ennooTə paRanju*
she this matter I Dat say past
'She told me this (matter).'

The copula *aaNə* 'be' is the cleft marker. The clefted constituent occurs to the left of the copula. I took the copula in the clefts to be an equative copula (with little semantics), and therefore it can be generated under the I node. I also assumed that the equative copula selects two complements: the XP (in the cleft focus) and a nominalized clause. Notice that the cleft clause has a particle *-atə* attached to the verb. This is a nominalizer; it can take overt case affixes.

2. Wh-typology

The languages of the world (it would seem) can be classified into three broad classes as regards the nature of wh-constructions. (a) those like Romanian and Serbo-Croatian that move all wh-phrases overtly to the Spec CP (b) those like Chinese and Korean in which all wh-phrases remain in-situ and (c) languages like English that move one and only one wh overtly to Spec CP and the rest remain in-situ. In the minimalist theory, the wh in order for it to receive interpretation has to undergo some kind of feature checking with a C head, either overtly or covertly. That much is clear. What is not well understood is the question: how does one retell in minimalist terms the story of LF movement of whs in-situ. There are four possibilities: one is to say that all whs in-situ actually move to Spec CP in covert syntax (move understood as copy plus merge). A second option is to say only the wh-feature needs move. A third possibility is in terms of Probe and Goal and a process called Agree. The fourth approach is in terms of unselective binding.

The introduction of phases into minimalist theory has actually compounded the problem for wh-in-situ phenomenon. As per Chomsky's PIC (Phase Impenetrability

Condition) any constituent that has to enter into any syntactic operation, including feature checking, has to get out of the complement domain of a phase before it is shipped off to PF. This necessitates 'transfer', a separate process in Chomsky (2005). Since that was found to be not an appealing move, linguists have tried other solutions. Thus Bošković (2007) has tried to show that PIC is not relevant to covert feature checking using Agree. He proposes that the conditions that constrain overt movement are not applicable to Agree. In overt movement, it is further hypothesized that there is an uninterpretable Q feature on a wh-element which is visible for movement and is checked as a reflex of the primary checking relation. In other words, when there is overt movement, the wh moves to satisfy the [+Wh] of the target C. For the wh-in-situ, Agree is enough. The probe sent by a higher C head will find a Goal in the first wh in its c-command domain. If there are more whs further down the line, they will also be undergoing Agree with the Probe of the C.

However, there is an inconvenient factor in this account. In languages of type (a) every wh is assumed to have an uninterpretable feature about it. Therefore, if there are 'n' whs in a sentence, all of them have this [+U] and so all of them move to Spec CP. As for type (c), none of the whs in-situ has a [+U] feature and so none needs to move. Their [+Wh] feature can be checked by Agree without overt movement. What about the (b) type? Here, since only the first wh moves, one has to say that only that one has a [+U] feature, the rest have [–U]. This is no more than restating the problem. Had there been no languages like English, a neat partition into types (a) and (b) would have been satisfactory, but the behaviour of multiple wh-constructions in English spoils the picture.

It is against the background of these puzzling and yet unresolved set of facts that I wish to examine the strategy of clefting used by Malayalam wh-questions. My contention is *that Malayalam is not a wh-in-situ language*, contrary to what has been generally assumed, not even in typological terms. Malayalam uses clefting of a wh-phrase (or alternatively of the whole clause that contains a wh) in a way quite similar to English moving a wh to the Spec CP. Obligatory clefting facilitates the wh-feature checking later on. I shall put off that to a later section and proceed to give a minimalist analysis of the cleft construction as a first step to discussing the main issue of the paper.

3. Clefts in a minimalist model

3.1 The English cleft

One reason why a GB theoretic analysis of the Malayalam cleft (or for that matter, the English cleft as per Chomsky (1977)) had to involve an empty operator movement was because of the D-Structure. In GB theory, D-Structure was an all-at-once level, and therefore all arguments had to be generated before any movement. Hence the appeal to an empty operator which gets linked to the constituent generated in the cleft focus by some sort of co-indexing. But in the minimalist model, the clause is built in a bottom-up fashion and move and merge can be freely interspersed. This, then, I think, allows for an analysis of a cleft where the clefted constituent can itself move to the cleft focus, instead of taking recourse to an empty operator. For the sake of concreteness let us take the following English sentence (9):

(9) It was *Aspects* that John taught in his syntax course.

After the basic clause *[that[John taught Aspects in his syntax course]]* has been built by successive select-and-merge, let the *be* select this clause as its complement and merge it. Now assume that *Aspects* has a [+Focus] feature with it. It is to be noted that in our analysis, the *be* in clefts is not the matrix verb, it is simply the Focus marker. (Naming the node as V is only for expository purposes.) That means, the *be* head has a [+Focus] feature to check.[3]

(10)

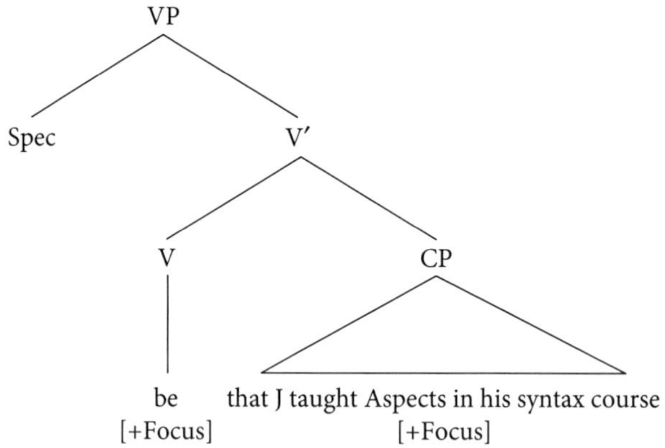

Now the clefted DP goes to the Spec for feature checking. After this movement, a T selects and merges the VP. Then V raises to T and finally a pleonastic *it* is merged

3. It has often been claimed that the fronted part in a cleft is the focus of the utterance. Rochemont (1986), Kiss (1998), among others. But it has also been argued that the clefted item need not necessarily be the focus. Thus, Szendroi (2006) gives the following examples to show that the clefted item need not be the focus of the utterance.

(i) I thought it was Peter who ate the pizza.
(ii) No, it was Peter who ate *the spaghetti.*

I am however ignoring this possibility.

in the Spec T. (Here I am ignoring the question of PIC. I will return to that in a later section)

While the above derivation seems to work for *that* clefts in English, notice that this does not cover the *who* clefts, like *It was John who taught Aspects in his syntax course*, where there is a clear case for a wh-movement.[4] I leave this issue open and turn to Malayalam clefts. Malayalam clefts seem to lend themselves to an analysis along the lines suggested here, as there are no clefts with overt wh-words, unlike in English.

3.2 Malayalam clefts: An analysis

Much the same can be said about the derivation of the Malayalam cleft. Consider Example (11):

(11) *awaL oru waliya wiiTə aaNə waaŋŋiyatə*
she one big house be buy past atə
'It was a big house that she bought'

Upto the point where the copula selects and merges a clause, the derivation proceeds as in the case of the English cleft. Then the XP from the inner clause raises to the Spec of the copula, for checking the feature [+Focus]. I take the Spec of the focus marking copula to be an A-bar position. As long as the copula remains under the Focus, it is a functional head and its Spec is undoubtedly an A' position. Then, T selects and merges this VP as its complement. At this point, for the checking of the nominative case of the matrix T, the cleft clause can optionally raise to its Spec position. Unlike the English *that* clause, the cleft clause of the Malayalam cleft can check nominative case, given the presence of the nominalizer *-atə*. If it does we get the order in which the clause comes initially followed by the cleft focus and the cleft marker *aaNə*. A second option for the grammar is to merge an empty pleonastic element in the Spec TP slot, which gives rise to the order where the cleft clause follows the focused constituent plus *aaNə*. See (11a and 11b).

(11) a. [awaL t waaŋŋiyatə] oru waliya viiTə aaNə
b. oru waliya viiTə aaNə [awaL t waaŋŋiyatə] = (11a)

The bracketed part is the cleft clause in (11 a–b). The *t* shows the position from where the clefted item was extracted. Notice that the exact word order in (11) is

4. Actually, either of the two analyses of the cleft, i.e. as involving a direct movement to the cleft focus/one mediated by the movement of an empty operator will be consistent with the main argument in this paper. One technical point is with regard to the need to move the clefted XP to the edge of the embedded CP in order to void the effects of PIC.

different from those in (11a) and (11b). (11a) is derived from (11b) by a further application of Move; it raises *awaL* 'she' to a Topic position in the left periphery.

One more technical detail needs to be mentioned here. After the XP moves to the Spec of the copula in the above derivation, the copula 'right cliticizes' to the XP. This is evident from the fact that nothing can intervene between the cleft focus and *aaNə*. This is what makes the *aaNə* act as the cleft marker.

It has been noticed that long distance clefting in Malayalam is syntactically distinct in nature from the clause bound clefting. There is a difference in the degree of freedom in word order. The cleft focus and the cleft marker combine can float down the clause and occupy any position, in the latter kind of clefts. But in the long distance clefts this is not possible, based on which Jayaseelan and Amritavalli (2005) argues that they arise out of two distinct operations. For relevant examples and arguments, see Jayaseelan and Amritavalli (2005). As this does not directly affect anything I say in this paper, I am not going into the details.

3.3 Questions

As mentioned in the introduction, questions in Malayalam usually appear as clefts. Why? We have seen that clefting moves a constituent to a Focus position. Now, wh-constituents are inherently focus bearing elements. Therefore, a wh going to the Spec of the copula in a clefted construction is nothing but an instance of overt focusing. Secondly, this movement to the focus position facilitates the need for a wh-phrase (a nonreferential XP) to get the required operator-variable interpretation. One parallel with English (and English like languages) needs to be noted here. The movement of wh to the Spec CP takes it out of the domain of Tense. Clefting also achieves the same. Therefore there are (at least) two options for the wh, English chooses one option, Malayalam the other. Why Malayalam doesn't choose the option of moving wh to Spec CP is not clear. Or put another way, why English doesn't resort to clefting, if the two options made available by UG are kind of equal. I suspect that the English choice is linked to the obligatory T to C movement in English interrogatives. Malayalam has no such phenomenon. More work need to be done before one can say anything categorically regarding this issue. Given below are the technical details of the cleft strategy. Consider (12), a clefted wh-question:

(12) *entə aaNe awaL waaŋŋiyatə*
what be she buy past atə
'what did she buy?'

entə 'what' is moved to the Spec of *be* as already explained in (11). The actual question interpretation of the wh is, we will argue in a later section, by an association with a disjunction operator in the C. (See Section 4).

3.4 Embedding

Consider now an embedded constituent question.

(13) **nii awaL entə waaŋŋi ennə wicaariccu*
you she what buy past that think past

(14) *entə aaNə nii awaL t waaŋŋi ennə wicaariccatə*
what be you she buy past that buy past

(15) *awaL entə waaŋŋi ennə aaNə nii t wicaariccatə*
she what buy past that be you think past atə
'What did you think she bought?'

In (13), *what* is in-situ and the structure is starred. (14) is the cleft version where only the *what* is clefted, while in (15) the whole clause containing *what* is undergoing clefting. Let us consider (14) first. For the wh to move out to the cleft focus, it has to first move to the outer Spec of the vP, then to the Spec CP, in order to avoid a PIC violation. Assume this to be so. After the copula has merged the CP with the wh in its Spec CP, it is possible for the wh to go to the Spec of the copula, for checking the [+Focus] feature. Recall that we are assuming a wh to have a [+Focus] feature with it.

Coming to (15), the derivation proceeds as follows. The verb *think* takes the whole clause as its complement *[awaL entə waaŋŋi ennə]*. It is this clause that is clefted (*t* shows the extraction site). For a constituent to undergo clefting, as per our assumptions, it has to have a [+Focus] feature. Now, the clause containing the *wh* has a [+Focus] feature, that is the [+Focus] feature of the wh-phrase. This feature can percolate to the head of the CP that is clefted which, in turn, facilitates the feature checking. Later the wh will associate with the disjunction operator in the head C to give the interrogative reading.

Comparing (14) with (15), we see that there are two ways in which the wh in embedded structures could get out: either by clefting only the wh (as in (14)) or by clefting the whole clause (as in (15)). In either case a direct question reading is available.[5]

5. In addition to (14) and (15), there is one more possibility, that is, to first have the wh word clefted and then the clause containing it can again undergo clefting, as in (i):

(i) *entə aaNə awaL waaŋŋiyatə ennə aaNə nii wicaariccatə*
what be she buy past atə that be you think past atə = 15

3.5 Mutiple wh-constructions

Now let us see what happens when there is more than one wh-phrase in an embedded clause. Consider (16) which has two wh-words *aarə* 'who' and *entə* 'what' in-situ.

(16) **nii aarə entə waaŋŋi ennə wicaariccu.*
'Who did you think bought what?'

(16) is predictably starred, the two whs in-situ cannot go out of the scope of T due to the familiar constraints on movement. (We will get back to the exact nature of this in the final section). The language therefore uses the stock strategy of clefting. However, in the case of (16), the only well-formed option is to cleft the whole clause (see (17)).

(17) *aarə entə waaŋŋi ennə aaNə nii wicaariccatə*
who what buy past that be you think past atə
'Who did you think bought what?'

Clefting of the wh-phrases alone runs into problems. Recall that a cleft construction can focus just one constituent. (This can be easily verified by non-question clefts.) Therefore, taking both *aarə* and *entə* to the cleft focus is not an option. Taking one or the other alone will result in a construction that has a wh-in-situ that cannot get out. These three cases are illustrated by (18–20) below:

(18) **aarə entə aaNə nii waaŋŋi ennə wicaariccatə*
who what be you buy past that think past atə

(19) **aarə aaNə nii entə waaŋŋi ennə wicaariccatə*
who be you what buy past that think past atə

(20) **entə aaNə nii aarə waaŋŋi ennə wicaariccatə*
what be you who buy past that think past atə

So we return to the grammatical (17) and see how the two whs, each bearing a [+Focus] feature, are allowed in the cleft focus. I have suggested that the [+Focus] feature of a single wh can 'climb' to the head of the clefted CP. When there are two phrases with this feature, we need to address two issues. One is the narrow, technical issue of feature checking. There shouldn't be any hitch as regards the [+Focus] feature on the copula – it can check (and delete) by valuing the feature on the phrase in the Specifier position. This might be analogous to the need for creating a composite [+Wh] for feature checking in the Comp of Slavic languages that stack all the whs overtly in the Spec CP. The second issue is this: what is getting a focused reading by means of clefting? We may answer this by saying that it is the CP, but within the CP there are two phrases which are inherently focused.

The well-formed multiple wh-question in (17) is one where both the whs are in the embedded clause, to begin with, but both acquire matrix scope by means of clefting. That is, the meaning conveyed by (17) is

(17') For which x and which y, you thought x bought y

3.6 Disambiguation

Another aspect of the obligatory clefting of questions is that it helps in the construal of adverbial modifiers. Consider (21):

(21) When did you think she bought the new house?

In (21), the adverb *when* can be construed as modifying either *think* or *buy*. The corresponding question in Malayalam can be framed in two ways, see (22) and (23).

(22) *eppooL aaNə nii awaL wiiTə waaŋŋi ennə wicaariccatə*
when be you she house buy past that think past atə
'For what time t, you thought at t that she had bought the house t ?'

(23) *awaL eppooL wiiTə waaŋŋi ennə aaNə nii wicaariccatə*
she when house buy past that be you think past atə
'You thought at what time t she bought the house at t?'

Notice that in (22) only the wh is clefted, while in (23) the whole clause is clefted. This dual option helps in showing explicitly where the adverb belongs. In (23) the wh is still within the embedded clause and therefore it is associated with the verb *buy*. (22) is arguably still ambiguous, but I suspect the preferred reading is one where it is construed with the matrix verb *think*, hence the gloss.

3.7 Wh-phrases in relative clauses

Consider (24):

(24) **nii aarə ezuthiya pustakam waaŋŋaNam ennə wicaariccu*
You who write rel. book buy should that think past atə
'Who did you want to buy the book written by?'

The sentence is starred because of the presence of a relative clause containing a wh-word. The wh cannot check its feature, buried as it is inside a complex NP. However, if the clause containing the complex NP is clefted, the sentence is fine, giving a direct question reading (see (25)). Another option is to cleft just the relative clause, as in (26).

(25) *[aarə ezutiya pustakam waaŋŋaNam ennə] aaNə nii wicaariccatə*
who write rel. book buy should that be you think past atə
'Who was it that you wanted to buy the book written by'

(26) [*aarə ezutiya pustakam*] *aaNə nii waaŋŋaNam ennə wicaariccate*?
who write rel. book be you buy should that think past atə
'Who was it that you wanted to buy the book written by?'

This demonstrates another facet of the clefting strategy the language employs.

4. The question interpretation

I have so far only shown that clefting takes the wh-constituent, or the clause containing the wh-constituent, out of the matrix clause and puts it in the of Focus, the Focus marker being the copula *aaNə*. How does this ensure a question interpretation in constituent questions? Actually, replacing a referential DP by a wh-phrase cannot in itself lend the sentence a question reading. Minimally, there should be a question intonation, seen in echo questions in English and unembedded wh-in-situ-questions in Malayalam. Syntactically, there should be some mechanism that signals a question as opposed to the default declarative reading. In English Yes/No questions, there is the obligatory subj-aux inversion. In a number of languages, there is an overt Q particle (like the *mo* in Japanese and *oo* in Malayalam) in the C. In Malayalam Yes/No questions the *-oo* which seems to be attached the clause final (inflected) verb can actually be analysed as situated in the head C. It is a disjunction operator, as argued for in Jayaseelan (2001). Jayaseelan (2001) further says that this disjunction operator, which is incidentally homophonous with the disjunction particle *oo* 'or', is present in not only Yes/ No questions, but in wh-questions as well. It is overt in the former, but covert in the latter. He further posits this covert disjunction operator in the C universally.[6] That is, even a language like English with overt wh-movement and a wh-in-situ language like Chinese have this. It is the presence of this disjunction operator that "by association with the focus" lends the sentence the interrogative reading. The disjunction operator's association with focus can be achieved by nonmovement means, says Jayaseelan. Wh-movement, overt or covert, only checks the [+Wh] feature of the C, it is independent of question interpretation (See Jayaseelan (2001) for details). I propose to adopt this analysis and modify it in the following way. The matrix C of the clefted questions that we considered in the earlier sections has a disjunction operator. The wh in the cleft focus can associate with this operator and effect a question reading.[7] The syntactic constraints, if any, on establishing this

6. More precisely, it is in the head of ForceP.

7. For the purposes of fixing the wh's scope, all we may need to say is that the C operator in Malayalam can only associate with elements in the smallest finite clause that contains the C. (I am obliged to an anonymous reviewer for this clarification.)

association, are not clear. Perhaps there is none. As long as the wh is in a focus position, it can associate with the disjunction operator.

5. Phase impenetrability condition and Agree

Now it is time to take stock. In sum, what we propose with regard to the obligatory clefting in embedded questions in Malayalam are the following:

a. Malayalam is not a wh-in-situ language like Korean or Chinese
b. Clefting is a strategy that takes the wh-constituent from inside a clause to the Specifier of the Focus projection, which is the copula *aaNə*.
c. It is the inherent [+Focus] feature of the wh-phrase that legitimizes its movement to the Spec Focus. It checks the [+Focus] feature in the Spec-Head configuration.
d. In addition to the [+Focus] feature checking, a wh-phrase has to check the [+Wh] feature, an uninterpretable feature, with the C head (i.e. $Force^0$) of an interrogative.
e. The question interpretation is effected not by the wh-feature, but by a disjunction operator (a null equivalent of *oo*) in C associating with the item in the Focus.
f. A wh-in-situ in an embedded clause in Malayalam cannot undergo feature checking by Agree.

The last point needs to be fleshed out. The question that we need to address is this: how does the wh-feature checking happen in multiple wh-constructions in English? Chomsky (2000) gets the second wh to check this uninterpretable feature by a making it undergo a special process called 'transfer' in order to avoid the prohibition caused by PIC. Bošković (2007), on the other hand, says that the wh-feature of the second wh-phrase in English is [+ interpretable] and therefore it can do the checking in-situ by means of Agree. He also argues that Agree in not constrained by PIC.[8] The Malayalam data analysed in this paper, I believe, throws interesting light on these issues. Had it been possible to do the checking of the wh-feature in-situ by Agree, in total disregard of PIC, as argued by Bošković (2007), then we have no good reason for obligatory clefting. The need for the disjunction operator to associate with the focus can perhaps be achieved by other means. Remember clefting is not the only focusing strategy, there can be a phonological Focus, with a special intonation. But that cannot save a wh-in-situ question in

8. For Boskovic (2007), PIC is not a principle of syntax, it is a consequence of Spell-out applying to the complement of a phase, at the completion of each phase.

the language. (13) with a question intonation on *entə* 'what' is as bad. So it boils down to the need to get the wh out of the clause because it has an uninterpretable feature, always. And a related point is that once it is in the Spec of Focus, PIC does not interfere, as the 'edge' of the phase is accessible to further syntactic operations.

Lastly, I wish to consider the unselective binding approach to wh-in-situ. Tsai (1999) has argued that wh-in-situ languages like Chinese, Japanese and Hindi need not resort to moving their wh-phrases as they can be bound by a null operator merged in the Spec CP. He also says that English cannot take this option as English wh-words are morphologically operator-variable combines. This obviates the Merger of a null operator in the Spec CP, a cheaper option, given the Merge-over-Move preference in minimalist architecture. The 'wh' part in question words like *what, when, where, why* etc. are morphological devices that facilitate feature checking in Spec CP. If Tsai's argument is on the right track, then unselective binding ought not be an option for Malayalam wh-phrases, as their morphological pattern is similar to that of pronouns, as is the case with English. In English, replacing *wh* with *th* gives the set of pronouns; in Malayalam, replacing *e* with *i*/*a* gives the set of pronouns. Compare (27) with (28):

English

(27)	what	that
	when	then
	where	there

Malayalam

(28)	eetə	'which'	itə	atə	'this/that'
	eppooL	'when'	ippooL	appooL	'now/then'
	ewiTe	'where'	iwiTe	awiTe	'here/there'
	eŋŋane	'how'	iŋŋane	aŋŋane	'this way/that way'
	ennə	'which day'	innə	annə	'today/that day'

This then seems to lend support to my position that Malayalam is not a wh in-situ language and that the wh needs to get out of its argument position in overt syntax for feature checking.

References

Bošković, Zeljko. 2007. On the locality and motivation of Move and Agree: an even more minimal theory. *Linguistic Inquiry* 38(4): 589–644.

Chomsky, Noam. 1977. On wh movement. In *Formal Syntax*, Peter Culicover, Tom Wasow & Adrian Akmajian (eds). New York NY: Academic Press.

Chomsky, Noam. 2000. Minimalist inquiries: The framework. In *Step by Step: Essays on Minimalism in Honor of Howard Lasnik*, Roger Martin, David Michaels, Juan Uriagereka & Samuel Jay Keyser (eds), 89–155. Cambridge MA: The MIT Press.

Chomsky, Noam. 2005. On phases. In *Foundational Issues in Linguistic Theory,* Robert Freidin, Carlos Peregrin Otero & Maria Luisa Zubizarreta (eds). Cambridge MA: The MIT Press.

É. Kiss, Katalan. 1998. Identification focus and information focus. *Language* 74: 245–273.

Jayaseelan, K.A. 2001. Questions and question word incorporating quantifiers in Malayalam. *Syntax* 4(2): 63–93.

Jayaseelan, K.A. & Amritavalli, Raghavachari. 2005. Scrambling in the cleft construction in Dravidian. In *The Free Word Order Phenomenon: The Syntactic Sources and Diversity*, Joachim Sabol & Mamoru Saito (eds), 137–162. New York NY: Mouton de Gruyter.

Madhavan, P. 1987. Clefts and psuedoclefts in Malayalam. Ph.D. dissertation. Central Institute of English Foreign Languages, Hyderabad, India.

Rochemont, Michael. 1986. *Focus in Generative Grammar* [Studies in Generative Linguistic Analysis 4]. Amsterdam: John Benjamins.

Szendroi, Kriszta. 2006. Focus movement. In *Blackwell Companion to Syntax,* Vol II, Martin Everaert & Henk van Riemsdijk (eds). London: Blackwell.

Tsai, Dylan. 1999. On economizing the theory of A-bar dependencies. New York NY: Garland.

Cleft partitionings in Japanese, Burmese and Chinese*

Daniel Hole & Malte Zimmermann
University of Stuttgart / University of Potsdam

The article presents the first comparative overview and analysis of clefting and related focusing strategies involving clauses with nominalizers in three (South) East Asian languages: Japanese, Burmese, and Mandarin Chinese. The three languages exhibit parametric variation as to whether focusing requires the overt partitioning into a focused cleft constituent and a background clause with a nominalizer (Mandarin) or not (Japanese, Burmese). A major finding is that syntactic partitioning is brought about in two different ways in the languages under discussion: Base-generated clefts (Japanese, Burmese) vs. movement clefts (Japanese, Mandarin). Semantically, cleft structures come with an exhaustive interpretation in all three languages. We hypothesize that, crosslinguistically, syntactic partitioning is a necessary, though not a sufficient condition for exhaustiveness effects with focus.

Keywords: Cleft; exhaustiveness; partitioning; *shì…de*-cleft; nominalizer; East Asian; South East Asian; Mandarin Chinese; Burmese; Japanese

1. Introduction

The article presents a first comparative overview and analysis of the syntax and semantics of clefting and focusing strategies in three (South) East Asian

* This work was carried out as part of the Collaborative Research Center SFB 632 "Information Structure". The financial support of the German Science Foundation (DFG) is gratefully acknowledged. We would like to express our gratitude to two anonymous reviewers, to our Japanese consultant Shinichiro ISHIHARA, our Mandarin consultants WANG Bei, CHENG Hsiu-Wen and CUI Jin, and our Burmese consultants SAW Nay Min Min Thaw and ZIN Kyaw Kyaw. We would also like to thank Uta GÄRTNER (HU Berlin) for establishing the contact to ZIN Kyaw Kyaw, and to Gunnar PETERS and Pavel OZEROV for invaluable help with the glossing of the Burmese data. Final thanks are due to Wolfram SCHAFFAR for much relevant discussion, and to the audience at the Cleft Workshop in November 2008 at ZAS/Berlin. All remaining mistakes are solely ours.

languages: Japanese, Burmese, and Mandarin Chinese.[1] The three languages exhibit typological variation in syntax (word order: SVO vs. SOV), phonology (tonal languages vs. pitch-accent languages), and morphological type (agglutinating vs. isolating), but they all feature clefting and related focusing strategies that involve backgrounded clauses headed by a nominalizing element. This is illustrated in (1) to (3).[2]

(1) *Clefts with nominalized clauses in Japanese and Burmese*

a. [*Taroo-ga* *Pari-de* *katta* no-*wa*] *tokee* da. (JAP)[3]
Taro-NOM Paris-LOC bought NLZ-TOP watch COP
'It was a watch that Taro bought in Paris.'/'What Taro bought in Paris was a watch.'

b. [*pol:* *pe:ris-hma.* *wekhe.*-ta] *naji-ta-loun:* hpji' *te.* (MYA)
Paul Paris-LOC bought-NLZ clock-one-CL COP RLS
'It was a watch that Paul bought in Paris.'/'What Paul bought in Paris was a watch.'

(2) *In-situ focusing structures with nominalized clauses in Japanese and Burmese*

a. [*Taroo-ga* *Pari-de* *tokee(-o)* *katta* no] (da). (JAP)
Taro-NOM Paris-LOC watch-ACC bought NLZ COP
'Taro bought a watch in Paris.'

b. [*pol*: *naji-ta-loun:-kou* *we* *nei* ta]. (MYA)
Paul clock-one-CL-OBJ buy PROG NLZ
'Paul is buying a watch.'

(3) *Clefts with nominalizers in Mandarin Chinese*

[Shì *Zhāngsān* *mǎi* *biǎo* de]. (CMN)
COP Zhangsan buy watch NLZ
'It is Zhangsan who bought a watch.'

Our central objective in this article is to show that the clefting and focusing strategies in (1) to (3) show considerable differences, which are somewhat

1. Unless indicated otherwise, data are from elicitations carried out in the project A5 'Focus marking, focus interpretation, and focus use from a cross-linguistic perspective' within the collaborative research center SFB 632 "Information Structure".

2. The following abbreviations are used in glosses: CL – classifier; COMP – complementizer; COP – copula; IRR – irrealis; LOC – locative; NEG – negation; NLZ – nominalizer; NOM – nominative; OBJ – object marker; POL – politeness; PRF – perfective; PROG – progressive; Q – question particle; RLS – realis; TOP – topic marker.

3. For abbreviated language names, the ISO 639–3 conventions are used throughout: 'MYA' for Burmese/Myanmar, 'JAP' for Japanese, and 'CMN' for Mandarin Chinese.

obscured by their surface similarities, and in particular by the presence of a nominalizing element heading a (nominalized) clause.[4] We argue that the three strategies exhibit variation along two dimensions: The first dimension concerns the question of whether focusing involving a nominalizer induces the syntactic partitioning into a focus part and a background part, as in (1) and arguably (3), or not, as in (2). The second concerns the question of whether or not the focus constituent in constructions involving a nominalizer *must* receive an exhaustive interpretation. We show that Japanese (pitch accent, SOV, agglutinating, +case) patterns with Burmese (tonal, SOV, agglutinating, weakly grammaticalized case/discourse role markers) in that both languages feature partition structures alongside non-partition structures, cf. (1) vs. (2). In Mandarin Chinese (tonal, mainly SVO, isolating, −case), by contrast, focus in clauses always induces a partitioning into focus and background in the overt or covert syntax. The data discussed show that, cross-linguistically, syntactic partitioning can be brought about in various ways. In the languages under discussion we find base-generated clefts (Japanese, Burmese), movement clefts (Japanese, Chinese), and LF-clefting (with a residual class of clefts in Mandarin Chinese). As for the semantic interpretation, it is shown that syntactic partitioning structures (here: cleft structures) come with an exhaustive interpretation in all three languages. Based on this finding, we hypothesize that syntactic partitioning is a necessary, though not a sufficient condition for exhaustiveness effects cross-linguistically.

A prominent feature of all three languages is the frequent use of clefting structures that are built around what is commonly referred to as *nominalizations* in the tradition of Matisoff (1972) or Lehmann (1982). Roughly, the term nominalization refers to predicates or clauses which acquire the distributional properties of nominals, or adnominal categories, by virtue of the presence of a functional element. For instance, the Mandarin Chinese nominalizer *de* yields nominal expressions when combined with a verbal category, as shown in (4).

(4) a. *zuótiān* *lái*-de (CMN)
yesterday come-NLZ
'the one who came yesterday'

b. *chī*-de (CMN)
eat-NLZ
'the thing eaten(/the one eating)'

4. We will not be concerned so much with the structural analysis of the cleft constructions in (1ab) as clefts or pseudoclefts, respectively, and thus paraphrase them by means of *it*-clefts in what follows; see the discussion in §§ 2.2 and 2.3, in which we adopt a pseudocleft analysis for the Japanese and Burmese cleft structures in (1ab).

Nominalizers are also frequently found in attributive constructions, where they are typically used to mark property-denoting expressions as adnominal modifiers. (5) presents Chinese examples with an adjective or stative verb (5a), and with a more complex relative clause attribute (5b), respectively.

(5) a. *nǔlì*-de *xuéshēng* (CMN)
hard.working-NLZ student
'hard-working student'

b. *zuótiān* *lái*-de *rén* (CMN)
yesterday come-NLZ person
'the person who came yesterday'

The data in (4) and (5) are typical of Chinese, and the same holds for parallel structures in Japanese. The parallelism in structure and interpretation between (5b) and (4ab) supports an analysis that postulates an empty head noun $\varnothing_N$ to be present in the structures in (4). This amounts to the claim that the particle *de* does not perform the nominalizing function by itself, but merely serves as forming adnominal attributes in both (4) and (5). For Burmese *ta* 'NLZ', the case is slightly different. Simpson (2008) has recently proposed that this element (and its irrealis counterpart *hma*) arose through a process of fusion between a Chinese-style attribute marker *te* (or *me* in the irrealis case) and a general head noun *ha* 'thing/fact'; see also Okell (1969) for a first proposal along these lines. On this analysis, then, the label 'NLZ' in our Burmese glosses would relate to a different function than the one performed by Chinese *de*, or Japanese *no*. Nonetheless, we will use the same descriptive label 'NLZ' for these functional elements in Japanese, Burmese and Chinese, in keeping with the widespread use of this terminology in East and South East Asian linguistics. We feel justified in doing so for the following reasons: First, none of the nominalizing structures investigated here has an attributive use. Irrespective of whether or not an empty head element is present in these structures, the complete structures show an overall resemblance with saturated expressions of the nominal (DP) or clausal type (CP), and not with attributes. Second, Hole (2011) proposes for the case of Mandarin *de* that instances of this marker in syntactic clefts are followed by an empty head. This is as in Simpson's (2008) analysis of nominalizers in Burmese, except that the fused specifying morpheme has phonetic content in Burmese.

The article is organized as follows: Section 2 discusses and analyzes the clefting and *in-situ* focus strategies in Japanese and Burmese, cf. (1), (2). Special attention is paid to the fact that Japanese has both base-generated and movement clefts (Hiraiwa & Ishihara 2002), where both types of Japanese clefts are interpreted exhaustively, same as their base-generated Burmese counterparts. Section 3 discusses and analyzes Mandarin *shì*...*de*-clefts, which also exhibit a nominalizing element, and which are interpreted exhaustively in spite of the seeming absence of a clear surface partition. In response to this finding, we adopt Hole's (2011) analysis of *shì…de*-clefts as partitioning structures that are partly obscured by the application of a phonology-driven reordering process. Section 4 concludes.

2. Focusing and clefting strategies in Japanese and Burmese

2.1 Background information on Japanese and Burmese

Japanese (isolate or Altaic) and Burmese/Myanmar (Sino-Tibetan/Southern Burmish) are spoken at quite some geographical distance, with Sinitic and other languages intervening, making the existence of direct contact phenomena highly implausible. Both languages are strictly OV and have agglutinative word formation, but, apart from that, the two languages differ in significant ways: Japanese has case-marking on DPs; as a pitch-accent language it only has some lexical tone features with low functional load; and it has a system of morphophonemics (consonant alternations) that is typical of Altaic languages. An example of an out-of-the-blue sentence with unmarked word order, which constitutes the basis for the focus variations to come, is given in (6).

(6) *Taroo-ga Pari-de tokee(-o) katta.* (JAP)
Taro-NOM Paris-LOC watch-ACC bought
'Taro bought a watch in Paris.'

More generally, Japanese shares many traits with Korean in spite of its disputed genetic classification. It was also subject to strong and long-lasting (lexical) influence from China, which – as will be shown – had no direct impact on its focusing and clefting system.

Burmese/Myanmar was subject to strong (lexical) influence from the (Indoeuropean) Pali superstrate, and it has diglossia between literary and colloquial Burmese (our examples are drawn from the colloquial variety). In contrast to Japanese, it has no fully syntacticized case-marking system, but still makes abundant use of particles for the marking of arguments and adjuncts. Among those particles, some appear to indicate hybrid categories that simultaneously signal syntactic/semantic role as well as discourse status in ways yet to be determined in more detail. Two such particles occur in our examples, namely *ka.* and *kou*, cf. (7); see Soe (1999: 94–116) and Vittrant (2008) for discussion. We gloss them as topic and object markers (TOP/OBJ), respectively, well aware of the preliminary character of these generalizations. In addition, Burmese has four lexical tones plus a complex system of segmental and tone sandhi. An unmarked neutral sentence, which again forms the basis for the focus variations to come, is shown in (7).

(7) *pol: naji-ta-loun:-kou pe:ris-hma wekhe.-te* (MYA)
Paul clock-one-CL-OBJ Paris-at bought-RLS
'Paul bought a watch in Paris.'

In the following sections, we first investigate focus clefts in Japanese (§2.2), which – as convincingly argued by Hiraiwa and Ishihara (2002) – come in two kinds, namely as base-generated pseudoclefts and as clefts derived by (focus) movement. It is also shown that either clefting strategy induces an exhaustive interpretation on the cleft constituent. We then turn to syntactic clefts in Burmese. Their syntactic status as base-generated or movement clefts is more difficult to establish, but they also trigger exhaustiveness effects (§2.3). §2.4 turns to the *in-situ* counterparts with nominalized clauses, which show flexible association with focus and no exhaustiveness effects in either language. §2.5 concludes with a tentative generalization about the relationship between overt syntactic partitioning in form of focus clefting and exhaustiveness effects in the semantic interpretation.

2.2 Overt syntactic partitioning in Japanese

2.2.1 *Syntactic structure*

Japanese has two ways of inducing an overt partition into focus and presupposition by means of cleft formation. Both cleft types allow for clefting of nominal constituents with various thematic roles (AG, TH, LOC, etc.), and their basic structure in terms of linear sequencing is as in (8). A topic-marked nominalized clause headed by the nominalizer *no*, which expresses the presupposed part of the utterance content, is followed by the cleft constituent in pre-copular position and the copula *da*. The same linearization pattern will be found in Burmese (but not in Mandarin Chinese); cf. §2.3.

(8) *Basic structure of Japanese cleft sentences*
[$_{\text{nominalization}}$ clause ***NLZ-TOP***] [cleft constituent$_{\text{DP/PP}}$] ***COP***
presupposition *cleft focus (phrase)*[5]

The first clefting strategy is illustrated in (9). Notice that the cleft constituent is invariably realized without overt case-marking no matter whether the cleft constituent corresponds to a subject, as in (9a), an object, as in (9b), or an adverbial, as in (9c).

5. The term *focus phrase* is used as in Krifka (2006) here and in the following. The focus phrase in the clefted position may also contain non-focused material (e.g. adpositions). Since cleft focus phrases are islands for movement they constitute minimal focus-containing constituents that are pied-piped along by focus-related movement; or they are simply juxtaposed to background material in base-generated information-structural partitions.

(9) a. [*Pari-de* *tokee-o* *katta* no-*wa*] <u>*Taroo*</u> da. [S]
Paris-LOC watch-ACC bought NLZ-TOP Taro COP
'It was Taro who bought a watch in Paris.'

b. [*Taroo-ga* *Pari-de* *katta* no-*wa*] <u>*tokee*</u> da. [O]
Taro-NOM Paris-LOC bought NLZ-TOP watch COP
'It was a watch that Taro bought in Paris.'

c. [*Taroo-ga* *tokee-o* *katta* no-*wa*] <u>*Pari*</u> da. [ADV]
Taro-NOM watch-ACC bought NLZ-TOP Paris COP
'It was in Paris that Taro bought a watch.'

As pointed out by Hiraiwa and Ishihara (2002), among others, there is a second clefting strategy, which is exemplified in (10ab) for OBJ- and ADJ-focus, respectively.

(10) a. [*Taroo-ga* *Pari-de* *katta* no-*wa*] <u>*tokee-o*</u> da. [O]
Taro-NOM Paris-LOC bought NLZ-TOP watch-ACC COP
'It was a *watch* that Taro bought in Paris.'

b. [*Taroo-ga* *tokee-o* *katta* no-*wa*] <u>*Pari-de*</u> da. [ADV]
Taro-NOM watch-ACC bought NLZ-TOP Paris-LOC COP
'It was in Paris that Taro bought a watch.'

Hiraiwa and Ishihara (2002) show that the two cleft variants differ in important ways that call for the assumption of two different underlying structures and derivational histories. Most strikingly, the cleft constituents in (10) show case, or postpositional, marking, which clearly marks them as arguments or adjuncts of the verbal predicates inside the nominalized clauses. Second, the cleft variant in (11ab) with an overtly case-marked cleft constituent exhibits island sensitivity; cf. (11b). No such island sensitivity is observed for the cleft variant without overt case-marking on the cleft constituent; cf. (11a).

(11) a. [*John-ga*[[e_i e_j *kaita*] *hito*$_i$]-*o* *hihansita* no]-*wa*
John-NOM wrote person-ACC criticized NLZ-TOP
<u>*kono-ronbun*</u>$_j$ da.
this-paper COP
'(lit.:) It is this paper$_j$ that John criticized the person who wrote e_j.'

b. *[*John-ga*[[e_i e_j *kaita*] *hito*$_i$]-*o* *hihansita* no]-*wa*
John-NOM wrote person-ACC criticized NLZ-TOP
<u>*kono-ronbun-o*</u>$_j$ da.
this-paper-ACC COP
'(int./lit.:) It is this paper$_j$ that John criticized the person who wrote e_j.'
(Hiraiwa & Ishihara 2002: 37)

Based on these differences and others, Hiraiwa and Ishihara conclude, correctly, we think, that the cleft variant with overt case-marking in (10) involves syntactic movement of the focus constituent to its surface focus position from a base-generated position inside the nominalized clause. This movement analysis captures the observed island sensitivity, and it accounts for the fact that the cleft constituent surfaces with its original adpositional or case marking, which marks it as an argument or adjunct of the nominalized predicate.

There are several ways of implementing this in terms of syntactic structure. For concreteness, we adopt Hiraiwa and Ishihara's (2002: 43) analysis, according to which Japanese movement clefts instantiate a mono-clausal structure with a Rizzi-style left periphery (Rizzi 1997). The overt cleft configuration is derived in two steps from the underlying *in-situ* focus structure with nominalizer in (12a), to be discussed in §2.4.[6] In a first step, the focus constituent XP moves from its base-generated position to the specifier of the functional projection Spec,FocP, cf. (12b). Subsequently, the nominalized clausal remnant moves around the focus constituent to Spec,TopP by means of remnant topicalization, cf. (12c). As a result, we arrive at a clear syntactic partitioning, with the focus constituent surfacing in pre-copular position. The syntactic structure of (10a) is shown in (13):[7]

(12) a. $[_{\text{TopP}}$ — wa $[_{\text{FocP}}$ — $[_{\text{FinP/CP}}$ $[_{\text{TP}}$ ...XP_{FOC} ...] no] da]]
b. $[_{\text{TopP}}$ — wa $[_{\text{FocP}}$ $\mathit{XP}_{FOC,1}$ $[_{\text{FinP/CP}}$ $[_{\text{TP}}$ ...t_1 ...] no] da]]
c. $[_{\text{TopP}}$ $[_{FinP/CP}$ $[_{TP}$ ...t_1 ...] $\text{no}]_2$ wa $[_{\text{FocP}}$ $\text{XP}_{\text{FOC},1}$ t_2 da]]

(13) $[_{\text{TopP}}$ $[_{FinP/CP}$ $[_{TP}$ Taroo-ga Pari-de t_1 katta] $\text{no}]_2$ wa
$[_{\text{FocP}}$ <u>*tokee-o*</u>$_{FOC,1}$ t_2 da]]

By contrast, the cleft-variants in (9) are not derived by focus movement. The cleft constituents are base-generated in their surface positions. The absence of focus

6. Based on data from NPI-licensing, Cho, Whitman and Yanagida (2008) argue that Japanese movement clefts must involve a bi-clausal structure with the copula element *da* in the matrix T-domain and long movement of the focused constituent into the matrix clause. Since nothing hinges on it for the intents and purposes of this article, we do not take a position on the correct syntactic analysis of Japanese movement clefts.

7. We leave it open whether the copular element *da* in (12) is base-generated in Foc, or whether it is base-generated in T, as in (14), and moved to its surface position in Foc by means of head movement. Both the assumption of free base-generation in Foc or T and the assumption of T-to-Foc-movement are in line with the ambiguous status of copula elements as focus markers and *vice versa*, which is cross-linguistically well-attested; cf. McWhorter (1994), Hartmann (2006).

movement accounts for the observed island insensitivity and for the fact that the cleft constituent invariably shows zero case-marking.[8] To be concrete, we take the cleft constituents in (9) to be generated as part of a pseudocleft in which the copula *da* relates the nominalized clausal topic DP and the focus constituent. This is depicted in (14), in which the focus constituent is base-generated as the predicate of the pseudocleft in pre-copular position, while the nominalized clause takes over the function of subject DP. This analysis is in line with the analysis of English *it*-clefts as concealed pseudoclefts in Percus (1997).

(14) *Base-generated Japanese pseudoclefts*

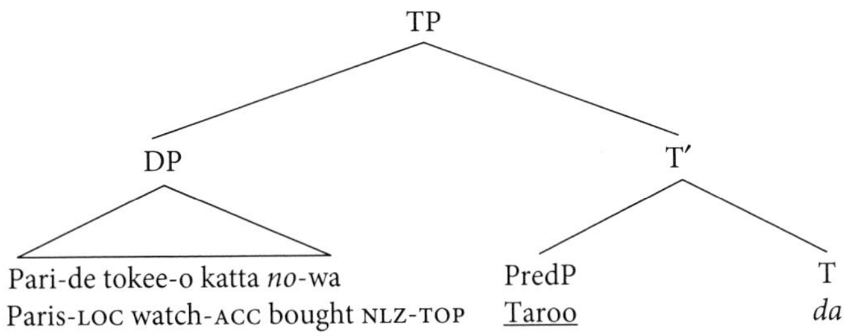

Taking stock, Japanese has two ways of bringing about a structural partition into focus and background material. The focus constituent can move from its base position to a designated pre-copular focus position, retaining its case features and obeying constraints on movement; or it is base-generated in pre-copular position as part of a pseudocleft in which the nominalized clause functions as the second argument of the copula *da*.

8. The non-movement analysis may overgenerate insofar as it would seem to predict island configurations, such as (11a), to be potentially ambiguous modulo additional selectional restrictions (which would block the non-sensical interpretation 'It is this paper that John critized the person that was written by it' for (11a)). Without movement, it should be possible, at least in principle, for the covert relative operator to bind either of the two empty categories inside the embedded relative clause in (11a). In response to this potential problem, one could introduce additional restrictions on the binding of empty categories, or, alternatively, one could resort to partial operator movement from within the relative clause to the edge of the nominalized background constituent; see Cho, Whitman and Yanagida (2008) and references therein. However, such partial operator movement would still constitute an island violation since Op-elements are otherwise blocked from leaving relative clauses (Watanabe 1992). For this reason, we favour an *in situ* account of Japanese non-movement clefts that relies on semantic binding – in accordance with recent work on semantic binding in Japanese (e.g. Kratzer & Shimoyama 2002).

2.2.2 *Exhaustiveness effects*

Both partitioning strategies in Japanese induce exhaustiveness effects on the (pseudo-)clefted focus constituent. In our view, the exhaustive meaning component of clefts is not truth-functional, but comes either in form of a presupposition (Percus 1997), or in form of a generalized conversational implicature (Horn 1981). Exhaustive cleft sentences thus differ semantically from sentences with the exclusive truth-functional operator *only*, which entail the falsity of sentences with alternative focus values. By contrast, a violation of the exhaustiveness requirement in Japanese cleft-sentences does not result in falsity, but rather in a presupposition failure, or in the cancellation of an exhaustiveness implicature.[9]

The exhaustive interpretation of Japanese clefts is witnessed by the fact that the cleft constituent cannot be the associate of additive focus particles, such as *mo* 'also' and scalar *sae* 'even', which trigger a presupposition to the effect that the background predicate does not exclusively hold of the individual denoted by the focused cleft constituent. This is shown for the pseudocleft variant in (15a) and for the focus movement variant in (15b). Notice that the cleft constituent is not in general immune to association with a focus particle, as association with the exclusive focus particle *dake* 'only' is compatible with the exhaustive cleft interpretation, and hence licit. (15c) shows that no exhaustiveness effect is present in *in-situ* focusing structures with nominalized clauses as introduced in (2).

---

9. That the exhaustiveness effect is not truth-functional can be seen from the fact that the coordination in (i) is infelicitous in the absence of the overt truth-functional exclusive operator *dake* 'only'. The infelicity of (i) can be attributed to the fact that the cleft sentence in the second conjunct is uninformative because it does not differ in truth-conditions from the first conjunct. With *dake* present, the exhaustive second conjunct is stronger in terms of truth-conditions, and hence felicitous.

(i) *Taroo-ga Pari-de tokee-o katta no-wa sitteita ga,*
Taro-NOM Paris-LOC watch-ACC bought NLZ-TOP knew alright,
Taroo-ga katta no-ga tokee-o-#(dake) da to-wa omowanakatta.
Taro-NOM bought NLZ-NOM watch-ACC-only COP COMP-TOP didn't.think
'I knew that Taro bought a watch in Paris, but I didn't think that it was #(only) a watch that he bought.'

Notice that the same holds for the English paraphrase, which has been taken as evidence for the non-truth-conditional nature of the exhaustiveness effect in English *it*-clefts by Horn (1981). See also Drenhaus, Zimmermann and Vasishth (2010) for experimental evidence to the same effect.

(15) a. [*Taroo-ga* *Pari-de* *katta* no-*wa*] *tokee*(?#*-mo*/#*-sae*/
Taro-NOM Paris-LOC bought NLZ-TOP watch-also/-even/
✓*-dake*) *da.*
-only COP
'It was (??#also/#even/✓only) a watch that Taro bought in Paris.'

b. [*Taroo-ga* *Pari-de* *katta* no-*wa*] *tokee-o*(#*-mo*/
Taro-NOM Paris-LOC bought NLZ-TOP watch-ACC-also/
#*-sae*/✓*-dake*) *da.*
-even/-only COP
'It was (#also/*even/✓only) a watch that Taro bought in Paris.'

c. [*Taroo-ga* *Pari-de* *tokee*(✓*-o-mo*/✓*-o-sae*/✓*-dake-o*)]
Taro-NOM Paris-LOC watch-ACC-also/-ACC-even/-only-ACC
katta no da.
bought NLZ COP
'Taro bought also/even/only a watch in Paris.'

The data in (15ab) suggests that the ban on additive focus particles is contingent on surface partitioning irrespective of whether it comes about by base-generation or by focus movement.[10] Anticipating the discussion in §2.4, this finding is corroborated by the fact that association of focus constituents with additive focus particles is indeed possible in the *in-situ* focus construction. Table 1 gives an overview of the grammatical and semantic properties of the three major focusing strategies in Japanese.

Table 1. Properties of Japanese *in-situ* and *ex-situ* focusing constructions/clefts

	Case marking on focus	Island sensitivity	Exhaustiveness
cleft	yes	yes	*yes*
pseudocleft	no	no	*yes*
nominalized *in-situ* focus construction	yes	no	no

The data summarized in Table 1 shows conclusively that a mandatory exhaustive interpretation is not a property of focus per se, but arises only when the focus constituent is clefted. We also see that the exhaustiveness effects cannot automatically be linked to the nominalizing head *no*, which is present in the *in-situ* focus

10. We have no analysis for the subtle, though robust, fact that *-mo* 'also' is slightly better in the (base-generated) pseudocleft (13a) than in the (movement) cleft in (13b).

construction as well. For this reason, we tentatively conclude that it is the syntactic partition into focus and background – in combination with topic marking on the background part – that is responsible for the exhaustive interpretation of focus constituents. The topic-marked background constituents establish a referential address in the common ground (Reinhart 1982; Krifka 2008; Endriss 2009), and can thus be conceived of as (definite) individual-denoting expressions of semantic type e. This is reflected by our choice of the category label DP on the background part in (14). Because of the topic semantics, Japanese cleft sentences can only be interpreted as identificational statements: the copula element equates the two type-e expressions denoted by the clefted focus constituent and the topic-marked background, respectively. Since the topical background constituent is semantically definite, the exhaustiveness effect arises from the interaction of the maximality presupposition of the topic expression, on the one hand, and the equative semantics of the copula element *da*, on the other. The semantic representation for the schematic cleft structure in (16a) is given in (16b).

(16) a. $[\text{YP}_{\text{BG}}$-NLZ-TOP$]$ $[\text{XP}_{\text{FOC}}]$ COP
b. $\iota x.\ [\![\text{YP}_{\text{BG}}]\!](x) = [\![\text{XP}_{\text{FOC}}]\!]$
'the unique x satisfying the background property is equal to the focus denotation'

The semantic representation of exhaustive Japanese clefts in (16b) is on a par with the semantic representations proposed for exhaustive focus constructions in Hungarian (Kenesei 1986; Szabolcsi 1994) and for *it*-clefts in English (Percus 1997). The difference with Japanese clefts is that the application of the iota operator is triggered by the presence of overt topic marking in Japanese. We will return to the issue of exhaustive interpretations in connection with Burmese clefts and with Burmese and Japanese *in-situ* foci in Sections 2.3 and 2.4, in which we show that exhaustiveness is always tied to the presence of an overt syntactic partition in these languages.

2.3 Overt syntactic partitioning in Burmese/Myanmar

The Burmese cleft structure parallels its Japanese counterparts both in terms of linear sequencing and in that the presupposed part is expressed by means of a nominalized clause. Compare (17) with (8) above:

(17) *Basic structure of Burmese cleft sentences*

$$\underbrace{[_{\text{nominalization}}\ \text{clause NLZ}]}_{\textit{presupposition}}\qquad \underbrace{[\text{cleft constituent}]}_{\textit{cleft focus (phrase)}}\ \text{COP}$$

(18a–c) exemplify this pattern with the Burmese counterparts of the Japanese clefts in (9a–c).

(18) a. [*pe:ris-hma. naji-ta-loun: wekhe.*-ta(-*ka.*)] *pol:* (hpji' *te*) [S]
Paris-LOC clock-one-CL bought-NLZ-TOP Paul COP RLS
'It is Paul who bought a watch in Paris.'

b. [*pol: pe:ris-hma. we-khe.*-ta(-*ka.*)] *naji-ta-loun:* (hpji' *te*) [O]
Paul Paris-LOC bought-NLZ-TOP clock-one-CL COP RLS
'It was a watch that Paul bought in Paris.'

c. [*pol: naji-ta-loun:-kou wekhe.*-ta(-*ka.*)]
Paul clock-one-CL-OBJ bought-NLZ-TOP
pe:ris-hma. (*hpji'* te) [LOC]
Paris-at COP RLS
'It was in Paris where Paul bought a watch.'

d. [*θu nɛ' cənɔ twe' Ta*] *məne'ka' pa* [TEMP]
3SG with 1SG meet NLZ yesterday POL
'It was yesterday that I met him.' (Vittrant 2008; her transcription)

The Burmese cleft constructions differ from Japanese clefts in a number of superficial ways. First, the presupposed nominalized clause need not be overtly topic-marked, as the topic marker *ka.* is optional. Second, unlike in Japanese, we find only one *ex situ* clefting strategy in Burmese, which gives rise to the question of whether the sentences in (18a–c) are instances of base-generated pseudoclefts or movement clefts. Since Burmese lacks regular case-marking, the absence of overt case-marking on the cleft constituent is not a reliable diagnostic for the pseudocleft analysis. The evidence from island configurations is univocal, though. *Wh*-and cleft-dependencies are easily established across island boundaries. This is shown for a complex DP in (19).[11,12]

11. We also encountered a variant of (19a) with the *wh*-word *in-situ*; cf. (i).

(i) [*pol: apji' sha khe.te.-lou ba wekhe.*-ta] *le:*
Paul criticized the.one.who-OBJ what bought-NLZ Q
lit.: 'What is [the thing]$_i$ such that Paul criticized the person who bought (it$_i$)?';
i.e. 'What is the x such that Paul criticized the person who bought x?'

The structure in (i) is actually the preferred way of expressing the intended question meaning and constitutes an instance of an *in-situ* focus structure as introduced in (2b). The *wh*-word occurs in its canonical preverbal focus position, but inside an island (the relative clause in the DP), whereas the question operator takes matrix scope. This suggests that the focused constituent in *in-situ* focusing structures is interpreted *in situ* as well.

12. Given the interpretations of (19ab), the embedded background *ta*-constituents exhibit the unexpected word order SVO instead of the typical order SOV. It would seem that the sentences in (19ab) are structurally ambiguous and give rise to a second (non-sensical) reading that is compatible with the normal SOV-order, and according to which (19a) could also mean something like 'What is the thing that bought the man whom Paul criticized' (Pavel Ozerov, p.c.).

(19) a. [*pol:* *apji' sha* *khe.te.-lou* *wekhe.*-ta] *ba* *le:*
Paul criticized the.one.who-OBJ bought-NLZ what Q
lit.: 'What is [the thing]$_i$ such that Paul criticized the person who bought (it$_i$)?';
i.e. 'What is the x such that Paul criticized the person who bought x?'

b. [*pol:* *apji' sha* *khe.te.-lou* *wekhe.*-ta] ti naji *pe.*
Paul criticized the.one.who-OBJ bought-NLZ this watch POL
lit.: 'It is this watch that Paul criticized the person who bought (it).';
i.e. 'It is this x, x = this watch, such that Paul criticized the person who bought x.

In light of these facts, we conclude that the Burmese clefts in (18) have the structure of pseudoclefts as depicted in (20). The analysis parallels the one for Japanese pseudoclefts in (14), except for the additional CP structure on top of TP, which is taken to host the sentence-final functional elements in Burmese.

(20) *Base-generated Burmese pseudoclefts*

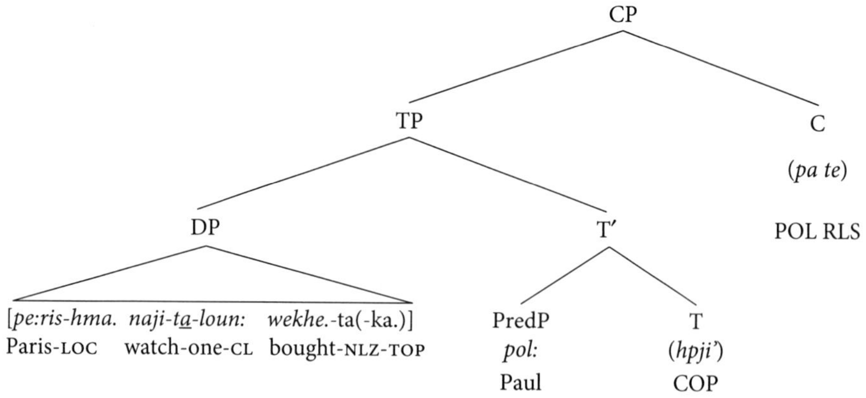

In spite of this, we feel confident about the validity of these data for the following reasons: (i.) the structures in (19ab) were volunteered by our consultants, which otherwise did not offer non-sensical translations that were unrelated in meaning to the English input; (ii.) on several occasions, our two consultants delivered converging data sets without hesitation, a situation not typically encountered with non-sensical statements; (iii.) the alternative *in-situ* construal of the *wh*-question in (i) in Footnote 11 clearly shows that an SVO-interpretation is available for this type of construction. In light of these facts, we consider the data in (19ab) to form an important source of information on the syntactic structure of clefts in Burmese.

Finally, the Burmese clefts in (18) pattern with their Japanese counterparts in that they, too, are interpreted exhaustively; cf. the Japanese cleft in (15a), repeated here as (21a), with the Burmese cleft in (21b). Neither sentence allows for association of the clefted focus constituent with additive or additive scalar particles.

(21) a. [*Taroo-ga* *Pari-de* *katta* *no-wa*] *tokee*(?#*-mo*/#*-sae*/
Taro-NOM Paris-LOC bought NLZ-TOP watch-also/-even/
✓*-dake*) da (JAP)
-only COP
'It was (?#also/#even/✓only) a watch that Taro bought in Paris.'

b. [*pol:* *pe:ris-hma.* *wekhe.-ta*] *naji-ta-loun:*(*#le:/#-taun/*✓*-be:*)
Paul Paris-LOC bought-NLZ watch-one-CL-also/-even/-only
hpji' *te* (MYA)
COP RLS
lit.: 'It was (#also/#even/✓only) a watch that Paul bought in Paris.'

The exhaustiveness of Japanese and Burmese clefts patterns with the semantic interpretation of pseudoclefts and *it*-clefts, which are commonly taken to be exhaustive in English and related languages; see, e.g. Krifka (2008), É. Kiss (1998, 1999), Percus (1997), and Delin and Obenauer (1995), among others; but see Horn (1981) and Dufter (2009) for an opposing view of clefts as not necessarily exhaustive. At the same time, Davis et al. (2004) and Koch and Zimmermann (2010) show that clefts are not interpreted exhaustively in several languages of the Salish family of Western Canada. Taking up an argument in Percus (1997), von Fintel and Matthewson (2008) link the absence of exhaustiveness or uniqueness effects in Salish to the general absence of definite determiners in these languages. In the same vein, we suggested above that the presence of exhaustiveness or uniqueness effects in Burmese and Japanese clefts is linked to the (optional) presence of the topic marker, which forces a definite interpretation on the presupposed nominalized clause. If this line of thinking proves correct, the overt syntactic partitioning into cleft constituent and presupposed background will only be a necessary, but not a sufficient condition for exhaustiveness effects, depending on independent grammatical properties of the language under discussion. We will come back to the relation between syntactic partitioning and exhaustive interpretation in Section 2.5.

2.4 Nominalized main clauses with *in-situ* focus in Japanese and Burmese

In addition to the cleft constructions investigated so far, Japanese and Burmese exhibit another focusing strategy involving nominalized clauses. This strategy involves a nominalized declarative main clause without overt partitioning into focus and background. The focus is a constituent of the nominalized clause instead, as shown schematically for Japanese in (22). As noted in §2.2, it is this structure from which Hiraiwa and Ishihara (2002) derive overt movement clefts.

(22) *Japanese **in-situ** focus with nominalized clauses*
[$_{CP/DP}$ [$_{TP}$ …[focus]…] *no*] (COP)

The focus constituent in (22) occurs in its base-generated (*in-situ*) position. In the absence of overt syntactic partitioning, the focus-background structure is indicated by prosodic means. The focus accent can be placed freely in the nominalized structure, as is typical of free association with (prosodic) focus. The nominalized *in-situ* focus structure in (23) is thus multiply focus-ambiguous and, depending on context and accent placement, can be used to express the focus-background structures in (24a–h), respectively (focus underlined):

(23)	[*Taroo-ga*	*Pari-de*	*tokee(-o)*	*katta*	no]	(da).
	Taro-NOM	Paris-LOC	watch-ACC	bought	NLZ	COP

(24) a. 'Taro bought a watch in Paris.' [S]
b. 'Taro bought a watch in Paris.' [O]
c. 'Taro bought a watch in Paris.' [ADV]
d. 'Taro bought a watch in Paris.' [S + O]
e. 'Taro bought a watch in Paris.' [V]
f. 'Taro bought a watch in Paris.' [VP]
g. 'Taro bought a watch in Paris.' [VP]
h. 'Taro bought a watch in Paris.' [clause]

Burmese, too, has a focus strategy in which the focus constituent occurs inside a nominalized main clause, but the resulting structures differ from their Japanese counterparts in three ways. First, unlike in Japanese, the copula is never overtly realized. Second, the nominalizing element appears in two forms, namely as realis *ta*, or irrealis *hma* (cf. §1). The third difference is more significant and concerns the fact that Burmese imposes an additional positional requirement on the position of the focus constituent inside the nominalized clause. The focus constituent must immediately precede the sentence-final verb, as shown for O focus in (25a), which is an infelicitous answer to a subject *wh*-question with the subject in sentence-initial position, and for S focus in (25b), which is an infelicitous answer to an object *wh*-question with the object in sentence-initial position.[13]

13. Notice that the focus constituent intervenes between the verb and other presupposed material to its left such that there is no clear bi-partition into focus and background material in (25ab).

(25) a. Q: <u>Who</u> is buying a watch? [S-wh]
A: {#*pol:*} *naji-ta-loun:-kou* {<u>*pol:*</u>} *we nei* ta
Paul clock-one-CL-OBJ Paul buy PROG NLZ
'<u>Paul</u> is buying a watch.'

b. Q: What is Paul buying? [O-wh]
A: {#*naji-ta-loun:-kou*} *pol:* {<u>*naji-ta-loun:-kou*</u>} *we nei* ta
clock-one-CL-OBJ Paul clock-one-CL-OBJ buy PROG NLZ
'Paul is buying <u>a watch</u>.'

The pattern in (25) replicates the preverbal focus constraint in canonical declarative clauses in Burmese (Simpson & Watkins 2005) and other SOV-languages; cf. (26ab).[14]

(26) a. *pol: pe:ris-hma* <u>*naji-ta-loun:-kou*</u> *wekhe.-te* [O]
Paul Paris-LOC clock-CL-OBJ bought-RLS
'Paul bought <u>a watch</u> in Paris.'

b. *pol: naji-ta-loun:-kou* <u>*pe:ris-hma*</u> *wekhe.-te* [LOC]
Paul clock-CL-OBJ Paris-LOC bought-RLS
'Paul bought a watch <u>in Paris</u>.'

Moreover, the preverbal focus constraint is also active in *wh*-question formation (cf. Simpson & Watkins 2005: 36, transcription theirs except for the proper name; cf. also Footnote 11).

(27) a. *pol:* <u>*ba*</u> *wje-dha le:?*
paul what buy-RLS Q
'What did Paul buy?'

b. *dihsa.aup.kou* <u>*bedhu*</u> *wje-dha le:?*
this.book.OBJ who buy-RLS Q
'Who bought this book?'

The active status of the preverbal focus constraint in Burmese nominalized *in-situ* focus constructions may therefore be taken as an indicator of a high degree of assimilation of this sentence type to the canonical declarative sentence type. The schematic structure of Burmese nominalized *in-situ* focus constructions with nominalizers *ta* and *hma* is given in (28).

(28) $[_{CP/DP}$ $[_{IP}$ …[<u>focus</u>] V] *ta/hma*]

On the semantic side, the nominalized *in-situ* focusing structures in Japanese and Burmese are unspecified regarding exhaustiveness. It follows that additive focus

14. Cf. Simpson and Watkins (2005) for factors that may override the adjacency constraint in individual cases.

particles can freely associate with the focus constituent inside the nominalized clause, as can scalar additive and exclusive particles.

(29) a. JAP: ✓Additive focus particles
Taroo-ga *Pari-de* *tokee(-o)-mo/(-o)-sae/dake(-o)* *katta*
Taro-TOP Paris-LOC watch-ACC-also/ACC-even/only-ACC bought
no da.
NLZ COP
'Taro bought also/even/only a watch in Paris.'

b. MYA: ✓Additive focus particles
pol: *pe:ris-hma* *naji-ta-loun:-le:* *wekhe.*-ta
Paul Paris-LOC clock-CL-*also* bought-NLZ
'Paul bought also a watch in Paris.'

As already noted in Section 2.2, the non-exhaustiveness of Japanese and Burmese *in-situ* focus structures stands in stark contrast to the mandatory exhaustiveness of the corresponding cleft constructions with overt syntactic partitioning. This suggests that it is indeed syntactic partitioning, possibly in interaction with additional factors, which has an effect on semantic interpretation.

2.5 Nominalized focusing structures in Japanese and Burmese: Summary

Japanese and Burmese exhibit a number of focusing strategies that involve nominalized clauses. Next to a pseudocleft construction (Japanese, Burmese) and a movement cleft construction (Japanese), which involve an overt syntactic partitioning into focus and background, there is also an *in-situ* strategy without partitioning. Its focus constituent is realized inside a nominalized clause. The semantic interpretation of the various focusing structures in the two languages is summarized in Table 2.

Table 2. Exhaustiveness in clefts and nominalized *in-situ* focus structures

Exhaustiveness effect	Japanese	Burmese
cleft/pseudo-cleft	yes	yes
nominalized *in-situ* focus construction	no	no

The table shows that exhaustiveness effects with focus structures are contingent on the overt partitioning of the clause into clefted focus and presupposition in Japanese and Burmese. At the same time, the occasional possibility of non-exhaustive readings in German, English and Romance cleft-sentences pointed out in Prince (1978), Horn (1981) and Dufter (2009), among others, as well as the non-exhaustive interpretation of clefts in the Salish languages, suggests that, universally, overt partitioning may only be a necessary, but not a sufficient condition for the exhaustive interpretation of focus constituents. We conclude the section on Japanese and Burmese with the tentative universal in (30), which remains subject to further cross-linguistic scrutiny.

(30) *EXH-Universal*
  (i) If a given language exhibits exhaustiveness effects with focus, and
  (ii) if that language has two different focusing structures X and Y, such that Y involves a syntactic partition into cleft focus and presupposition, but X does not, then the exhaustiveness effects will show up in Y.

The EXH-universal in (30) only postulates a one-way entailment between syntactic structure and semantic interpretation, and it is thus weaker than the bi-directional entailment between clefting and exhaustive interpretation that is standardly assumed (e.g. É. Kiss 1998; Krifka 2008). In particular, (30) only makes the emergence of exhaustive foci dependent on syntactic partitioning, but it does not require all cleft-structures to be exhaustive. At the same time, it makes no predictions about the exhaustiveness of focus for languages that have only one focusing structure at their disposal.

3. Chinese

3.1 Basic facts about Mandarin Chinese

Mandarin Chinese is a VO language with some OV traits. Its DP and PP syntax conforms to the OV type insofar as it has several postpositions and preposed relative clauses (Comrie 2008).[15] The language is mostly isolating with some agglutinating tendencies in aspect and noun formation. Compounding abounds. Mandarin Chinese is a lexical tone language with four tones.

A neutral S ADV V O sentence in correspondence with the Japanese and Burmese sentences in Section 2 is given in (31).

(31) *Zhāngsān zài Bālì mǎi le biǎo.*
Zhangsan at Paris buy PRF watch
'Zhangsan bought a watch in Paris.'

15. It is still unclear to what extent the OV tendencies of Mandarin Chinese can be explained in terms of structural influence from other languages; cf., e.g. the discussion of the Altaic influence in the early years of the Manchu Qing dynasty (1644–1911) in Norman (1982), Hashimoto (1986), and Okada (1992).

In (31), the VO constituent is preceded by the adverbial, which is, in turn, preceded by the subject. The only difference to Japanese and Burmese in terms of linearization is the VO order (as opposed to the OV order of Japanese and Burmese).

3.2 Comparing the basic structure of clefts in Mandarin Chinese with Japanese and Burmese pseudoclefts

(32a) presents the counterpart of (31) with the locative phrase clefted. (32b) is the corresponding subject cleft.

(32) a. *Zhāngsān* shì *zài Bālì* *mǎi biǎo*-de. [LOC]
Zhangsan COP at Paris buy watch-NLZ
'It was in Paris where Zhangsan bought a watch.'

b. *Zài Bālì* shì *Zhāngsān* *mǎi biǎo*-de. [S]
at Paris COP Zhangsan buy watch-NLZ
'In Paris it was Zhangsan who bought a watch.'

The functional elements involved in projecting the cleft pattern in Chinese are the same as in Japanese and Burmese; (32ab) each feature a copula and a nominalizer. Still, the overall make-up of clefts in Chinese differs from the one in the other two languages. First, the copula is not clause-final, this being a reflex of the SVO nature of Mandarin Chinese. More importantly, researchers converge on the point that, in Mandarin, the copula does not intervene between the focus presupposition and the clefted phrase, as it does in Japanese or Burmese. Instead, the copula links the topical constituent to its left with the cleft-plus-presupposition part to its right. Given this, and since the nominalizer *de* follows the cleft-plus-presupposition string, the boundary between focal and presupposed material in Chinese clefts is not clearly demarcated – at least insofar as morphological marking is concerned. Another difference between Chinese and the other two languages concerns the fact that the string between the cleft focus and the nominalizer does not refer to a definite topical entity, as was the case with the NLZ-marked constituents in Japanese and Burmese.[16] This generalization is not just warranted by speakers'

16. Apart from the clefts discussed in the main text, Mandarin also has pseudoclefts that are structurally and functionally analogous to the Japanese and Burmese pseudoclefts discussed in §§2.1–2.3; cf. (i).

(i) [*Zhángsān zài Bālì mǎi*-de (*dōngxi*)] shì *biǎo*.
Zhangsan at Paris buy-NLZ thing COP watch
'What Zhangsan bought in Paris was a watch.'

Given the analysis of Japanese and Burmese pseudoclefts in the previous sections, sentences as in (i) receive a straightforward analysis (cf. Hedberg & Jhang 1994). By contrast, the Mandarin

intuitions, but also by a clear distributional characteristic: the *de*-marked constituent in the Chinese clefts discussed here never occurs in the topical position in the left periphery. This position is filled by the outer topical argument of the copula, as pointed out above. Moreover, while the missing head noun of Mandarin pseudoclefts as in (i) of Footnote 16 can be rendered explicit, it is impossible to use any overt head nouns in the Mandarin clefts under scrutiny here. Researchers thus widely agree that *de* marks a verbal or clausal category instead (cf. Simpson & Wu 2002 for their C-headed cleft types, Paul & Whitman 2008; Cheng 2008). Hole (2011) adopts Simpson and Wu's (2002) analysis which proposes that the "nominalizer" structure found in Mandarin clefts is really a structure in which *de* links the cleft presupposition to an empty C head (labeled C_2 in (33)). This empty C head belongs to a paradigm of C categories heading conditional, temporal, reason and other clauses.[17] (33) contrasts a cleft sentence with its zero C_2 head with a conditional clause in which the C_2 head has phonetic content. (We will leave it open here whether CP and C_2P can be assimilated to Rizzi's 1997 FocP and FinP, respectively, as suggested by a reviewer.)

(33) a. *Zhāngsān*$_j$ shì [$_{CP}$ <u>*zài*</u> <u>*Bālì*</u> *pro*$_j$ *mǎi* *biǎo* [$_{C'}$ de$_C$ ∅$_{C2}$]].
Zhangsan COP at Paris buy watch NLZ
'It was in Paris where Zhangsan bought a watch.'

b. [$_{CP}$ [*Tā* *bù* *lái*] [de$_C$ huà$_{C2}$]] (conditional clause)
(s)he not come NLZ if
'If (s)he doesn't come ...'

The fact that the C head follows its hypothesized complement may be surprising in light of the overall SVO character of Mandarin Chinese. Still, as was mentioned in Section 3.1 above, Mandarin Chinese does have some OV traits, and therefore clause-final C heads are not entirely unexpected. Note that clause-typing particles in Mandarin-Chinese are likewise clause-final (Cheng 1997), as shown in (34).

(34) *Zhāngsān* *mǎi-le* *biǎo* *ma/a*!
Zhangsan buy-PRF watch Q/EXCLAMATIVE
'Did Zhangsan buy a watch?'/ 'Hey, Zhangsan bought a watch!'

---

cleft structure to be analysed in the main text requires an analysis which is different from the one given for the pseudoclefts in Japanese and Burmese, even though it is based on the same functional expressions, viz. a nominalizer and a copular element.

17. Cf. Zhang (2009) for independent evidence that *de* occurs in structures with iterated heads of a single general type.

We will return to the syntactic derivation of Mandarin clefts below. What matters at the present point is that a general case can be made for the analysis of *de*-marked clefts in Mandarin as involving a clausal category that is headed by *de*; the copula in the structure links the topic constituent (frequently a subject as in (32a)/(33a)) to the cleft-plus-presupposition part. This is depicted in (35). The nominalizer element in (35) is marked by scare quotes to remind the reader that the presence of the nominalizer in (35) does not yield a nominalized complement of the copula, unlike in Japanese and Burmese. As pointed out in Section 1, we stick with the terminological tradition in this respect because the range of polysemy of the Chinese nominalizer *de* overlaps to a great extent with that of Japanese *no* and Burmese *ta/hma*.

(35) *Basic structure of Chinese cleft sentences*

[topic/subject] *COP* [$_{CP}$ clause "*NLZ*"]

topic *cleft focus (phrase) + cleft presupposition*

The syntax of the post-copular part of the cleft structure in (35) is a controversial issue. Despite intensive research efforts made over the past thirty years or so, no consensus has been arrived at in this domain (Simpson & Wu 2002; Cheng 2008; Paul & Whitman 2008). Here, we adopt Hole's (2011) recent proposal for the analysis of Chinese clefts, but we do so against the background of competing theories.

3.3 Exhaustiveness and positional restrictions with Chinese clefts

There are two basic generalizations to be accounted for by any theory of Chinese clefts. First, Chinese clefts display exhaustiveness effects. Second, there are positional restrictions on the cleft focus phrase. We will look at each of these generalizations in turn.

The exhaustiveness effect of Chinese clefts is evinced by the example in (36) (cf. Paul & Whitman 2008: 420).

(36) *Tā* shì *zài Běijīng xué yǔyánxué* de, #*dàn yě* shì *zài*
(s)he COP at Beijing study linguistics NLZ but also COP at
Shànghǎi xué de.
Shanghai study NLZ
'It's in Beijing that (s)he studied Chinese, #but also in Shanghai.'

The effect is absent with the sentence-medial variant of the so-called *Bare-*shì *Focus Construction*. This construction is, correctly, we believe, analyzed as an *in-situ* association-with-focus pattern by Paul and Whitman (2008). The Bare-*shì* counterpart of (36) is shown in (37). (38) illustrates the free focusing options found with this construction.

(37) *Tā* shì *zài Běijīng xué-guo yǔyánxué, dàn yě zài*
(s)he COP at Beijing study-ASP linguistics but also at
Shànghǎi xué-guo.
Shanghai study-ASP
'(S)he studied Chinese in Beijing, but also in Shanghai.'

(38) *Tā* shì [*zài Běijīng* [*xué-guo yǔyánxué*]].
(s)he COP at Beijing study-ASP linguistics
'(S)he studied linguistics in Beijing.' [LOC]
'(S)he studied linguistics in Beijing.' [O]
'(S)he studied linguistics in Beijing.' [V]
'(S)he studied linguistics in Beijing.' [VP]
'(S)he studied linguistics in Beijing.' [LOC+VP]

The Bare-*shì* Focus construction thus patterns with the *in-situ* focusing structures discussed for Japanese and Burmese in Section 2.4. Given that we have two focusing constructions in Mandarin Chinese, only one of which displays exhaustiveness effects, the EXH-universal makes us expect that, if there is a syntactic partition involed in focus marking, it ought to show up with the *shì...de* construction, and not with the Bare-*shì* Focus Construction. Provided that the order of constituents in the *shì...de* clefts considered so far is identical to the one found in canonical sentences and in the Bare-*shì* Focus Construction, the existence of a syntactic partition in Chinese *shì...de* clefts is not immediately transparent (see above). However, there is an additional positional restriction that allows us to make a case for the presence of a syntactic partition in Chinese clefts as well. This restriction concerns the fact that the large majority of Chinese cleft sentences only allow for cleft focus phrases to be located adjacent to the copula (see Section 3.4 for a regular class of exceptions to this generalization). This generalization is illustrated in (39).[18]

18. Cheng (2008) presents an analysis of Chinese *shì...de*-clefts in terms of free focus. According to her analysis, the focus may be expressed by any constituent within the complement of the copula *shì*. However, this view is at odds with the traditional view that most clefted foci in Chinese clefts must be adjacent to the copula. Hole (2011:1712) aims at reconciling Cheng's (2008) intuition of free focus with the traditional view. He argues that Cheng's (2008) free foci in cleft sentences are, for the most part, corrective foci that supersede (second-occurrence) cleft foci in the position adjacent to the copula.

(39) a. *Zhāngsān* shì <u>*zuótiān*</u> *zài bàngōngshì xiě shī* de.
Zhangsan COP yesterday at office write poem NLZ
'It was yesterday that Zhangsan wrote poems in his office.'

b. *Zhāngsān* shì (#*zuótiān*) <u>*zài bàngōngshì*</u> *xiě shī* de.
Zhangsan COP yesterday at office write poem NLZ
int.: 'It was in his office that Zhangsan wrote poems (#yesterday).'

c. *Zuótiān Zhāngsān* shì <u>*zài bàngōngshì*</u> *xiě shī* de.
yesterday Zhangsan COP at office write poem NLZ
'Yesterday it was in his office that Zhangsan wrote poems.'

d. *Zuótiān* shì <u>*Zhāngsān*</u> *xiě shī* de.
yesterday COP Zhangsan write poem NLZ
'Yesterday it was Zhangsan who wrote poems.'

(39a) has the immediately post-copular adverb as a cleft focus. If we were to try to interpret the second post-copular constituent as focused instead, as in (39b), the result would be infelicitous. (39c) provides a way of expressing the intended cleft partition of (39b), with the intervening adverb of (39b) being realized in topic position, and with the cleft constituent adjacent to the copula. Finally, (39d) demonstrates that subjects may likewise be clefted.

3.4 The syntax of Chinese clefts

We take the positional requirement introduced in the previous subsection to be indicative of a syntactic partition at the surface of Chinese clefts. We thus start out from the hypothesis that there is a syntactic position in the complement of the copula in Chinese clefts which is designated to host clefted constituents. At the same time, we saw in the previous subsection that the functional element differentiating between the *in-situ* focusing Bare-*shì* Focus Construction and cleft sentences is the nominalizer *de*. Hence it is natural to assume that the projection of clefts in Chinese is triggered by *de* and by the structure that comes with it. This conclusion brings us back to a challenge that we left unresolved in Section 3.2 in the context of clause-final C heads in the SVO language Chinese. There, we argued that there is evidence to the effect that *de* and other clause-final elements instantiate such clause-final C heads. What adds to this challenge at the present point is our claim that *de* partakes in the projection of the syntactic cleft configuration even though *de* is not in a syntactic position where it could indicate the cleft-and-presupposition divide in a perspicuous manner.

In response to this twofold challenge, we assume with Hole (2011:1720) that the clause-final position of *de* is the result of PF movement. At spell-out, and also at LF, the structure of Chinese clefts is as in (40).

(40)

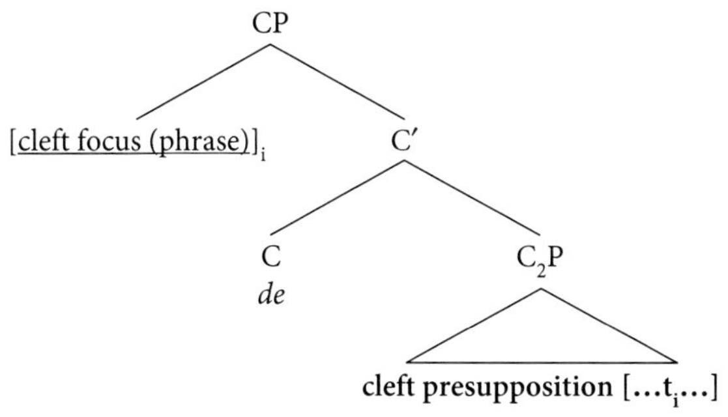

The PF linearization with the presuppositional constituent preceding *de* is derived in the following manner: *de* is an enclitic that must attach to a deaccented host.[19] Since the material in the cleft focus phrase is not deaccented, LF-preposing of the cleft presupposition is the only way to abide by the cliticization requirements of *de*.

There is a variant of Chinese clefts that, according to our analysis, displays a slightly larger discrepancy between its PF and LF representations than the cleft constructions looked at so far. This variant is mainly found in Northern dialects (Paul & Whitman 2008: 427), and it allows for object foci at the right edge of the clause; cf. (41).

(41) *Zhāngsān* shì *chàng*-de <u>*shénme*</u> <u>*gē*</u>?
Zhangsan COP sing-NLZ what song
As for Zhangsan$_i$, [what was the song]$_{\text{Cleft Focus Phrase}}$ he$_i$ sang?
(cf. Paul & Whitman 2008: 428)

Notice that the availability of object focus interpretations with *shì...de* clefts is restricted to this marked clefting option with the word order V NLZ O and the peculiar surface linearization of the nominalizer *de* preceding the object. By contrast, *shì...de* clefts with the unmarked word order V O NLZ (if there is an object) can never express object focus. In addition to object cleft readings, V *de* O clefts also allow for the interpretation of subjects and adjuncts in immediately post-copular position as clefted foci, same as in clefts with clause-final *de*.[20]

19. Cf. Xu (1999) for phonetic correlates of deaccentuation in Mandarin Chinese (lowering of f_0 and compression of f_0 range). Cf. Hole (2011) for the complete picture of *de*-cliticization including a class of principled exceptions to the deaccentuation requirement.

20. See Lee (2005), Paul and Whitman (2008) and Hole (2011) for further discussion of the distribution of V *de* O clefts, which is still poorly investigated and controversial.

Hole (2011:1721–3) argues that V *de* O clefts as in (41) and (42) can, to a large extent, be assimilated to the canonical V O *de* pattern if it is assumed that, in V *de* O clefts, object shift precedes the cliticization of *de* to the verb. A derivation of (42) along these lines is schematically shown in (43).

(42) *Wǒ* shì *xiě*-de <u>*shī*</u>.
I COP write-DE poem
'It's poems that I write.'

(43) a. Object Shift
$[_{AspP}$ shī$_i$ ... $[_v$ v xiě t$_i$]]]
poem write

b. Remnant PF Movement
[(xiě)$_{PF}$ $[_C$ *-de* ... $[_{Asp}$ shī$_i$ ...(xiě)$_{spell\text{-}out}$]]]]
write DE poem write

Since object shift in Mandarin is restricted to finite clauses (Paul 2002), it is plausible to assume that the position of the shifted object is the specifier position of some inflectional category. For the sake of concreteness, and given that Mandarin has grammaticalized aspect, we take this position to be Spec,Asp. In (43a), the object has moved to Spec,Asp. (43b) shows the result of PF movement, where the remnant constituent has moved around the shifted object to the specifier position of the C-category headed by *de*. Similar proposals have been made by Cho and Nishiyama (2000: 40) for VP-fronting without objects in Yoruba (Kwa, Niger-Kongo), and by Simpson (2001: 109) for Thai VP-fronting without objects across modal verbs. The fact that *de* attracts the verb (and not the object) as clitic host is accounted for by *de*'s aforementioned restriction to cliticize onto deaccented material. Note that the V *de* O pattern does not allow for verb clefts. This is expected since, if the verb was focused, it would be accented and would thus not be a potential host for the cliticization of *de*.

The proposed analysis derives the V *de* O pattern, and it does so in a plug-in fashion that simply adds one extra operation – object shift – to the analysis of V O *de* clefts. We take this to be an advantage of the general proposal. Moreover, the grammaticality patterns observed with V *de* O clefts correspond in part to those found with mere object shift in Mandarin. Most importantly, neither V *de* O clefts nor object shift structures allow for overtly marked indefinites as objects; cf. Shyu (2001) on object shift, and Lee (2005), Paul and Whitman (2008) and Hole (2011) for the same restriction found with the V *de* O pattern.

Notice finally that the combination of object shift and PF remnant movement derives the surface V *de* O pattern, but it does not yet assimilate V *de* O object clefts as in (41) to the syntactic representation in (40). In response to this situation we assume that the shifted object moves on to spec,C of (40) in the LF branch of grammar if it is a cleft focus.[21]

For the copula-headed structure above the cleft structure proper we propose, again following Hole (2011), that the copula is a verbal element which embeds the cleft CP inside a higher clausal layer. A parallel assumption is made by Simpson and Wu (2002) and, similarly, by Paul and Whitman (2008). Simpson and Wu (2002) argue that the copula has present-tense implications of its own, thereby justifying a doubly tensed structure for Chinese clefts; see Simpson and Wu (2002) and Hole (2011:1730–1) for details. (44b) depicts the resulting biclausal structure of (44a). The internal structure of the CP node in (44b) is again as in (40).

(44) a. *Zhāngsān*$_{\text{SUBJECT/TOPIC}}$ shì [<u>*zuótiān*</u> *lái*-de]$_{\text{COMMENT}}$
Zhangsan COP yesterday come-DE
'As for Zhangsan, it was yesterday that he came.'

b.

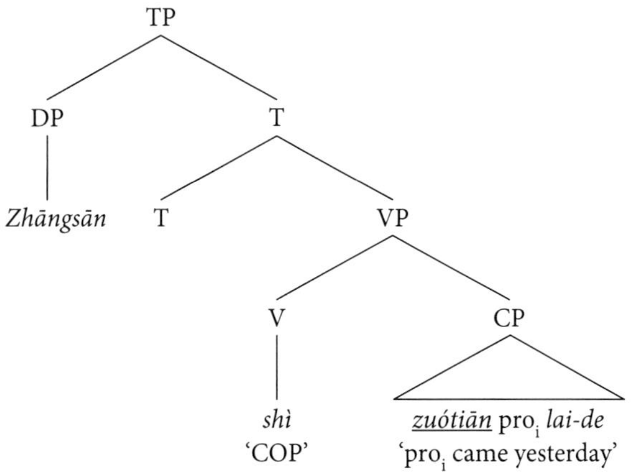

To conclude this subsection, we argue for a syntactic partition underlying Chinese *shì…de* clefts. The partition is brought about by the nominalizer *de*. At spell-out and at LF, the presupposition is the complement of *de*; the cleft focus phrase has moved out of the complement of *de* to its specifier. Since *de* comes with a requirement to cliticize onto deaccented material the presupposition is preposed before *de* at PF. In the case of V *de* O clefts, this PF movement step is preceded by

21. The assumption that the object in object V *de* O clefts moves to spec,C only in the LF branch is not trivial. Hole (2011) proposes, in line with Fox and Pesetsky (2005) in their analysis of Scandinavian object shift, that PF-true linearization constraints are active in V *de* O clefts. If the object moved to spec,C before spell-out, the result would be an OV order at PF. This order, albeit available in Chinese, is not canonical. Chinese clefts, however, always display the canonical word order.

object shift before spell-out. If the object in the V *de* O cleft is in focus, it moves to the specifier position of *de* in the LF part of the syntax, thereby preserving the canonical surface syntax of Chinese clefts. The copula *shì* embeds the cleft CP in a tensed structure of its own with the subject of the copula in spec,T.

3.5 The source of exhaustiveness in Chinese *shì…de*-clefts: Event presuppositions

As discussed in Sections 1 and 3.2 above, the presupposition part headed by *de* in Chinese clefts is a verbal or sentential category. As such, we do not expect it to denote an individual, as was the case with Japanese and Burmese cleft structures. Consequently, we cannot rely on an identificational semantics along the lines of (16b) in Section 2.2.2 to produce the exhaustiveness effect in Chinese. What Hole (2011:1729) proposes instead is that *de* comes with a presupposition that is very much akin to the uniqueness presupposition of the definite article. However, instead of quantifying over individuals, the existence and uniqueness presuppositions induced by *de* affect the ontological domain of events. What *de* presupposes is that there is just a single contextually salient event of the presupposition type.[22] *De* thus bears a certain resemblance with definite event markers in other languages, such as Fongbe or Haitian Creole (Larson 2003), and also Mohawk (Baker & Travis 1997). However, apart from introducing a presupposition over the domain of events, *de* is semantically inert and denotes the identity function at the level of truth-functional meaning. The exhaustiveness effect eventually arises as a result of a maximality presupposition over (minimal) events that comes at no theoretical cost (Kratzer 2007, 2009). If one says that Paul is the agent of an event e, then it is presupposed that *only* Paul acted as the agent of e. To be sure, there may be a larger event e′ that has e as a proper part and in which Paul may have acted as part of a group agent. But even under such circumstances Paul will remain the sole agent of the original smaller event e, thus satifying e's maximality presupposition. Now, if *de* has a presupposition that restricts the number of events of the background type to one, then it will follow that no alternative to the focus value yields a true predication when it is combined with the background predicate. Put differently, it is the eventive nature of the cleft presupposition, together with the fact that (minimal) events

22. The formal definition of the meaning of *de* fused with the empty C head is given in (i) (Hole 2011:1729).

(i) $\lambda f_{\langle \tau,\langle s,t\rangle\rangle} : \exists! e_{max} \in C\ \exists u_{\tau}\ [f(u)(e)=1]\ \lambda u_{\tau}'.\ \lambda e'.\ f(u')(e')=1$,
where f is the denotation of the cleft presupposition,
τ is a variable over available semantic types of cleft focus phrases, and
u is a variable over the semantic domain of the cleft focus phrase

only allow for a single (group) participant per thematic role, that is responsible for the exhaustive interpretation of cleft foci in Mandarin Chinese.

4. Conclusion

The article provides the – to our knowledge – first comparative overview of the syntax and semantics of focusing strategies involving a nominalizing element in three typologically different (South) East Asian languages, namely Burmese, Japanese, and Mandarin Chinese. We have shown that, despite first appearances, syntactic partitioning in form of clefting involving a backgrounded clause with a nominalizer is not only found in Japanese and Burmese, but also in Mandarin Chinese in the form of *shì…de*-clefts.

There are two major syntactic differences between the investigated focusing structures of Japanese and Burmese, on the one hand, and of Mandarin Chinese, on the other. The first is that, alongside cleft structures featuring nominalizations, Japanese and Burmese have nominalized clauses with *in-situ* focusing. This type of structure is unattested in Mandarin, because the *in-situ* Bare-*shì* Focus Construction features no nominalizing element. The second difference concerns the different mappings between the two information-structural parts of the cleft constructions, on the one hand, and the functional elements used to mark them on the other. All three languages make use of copulas and nominalizers in their cleft structures, but they do so in different ways. In this respect, too, Japanese and Burmese pattern alike. Being head-final languages, the copula in these languages follows the (pseudo)cleft presupposition and the cleft focus phrase. The cleft focus phrase forms a constituent with the copula, and this constituent is opposed to the cleft presupposition, thereby instantiating the syntactic cleft partition. The nominalizer heads the presupposition part and is itself followed by a topic marker. In this way, the nominalizer is the functional element associating directly with the cleft presupposition, and the function of the copula is to link the cleft focus with the cleft presupposition. In Mandarin Chinese, by contrast, the syntactic partition into cleft focus and cleft presupposition is brought about by the nominalizer itself. It takes the cleft presupposition as complement, just as in Japanese and Burmese. However, in contradistinction to these languages it is also pivotal for the whole cleft structure as, according to our analysis, it hosts the cleft focus in its specifier. Since the nominalizer *de* is phonologically enclitic in Chinese it cannot surface in its LF-interpretation position between cleft focus phrase and cleft presupposition, but it must cliticize onto the preposed cleft presupposition. This independent phonological property of *de* thus renders the surface syntax of Mandarin clefts superficially similar to Japanese and Burmese clefts, where the nominalizer likewise follows the presupposition part. In its clause-final position, the Chinese nominalizer does not separate the cleft focus from the cleft presupposition at PF in the way it does at LF. All in all, the overall syntactic function of the nominalizer in Chinese clefts is more like that of the copula in Japanese and Burmese clefts. The Chinese copula, by contrast, precedes and c-commands the complete cleft structure and projects a further clausal layer on top of the cleft structure.

Concerning the syntax-semantics interface, we have tentatively proposed an exhaustiveness universal. This universal restricts the occurrence of exhaustiveness effects in languages with partitioned and non-partitioned focusing constructions to the variant with syntactic partitioning, but without postulating a bi-unique dependency between syntactic partitioning and exhaustive interpretation. We have also shown that syntactic partitioning in form of clefting gives rise to presuppositional exhaustiveness effects in all three languages, while the corresponding *in-situ* focusing structures can receive non-exhaustive interpretations as well. Still, there are semantic differences: For Japanese and Burmese, we concluded that exhaustiveness is *not* tied to the nominalizing element. Instead, it is the topic marker attaching to the nominalized constituent that induces a (type e) individual interpretation of this constituent. Together with the presence of the copula, the complete cleft structure will receive an identificational interpretation, i.e. $a = b$. The denotation of the cleft focus thus inherits its unique reference from the background individual qua identification. In Mandarin Chinese, by contrast, the cleft presupposition is not-topic marked, for which reason it does not receive a topical (type e) interpretation. Instead, we proposed that the observed exhaustiveness effects are intimately tied to the presence of the nominalizer *de*. The nominalizer introduces a uniqueness presupposition over events, from which the exhaustiveness effect can be derived at no additional costs.

At a more general level, both individuals (as in the Japanese and Burmese cases) and events (as in the Chinese case) can be conceived of as particulars. Hence, we tentatively propose that an account of exhaustiveness in terms of the presupposed uniqueness of particulars is a promising way to account for the similarities and the differences in the interpretation of clefting structures in East and South East Asian languages.

References

Baker, Mark & Travis, Lisa. 1997. Mood as verbal definiteness in a "tenseless" language. *Natural Language Semantics* 5(3): 213–69.

Cheng, Lisa Lai-Shen. 1997. *On the Typology of Wh-Questions*. New York NY: Garland

Cheng, Lisa Lai-Shen. 2008. Deconstructing the *shì...de* construction. *Linguistic Review* 25(3–4): 235–266.

Cho, Eun & Nishiyama, Kunio. 2000. Yoruba predicate clefts from a comparative perspective. In *Advances in African Linguistics*, Vicki Carstens & Frederick Parkinson (eds), 37–49. Trenton NJ: Africa World Press.

Cho, Sungdai, Whitman, John & Yanagida, Yuko. 2008. Clefts in Japanese and Korean. *Proceedings from the Annual Meeting of the Chicago Linguistic Society* 44(1): 61–77.

Comrie, Bernard. 2008. The areal typology of Chinese: Between North and Southeast Asia. In *Chinese Linguistics in Leipzig*, Redouane Djamouri, Barbara Meisterernst & Rint Sybesma (eds), 1–21. Paris: École des Hautes Études en Sciences Sociales, Centre de Recherches Linguistiques sur l'Asie Orientale.

Davis, Henry, Matthewson, Lisa & Shank, Scott. 2004. Clefts vs. nominal predicates in two Salish languages. In *Studies in Salish Linguistics in Honor of Dale Kinkade*, Donna B. Gerdts & Lisa Matthewson (eds), 100–117. Missoula MT: University of Montana Occasional Papers in Linguistics.

Delin, Judy & Obenauer, Jon. 1995. Syntactic constraints on discourse structure: The case of it-clefts. *Linguistics* 33(3): 465–500.

Drenhaus, Heiner, Zimmermann, Malte & Vasishth, Shravan. 2010. Exhaustiveness effects in clefts are not truth-functional. Ms, University of Potsdam.

Dufter, Andreas. 2009. Clefting and discourse organization: Comparing Germanic and Romance. In *Focus and Background in Romance Languages* [Studies in Language Sciences 112], Andreas Dufter & Daniel Jacob (eds), 83–122. Amsterdam: John Benjamins.

É. Kiss, Katalin. 1998. Identificational focus versus information focus. *Language* 74 (2): 245–273.

É. Kiss, Katalin. 1999. The English cleft-construction as a focus phrase. In *Boundaries of Morphology and Syntax* [Current Studies in Linguistic Theory 180], Lunella Mereu (ed.), 217–229. Amsterdam: John Benjamins.

Endriss, Cornelia. 2009. *Quantificational Topics – A Scopal Treatment of Exceptional Wide Scope Phenomena*. Dordrecht: Springer.

von Fintel, Kai & Matthewson, Lisa. 2008. Universals in semantics. *The Linguistic Review* 25(1–2): 139–201.

Fox, Danny & Pesetsky, David. 2005. Cyclic linearization of syntactic structure. *Theoretical Linguistics* 31(1–2): 1–46.

Hartmann, Katharina. 2006. Focus constructions in Hausa. In *The Architecture of Focus*, Valeria Molnár & Susanne Winkler (eds), 579–607. Berlin: Mouton de Gruyter.

Hashimoto, Mantaro. 1986. The altaicization of northern Chinese. In *Contributions to Sino-Tibetan Studies*, John MacCoy (ed.), 76–97. Leiden: Brill.

Hedberg, Nancy & Jhang, Sea-Eun. 1994. Clefts and pseudoclefts in Korean and Mandarin. *Proceedings of the 1994 Annual Conference of the Canadian Linguistic Association*, 247–256.

Hiraiwa, Ken & Ishihara, Shinichiro. 2002. Missing links: Cleft, sluicing, and "No da" construction in Japanese. *MIT Working Papers in Linguistics* 43: 35–54.

Hole, Daniel. 2011. The deconstruction of *shì...de* clefts revisited. *Lingua* 121:1707–1733.

Horn, Lawrence. 1981. Exhaustiveness and the semantics of clefts. In *Papers from the* 11th *Annual Meeting of the Northeastern Linguistics Society*, Victoria Burke & James Pustejovsky (eds), 124–142. Amherst MA: GLSA.

Kenesei, István. 1986. On the logic of word order in Hungarian. In *Topic, Focus, and Configurationality* [Linguistik Aktuell/Linguistics Today 4], Werner Abraham & Sjaak de Meij (eds), 143–159. Amsterdam: John Benjamins.

Koch, Karsten & Malte Zimmermann. 2010. Focus-sensitive operators in Nłeʔkepmcin. In *Proceedings of Sinn und Bedeutung* 14, Sarah Zobel (ed.), 237–255. Vienna: Dept. of Linguistics, University of Vienna.

Kratzer, Angelika. 2007. Situations in Natural Language Semantics. In *The Stanford Encyclopedia of Philosophy (Spring 2007 edition)*, Edward N. Zalta (ed.), URL=<http://plato.stanford.edu/archives/spr2007/entries/situations-semantics/>.

Kratzer, Angelika. 2009. Pragmatic strengthening for free. Presentation at the annual DGfS-Meeting, Universität Osnabrück, March, 4, 2009.

Kratzer, Angelika & Shimoyama, Junko. 2002. Indeterminate pronouns: The view from Japanese. In *The Proceedings of the Third Tokyo Conference on Psycholinguistics* (TCP 2002), Y. Otsu (ed.), 1–25. Tokyo: Hituzi Syobo.

Krifka, Manfred. 2006. Association with focus phrases. In *The Architecture of Focus*, Valeria Molnár & Susanne Winkler (eds), 105–136. Berlin: Mouton de Gruyter.

Krifka, Manfred. 2008. Basic notions of information structure. *Acta Linguistica Hungarica* 55(3–4): 243–276.

Larson, Richard. 2003. Event descriptions in Fon and Haitian Creole. In *Creole Languages from a Generative Perspective*, Dany Adone (ed.). Tübingen: Niemeyer.

Lee, Huichi. 2005. On Chinese Focus and Cleft Constructions. Ph.D. dissertation, National Tsing Hua University.

Lehmann, Christian. 1982. Nominalisierung: Typisierung von Propositionen. In *Apprehension. Das sprachliche Erfassen von Gegenständen*, Hansjakob Seiler & Christian Lehmann (eds), 66–83. Tübingen: Narr.

Matisoff, James. 1972. Lahu nominalization, relativization, and genitivization. In *Syntax and Semantics*, Vol. 1, John Kimball (ed.), 237–257. New York NY: Seminar Press.

McWhorter, John. 1994. From focus marker to copula in Swahili. *Berkeley Linguistics Society: Special Session on Historical Issues in African Languages*, 57–66.

Norman, Jerry. 1982. Four notes on Chinese-Altaic linguistic contacts. *Tsing Hua Journal of Chinese Studies* 1–2: 243–247.

Okada, Hidehiro. 1992. Mandarin, a language of the Manchus: How Altaic? In *Historische und bibliographische Studien zur Mandschuforschung/Studi mancesi storici e bibliografici/Issledovanija po man'chzhurskoj istorii i bibliografii*, Martin Gimm, Giovanni Stary & Michael Weiers (eds), 165–187. Wiesbaden: Harrassowitz.

Okell, John. 1969. *A Reference Grammar of Colloquial Burmese*, 2 Vols. Oxford: OUP.

Paul, Waltraud. 2002. Sentence-internal topics in Mandarin Chinese: The case of object preposing. *Language and Linguistics* 3(4): 695–714.

Paul, Waltraud & Whitman, John. 2008. *Shi...de* focus clefts in Mandarin Chinese. *Linguistic Review* 25 (3–4): 413–51.

Percus, Orin. 1997. Prying open the cleft. In *Papers from the* 27th *Annual Meeting of Northeastern Linguistics Society*, Kiyomi Kusumoto (ed.), 337–351. Amherst MA: GLSA.

Prince, Ellen F. 1978. A comparison of WH-clefts and IT-clefts in discourse. *Language* 54(4): 883–906.

Reinhart, Tanya. 1982. *Pragmatics and Linguistics: An Analysis of Sentence Topics.* Bloomington IN: Indiana University Linguistics Club.

Rizzi, Luigi. 1997. The fine structure of the left periphery. In *Elements of Grammar: Handbook of Generative Syntax*, Liliane Haegeman (ed.), 281–337. Dordrecht: Kluwer.

Shyu, Shu-ing. 2001. Remarks on object movement in Mandarin SOV order. *Language and Linguistics* 2(1): 93–124.

Simpson, Andrew. 2001. Focus, presupposition and light predicate raising in East and Southeast Asia. *Journal of East Asian Linguistics* 10(2): 89–128.
Simpson, Andrew. 2008. The grammaticalization of nominalizers in Burmese. In *Rethinking Grammaticalization: New Perspectives* [Typological Studies in Language 76], María José López-Couso & Elena Seoane, in collaboration with Teresa Fanego (eds), 265–288. Amsterdam: John Benjamins.
Simpson, Andrew & Watkins, Justin. 2005. Constituent focus in Burmese: A phonetic and perceptual study. In *Studies in Burmese Linguistics*, Justin Watkins (ed.), 27–66. Canberra: Pacific Linguistics.
Simpson, Andrew & Wu, Zoe Xiu-Zhi. 2002. From D to T – determiner incorporation and the creation of tense. *Journal of East Asian Linguistics* 11(2): 169–209.
Soe, Myint. 1999. A Grammar of Burmese. Ph.D. dissertation, University of Oregon.
Szabolcsi, Anna. 1994. All quantifiers are not equal: The case of focus. *Acta Linguistica Hungarica* 42: 171–187.
Vittrant, Alice. 2008. Information structure in Colloquial Burmese, a highly contextual language. Paper presented at Syntax of the World's Languages 3, Freie Universität/Berlin, September 25–28.
Watanabe, Akira. 1992. Subjacency and S-structure movement of *wh*-in-situ. *Journal of East Asian Linguistics* 1: 255–291.
Xu, Yi. 1999. Effects of tone and focus on the formation and alignment of f0 contours. *Journal of Phonetics* 27: 55–105.
Zhang, Niina Ning. 2009. *Coordination in Syntax*. Cambridge: CUP.

Italian clefts and the licensing of infinitival subject relatives*

Petra Sleeman
University of Amsterdam

This paper investigates the licensing of infinitival subject relative clauses by clefted constituents. It is claimed that in Italian clefted constituents license infinitival subject relatives because in this language clefts function as contrastive foci. This claim is supported by the syntactic analysis of the position of clefted constituents that license infinitival subject relatives in Italian. It is argued that they occupy a left-peripheral Focus position in the clause. On the basis of extraction data, it is argued that the infinitival subject relative itself is a complement.

Keywords: cleft; infinitival relative clause; contrastive focus; Italian; left-periphery

1. Introduction

Infinitival relatives are relative clauses containing an infinitive instead of an inflected verb. With infinitival subject relatives, the head noun is interpreted as the subject of the relative clause. The infinitive in the subject relative clause can be an active or a passive verb. In the literature it is shown that infinitival subject relatives are licensed by a head noun modified by a superlative or a comparable modifier, such as *only* or the superlative ordinals *first* or *last* (Kjellmer 1975; Geisler 1995; Bhatt 1999, 2006):

(1) At age 60 years, Dolly Parton became the oldest woman to have a no. 1 song on the Billboard Hot Country Songs.

* This paper was presented at a meeting of the research group X-linguistic SemantiX at the University of Amsterdam (September 2008), at the Workshop on Clefts at ZAS in Berlin (28–29 November 2009), and at the 11th annual conference of the department of English of the University of Bucharest (4–6 June 2009). I thank the audiences for their useful remarks. I furthermore thank Enoch Aboh, Maria Aloni, Roberto Bacchilega, Marcel den Dikken, Josep Quer, and Mauro Scorretti for their grammaticality judgments and/or comments on an earlier version of this paper. In addition, I am grateful to the anonymous reviewers for their careful reading of my paper and their useful remarks, which helped me to improve the paper. All remaining errors are my own.

(2) Pauling remains the only person to have been awarded two unshared Nobel Prizes, one for chemistry in 1954 and one for peace in 1962.

(3) The ancient Greeks were the last to have true democracy.

Infinitival subject relatives are not only licensed by superlatives and comparable modifiers in English, but also in French (4–6) and Italian (7–9):

(4) *Il est le soliste le plus jeune à avoir joué avec cet orchestre.*
'He is the youngest soloist to have played with this orchestra.'

(5) *Suis-je le seul à avoir ce problème?*
'Am I the only one to have this problem?'

(6) *Armstrong fut le premier à avoir marché sur la lune.*
'Armstrong was the first to have walked on the moon.'

(7) *Il più giovane a raggiungere la cima è stato un giovane di 11 anni.*
'The youngest one to reach the top was an 11 year old child.'

(8) *Non sono il solo a pensare così.*
'I am not the only one to think so.'

(9) *Il primo a entrare è il primo a uscire.*
'First in, last out.'

According to Kjellmer (1975: 325), "it seems that it is the selective function of superlatives that is operative here": *oldest* in (1) selects one out of many women, *only* in (2) selects one out of many men, and *last* in (3) selects one nation out of many nations. Kjellmer furthermore notes that superlatives mark the end of a scale.

However, infinitival subject relative clauses are not only licensed by superlatives and equivalent modifiers, which have a selective function and mark the end of scale. In Italian, but not in English or French, clefts are also able to license infinitival subject relatives:

(10) *È stato Gianni a darmi la chiave.*
is been Gianni to give-me the key
'It was Gianni who gave me the key.'

(11) *It was John to have given me the key.

(12) **C'est Jean à m'avoir donné la clé.*

The licensing of the infinitival subject relative by the cleft in (10) raises two questions:

(i) Why is the cleft in (10) able to license the infinitival subject relative, and
(ii) Why is the cleft able to license the infinitival relative in Italian, but not in English or French?

Sleeman (2010) claims that superlatives and equivalent modifiers license infinitival subject relatives because they express a contrastive focus. This seems to be a mere reinterpretation of Kjellmer's notions of 'selective function' and 'end of the scale', but it is motivated in Sleeman (2010) by several linguistic properties of the construction.[1] In this paper I make the same claim for Italian clefts. On the basis of answering strategies used by Italian, English and French native speakers to answer a *wh*-question (Belletti 2005, 2008), I argue that in Italian (but not necessarily in English or French) clefts express a contrastive focus, which makes them able to license infinitival subject relative clauses. I argue furthermore that the constituents licensing infinitival relative clauses, including clefted constituents in Italian, are in a high position. I analyze the infinitival relative clause as their complement, showing that it allows extraction from it.

The paper is organized as follows. In Section 2, I argue that infinitival subject relatives are licensed by a contrastive focus. In Section 3, it is shown that Italian clefts, but not English or French clefts, express a contrastive focus. In Section 4, I argue that the clefted constituents licensing infinitival relative clauses are in a high position in the clause. In Section 5, I discuss the syntactic relation between the clefted constituent and the coda. Finally, in Section 6, the results of this paper are summarized.

1. Both reviewers observed that contrastiveness is not a sufficient condition for the licensing of infinitival subject relatives, as can be seen from the fact that infinitival subject relatives are ungrammatical in languages like German. As one of the reviewers pointed out, Frey (2004) convincingly argues for the existence of a contrast position in the left periphery of German sentences, which would show that contrastiveness does play a role in German. It is true that there must be more that blocks infinitival subject relatives in Germanic languages, but it should be noticed that they are not totally excluded. The following sentences, from Dutch, show that with the ordinals 'first' or 'last', in special contexts, infinitival subject relatives can be used. Although these sentences, and especially sentence (i), differ in interpretation from the sentences with superlative ordinals discussed in Sleeman (2010), there ís a contrast expressed by these sentences. Sentence (i) means that every person might say this, but we would not. Sentence (ii) means that it might be the case that no one else admits this, but we will.

(i) *Wij zullen de laatsten zijn om dat te beweren.*
we will the last be to that to state
'We do not say that.'

(ii) *Wij zullen de eersten zijn om dat te beamen.*
we will the first be to that to admit
'We certainly agree.'

2. Licensing of infinitival subject relatives by contrastive focus

In the previous section we saw that infinitival subject relatives are licensed by superlatives, *only* and the superlative ordinals *first* and *last*. We saw furthermore that according to Kjellmer (1975), superlatives and equivalent modifiers have a 'selective function', selecting one or a subset of elements out of a larger set. Kjellmer notices furthermore that superlatives and equivalent modifiers "mark the end of a scale". Sleeman (2010) identifies the first property with Kiss' (1998) notion of 'identificational focus' and the second property with her notion of 'contrastive focus'.

Kiss distinguishes 'identificational focus' from 'information focus'. Whereas information focus merely conveys non-presupposed information, identificational focus is a quantification-like operation, it "represents a subset of the set of contextually or situationally given elements for which the predicate phrase can potentially hold" (Kiss 1998: 245). Kiss notices furthermore that an identificational focus "is identified as the exhaustive subset of the set for which the predicate phrase can potentially hold". An information focus does not express exhaustive identification.

Kiss uses a test to determine whether a focus expresses exhaustivity. A non-exhaustive focus can be part of an enumeration, whereas an exhaustive focus cannot. In the context of (13a), the answer (13b) contains an information focus, whereas (13c) contains an identificational focus. Kiss claims that the English cleft construction, as in (13c), always expresses identificational focus and not information focus:

(13) a. Where did you go in the summer?
b. I went to Italy (among other places).
c. It was to Italy where I went (and nowhere else).

Besides the cleft, phrases with which the operator *only* associates also have an exhaustive interpretation. Kiss (1998: 259) supposes that "*only* lends them an identificational focus feature". She argues that *only*-phrases are scalar: the elements of the set on which exhaustive identification is performed are ordered along a scale, and the element identified as that for which the predicate exclusively holds represents a low value on this scale.

A third notion that Kiss defines is that of "contrastive focus". Kiss considers an identificational focus to be contrastive "if it operates on a closed set of entities whose members are known to the participants of the discourse" (Kiss 1998: 267). The identification of a subset of a given set also identifies the contrasting complementary subset, as in (14):

(14) a. I heard you invited John and Mary.
b. I only invited John (and not Mary).

A non-contrastive identificational focus, on the other hand, operates on an open set of entities. It does not identify a contrasting complementary subset:

(15) a. Who wrote War and Peace?
b. It was Tolstoy who wrote War and Peace.

Sleeman (2010) argues that superlatives and equivalent modifiers licensing infinitival subject relatives create identificational foci, because they "have a selective function". They identify a subset from a scalar set of elements: the highest or the lowest subset. Sleeman (2010) argues furthermore that the constituents licensing infinitival subject relatives, "marking the end of a scale", express a [+contrastive] identificational focus. Superlatives and equivalent modifiers can also express a [–contrastive] identicational focus, but they only license infinitival subject relatives in their [+contrastive] use. In Sleeman (2010), a superlative is taken to create a [+contrastive] focus, if it identifies an (empty) contrasting complementary set consisting of members that represent a still higher or lower value than the end of the scale. Since superlatives represent the end of the scale, a still higher or lower value on the scale is naturally excluded. Superlatives express a [–contrastive], i.e. simply identificational focus, if only their selective function is stressed, but not the exclusion of an (empty) set of elements that represents a still higher or still lower value on the scale.

One might wonder what distinguishes my use of this notion 'constrastive focus' and Kiss' use of the notion 'identificational focus'. We saw that Kiss associates 'identificational focus' with exhaustivity. By exhaustivity Kiss means that there is no other element within the set of alternatives for which the predicate phrase holds: the identification of a subset goes together with the exclusion of the complementary subset. In my use of the notion 'contrastive focus' a complementary subset is also excluded. There is, however, a difference. Sleeman (2010) assumes, following Kampers-Manhe (1991) for French, that in languages such as Italian or French only subjunctive clauses, but not indicative clauses, can replace infinitival subject relatives:[2]

(16) *C' est la femme la plus âgée à avoir eu un enfant.*
this is the woman the most old to have had a child
'She is the oldest woman to have given birth.'

---

2. Just as in French (and in English), in Italian non-modal infinitival relative clauses are licensed by adjectives that represent the end of a scale. Just as in French, in Italian only subjunctive clauses can replace infinitival subject relatives:

(i) *E' la donna più anziana a aver partorito.*
She-is the woman most old to have given-birth.
'She is the oldest woman to have given birth.'

(ii) *E' la donna più anziana che abbia partorito.* (= i)
'She is the oldest woman that has.SUBJ given birth.'

(iii) *E' la donna più anziana che ha partorito.* (≠ i).
'She is the oldest woman that has.IND given birth.'

(17) a. *C' est la femme la plus âgée qui ait eu*
this is the woman the most old who has.SUBJ had
un enfant. (= 16)
a child

b. *C' est la femme la plus âgée qui a eu*
this is the woman the most old who has.IND had
un enfant. (≠ 16)
a child

Farkas (1985) suggests that a negative existential is involved in sentences containing superlatives and associated modifiers and that this negative existential is responsible for the possibility of using subjunctive relatives in such cases. In Romance languages the subjunctive in relative clauses is licensed by a head noun whose existence is negated, almost negated or at least questioned.[3] Part of the meaning of (16) and (17a) is that there has never been a woman older than this one that has given birth. This means that an extra set of alternatives is created, which is, however, a set of potential alternatives, because their existence is denied. I take a contrastive focus therefore to imply that there is domain widening and to exclude any possible alternative.[4]

This interpretation is supported by the following fact. Besides stating that superlatives "have a selective function" and "mark the end of a scale", Kjellmer (1975) points out that the adverb *ever* can be used in infinitival subject relative clauses. Kjellmer states that *ever* is normally non-assertive, occurring in negative and/or interrogative clauses. Kjellmer observes that (18) means 'I haven't ever

3. This is illustrated by the following examples from French:

(i) *Il n'y a personne qui le sache.*
'There is no one who knows.SUBJ.'

(ii) *Il n'y a que peu de personnes qui le sachent.*
'There are only few people who know.SUBJ.'

(iii) *Y a-t-il quelqu'un qui le sache?*
'Is there anyone who knows. SUBJ?'

(iv) *Je cherche quelqu'un qui le sache.*
'I am looking for someone who knows.SUBJ.'

4. Although superlative ordinals can be combined with a subjunctive clause, non superlative ordinals such as *third* or *seventh* cannot. Although in the literature some examples are given of infinitival subject relatives licensed by non superlative ordinals, I take these examples to be rather marginal. The marginality results from the fact that the non-superlative ordinals do not represent the end of the scale and that therefore there is no negative existential involved.

tasted a better wine than this', and states that it is therefore natural that 'ever' should be found in infinitival relative clauses depending on head nouns modified by a superlative:[5]

(18) This is the best wine I've ever tasted.

Sleeman (2010) claims that it is the negative interpretation entailed by the superlative and equivalent modifiers that makes them create a [+contrastive] identificational focus, a contrast being expressed with an empty complementary set, which is entailed by the meaning of the superlative denoting the extreme value on a scale and which is therefore known to the participants of the discourse (see Kiss' definition of contrastive focus above).[6]

In the introduction to this paper I showed that not only in English, but also in Italian and French, superlatives and equivalent modifiers license infinitival subject relative clauses. Some examples are repeated below:

(19) *Il più giovane a raggiungere la cima è stato un giovane di 11 anni.*
'The youngest one to reach the top was an 11 year old child.'

(20) *Armstrong fut le premier à avoir marché sur la lune.*
'Armstrong was the first to have walked on the moon.'

However, in the introduction I also showed that whereas in Italian clefts can license infinitival subject relatives, in English and French they cannot do so. The relevant examples are repeated below:

(21) a. *È stato Gianni a darmi la chiave.*
is been Gianni to give-me the key
'It was Gianni who gave me the key.'

b. *It was John to have given me the key.

c. **C'est Jean à m'avoir donné la clé.*

5. Cf. Giannakidou (1997), who argues that in Greek polarity items are licensed, among others, by superlatives, because of the negative part of their meaning.

6. One of the reviewers wondered why the other elements on the scale cannot count as alternatives. It is true that in the case of, e.g. *last*, all preceding elements could count as alternatives. What, in my analysis, is important in the licensing of infinitival subject relatives by superlatives, however, is the negative existential that is created by the absence of elements following *last*. This is supported by the use of the superlative ordinal *first*. The sentence *John is the first New Zealander to have won this prestigious tournament* may be uttered without there being a person that has won the tournament after John. There is therefore only a contrast with any other person that might have won the tournament before John but whose existence is denied.

Kiss argues that there is parametric variation in the feature content of identificational focus. In English, identificational focus is [±contrastive]. The *only*-phrase in (14b) expresses a [+contrastive] identificational focus, but in another context it can also express a [−contrastive] focus. The cleft in (15b) expresses a [−contrastive] identificational focus. However, if the interpretation as [+contrastive] depends on the possibility of the identification of a complementary subset, which is possible within a closed set of elements, as Kiss states, the cleft can also express a [+contrastive] focus:

(22) a. Who wrote War and Peace: Tolstoy or Dostoyevsky?
b. It was Tolstoy who wrote War and Peace (and not Dostoyevsky).

For Italian Kiss claims that identificational focus is always [+contrastive]. I assume that it is the necessarily [+contrastive] interpretation of the cleft in Italian which allows it to license infinitival subject relative clauses. In the next section I provide support for the claim that the Italian cleft, as opposed to the English and French cleft, expresses a [+contrastive] identificational focus, allowing it to license infinitival subject relatives.

3. Parametric variation in the feature content of clefts

In the previous section we saw that in Italian, but not in English or French, the cleft is able to license an infinitival subject relative clause. The question is why this should be so: why is the cleft able to license the infinitival relative in Italian, but not in English or French? In the previous section I claimed that if the cleft licenses an infinitival relative clause in Italian, it does so because it expresses a [+contrastive] focus. In English and French the cleft expresses an identificational focus that is [±contrastive].

Evidence for these claims is provided by preferred answering strategies used to answer questions concerning the identification of the subject of the clause (Belletti 2005, 2008). Belletti states that in order to answer questions about a video they had seen native speakers of Italian, French and English used different answering strategies. In order to answer the questions in the (a)-sentences of (23) A, B, and C formulated below, native speakers of Italian used a subject inversion strategy, native speakers of French used a truncated cleft or a full cleft, and native speakers of English used an SV order with a pitch accent on the subject. According to Belletti, although a (truncated) cleft is the preferred option in French, an SV order with a pitch accent on the subject is not excluded.

Although a pitch accent on the subject is the preferred option in English, the cleft is not excluded either:

(23) A.
  a. Chi è partito/ha parlato? Italian: VS ("free inversion")
  b. E' partito/ha parlato Gianni.

  B.
  a. Qui est parti/a parlé? French: ((reduced) cleft, also C)
  b. C'est Jean (qui est parti/a parlé).

  C.
  a. Who came/spoke? English: SV/(*in situ* focalization, also B)
  b. *John* came/spoke
  c. *John* did

According to Belletti, a (reduced) cleft, normally disfavored, is possible in Italian and may become the preferred option when either a cleft is contained in the question, as in (24),

(24) a. *Chi è (stato) che ha rotto il vaso?*
  Who it-is (been) that has broken the vase
  'Who broke the vase?'

  b. *E' (stato) Gianni.*
  it-is (been) Gianni
  'It was Gianni.'

or with agentive predicates expressing a somewhat negative presupposition, as in (25):[7]

(25) a. *Chi ha urlato?*
  who has screamed
  'Who screamed?'

  b. *E' stato Gianni.*
  it-is been Gianni
  'It was Gianni.'

7. Mara Frascarelli (p.c.) pointed out to me that the question in (24) is not necessarily contrastive. Belletti's main argument for the contrastive interpretation comes indeed mainly from (25), the cleft in the question in (24) rather seems to be a grammaticalized structure.

Belletti does not explain what she means by "agentive predicates expressing a somewhat negative presupposition". I take it to mean that by asserting that someone has done something, other possible agents are excluded. If I utter (25b), asserting that it was Gianni who screamed, the presupposition is that the one who screamed might have been me (or someone else present). By uttering (25b), this possible alternative is excluded.

Belletti shows that with object questions, Italian, French and English do not manifest any difference in the answering strategies, when answers are provided with a full clause:

(26) Italian
  a. *Che cosa hai comprato?*
     'What have you bought?'
  b. *Ho comprato un libro.*
     'I have bought a book.'

(27) French
  a. *Qu'as-tu acheté/Qu'est-ce-que tu as acheté?*
  b. *J'ai acheté un livre*

(28) English
  a. What have you bought?
  b. I have bought a book.

Belletti shows that, in all three languages, with object questions a cleft can also be used, with a contrastive meaning (examples are from Italian, where "–" indicates the base position of the moved constituent):

(29) *E' Gianni [che (Maria) ha incontrato (Maria) –]*
     it-is Gianni that Maria has met (Maria)
     'Mary met GIANNI.'

(30) *E' con Gianni [che Maria ha parlato –]*
     it-is with Gianni that Maria has spoken
     'Mary spoke with GIANNI.'

Belletti's discussion of answering strategies shows thus that in Italian not only object clefts but also subject clefts, both involving a negative presupposition, have a contrastive interpretation:

(31) a. *E' MARIA che ha parlato con Gianni (non Francesca).*
     'It is Maria that has spoken with Gianni (not Francesca).'

b. *E' MARIA che Gianni abbracciava (non Francesca).*
'It is Maria that Gianni kissed (not Francesca).'

c. *E' CON GIANNI che Maria ha parlato (non con Piero).*
'It is with Gianni that Maria has spoken (not with Piero).'

In English and French, only object clefts have a contrastive interpretation. In French a subject cleft is the canonical strategy used to answer a *wh*-question. In English it can also be used, although a pitch accent on the subject is the preferred strategy. In both languages, a subject cleft is thus not necessarily contrastive.

This discussion of answering strategies supports my claim that in Italian (subject) clefts are able to license infinitival subject relatives, because they express a [+contrastive] focus. Since, in French and English, subject clefts express a [±contrastive] focus, the contrastive interpretation just being a side effect of the identificational focus interpretation, they cannot license infinitival relative clauses.[8]

In this section and the preceding one, I have argued that, in Italian, a cleft is able to license infinitival subject relative clauses because it expresses a [+contrastive] focus. In the next section, I provide syntactic evidence for my claim.

4. Syntactic evidence for the feature [+contrastive]

As Kiss (1998) shows, a non-contrastive identificational focus is in a high position in Hungarian:

(32) *Mari egy* ***kalapot*** *nézett ki magának.*
Mary a hat.ACC picked out herself.ACC
'It was a hat that Mary picked for herself.'

Kiss claims that the English realization of identificational focus is the cleft construction. She adopts Brody's (1990, 1995) analysis of the cleft construction. IP in the main clause is filled by expletive *it* and the copula *be*. I^o takes the subordinate

8. One of the reviewers wondered why superlatives, also being [±contrastive], can license infinitival subject relatives in French and English, whereas clefts cannot. As I argued above, however, superlatives have two clearly distinguished uses, one in which the relative clause contains an indicative, and one in which the relative clause contains a subjunctive or has the form of an infinitival relative. In the first case the nominal head modified by the superlative simply expresses an identificational focus and is therefore [−contrastive], in the second case it is [+contrastive] and expresses a contrastive focus. Therefore, it is not [±contrastive], but [+contrastive] or [−contrastive].

clause as its complement. The subordinate clause is dominated by FocusP to the Spec of which the clefted constituent moves:[9]

(33) $[_{CP}$ $[_{IP}$ it $[_{I}$ is$_i$ $[_{FocusP}$ me$_j$ $[_{Focus'}$ $[_{Focus^0}$ t$_i$ $[_{CP}$ t$_j$ $[_{C'}$ $[_{C}$ that $[_{IP}$ t$_j$ is sick]]]]]]]]]]

Kiss (1998) states that in many languages a focus in a high position in the sentence is a [+contrastive] focus. Belletti (2008) claims that this is also the case in Italian. Whereas in Sicilian, a sentence-initial focus is not necessarily [+contrastive] (Cruschina 2004), in standard Italian it is, according to Belletti.[10]

In Belletti's analysis, contrastive clefts involve the left peripheral focus position of the CP complement of a copula, *che* occupying the head of FinP:

(34) E' $[_{CP}$ $[_{FocusP}$ MARIA....[che [*pro* ha parlato – con Gianni]]]]

(35) a. E' $[_{CP}$ $[_{FocusP}$ MARIA ...[che [Gianni abbracciava –]]]]
b. E' $[_{CP}$ $[_{FocusP}$ con GIANNI ....[che [Maria ha parlato –]]]]

According to Belletti, it might be that there is no real semantic difference between sentences like (36) and (37), where the crucial distinction between the two pairs is that the latter instantiates left peripheral contrastive focalization in a root clause with no overt copula:

(36) a. *E' MARIA che Gianni abbracciava.*
'It is Maria that Gianni kissed.'

b. *E' con GIANNI che Maria parlava.*
'It is with Gianni that Maria spoke.'

(37) a. *MARIA Gianni abbracciava.*
Maria Gianni kissed

b. *Con GIANNI Maria parlava.*
With Gianni Maria spoke

9. The constituent in Spec,FocusP can also be base-generated, and linked to a corresponding *wh*-pronoun in the embedded CP at LF:

(i) It is me$_i$ who$_i$ is sick.

10. In Sicilian (i) can be used to answer the question 'What did you write yesterday?' (Cruschina 2004):

(i) *N' articulu scrissi.*
an article I-have-written
'I wrote an article.'

In Belletti's analysis, a [+contrastive] focus occupies thus a high position in the complement clause of the copula, just as in Brody's analysis of the English [±contrastive] cleft in (33). In Belletti's analysis, a [±contrastive] focus, however, occupies a low position in the clause. In her analysis of the French subject cleft (23B), the [±contrastive] cleft involves the low new information focus position in the periphery of the vP domain. Since, in English, instead of a (more preferred) SV construction with a subject bearing a pitch accent, as in (23C), a cleft can also be used, this analysis would also hold for the English cleft construction.[11] In Belletti's analysis, the copula in vP takes a small clause (sc) as its complement. The small clause is a subject – predicate structure, where the predicate is a (relative like) CP:

(38) $[_{TP}$ Ce … $[_{TopP}$ $[_{FocusP}$ $[_{TopP}$ $[_{vP}$ être $[_{sc}$ Jean $[_{CP}$ ~~qui a parlé~~]]]]]]

(39) $[_{TP}$ Ce être $[_{TopP}$ $[_{FocusP}$ Jean $[_{TopP}[_{vP}$ $t_{\text{être}}$ $[_{sc}$ t_{Jean} $[_{CP}$ ~~qui a parlé~~]]]]]]

(40) $[_{TP}$ It be $[_{TopP}$ $[_{FocusP}$ John $[_{TopP}[_{vP}$ t_{be} $[_{sc}$ t_{John} $[_{CP}$ ~~that spoke~~]]]]]]

In Belletti's analysis, the clefted constituent in French (and English) occupies the same position as the postverbal subject in Italian, viz. the low focus position in the periphery of the vP domain:

(41) $[_{CP}$ ..$[_{TP}$ *pro*..è..partito/ha parlato $[_{TopP}$ $[_{FocusP}$ Gianni $[_{TopP}$ $[_{vP}$ ….]]]]]]

For the English SV construction Belletti claims that focalization of the preverbal subject is brought about by activation of a DP internal (new information) focus position (Aboh 2004).

Belletti claims thus that Italian clefted constituents, being [+contrastive], occupy a position in the left periphery of the clause, which is the complement of the copula, whereas French and English clefted constituents (at least subjects), being [±contrastive], occupy the left periphery of the vP phase.

In this paper I claim that Italian clefted constituents license infinitival subject relatives because they are [+contrastive]. In Belletti's analysis of clefts, a contrastive interpretation is related to a high position in the clause. In what follows I show that there is indeed evidence that clefted constituents licensing infinitival relative clauses are in a high position in the clause. This supports my claim that infinitival relative clauses are licensed by a contrastive interpretation.

---

11. Since in English and French object clefts are constrastive, just as in Italian, they would occupy a high peripheral position in Belletti's analysis. In Belletti's view, Brody's analysis of English clefts would thus only hold for object clefts:

(i) $[_{CP}$ $[_{IP}$ it $[_{I}$ was$_i$ $[_{FocusP}$ to John$_j$ $[_{Focus'}$ $[_{Focus^0}$ t_i $[_{CP}$ t_j $[_{C'}$ $[_{C}$ that $[_{IP}$ I spoke t_j]]]]]]]]]].

Besides clefted DPs, there are two other clefted constituents in Italian that can license infinitival subject relatives, both involving quantifiers:[12,13]

(42) *Sono molte le persone a farne uso in Italia.*
are many the persons to make-of it use in Italy
'Many people in Italy use it.'

(43) *Siamo in molti a pensare questo.*
we-are in many to think this
'Many of us believe it.'

---

12. The construction in (42) exists next to a structure in which the quantifier is preposed with respect to the copular verb:

(i) *Molte sono le persone a farne uso in Italia.*

In French (but not in English) preposed quantifiers can also license infinitival subject relative clauses, see Sleeman (2010):

(ii) *Nombreux sont ceux à avoir voulu tenter l'expérience.*
numerous are those to have wanted try the experiment
'Those who wanted to try the experiment are numerous.'

(iii) *Rares sont les personnes à avoir les trois quarts des produits.*
rare are the persons to have the three quarters of-the products
'The people that have three quarters of the products are rare.'

(iv) *Elles sont trois à avoir remporté les premiers prix.*
they are three to have taken the first prizes
'Three have taken the first prizes.'

The distinction between French and English suggests that the proposed analysis needs to be refined. I will leave this for future research.

13. Marcel den Dikken (p.c.) pointed out to me that one might wonder whether the constructions in (42–43) are clefts or simply inverted sentences. Den Dikken (this volume) considers the specificational sentence in (i) to be a (pseudo)cleft, because (i) "'cleaves' the sentence *Brian is important to himself* into two portions on either side of the copula, with *important to himself* specifying a value for the variable in the *wh*-clause".

(i) What Brian$_i$ is is important to himself$_i$.

Analogously, in a canonical cleft sentence, there are two portions: the clefted constituent specifying a value for 'it', and the relative clause, cf. Den Dikken's (this volume) analysis. In the same spirit, in (43), there are two portions: the quantifier specifying a value for the (empty) subject of the copula and the relative clause. (42) can also be considered to be a cleft and to contain two portions, but in a slightly different way: whereas the first portion is the quantifier specifying a value for the (empty) subject of the copula, as in (43), the other portion is not the relative clause alone, but the whole DP (see also Footnote 21). The French equivalent (ii–iii) in Footnote 12, however, can be considered to be a simple inversion structure.

The construction in (42) can be used with preposed 'many' or 'few':

(44) *Sono poche le persone a conoscere la storia di questa città.*
are few the persons to know the story of this city
'There are few persons who know the story of this city.'

When the quantifier is not preposed, the use of the infinitival relative is ungrammatical:

(45) **Le persone a farne uso in Italia sono molte.*

(46) **Le persone a conoscere la storia di questa città sono poche.*

It is only possible to leave the quantifier in its base position if a finite relative clause is used instead of an infinitival relative clause:[14]

(47) *Le persone che ne fanno uso in Italia sono molte.*
the persons that of-it make use in Italy are many
'Many people in Italy use it.'

(48) *Le persone che conoscono la storia di questa città sono poche.*
the persons that know the story of this city are few
'There are few persons who know the story of this city.'

Departing slightly from Brody's (33) and Belletti's (34) analyses of the clefted DP-construction, I propose that the quantifier in (42) and (44) moves to a FocusP in the left periphery of the clause (Rizzi 1997) and that the copular verb moves to a position dominating FocusP:[15]

(49) Sono $[_{\text{FocusP}}$ molte $[_{\text{vP}}$ t_{essere} $[_{\text{SC}}$ le persone a farne uso in Italia $[t_{\text{molte}}]]]]$.

14. With the preposed quantifier the finite relative clause can also be used, with an indicative verb and not a subjunctive verb (i). The subjunctive is only used in relative clauses depending on a (quasi-) negative head noun (such as nouns modified by a superlative), but not in clauses depending on an indirectly quantified noun as in (i) or depending on a clefted noun as in (ii):

(i) *Molte sono/Sono molte le persone che ne fanno /*ne*
many are/are many the persons that of-it make.IND /of-it

facciano uso.
make.SUBJ use

'Many people use it.'

(ii) *E' stato Gianni che mi ha /*mi abbia dato la chiave.*
is been Gianni that mi has. IND/me has.SUBJ given the key
'It was John who gave me the key.'

15. In Belletti's (2008) analysis of the canonical Italian cleft, as in (34), FocusP is in the left periphery of the subordinate clause, whereas in Brody's analysis of the canonical cleft presented in (33) it is on top of the subordinate clause. For all types of clefts, I rather assume that the focalized constituent moves to a position outside its (small) clause, which is more in line with Brody's

The quantifiers that license the use of the infinitival subject relative, i.e. 'many' and 'few', are proportional quantifiers. They denote high or low values on the scale. I suggest that preposing, i.e. focalization, makes their position on the scale even "more peripheral". Just like superlatives, they have a contrastive interpretation, asserting that there is (almost) no one or nothing else (not) having the property under consideration, which licenses the infinitival clause.

The second type of clefted quantificational constituent that licenses infinitival subject relatives, as in (43), does not necessarily denote the end of a scale:

(50) *Siamo in tre a sapere la verità.*
we-are in three to know the truth.
'Three of us know the truth.'

(51) *Sono in diversi a voler lottare.*
they-are in several to want fight.
'Several want to fight.'

(52) *Siete in troppi a visitare il sito.*
you-are in too-many to visit the site
'Too many of you visit this site.'

(53) *Molte persone sono sole a gestire una famiglia.*
many persons are only to manage a family
'Many people manage a family on their own.'

This construction comes close to the clefted DP construction:[16]

(54) *Siete voi a decidere.*
you-are you to decide
'You may decide.'

Whereas in the construction in (49) the relative clause contains an overt subject DP, both in (54) and in (50–53) it does not (cf. Footnote 13). However, just as

analysis or with Belletti's analysis of the English and French cleft (38–40), the difference being that the clefted consituent moves to the high focus position and not to the low focus position.

16. In both cases a relative clause with an inflected (indicative) verb instead of an infinitive can also be used:

(i) *Siamo in tre che sappiamo la verità.*
we-are in three that know the truth.
'The three of us know the truth.'

(ii) *Siete voi che decidete.*
you-are you that decide
'You decide.'

in (49), in (50–53) it is the quantifier, and not a DP as in (54), that moves to FocusP in the left periphery of the clause (Rizzi 1997):

(55) *pro* siamo $[_{\text{FocusP}}$ in tre $[_{\text{vP}}$ t_{essere} $[_{\text{SC}}$ t_{pro} a sapere la verità $[t_{\text{in tre}}]]]]$

If it is correct to claim that syntactically the construction in (50–53) comes close to the cleft construction in (54), there should also be a semantic correspondence.[17] We have seen that a clefted DP in Italian can be interpreted as [+constrastive]. I suggest that the same holds for the clefted quantificational expression in (50–53). The focalization of the quantificational expression in (56) entails that other numbers than three are excluded. This is why infinitival subject relatives are licensed, even if the quantifiers themselves do not refer to the end of the scale:

(56) *Siamo in tre a sapere la verità (e non in quattro).*
We-are in three to know the truth (and not in four).
'Three of us know the truth (and not four).'

In this section I have shown that there is syntactic evidence for my claim that infinitival subject relatives are licensed by a [+contrastive] focus. We have seen that infinitival subject relatives are not only licensed by canonical DP-clefts, but also by clefted quantifiers, moving all to a position in the left periphery in the clause. In the next section I discuss the syntactic relation between the clefted constituent and the coda, i.e. the relative clause.

5. Syntactic analysis of the cleft constructions

In the previous section we saw that three types of cleft constructions license infinitival subject relative clauses. The relevant examples are repeated below for convenience:

(57) *È stato Gianni a darmi la chiave.*
is been Gianni to give-me the key
'It was Gianni who gave me the key.'

(58) *Siete voi a decidere.*
you-are you to decide
'You may decide.'

17. Mara Frascarelli (p.c.) pointed out to me that the construction in (55) is not necessarily contrastive. Although it might be the case that because of grammaticalization the structure is losing its contrastive interpretation, some other native Italian speakers that I consulted still felt it to be there.

(59) *Sono molte le persone a farne uso in Italia.*
are many the persons to make-of it use in Italy
'Many people in Italy use it.'

(60) *Siamo in tre a sapere la verità.*
we-are in three to know the truth
'Three of us know the truth.'

For all three constructions there exists a cleft construction with an inflected verb instead of an infinitive (cf. 31a, Footnote 14, and Footnote 16):

(61) *È stato Gianni che mi ha dato la chiave.*
is been Gianni that me has given the key
'It was Gianni who gave me the key.'

(62) *Siete voi che decidete.*
you-are you that decide
'You decide.'

(63) *Sono molte le persone che ne fanno uso in Italia.*
are many the persons that of-it make use in Italy
'Many people in Italy use it.'

(64) *Siamo in tre che sappiamo la verità.*
we-are in three that know the truth.
'The three of us know the truth.'

In the previous section I presented two analyses of clefted DPs (with an inflected verb) that have been made in the literature. In both analyses the cleft sentence consists of a main and a subordinate clause. In the analysis Kiss adopts the clefted DP is on top of the subordinate clause (65) and in Belletti's analysis it is in the left periphery of the subordinate clause (66):[18]

(65) [$_{CP}$ [$_{IP}$ [$_{I}$ è$_{i}$ [$_{FocusP}$ MARIA$_{j}$ [$_{Focus'}$ [$_{Focus^0}$ t$_{i}$ [$_{CP}$ t$_{j}$ [$_{C'}$ [$_{C}$ che [$_{IP}$ *pro* ha parlato – con Gianni]]]]]]]]]]

(66) E' [$_{CP}$ [$_{FocusP}$ MARIA ....[che [*pro* ha parlato – con Gianni]]]

In both analyses, the relative clause is a complement, in line with Kayne's (1994) Antisymmetry theory, and not an adjunct, as in, e.g. Clech-Darbon, Rebuschi and

18. In line with my analysis of the clefted quantifier-constructions in (49) and (55), I rather assume that the focalized DP in (65–66) moves to a FocusP in the left periphery of the main clause (Rizzi 1997) and that the copular verb moves to a position dominating FocusP.

Rialland's (1999) analysis.[19] In this section I argue that infinitival relative clauses provide indeed evidence for the assumption that the coda of clefted constituents is a complement.

In the introduction to this paper I showed that infinitival subject relative clauses are not only licensed by clefts, but also by a head noun modified by a superlative or an equivalent modifier.[20] The infinitival subject relative can be replaced by a relative clause containing an inflected (subjunctive) verb:

(67) *Gianni è stato il solo a parlare con la stampa.*
'Gianni was the only one to speak with the press.'

(68) *Gianni è il solo che abbia raggiunto un risultato vero.*
Gianni is the only that has.SUBJ obtained a result true
'Gianni is the only one that has obtained a true result.'

Sleeman (2005) analyzes both the inflected relative clause and the infinitival relative clause as a complement, but shows that extraction is only possible from the infinitival relative clause:

(69) *Con chi Gianni è stato il solo (giornalista) a parlare –?*
'With whom was Gianni the only (reporter) to speak?'

(70) **Con chi Gianni è stato il solo (giornalista) che*
with whom Gianni is been the only (reporter) that
abbia parlato?
has.SUBJ spoken

Sleeman (2005) claims that the prepositional complementizer *a* is located, within the articulated C-domain (Rizzi 1997), in the lower complementizer position, viz. Fin^0, which reflects certain properties of the verbal system of the clause, such as mood. The noun or empty pronoun moves to the Spec of FinP, leaving Spec,ForceP empty so that another constituent can move through this position:

(71) [$_{ForceP}$ Con chi$_j$ Gianni è stato il solo [$_{ForceP}$ t$_j$ [$_{FinP}$ giornalista$_i$/*pro*$_i$ a parlare t$_i$ t$_j$]]]?

19. In Clech-Darbon, Rebuschi and Rialland's (1999) analysis, the post-focal coda, i.e. the relative clause, is adjoined to IP and is interpreted as a predicate that binds a predicate variable associated with the translation of the [Spec, IP] pronoun:

(i) [[$_{IP}$ C'est un/le dictionnaire] [$_{CP}$ Op que j'ai acheté t]].
'It's a/the dictionary that I've bought.'

20. If infinitival subject relatives are licensed by a "high" focus, it might be assumed that in (67)–(68) the superlative or equivalent modifier moves to a (maybe "high") DP-internal focus position (Aboh 2004; Corver & van Koppen 2009), probably at LF (Sleeman 2010).

For the full relative clause Sleeman (2005) assumes that it is also dominated by ForceP, but this time the (empty) noun has to move to Spec,ForceP, which contains the complementizer *che* in its head position. This means that there is no empty Spec left that could be used for the extraction of a constituent out of the relative clause, which is the complement of *solo*, just as in (72):

(72) *Con chi$_j$ Gianni è stato il solo [$_{ForceP}$ giornalista$_i$ /*pro*$_i$ [$_{Force'}$ che [$_{FinP}$ abbia parlato t$_i$ t$_j$]]]]?

For the three types of clefts I assume that the infinitival relative clause and the finite clause occupy the same position. The following examples show that extraction from the finite clause is excluded:

(73) **l' orchestra strabiliante che è stato lui che ha plasmato*
the orchestra extraordinary that is been he that has modeled

(74) **un lusso che siamo in pochi che ci possiamo permettere*
a luxury that we-are in few that us can permit

(75) **una storia che sono poche le persone che conoscono*
a story that are few the persons that know

Extraction from the infinitival relative clause corresponding to (73–74), however, is much better:

(76) *l' orchestra strabiliante che è stato lui a plasmare*
the orchestra extraordinary that is been he to model
'the extraordinary orchestra that he has modeled'

(77) *un lusso che siamo in pochi a poterci permettere*
a luxury that we-are in few to can-us permit
'a luxury that few can afford'

Assuming Kayne's (1994) raising analysis of relative clauses, we can account for the difference between (73) and (76) in the following way. In (73), both *lui* and *l'orchestra strabiliante* have to pass through the most embedded Spec,ForceP: when *lui* has moved to Spec,ForceP, this position cannot be used anymore for the movement of *l'orchestra strabiliante* (78). In (79), however, *a* occupies Fin^0 and Spec,FinP can be used for the movement of *lui*, leaving Spec,ForceP available for the movement of *l'orchestra strabiliante*:

(78) *l'orchestra strabiliante$_j$ che *pro* è stato [$_{FocusP}$ lui$_i$ [$_{IP}$ [$_{vP}$ t$_{essere}$ [$_{ForceP}$ t$_i$ che ha plasmato t$_i$ t$_j$]]

(79) l'orchestra strabiliante$_j$ che *pro* è stato [$_{FocusP}$ lui$_i$ [$_{IP}$ [$_{vP}$ t$_{essere}$ [$_{ForceP}$ t$_j$ [$_{FinP}$ t$_i$ a [plasmare t$_i$ t$_j$]]]]

For (74) I assume a structure as in (80). Since *pro* moves to the Spec of the embedded ForceP (and subsequently to Spec,IP of the copular verb), this position cannot be used to move *un lusso*. In (81), however, Spec,FinP is used for the movement of *pro*, and Spec,ForceP is available for the movement of *un lusso*:

(80) *un lusso$_j$ che *pro*$_i$ siamo [$_{FocusP}$ in pochi [$_{IP}$ [$_{vP}$ t$_{essere}$ [$_{SC}$ [$_{ForceP}$ t$_i$ che ci possiamo permettere t$_i$ t$_j$] [t$_{in\ pochi}$]]]]].

(81) un lusso$_j$ che *pro*$_i$ siamo [$_{FocusP}$ in pochi [$_{IP}$ [$_{vP}$ t$_{essere}$ [$_{SC}$ [$_{ForceP}$ t$_j$ [$_{FinP}$ t$_i$ a poterci permettere t$_i$ t$_j$]] [t$_{in\ pochi}$]]]]].

Extraction from the infinitival relative clause corresponding to the third type of *che*-cleft, (75), is, however, ungrammatical:

(82) **una storia che sono poche le persone a conoscere*
a story that are few the persons to know
'a story that few people know'

The difference between (79) and (81) on the one hand, and (82) on the other, is that in (79) and (81) there is a trace in Spec,FinP, whereas in (82) a DP fills Spec,FinP:

(83) *una storia$_j$ che *pro* sono [$_{FocusP}$ poche [$_{IP}$ [$_{vP}$ t$_{essere}$ [$_{SC}$ [$_{ForceP}$ t$_j$ [$_{FinP}$ le persone$_i$ a conoscere t$_i$ t$_j$]] [t$_{poche}$]]]]].

I propose that (83) is ruled out by the Minimal Link Condition, i.e. Shortest Move (Chomsky 1995), which is incorporated in Attract: Spec,ForceP of the main clause should attract the closest DP in the lower ForceP, which is *le persone*, and not *una storia*, which is not the closest DP.[21,22]

21. Ignazio Mauro Mirto (p.c.) pointed out to me that there is another difference between the two types of quantifier clefts: whereas fronting of the infinitival relative clause is acceptable in (i), it is not in (ii):

(i) *A pensare questo siamo in molti.*
to think this we-are in many
'Many people believe it.'

(ii) **A farne uso in Italia sono molte le persone.*
to make-of it use in Italy are many the persons
'Many people in Italy use it.'

The difference in grammaticality might result from the fact that in (i) the whole FinP including the trace of *pro* (cf. 81) is moved, whereas in (ii) only part of FinP, viz. the infinitival relative clause is moved (cf. 83).

22. For some of the native Italian speakers that I consulted the insertion of a resumptive pronoun in (83) improved its acceptability (i). This suggests that the unacceptability of (83) is syntactic in nature:

(i) *?* *una storia che sono poche le persone a conoscerla*
a story that are few the persons to know it

In this section I have claimed that the subordinate clauses in *a*-clefts and *che*-clefts do not differ w.r.t. their position in the sentence. In principle extraction is possible from both, but in *che*-clefts movement through Spec,ForceP is not possible because this position is used for the movement of another constituent. In *a*-clefts, Spec,ForceP is available for movement, because Spec,FinP is used for movement of another constituent. An overt DP in Spec,FinP, however, can block movement because of the Minimal Link Condition. For all cases I have adopted an analysis in which the clefted constituent moves to a high focus position dominating the subordinate clause.

6. Conclusion

In this paper, I have claimed that infinitival subject relatives are licensed by clefted constituents if these express a [+contrastive] focus, which I have taken to mean 'excluding any possible alternative'. I have shown that whereas in English and especially in French the use of clefts is a normal strategy used to answer a question concerning the identification of the subject of the clause, in Italian the use of a cleft in this case is associated with a somewhat negative presupposition and expresses thus a [+contrastive] focus (Belletti 2008).

I have shown that three types of clefts license infinitival subject relative clauses: the canonical cleft with a clefted DP, and two types of clefts with a clefted quantificational expression. I have argued that all three types express a [+contrastive] focus. For all three types of clefts, I have adopted a structure in which the clefted constituent, being a [+contrastive] focus, is located in the left periphery of the clause. Following Belletti (2008), I have assumed that clefted constituents in English and French, expressing a [±contrastive] focus, are in a low focus position, viz. in the left periphery of the vP phase.

For the coda, i.e. the infinitival relative clause, I have assumed that, just like the finite relative clause, it is a complement rather than an adjunct, in line with Kayne's (1994) Antisymmetry theory. I have shown that extraction is possible from the infinitival relative clause with the canonical DP-cleft and with one type of quantifier-cleft. I have argued that extraction is possible because Spec,ForceP is available as an extraction site. I have attributed the impossibility of extraction from the second type of quantifier-cleft, a type involving subject inversion, to Chomsky's (1995) Minimal Link Condition.

In this paper I have shown that, besides clefts, infinitival subject relatives are licensed by a head noun modified by a superlative or an equivalent expression, not only in Italian, but also in English and French. I have argued that the superlative or the equivalent expression expresses a [+contrastive] focus, which suggests that it moves to a FocusP in the left periphery of the DP, probably at LF. I have also argued that a superlative does not necessarily have to express a [+constrastive] focus, but I have claimed that in that case it does not license an infinitival subject relative. In line with Belletti's distinction between a high and a low focus position in the clause, a question that comes to mind is whether two types of focus position can be motivated within the DP: a high focus position in the left periphery of the DP and a low focus position just dominating NP. I leave this question for future research.

References

Aboh, Enoch. 2004. Topic and focus within D. *Linguistics in the Netherlands* 2004. 1–12.

Belletti, Adriana. 2005. Answering with a cleft: the role of the null subject parameter and the VP periphery. In *Proceedings of the Thirtieth Incontro di Grammatica Generativa*, Laura Brugè, Giuliana Giusti, Nicola Munaro, Walter Schweikert & Giuseppina Turano (eds), 63–82. Venice: Cafoscarina.

Belletti, Adriana. 2008. Answering strategies: New information subjects and the nature of clefts. Chapter 10 of *Structures and Strategies*. London: Routledge.

Bhatt, Rajesh. 1999. Covert Modality in Non-finite Contexts. Ph.D. dissertation, University of Pennsylvania. Also published as Bhatt 2006.

Bhatt, Rajesh. 2006. *Covert Modality in Non-finite Contexts*. Berlin: Mouton de Gruyter.

Brody, Michael. 1990. Some remarks on the focus field in Hungarian. *UCL Working Papers in Linguistics* 2: 201–25.

Brody, Michael. 1995. Focus and checking theory. In *Approaches to Hungarian*, V: *Levels and Structures*, István Kenesei (ed.), 29–44. Szeged: JATE.

Chomsky, Noam. 1995. *The Minimalist Program*. Cambridge MA: The MIT Press.

Clech-Darbon, Anne, Rebuschi, Georges & Rialland, Annie. 1999. Are there cleft sentences in French? In *The Grammar of Focus* [Linguistik Aktuell/Linguistics Today 24], Laurie Tuller & Georges Rebuschi (eds), 83–118. Amsterdam: John Benjamins.

Corver, Norbert & van Koppen, Marjo. 2009. Let's focus on noun phrase ellipsis. *GAGL (Groninger Arbeiten zur Germanistischen Linguistik)* 4: 3–26.

Cruschina, Silvio. 2004. Il focus di nuovo informazione e la periferia sinistra: La struttura informative della frase in Siciliano. Ph.D. dissertation, University of Siena.

Farkas, Donka. 1985. *Intensional Descriptions and the Romance Subjunctive Mood*. New York NY: Garland.

Frey, Werner. 2004. The grammar-pragmatics interface and the German prefield. *Sprache & Pragmatik* 52: 1–39.

Geisler, Christer. 1995. Relative Infinitives in English. Ph.D. dissertation, Uppsala University.

Giannakidou, Anastasia. 1997. The Landscape of Polarity Items. Ph.D. dissertation, Groningen University.

Kampers-Manhe, Brigitte. 1991. *L'opposition Subjonctif/Indicatif dans les Relatives*. Amsterdam: Rodopi.

Kayne, Richard. 1994. *The Antisymmetry of Syntax*. Cambridge MA: The MIT Press.

É. Kiss, Katalin. 1998. Identificational focus versus information focus. *Language* 74(2): 245–73.
Kjellmer, Göran. 1975. Are relative infinitives modal? *Studia Neophilologica* 47: 323–32.
Rizzi, Luigi. 1997. The fine structure of the left periphery. In *Elements of Grammar: Handbook of Generative Grammar*, Liliane Haegeman (ed.), 281–339. Dordrecht: Kluwer.
Sleeman, Petra. 2005. The com(p)-position of DP-internal infinitival clauses. In *Contributions to the thirtieth Incontro di Grammatica Generativa*, Laura Brugè, Giuliana Giusti, Nicola Munaro, Walter Schweikert & Giuseppina Turano (eds), 333–49. Venice: Cafoscarina.
Sleeman, Petra (2010). Superlative adjectives and the licensing of non-modal infinitival subject relatives. In *Adjectives. Formal Analyses in Syntax and Semantics* [Linguistik Aktuell/Linguistics Today 153], Patricia Cabredo-Hofherr & Ora Matushansky (eds), 233–64. Amsterdam: John Benjamins.

Language index

Subject index